Lecture Notes in Computer Science   15915

Founding Editors

Gerhard Goos
Juris Hartmanis

The series Lecture Notes in Computer Science (LNCS), including its subseries Lecture Notes in Artificial Intelligence (LNAI) and Lecture Notes in Bioinformatics (LNBI), has established itself as a medium for the publication of new developments in computer science and information technology research, teaching, and education.

LNCS enjoys close cooperation with the computer science R & D community, the series counts many renowned academics among its volume editors and paper authors, and collaborates with prestigious societies. Its mission is to serve this international community by providing an invaluable service, mainly focused on the publication of conference and workshop proceedings and postproceedings. LNCS commenced publication in 1973.

Christos Mousas · Hyewon Seo ·
Daniel Thalmann · Frederic Cordier
Editors

Computer Animation and Social Agents

38th International Conference, CASA 2025
Strasbourg, France, June 2–4, 2025
Proceedings

 Springer

Editors
Christos Mousas (iD)
Purdue University
West Lafayette, IN, USA

Hyewon Seo
CNRS, University of Strasbourg
Strasbourg, France

Daniel Thalmann (iD)
EPFL
Lausanne, Switzerland

Frederic Cordier
University of Haute-Alsace
Mulhouse, France

ISSN 0302-9743   ISSN 1611-3349 (electronic)
Lecture Notes in Computer Science
ISBN 978-981-95-0099-4   ISBN 978-981-95-0100-7 (eBook)
https://doi.org/10.1007/978-981-95-0100-7

This Springer imprint is published by the registered company Springer Nature Singapore Pte Ltd.
The registered company address is: 152 Beach Road, #21-01/04 Gateway East, Singapore 189721, Singapore

If disposing of this product, please recycle the paper.

Preface

CASA is the oldest international conference on computer animation and social agents in the world. It was founded in Geneva in 1988 under the name of Computer Animation (CA) by the Computer Graphics Society (CGS). In the past few years, CASA has been held in Europe (Belgium, Netherlands, France, Switzerland, UK, etc.), Asia (South Korea, China, Singapore), and the USA. CASA 2025 provided a great opportunity to interact with leading experts, share your own work, and educate yourself through exposure to the research of your peers from around the world. The 38th International Conference on Computer Animation and Social Agents (CASA 2025) was held on June 2–4, 2025, in Strasbourg, France. The conference was organized by the University of Strasbourg and the ICube laboratory. These CASA 2025 LNCS proceedings are composed of 17 papers from a total of 65 submissions. To ensure the high quality of the publications, each paper was double-blindly reviewed by at least two experts in the field, and authors of accepted papers were asked to revise their papers according to the review comments prior to publication.

The 6th Workshop on Next-Generation Computer Animation Techniques (AniNex) was organized in conjunction with CASA 2025. The workshop focused on cutting-edge research from all perspectives of computer animation, including interdisciplinary approaches and applications. A special section comprising 3 papers from the AniNex workshop is included in this edition, selected from a total of 17 submissions. The same rigorous review process was applied as in the main conference. We are grateful for the support and invaluable contributions from the workshop chairs (Jian Chang, Anil Bas, Shihui Guo, Jian Jun Zhang), the workshop's review committee, the authors, and the main conference organizers. We acknowledge that this workshop received support from the EU H2020 Marie Skłodowska-Curie Scheme (CfACTs, 900025).

We would like to express our deepest gratitude to all the PC members and external reviewers who provided timely and high-quality reviews. We would also like to thank all the authors for contributing to the conference by submitting their work.

May 2025

Christos Mousas
Hyewon Seo
Daniel Thalmann
Frederic Cordier

Organization

Organizing Committee

Conference Co-chairs

Frederic Cordier	University of Haute-Alsace, France
Kun Zhou	Zhejiang University, China
Nadia Magnenat-Thalmann	University of Geneva, Switzerland

Program Co-chairs

Christos Mousas	Purdue University, USA
Hyewon Seo	CNRS, University of Strasbourg, France
Daniel Thalmann	EPFL, Switzerland

International Coordinator

Bin Sheng	Shanghai Jiao Tong University, China

Publicity Chair

Xiaosong Yang	Bournemouth University, UK

Program Committee

Domna Banakou	New York University Abu Dhabi, UAE
Sahba Zojaji	Chinese University of Hong Kong, Shenzhen, China
Sung-Hee Lee	Korea Advanced Institute of Science and Technology, South Korea
Junyong Noh	Korea Advanced Institute of Science and Technology, South Korea
Jian Chang	Bournemouth University, UK
Sylvie Gibet	Université Bretagne Sud, France
Brandon Haworth	University of Victoria, Canada
Banafsheh Rekabdar	Portland State University, USA

Eduardo Alvarado   LIX, École Polytechnique/CNRS, Institut
                               Polytechnique de Paris, France
Aikaterini Mania   Technical University of Crete, Greece
Alessandro Artusi   CYENS Center of Excellence, Cyprus
Amit Bermano   Princeton University, USA
Tamar Shinar   University of California Riverside, USA
Özge Nilay Yalçın   Simon Fraser University, Canada
Etienne Vouga   University of Texas at Austin, USA
Mohammed Safayet Arefin   Colorado State University, USA
John McGhee   UNSW Art & Design, Australia

Contents

**The 6th Workshop on Next-Generation Computer Animation
Techniques (AniNex 2025)**

Computer Animation and Social Agents (CASA 2025)

Speech-Driven 3D Facial Animation with Regional Attention for Style Capture

Bailin Yang$^{(\boxtimes)}$, Jiahao Pan, Fangzhe Nan, and Jiajie Wu

Department of Computer Science and Technology, Zhejiang Gongshang University, Hangzhou, China
ybl@zjgsu.edu.cn

Abstract. Speech-driven 3D facial animation has achieved significant progress, producing increasingly realistic results. However, animations generated solely from audio input often lack expressive style. Current research predominantly focuses on style control using video or mesh sequences, neglecting scenarios relying exclusively on audio input, which results in less expressive outcomes. To address this limitation, we propose a novel method that employs a regional attention mechanism guided by a single identity vector, enabling the generation of stylistically consistent and highly expressive animations. Our approach customizes facial attention mask regions for individual speakers and incorporates two loss functions, L_{mask} and L_{normal}, to capture detailed style information through vertex movements and geometric variations. Extensive experiments and user studies demonstrate that our method outperforms existing approaches in qualitative and quantitative evaluations.

Keywords: Speech-Driven 3D face animation · style · regional attention

1 Introduction

Owing to its applications in virtual reality, film production and gaming, speech-driven 3D facial animation has garnered significant interest. This research aims to generate realistic and vivid 3D facial animations from arbitrary speech signals, potentially reducing production costs in related industries, swiftly generating high-quality animations, and enhancing the immersion and authenticity of virtual experiences.

Early works focused on mapping phonemes to visual expressions but were limited in animation quality [31,39]. With advancements in deep learning, methods like VOCA [8], which uses temporal convolution to regress facial movements from audio, and MeshTalk [29], which uses a UNet-style decoder to decode facial expressions from latent space, have emerged. FaceFormer [13] leverages a transformer-based autoregressive model to produce facial animations sequentially.

C. Mousas et al. (Eds.): CASA 2025, LNCS 15915, pp. 3–20, 2026.
https://doi.org/10.1007/978-981-95-0100-7_1

A speaker's unique speaking style is reflected not only in the spectral features of the speech signal but also in the associated facial movements. These movements, closely linked to a speaker's physiology and linguistic habits, are critical for creating expressive animations. Neglecting these style differences can make animations appear stiff and unnatural. While some methods [5,32] have explored personalized styles using video or mesh sequences, they rely on additional modal inputs. In scenarios where only audio input is available, the animations often lack expressiveness and fail to capture stylistic nuances.

We propose a speech-driven facial animation method that leverages a regional attention mechanism to effectively capture personalized styles from existing speakers and represent them using an identity vector. The method focuses on vertex displacement and geometric variations. For vertex displacement, our method identifies facial attention mask areas through analysis of facial vertex motion for different speakers and applies a specific loss function L_{mask} to capture style nuances. For geometric variations, we use face normal deflection with a specially designed loss function L_{normal} and an automated threshold strategy to capture style information, thereby enhancing the detail and expressiveness of animations. We employ a non-autoregressive transformer-based network [34], which achieves superior performance. Additionally, the ablation study in Sect. 4.5 demonstrates our method's adaptability and its enhancement of mesh-based speech-driven technologies. Our contributions can be summarized as follows:

- We propose a regional attention mechanism that customizes focus on facial stylized areas for different speakers, effectively capturing personalized style from vertex displacements.
- We introduced a face normal loss function with an angular threshold strategy, automating its activation. This effectively captures personalized style information within geometric variations and enhances the geometric detail of face animations.
- Extensive experiments show that our method has superior performance and can be effectively transferred to other methods.

2   Related Work

2.1   Speech-Driven 3D Facial Animation

Facial animation, as a classic field in computer graphics, has attracted significant research attention over the years [3,15,21–23,33]. Speech-driven 3D facial animation is a branch within facial animation, aiming to generate realistic facial animations from an audio signal. Our research is dedicated to 3D talking faces that utilize 3D models, which are broadly categorized into viseme-based and learning-based approaches.

Viseme-Based 3D Face Animation. primarily appears in earlier methods and integrates easily into existing animation pipelines, making it animator-friendly. These methods animate by mapping phonemes to visemes, which are facial expressions corresponding to phonemes. For example, Taylor et al. [31] developed a dynamic visemes model to handle the complex many-to-many relationships between phonemes and visemes. Xu et al. [39] linked animation curves with sequential phoneme pairs using a standard set of visemes to produce synchronized facial movements. JALI [12] enhanced mouth movements by integrating lip and jaw rig animations and establishing co-articulation rules for more natural results. While these viseme-based methods are semantically strong, they often lack precision and require adjustments by animators.

Learning-Based 3D Face Animation. [5,8,10,13,20,27–29,32,37,38] has shown promise in data-driven approaches. Karras et al. [20] integrated learnable emotion vectors with convolutional networks to create 3D mesh animations from speech. Emotalk [28] utilizes an emotion decoupling module to distinguish between speech content and emotions, generating emotional facial expressions with blendshape coefficients, while FaceTalk [1] employs a latent diffusion model for high-fidelity volumetric head animations. Unlike FaceTalk, we focus on Mesh-based methods.

Next, we will review works most relevant to our research that convert audio into 3D mesh outputs. MeshTalk [29] uses a cross-modality loss to separate audio-correlated and uncorrelated information for lip and upper face animations, respectively. FaceFormer [13] approaches facial animation as a sequence-to-sequence learning problem, leveraging transformers to holistically consider the context. CodeTalker [38] addresses cross-modal uncertainty by discretizing the facial motion space, and SelfTalk [27] enhances lip-readability with a commutative training diagram for more accurate lip shapes. Imitator [32] adapts to new users by combining generalized viseme generation with personalized motion decoding. Yang et al. [40] proposed a probabilistic model using a vector-quantized codebook to achieve diverse yet speech-synchronized animations. Song et al. [30] propose a diffusion-based framework integrating LG-LDM and emotion-centric VQ-VAE for expressive speech-driven 3D facial animation. Jung et al. [19] introduced a speed-aware adaptive window-based approach with a multi-window mechanism, enabling the network to capture fine and coarse temporal features across varying speaking rates. AdaMesh [6] separately models facial expression and head pose styles via MoLoRA and semantic-aware retrieval, enabling high-quality personalized adaptation from a reference video about 10 s.

These methods enhance facial animation performance from various perspectives, such as emotion [10,28] and lip-reading [27]. Although existing methods [5,32] have explored style information, they typically rely on additional modal inputs for style control, such as video or facial mesh sequences. In contrast, our method requires only an identity vector for control and effectively displays personalized style characteristics consistent with the identity vector in face animations generated from a single audio input.

2.2 Attention Mechanisms

Attention mechanisms are widely used in computer vision [4,7,9,17,35] to help deep learning models selectively focus on crucial content, enhancing their performance in complex tasks. Initially, RAM [26] integrated attention with RNNs to recursively predict important areas. Subsequently, Jaderberg et al. [18] proposed the STN, which explicitly predicts important regions through learning affine transformations. Later, SENet [17] introduced a channel-attention network that adaptively predicts potentially important features. The advent of transformers [34] has spurred advancements in self-attention [11,25,36], enhancing speed, quality, and generalizability in computer vision. We refer readers to the survey by Guo et al. [16] for a comprehensive understanding, .

Some works on speech-driven 3D facial animation have leveraged attention mechanisms effectively. FaceFormer [13] uses a transformer model to prioritize important elements in long-term audio content. Imitator [32] enhances attention on bilabial consonants to refine lip closure, while SelfTalk [27] focuses on the lip region to produce more accurate lip shapes. Given the success of the attention mechanism, we have incorporated it to thoroughly capture personalized style information.

3   Methodology

This section outlines our proposed method and training model, including the regional attention mechanism and the normal threshold strategy. Detailed explanations of these two modules are provided in Sects. 3.2 and 3.3.

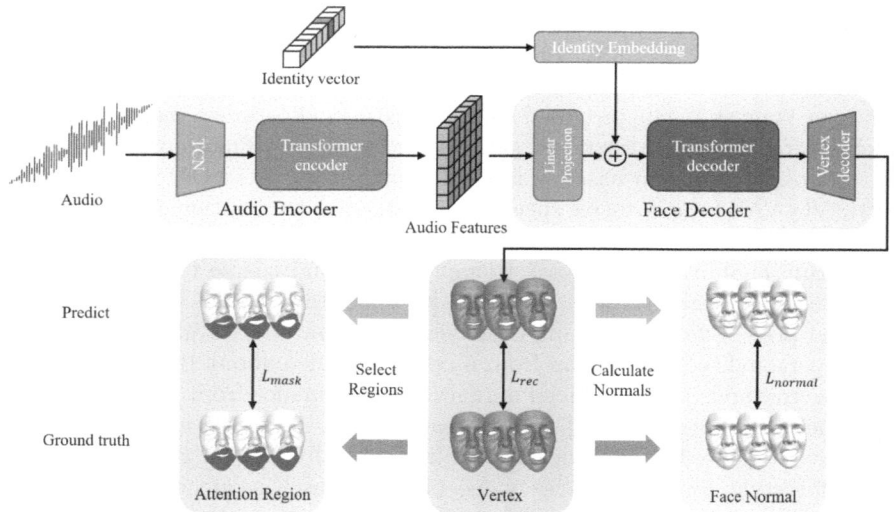

Fig. 1. Overview of our method: Using audio and an identity vector as inputs, our non-autoregressive model predicts vertex offsets and generates facial animations with stylistic expression. The model is constrained by two loss functions, L_{mask} and L_{normal}, alongside a personalized facial region attention mask. This setup effectively captures the speaker's style characteristics through vertex motion and geometric variations.

3.1   Problem Formulation and Overview

Problem Formulation. Let $Y_{1:T} = (y_1, \ldots, y_T)$, where each $y_t \in \mathbb{R}^{V \times 3}$, be a sequence of facial vertex offsets from a template face mesh $m \in \mathbb{R}^{V \times 3}$, representing the target facial animation. Let $A_{1:T} = (a_1, \ldots, a_T)$, where each $a_t \in \mathbb{R}^D$, be a sequence of D-dimensional audio features corresponding to each visual frame y_t. Our goal is to synthesize realistic and detailed 3D facial animations $Y_{1:T}$ from the audio $A_{1:T}$, animating a neutral template face m through the transformation $M_{1:T} = (m + y_1, \ldots, m + y_T)$.

To achieve this objective, we employ a non-autoregressive network architecture based on a transformer (see Fig. 1), which greatly enhances both inference and training speeds. Following prior work [13,27,38], we use the self-supervised pre-trained speech model, wav2vec 2.0 [2], as our audio encoder. This model uses a Temporal Convolution Network (TCN) to transform raw speech waveforms into feature vectors and a transformer encoder to refine these into meaningful speech representations. By masking parts of the audio features, wav2vec 2.0 encourages the model to predict these masked areas, enhancing the accuracy and efficacy of the feature extraction.

The overview of our method is as follows: Given a raw audio signal R and an identity vector s, the audio encoder extracts features $A_{1:T}$ from R. These audio features and the identity vector s are input into the face decoder. In the decoder, s is embedded into $A_{1:T}$ using an embedding layer, enhancing the data used to predict vertex offsets for facial animations. The process is outlined as:

$$\hat{Y} = D_{face}(E_{audio}(R), s) \tag{1}$$

3.2   Regional Attention Mechanism

Each individual exhibits a unique personalized style in facial movements while speaking, which is reflected in the face animation as shifts in vertex positions and changes in geometric shapes. In other words, this personalized style can be characterized as facial movements corresponding to phonemes that are strongly associated with the speaker.It is noteworthy that even with the same speech segment, the distribution of facial vertex movements can vary significantly among different speakers. Based on this observation, we posits a hypothesis: the most active areas in facial movements largely encapsulate the speaker's personalized style information.

To fully capture the style information inherent in facial movements, we propose a regional attention mechanism. This mechanism selects certain areas based on the activity level of facial vertex movements as representative regions of a speaker's personalized style, namely the facial attention mask areas. Since the style characteristics vary among different speakers, the facial attention mask areas are also unique to each individual.

Our method can be generally divided into two steps: first, quantify the activity of facial regions; second, segment the facial regions based on the quantification results. To quantify the activity level of vertex movements, we measure it

8   B. Yang et al.

by the sum of the inter-frame vertex offsets. The specific calculation formula is
as follows:

$$distance_v = \sum_{t=1}^{T-1} \|y_{t+1,v} - y_{t,v}\|_2 \tag{2}$$

where v represents the v-th vertex, and $y_{t,v}$ denotes the position of vertex v in
frame t. Based on the above calculation method, we computed the distribution of
facial vertex movements for all speakers in both the BIWI [14] and VOCASET
[8] datasets.Considering that the calculation is for individual characters, and
all vertices share the same number of intervals between frames, we opt not to
calculate the average to speed up the calculation. Figure 2 shows the distribution
of facial vertex movements for two speakers from the BIWI dataset. We ranked
the vertices based on their activity levels and generated heatmaps, where red
areas indicate vertices with higher activity, and blue areas represent relatively
inactive vertices.

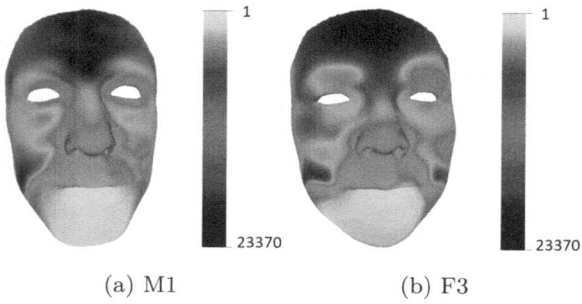

(a) M1   (b) F3

Fig. 2. Visualization of vertex activity rankings across different subjects in the BIWI
Dataset. Colors represent activity levels: red (high), green (medium), blue (low). (Color
figure online)

After calculating the activity levels of all vertices in the facial regions, the
next step is to delineate personalized facial attention mask areas for each speaker
based on their activity levels. This segmentation must not only accurately represent the unique style of the speaker but also ensure obvious differences from
the mask areas of others.To this end, we propose a threshold-based segmentation method. Specifically, we set a proportional threshold φ , where a vertex is
considered part of the attention mask area only if its activity level is among
the top φ percent of all vertex activity levels. Using this method, we successfully modeled the style information in the facial movements of all speakers in
the dataset, thereby ensuring that the final generated face animations vividly
reflect personalized style characteristics.The overall process can be summarized
as Algorithm 1.

Algorithm 1. Regional Attention Mechanism

1: **Input:** Dataset, proportion threshold φ
2: **Output:** $FaceMask$
3: **for all** character i **do**
4:      $FaceMask_i \leftarrow \{\}$
5:      $Face_i \leftarrow \{\}$
6:      **for all** vertex v **do**
7:          calculate $distance_v$
8:          Add $distance_v$ to $Face_i$
9:      **end for**
10:     $Face_i^{top\,\varphi} \leftarrow$ top φ elements $\in Face_i$
11:     **for all** $distance_v$ in $Face_i$ **do**
12:         **if** $distance_v \in Face_i^{top\,\varphi}$ **then**
13:             Add v to $FaceMask_i$
14:         **end if**
15:     **end for**
16: **end for**

Figure 3 illustrates the finalized facial attention mask areas for two different speakers in BIWI dataset. The figure clearly shows significant differences between the two, which are attributable to the distinct personalized styles of the speakers.

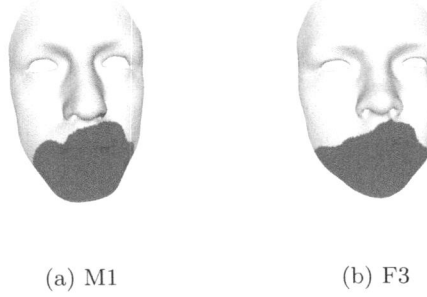

(a) M1   (b) F3

Fig. 3. Visualization of facial attention mask areas for different subjects in BIWI dataset.

Based on the computed attention mask areas, we propose a new loss function L_{mask}, designed to impose additional attention on the vertex movements within these areas, thereby encouraging the model to better learn the personalized style characteristics of the speakers. The specific formula is as follows:

$$L_{mask} = \frac{1}{T} \frac{1}{|V_{mask}|} \sum_{t=1}^{T} \sum_{v \in V_{mask}} \|y_{t,v} - \hat{y}_{t,v}\|^2 \tag{3}$$

where V_{mask} denotes vertices that belong to the attention mask area. Although these areas primarily cover the lower face, the inherent correlation between upper and lower face during speech enables the capture of style variations in the upper face as well. By leveraging a regional attention mechanism,, we can give extra focus to stylistically representative areas to generate face animations with more pronounced style characteristics.

3.3   Face Normal Threshold Strategy

Capturing personalized style characteristics involves more than just focusing on vertex positions, as this approach lacks effective modeling of facial geometric shape changes. In fact, the unique variations in facial geometry during speech are crucial representations of personalized styles, which are determined by both the displacement of vertex positions and the deflection of triangular faces. Vertices define the basic shape of the face, while triangular faces construct the details of the facial geometry; both are essential and complement each other. Focusing solely on vertex positions while ignoring the information about the deflection of triangular faces may result in generated face animations that lose geometric details, thereby failing to accurately replicate the speaker's personalized style. To better capture stylistic expressions, we propose a loss function based on face normals that increases attention and supervision on the deflection of triangular faces, encouraging the model to generate face animations that more accurately reflect geometric shape changes consistent with the speaker's style.

Normals are an integral component of the 3D mesh that effectively reflect the geometric shape and are highly sensitive to geometric variations. When these variations occur, the normals correspondingly undergo angular deviations. We choose face normals over vertex normals because they are perpendicular to the plane of triangular faces, enabling them to sensitively capture changes in face deflection. This makes face normals an ideal choice for characterizing changes in geometric shape. We construct a new loss function using Face Normals, the formula is as follows:

$$L_{normal} = \frac{1}{T} \frac{1}{|F_{mask}|} \sum_{t=1}^{T} \sum_{f \in F_{mask}} \|1 - \cos(n, \hat{n})\| \tag{4}$$

where $\hat{n}$ and n represent the predicted and ground-truth normal respectively, F_{mask} denotes faces under the coverage of attention mask areas.

Due to the larger magnitude of the normal cosine loss compared to the vertex distance loss, and the sensitivity of normals to geometric variations, the influence of normal loss is significant during training, which increases the difficulty of model training. To address this issue, we propose the Face Normal Threshold Strategy: Specifically, we define the angle between the predicted and ground-truth Face Normals as θ, as illustrated in Fig. 4. And we set a threshold angle θ_{max}. When θ exceeds θ_{max} during training, the value of θ will be set to π, which means the directions of Face Normals are opposite.

Through this simple yet effective approach, we automatically control when the loss of face normal comes into play. As the training progresses, the accuracy of the vertex positions increases, and the angle between the normals gradually decreases. When θ is less than θ_{max}, it also indicates that the foundation of the

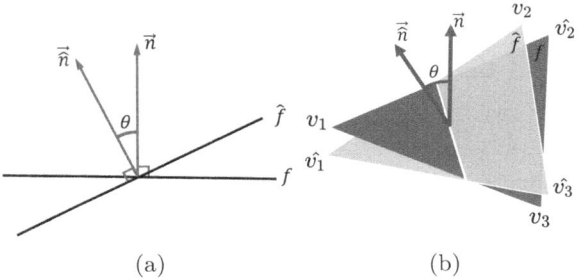

Fig. 4. Angle between predicted and ground-truth Face Normals from two perspectives. $\hat{n}$ and n denotes predicted and ground-truth face normal respectively; similarly for $\hat{f}$ and f.

facial shape has been established. At this point, the normal loss automatically takes effect, thereby sculpting more refined facial geometric details.By doing so, we not only reduce the complexity of model training but also fully utilize the geometric information contained in face normals. As a result, the final generated face animations exhibit a more refined and realistic representation of personalized style characteristics.

3.4 Loss Function

Our loss function consists of four components. In addition to the L_{mask} and L_{normal} mentioned above, there is also reconstruction loss L_{rec} and velocity loss L_{vel}. The reconstruction loss measures the vertex deviation between predicted and ground truth, the velocity loss measures the difference of adjacent frames between predicted and ground truth. These two loss functions can be formulated as follows:

$$L_{rec} = \frac{1}{T}\frac{1}{V}\sum_{t=1}^{T}\sum_{v=1}^{V}\|y_{t,v} - \hat{y_{t,v}}\|^2 \tag{5}$$

$$L_{vel} = \frac{1}{T}\frac{1}{V}\sum_{t=1}^{T}\sum_{v=1}^{V}\|(y_{t,v} - y_{t-1,v}) - (\hat{y}_{t,v} - \hat{y}_{t-1,v})\|^2 \tag{6}$$

The final loss is the weighted sum of the four losses:

$$Loss = \lambda_1 L_{rec} + \lambda_2 L_{vel} + \lambda_3 L_{mask} + \lambda_4 L_{normal} \tag{7}$$

where $\lambda_1 = 1000.0, \lambda_2 = 1000.0, \lambda_3 = 100.0, \lambda_4 = 0.001$ in our experiments.

3.5 Training Details

We train our model on an NVIDIA RTX 4090, completing 100 epochs in about 1 h. For BIWI and VOCASET, we set the proportion thresholds φ to 30% and 10%, targeting the mouth and chin areas. The learning rate is fixed at 1e-5 for both datasets, with θ_{max} set to $\pi/4$.

4   Experiments and Results

4.1   Datasets and Implementations

We train and test different methods using two public datasets, BIWI [14] and VOCASET [8]. Both datasets contain content of audio-mesh pairs based on English spoken utterances. BIWI includes 40 unique sentences shared by all speakers. VOCASET contains 255 unique sentences, with some sentences shared among the speakers. Compared to VOCASET, BIWI contains fewer phonemes, making tasks using this dataset more challenging.

BIWI Dataset. BIWI is a 3D audio-visual corpus for studying affective communication, consisting of affective speech and corresponding dense dynamic 3D face geometries. It includes 40 unique English sentences spoken by 14 participants (eight females and six males), recorded in both emotional and neutral states, with an average length of 4.67 s per sentence. The 3D facial geometries are captured at 25fps and consist of 23,370 vertices per face. Following previous methods [13,27,38], we use only the emotional subset. The dataset is divided as follows: 192 sentences in the training set (BIWI-Train), 24 in the validation set (BIWI-Val), and the test set split into BIWI-Test-A with 24 sentences by subjects seen in training, and BIWI-Test-B with 32 sentences by eight unseen subjects. BIWI-Test-B is ideal for qualitative evaluations, while BIWI-Test-A supports both qualitative and quantitative assessments.

VOCASET Dataset. VOCASET includes 480 facial motion sequences from 12 participants, each captured at 60fps and lasting 3 to 4 s. The face mesh, registered to the FLAME [24] topology, consists of 5023 vertices. For consistency with prior studies [8,13,27,38], we use the same data split: VOCA-Train, VOCA-Val, and VOCA-Test.

Implementations. We conducted experiments on BIWI and VOCASET, comparing our method with three mainstream methods: FaceFormer [13], CodeTalker [38], and SelfTalk [27]. We used pre-trained models and official implementations for ablation studies and training comparisons. Our method, along with FaceFormer and CodeTalker, requires speaking style inputs during testing. For seen subjects, we use the corresponding speaking style, and for unseen subjects, we employ the same the speaking style to ensure a fair comparison.

4.2   Quantitative Evaluation

We conducted quantitative evaluations focusing on lip synchronization and facial dynamics. Following previous methods [13,27,29,38], we assessed lip synchronization quality using the maximal lip vertex error (L_{max}^{lip}), which calculates the maximum L2 error across all lip vertices per frame, averaged over all frames. We also measured the mean lip vertex error (L_{mean}^{lip}) to provide a comprehensive evaluation, quantifying the mean L2 error of vertices in the lip region.

To quantitatively evaluate facial dynamics, we use the maximal face vertex error (L_{max}^{face}), the mean face vertex error (L_{mean}^{face}), and the upper-face dynamics deviation (FDD) as employed in CodeTalker [38] and SelfTalk [27]. Both L_{max}^{face} and L_{mean}^{face} measure the maximum and mean errors across all facial vertices per frame, averaged over all frames.

Table 1. Quantitative metrics on BIWI-Test-A

Method	$L_{max}^{lip} \downarrow$ $\times 10^{-4}$	$L_{mean}^{lip} \downarrow$ $\times 10^{-4}$	$L_{max}^{face} \downarrow$ $\times 10^{-4}$	$L_{mean}^{face} \downarrow$ $\times 10^{-5}$	FDD$\downarrow$ $\times 10^{-5}$
FaceFormer	5.3182	1.5162	6.5051	8.8173	4.6480
CodeTalker	4.8133	1.3582	6.0381	8.3052	4.1244
SelfTalk	4.2392	1.1927	**5.1419**	7.1895	3.5945
Ours	**4.1283**	**1.1855**	5.1470	**7.1556**	**2.9876**

We calculated the above metrics for all sequences in BIWI-Test-A and compared them with FaceFormer [13], CodeTalker [38], and SelfTalk [27]. As shown in Table 1, our method exhibits lower maximal and mean errors, indicating more accurate lip movements than mainstream methods. In facial dynamics, our approach surpasses others in L_{mean}^{face} and FDD, and matches the best in L_{max}^{face}, demonstrating that our facial dynamics align closely with the Ground Truth and produce more vivid facial animations.

4.3   Qualitative Evaluation

Besides quantitative assessment, qualitative evaluations are essential for speech-driven 3D facial animation. We conducted visual comparisons, as shown in Figs. 6 and 5. Figure 5 displays heatmaps for an intuitive analysis of Euclidean distance errors between method predictions and the Ground Truth for BIWI-Test-A and VOCA-Test. We employ BIWI-Test-A to evaluate the accuracy of style capture for speakers seen during training, and VOCA-Test to assess the visual performance on unseen speakers. In the former case, the corresponding speaker style is provided as input. In the latter, a consistent speaker style input is used across all methods to ensure a fair comparison. These heatmaps visualize max and mean vertex distance errors across all frames. The heatmap results demonstrate that our method yields lower vertex errors, indicating its effectiveness in capturing the styles of seen speakers and in generating high-quality facial animations for unseen speakers.

To evaluate geometric details in generated facial expressions, we used the same wild speech segment and speaking style from BIWI-Train as input for visual comparisons across methods. The results, shown in Fig. 6, include sampled frames at various pronunciation moments with magnified facial regions for clarity. Our method accurately captures facial undulations, particularly during phonemes like 'I' and the beginning of 'time,' where cheeks bulge. In contrast, methods like CodeTalker [38] and SelfTalk [27] struggle with these details and

14 B. Yang et al.

often produce uneven surfaces, while our method maintains smoother surfaces. This demonstrates that our method effectively captures the speaker's personalized style in geometric details.

Additionally, we analyzed speaking style differences in Fig. 7 using a wild speech segment and different VOCA-Train style inputs to drive the animations. We calculated the average lip vertex offsets under various styles for comparison. Figure 7 shows that different speaking styles lead to varying lip vertex offsets, which interlace rather than remain constant across styles. This suggests our method captures not just the amplitude of lip movements but the nuanced personal speaking styles, largely attributed to our regional attention mechanism that effectively distinguishes between speaking styles.

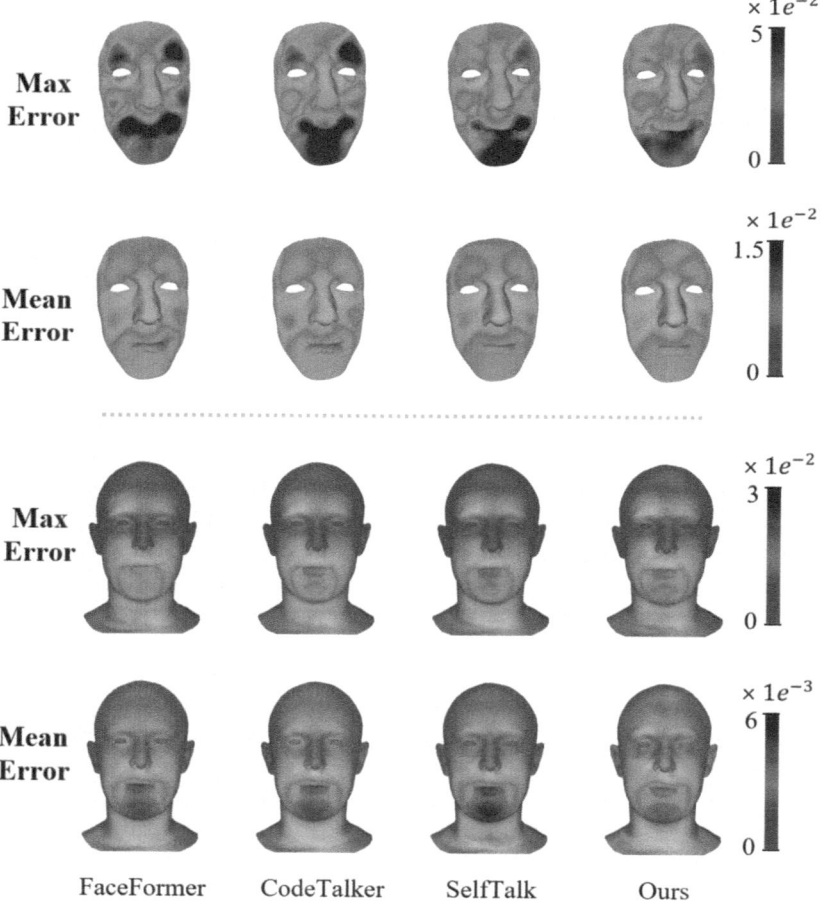

Fig. 5. Visualization of vertex error on BIWI-Test-A(upper) and VOCA-Test(lower), showing maximal and average Euclidean distance errors per vertex temporally.

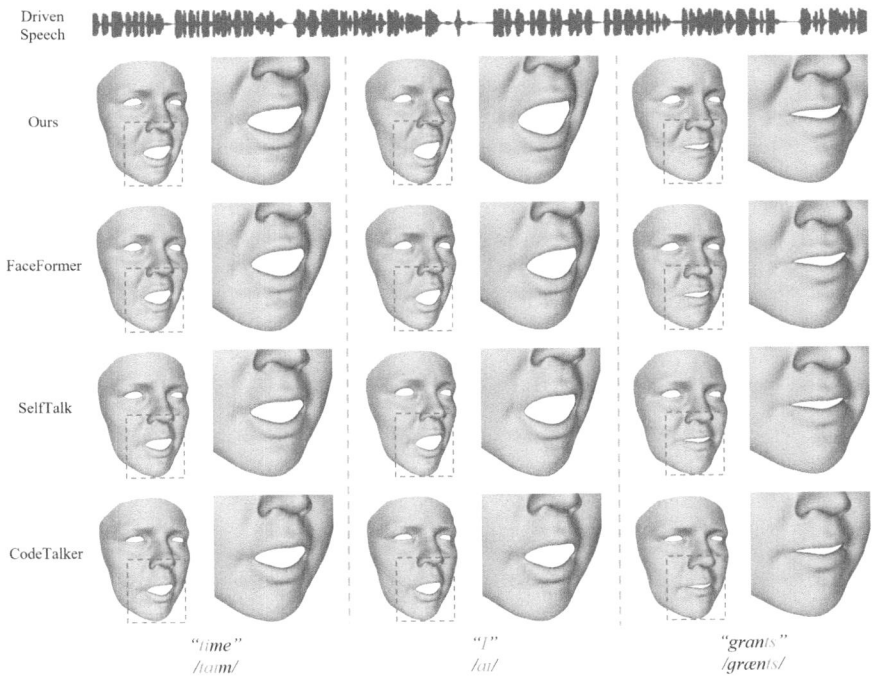

Fig. 6. Visual comparisons of sampled facial frames driven by the same external speech and the speaking style in BIWI-Train, illustrating the facial details with different speech segments.

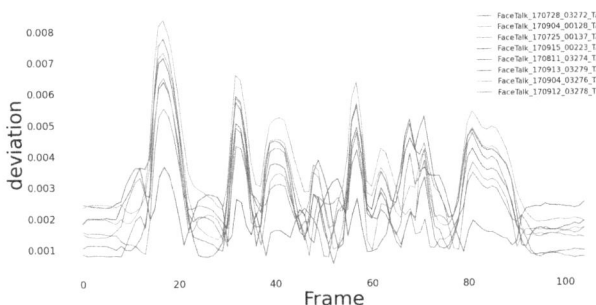

Fig. 7. Average lip vertex offset for our predicted sequence with the same driven speech and conditioned on different speaking styles in VOCA-Train.

4.4   User Study

We conducted user studies using A/B tests to compare our method with Face-Former [13], CodeTalker [38], SelfTalk [27], and Ground Truth, focusing on perceptual lip synchronization and animation realism. For BIWI, we selected 20 random samples from BIWI-Test-B for each of the four comparisons, totaling 80 A vs. B pairs. For VOCASET, we chose 20 samples from VOCA-Test, also resulting in 80 A vs. B pairs, but selected 10 samples per character due to only two characters being present, ensuring comprehensive character coverage. We invited 20 participants to assess lip synchronization and realism, offering choices between A, B, or equal due to the close quality of competing methods.

The percentage of user study participants who rated our method as equal to or better than competing methods is detailed in Table 2. In A/B tests against various methods, our approach is frequently seen as at least equal, particularly in 'Lip Sync' and 'Realism'. For instance, 58.75% and 61% of participants judged our method as equal or superior to SelfTalk in these aspects, respectively. This demonstrates that our method achieves good naturalness and realism in visual perception.

Table 2. User study results: Percentage of A/B tests where our method was chosen as equal or better than others on BIWI-Test-B and VOCA-Test

Competitors	BIWI-Test-B				VOCA-Test			
	Lip Sync		Realism		Lip Sync		Realism	
	Better	Equal	Better	Equal	Better	Equal	Better	Equal
Ours vs. FaceFormer	40.50%	11.00%	41.50%	18.00%	36.50%	28.50%	36.25%	32.50%
Ours vs. CodeTalker	48.25%	12.00%	48.50%	15.25%	32.25%	22.50%	31.75%	23.50%
Ours vs. SelfTalk	37.50%	17.20%	43.25%	10.75%	38.25%	20.50%	36.75%	24.25%
Ours vs. Ground Truth	37.75%	13.50%	38.00%	10.50%	17.75%	19.75%	16.50%	22.50%

4.5   Ablation Study

Two ablation experiments were conducted to assess the adaptability of our method and the impact of each component, with results in Table 3. For adaptability analysis, we modified the official implementations of FaceFormer [13], CodeTalker [38], and SelfTalk [27] by integrating our loss functions. Since CodeTalker operates in two stages, where stage 2 depends on stage 1's discrete space model, we used its pretrained stage 1 model to retrain stage 2, ensuring a fair evaluation. Experiments on BIWI-Test-A showed that incorporating our loss functions improved most metrics in other methods, with some remaining comparable (e.g., L_{mean}^{lip} in CodeTalker and FDD in SelfTalk). These results demonstrate our method's adaptability in mesh-based speech-driven 3D facial animation, enhancing lip accuracy and facial expressiveness.

In another ablation study, removing L_{mask} caused a greater FDD decline than L_{normal}, highlighting the importance of regional attention in speech-independent facial expressions. Removing both loss functions led to a significant drop in all metrics, further validating our method's effectiveness.

Table 3. Ablation study results for the adaptability of our method and the impact of components on BIWI-Test-A.

Method	$L_{max}^{lip}\downarrow$ $\times 10^{-4}$	$L_{mean}^{lip}\downarrow$ $\times 10^{-4}$	$L_{max}^{face}\downarrow$ $\times 10^{-4}$	$L_{mean}^{face}\downarrow$ $\times 10^{-5}$	FDD$\downarrow$ $\times 10^{-5}$
FaceFormer	5.3182	1.5162	6.5051	8.8173	4.6480
w/ our method	**4.8265**	**1.3309**	**5.9444**	**7.9894**	**3.6343**
CodeTalker	5.1438	**1.4134**	6.6119	8.7667	4.0687
w/ our method	**5.0583**	1.4175	**6.3037**	**8.6198**	**3.7911**
SelfTalk	4.2392	1.1927	5.1419	7.1895	**3.5945**
w/ our method	**4.0385**	**1.1096**	**4.8804**	**6.6839**	3.7311
Ours	**4.1283**	**1.1855**	**5.1470**	**7.1556**	**2.9876**
w/o L_{mask}	4.3699	1.2604	5.3282	7.4429	4.2447
w/o L_{normal}	4.2871	1.2328	5.3003	7.4070	3.5264
w/o both losses	4.4542	1.2373	5.4394	7.4673	4.2870

5   Discussion and Conclusion

In this paper,we propose a speech-driven facial animation method with Regional Attention mechanism, capable of generating highly expressive animations that align with the input style using only speech and an identity control vector. By customizing facial attention areas for different speakers, we effectively capture style information. Extensive experiments demonstrate its superior performance in both quantitative metrics and qualitative analysis, as well as its adaptability to mesh-based deep-learning frameworks. However, limitations remain, such as the lack of emotional modeling and real-time support, which will be further improved in future work.

Acknowledgements. This work was supported in part by the National Natural Science Foundation (Grant No. 62172366) and the Zhejiang Province Natural Science Foundation (Grant No. LD24F020003).

References

1. Aneja, S., Thies, J., Dai, A., Nießner, M.: Facetalk: audio-driven motion diffusion for neural parametric head models. arXiv preprint arXiv:2312.08459 (2023)
2. Baevski, A., Zhou, Y., Mohamed, A., Auli, M.: wav2vec 2.0: A framework for self-supervised learning of speech representations. In: Advances in Neural Information Processing Systems 33: Annual Conference on Neural Information Processing Systems 2020, NeurIPS 2020, December 6-12, 2020, virtual (2020)
3. Cao, C., Wu, H., Weng, Y., Shao, T., Zhou, K.: Real-time facial animation with image-based dynamic avatars. ACM Trans. Graphics **35**(4) (2016)

4. Carion, N., Massa, F., Synnaeve, G., Usunier, N., Kirillov, A., Zagoruyko, S.: End-to-end object detection with transformers. In: European Conference on Computer Vision. pp. 213–229. Springer (2020)
5. Chai, Y., Shao, T., Weng, Y., Zhou, K.: Personalized audio-driven 3d facial animation via style-content disentanglement. IEEE Trans. Visual. Comput. Graphics (2022)
6. Chen, L., et al.: Adamesh: personalized facial expressions and head poses for adaptive speech-driven 3d facial animation. IEEE Trans. Multimedia (2025)
7. Chu, X., Yang, W., Ouyang, W., Ma, C., Yuille, A.L., Wang, X.: Multi-context attention for human pose estimation. In: Proceedings of the IEEE Conference on Computer Vision and Pattern Recognition. pp. 1831–1840 (2017)
8. Cudeiro, D., Bolkart, T., Laidlaw, C., Ranjan, A., Black, M.J.: Capture, learning, and synthesis of 3d speaking styles. In: Proceedings of the IEEE/CVF Conference on Computer Vision and Pattern Recognition. pp. 10101–10111 (2019)
9. Dai, T., Cai, J., Zhang, Y., Xia, S.T., Zhang, L.: Second-order attention network for single image super-resolution. In: Proceedings of the IEEE/CVF Conference on Computer Vision and Pattern Recognition. pp. 11065–11074 (2019)
10. Daněček, R., Chhatre, K., Tripathi, S., Wen, Y., Black, M., Bolkart, T.: Emotional speech-driven animation with content-emotion disentanglement. In: SIGGRAPH Asia 2023 Conference Papers. pp. 1–13 (2023)
11. Dosovitskiy, A., et al.: An image is worth 16x16 words: transformers for image recognition at scale. arXiv preprint arXiv:2010.11929 (2020)
12. Edwards, P., Landreth, C., Fiume, E., Singh, K.: Jali: an animator-centric viseme model for expressive lip synchronization. ACM Trans. graphics (TOG) **35**(4), 1–11 (2016)
13. Fan, Y., Lin, Z., Saito, J., Wang, W., Komura, T.: Faceformer: speech-driven 3d facial animation with transformers. In: IEEE/CVF Conference on Computer Vision and Pattern Recognition, CVPR 2022, New Orleans, LA, USA, June 18-24, 2022. pp. 18749–18758 (2022)
14. Fanelli, G., Gall, J., Romsdorfer, H., Weise, T., Van Gool, L.: A 3-d audio-visual corpus of affective communication. IEEE Trans. Multimedia **12**(6), 591–598 (2010)
15. Fried, O., et al.: Text-based editing of talking-head video. ACM Trans. Graphics (TOG) **38**(4), 1–14 (2019)
16. Guo, M.-H., et al.: Attention mechanisms in computer vision: a survey. Comput. Visual Media , 1–38 (2022). https://doi.org/10.1007/s41095-022-0271-y
17. Hu, J., Shen, L., Sun, G.: Squeeze-and-excitation networks. In: Proceedings of the IEEE Conference on Computer Vision and Pattern Recognition. pp. 7132–7141 (2018)
18. Jaderberg, M., Simonyan, K., Zisserman, A., et al.: Spatial transformer networks. Adv. Neural Inf. Process. Syst. **28** (2015)
19. Jung, S., et al.: Speed-aware audio-driven speech animation using adaptive windows. ACM Trans. Graphics **44**(1), 1–14 (2024)
20. Karras, T., Aila, T., Laine, S., Herva, A., Lehtinen, J.: Audio-driven facial animation by joint end-to-end learning of pose and emotion. ACM Trans. Graphics (TOG) **36**(4), 1–12 (2017)
21. Kim, H., et al.: Deep video portraits. ACM Trans. Graphics (TOG) **37**(4), 1–14 (2018)

22. Lahiri, A., Kwatra, V., Frueh, C., Lewis, J., Bregler, C.: Lipsync3d: data-efficient learning of personalized 3d talking faces from video using pose and lighting normalization. In: Proceedings of the IEEE/CVF Conference on Computer Vision and Pattern Recognition. pp. 2755–2764 (2021)
23. Li, H., Yu, J., Ye, Y., Bregler, C.: Realtime facial animation with on-the-fly correctives. ACM Trans. Graph. **32**(4), 42–1 (2013)
24. Li, T., Bolkart, T., Black, M.J., Li, H., Romero, J.: Learning a model of facial shape and expression from 4d scans. ACM Trans. Graph. **36**(6), 194–1 (2017)
25. Liu, Z., et al.: Swin transformer: hierarchical vision transformer using shifted windows. In: Proceedings of the IEEE/CVF International Conference on Computer Vision. pp. 10012–10022 (2021)
26. Mnih, V., Heess, N., Graves, A., et al.: Recurrent models of visual attention. Adv. Neural Inf. Process. Syst. **27** (2014)
27. Peng, Z., et al.: Selftalk: a self-supervised commutative training diagram to comprehend 3d talking faces. In: Proceedings of the 31st ACM International Conference on Multimedia, MM 2023, Ottawa, ON, Canada, 29 October 2023- 3 November 2023. pp. 5292–5301 (2023)
28. Peng, Z., et al.: Emotalk: speech-driven emotional disentanglement for 3d face animation. In: Proceedings of the IEEE/CVF International Conference on Computer Vision. pp. 20687–20697 (2023)
29. Richard, A., Zollhöfer, M., Wen, Y., De la Torre, F., Sheikh, Y.: Meshtalk: 3d face animation from speech using cross-modality disentanglement. In: Proceedings of the IEEE/CVF International Conference on Computer Vision. pp. 1173–1182 (2021)
30. Song, W., et al.: Expressive 3d facial animation generation based on local-to-global latent diffusion. IEEE Trans. Visual. Comput. Graph. (2024)
31. Taylor, S.L., Mahler, M., Theobald, B.J., Matthews, I.: Dynamic units of visual speech. In: Proceedings of the 11th ACM SIGGRAPH/Eurographics Conference on Computer Animation. pp. 275–284 (2012)
32. Thambiraja, B., Habibie, I., Aliakbarian, S., Cosker, D., Theobalt, C., Thies, J.: Imitator: personalized speech-driven 3d facial animation. In: Proceedings of the IEEE/CVF International Conference on Computer Vision. pp. 20621–20631 (2023)
33. Thies, J., Elgharib, M., Tewari, A., Theobalt, C., Nießner, M.: Neural Voice Puppetry: Audio-Driven Facial Reenactment. In: Vedaldi, A., Bischof, H., Brox, T., Frahm, J.-M. (eds.) ECCV 2020. LNCS, vol. 12361, pp. 716–731. Springer, Cham (2020). https://doi.org/10.1007/978-3-030-58517-4_42
34. Vaswani, A., Shazeer, N., Parmar, N., Uszkoreit, J., Jones, L., Gomez, A.N., Kaiser, Ł., Polosukhin, I.: Attention is all you need. Advances in neural information processing systems **30** (2017)
35. Wang, Q., Wu, T., Zheng, H., Guo, G.: Hierarchical pyramid diverse attention networks for face recognition. In: Proceedings of the IEEE/CVF Conference on Computer Vision and Pattern Recognition. pp. 8326–8335 (2020)
36. Wang, X., Girshick, R., Gupta, A., He, K.: Non-local neural networks. In: Proceedings of the IEEE Conference on Computer Vision and Pattern Recognition. pp. 7794–7803 (2018)
37. Wu, H., Zhou, S., Jia, J., Xing, J., Wen, Q., Wen, X.: Speech-driven 3d face animation with composite and regional facial movements. In: Proceedings of the 31st ACM International Conference on Multimedia. pp. 6822–6830 (2023)

38. Xing, J., Xia, M., Zhang, Y., Cun, X., Wang, J., Wong, T.: Codetalker: speech-driven 3d facial animation with discrete motion prior. In: IEEE/CVF Conference on Computer Vision and Pattern Recognition, CVPR 2023, Vancouver, BC, Canada, June 17-24, 2023. pp. 12780–12790 (2023)
39. Xu, Y., Feng, A.W., Marsella, S., Shapiro, A.: A practical and configurable lip sync method for games. In: Proceedings of Motion on Games, pp. 131–140 (2013)
40. Yang, K.D., Ranjan, A., Chang, J.H.R., Vemulapalli, R., Tuzel, O.: Probabilistic speech-driven 3d facial motion synthesis: new benchmarks, methods, and applications. arXiv preprint arXiv:2311.18168 (2023)

Perspective Matters: Investigating the Effects of Vibrotactile Mode Design on User Experience in Action-Role Playing Game and Media

Hongyu Liu$^{\text{ⓘ}}$ and Zhenyu Gu$^{(\boxtimes)}$ⓘ

Shanghai Jiao Tong University, Shanghai, China
{liuhongyu9686,zygu}@sjtu.edu.cn

Abstract. Vibrotactile feedback is widely held to make medias attractive and enjoyable, but excessive vibrotactile feedback can lead to negative effects. Designing suitable vibrotactile feedback modes is challenging in games with intense interactions, such as action role-playing game (ARPG). This study investigates the impact of vibrotactile feedback designed from different perspectives on player and media audience's user experience. We designed three vibrotactile feedback modes based on player's perspective mode (PPM), boss's perspective mode (BPM), and global perspective mode (GPM), and created haptic video clips based on ARPG game (Black myth: Wukong) recordings. We evaluated these three feedback modes in a qualitative user study (N = 52) and conducted interviews with participants. The results indicate that PPM is universally applicable, while BPM is friendly for beginner players, and GPM is suitable for in-game cinematics and haptic streaming media. These findings inform game developers' decisions on tailoring vibrotactile feedback modes to specific game segments or player skills, and enhancing game transmission through haptic media.

Keywords: Game experience · Haptic experience · Multimodal interaction · Haptic streaming media · Action-role playing game

1 Introduction

In August 2024, Black Myth: Wukong set a record with 2.4 million concurrent players, making it the most-played single-player game in history [4]. Game-related videos and live streams gained immense popularity [20]. In action games, effective feedback design is vital to player experience [24].

Vibrotactile feedback enhances impact perception in action games, complementing visual and auditory cues while adding a physical dimension [30]. Its role in game and media design is increasingly prominent. Vibrotactile feedback in action games conveys information, confirms actions, and simulates virtual physicality [3,29]. Recent studies suggest decorative vibrotactile effects can enhance user experience [38].

C. Mousas et al. (Eds.): CASA 2025, LNCS 15915, pp. 21–38, 2026.
https://doi.org/10.1007/978-981-95-0100-7_2

In streaming and live broadcasts, haptic feedback enhances expressiveness and audience engagement, though excessive vibration may negatively impact user experience [7]. In high-intensity ARPGs, prolonged boss battles create frequent, intense interactions, posing challenges for haptic design [5].

To refine haptic feedback in high-frequency interactions, we developed three models: Player Perspective Model (PPM), Boss Perspective Model (BPM), and Global Perspective Model (GPM), offering distinct viewpoints. This study examines how vibration modes affect gaming experience and haptic media consumption, focusing on:

(1) How do different vibration perspectives influence player and audience experience?

(2) Do players of varying skill levels perceive vibration feedback differently?

We recruited 52 participants (36 players, 16 viewers) to evaluate these feedback models. Results indicate that PPM is the most preferred vibration mode among players, BPM boosts novice confidence, and GPM enhances spectating and haptic streaming engagement.

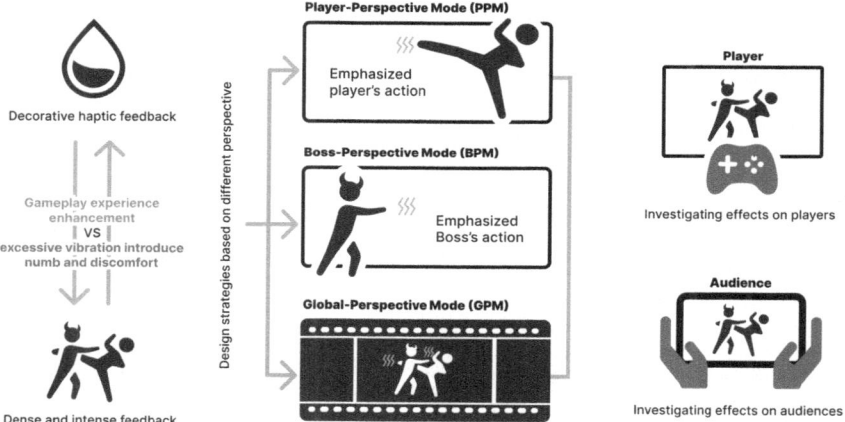

Fig. 1. Perspective-Based Vibrotactile Mode Design Strategies. This figure shows the problem of haptic in action role-playing games, and our design of vibrotactile modes from the perspectives of in game (player and boss) or out of game (audience), as well as our investigation of the impact of these modes on the user experience of game players and streaming media audiences.

2   Related Works

2.1   Decorative Vibrotactile Feedback

The concept of juice frequently arises in game experience discussions, referring to the excessive use of feedback in response to player input [31]. It is considered a component of game feel, where amplified feedback enhances expected gameplay sensations [31]. K. Hicks explored visual juiciness in player experience and proposed a juicy design framework for developers [13,14]. Smets et al. examined how juicy audio influences player experience [39]. More recently, juicy haptic design has gained attention, with designers leveraging vibrotactile feedback to create immersive sensations that simulate various game effects [37].

In ARPGs, boss battles are central to gameplay. Bosses serve as major non-player characters (NPCs) designed for player challenges, featuring stylized appearances and carefully crafted movements [15]. Some ARPGs revolve entirely around consecutive boss fights, a format known as boss rush. These battles are typically difficult, requiring multiple attempts to succeed [21]. Players engage in two primary actions: attacking and dodging [24]. Success depends on recognizing attack patterns, avoiding damage, and striking at opportune moments [2]. After several cycles, accumulated damage leads to victory. Combat feedback significantly impacts player performance, making the design of vibrotactile feedback for intense encounters a complex task. Designers must balance enhancing performance with ensuring a cohesive haptic experience. Thus, the role of excessive haptic design in action games, particularly in high-intensity player-enemy interactions, remains an important subject for exploration.

2.2   Strategies of Haptic Design

Feedback needs to serve the design purpose, and the design of feedback needs to be reviewed from a bigger picture. In game design, different perspectives are also employed to enhance the player experience. For instance, a first-person perspective is used to increase immersion, while a third-person perspective provides a broader view of the environment, helping players better understand their avatar's position and appearance within the virtual world [6,9]. We investigated the design of vibrotactile feedback in interactive media and summarized their design strategies:

On one hand, one of the key roles of vibrotactile feedback is to enhance the player's sense of presence and immersion, allowing them to enter the avatar's perspective. Designers use vibrotactile feedback to associate the player's input with the avatar's actions, thereby creating a sense of embodiment that supports immersive interactive experiences [32]. Embodiment can alter haptic perception [11], and these studies typically use vibrotactile feedback to associate with multiple inputs [8,25]. Additionally, using vibrotactile feedback to enhance weight perception in virtual environments or to improve spatial awareness [17,42]. This strategy enables users to feel more controllable in their actions. Vibrotactile feedback is used to enhance their roprioception sensations, making users feel that their virtual avatars are more like their own bodies.

On the other hand, haptic feedback design can also be expressed from an external perspective. For example, rendering the physical properties of interactive, such as objectsstiffness, roughness [23,27]. These vibrotactile feedback is used to emphasize external objects, improving the hedonic and emotional experience in interaction [10,18]. And vibrotactile feedback can enhance the experience of immersive audio or increase environmental realism in games, thereby improve user immersion [34,40]. This strategy improves the overall experience by using vibrotactile to emphasize externalize factors. They place the design focus on objects outside the user, enhancing the user's experience from the outside in, making interactive objects or environments more expressive. Sound and haptic feedback in games can be used to reinforce perspective-based design.

The related works above inspired our design of vibrotactile modes based on different perspectives. We found that current haptic feedback in games and media primarily focuses on rendering realistic tactile sensations for individual objects. However, little research attention has been given to how these numerous haptic feedback elements can be integrated in a more appropriate and comfortable manner. Building on this, we designed three haptic feedback perspectives–Player Perspective Mode(PPM), Boss Perspective Mode(BPM), and Global Perspective Mode(GPM)—to emphasize the actions of different roles in the game through vibration feedback (Fig. 1).

3   Methods

3.1   Feedback Mode Design

Building upon related work, we analyzed boss battles in ARPGs from three distinct perspectives.

In these encounters, both the player and the boss serve as central figures, with haptic feedback playing a crucial role in enhancing their expressiveness. The frequent interactions between them create numerous opportunities for vibration feedback. However, excessive vibrations pose a risk–overstimulation can lead to sensory fatigue, ultimately diminishing the player's experience. To mitigate this, a structured approach to combat design is necessary.

To address this challenge, we propose a vibration feedback framework based on three perspectives—the player perspective, boss perspective, and global perspective. This framework systematizes haptic feedback, ensuring it conveys clear design intentions while maintaining an optimal balance of stimulation. Building on this foundation, we developed vibrotactile feedback patterns for each perspective (Fig. 1).

PPM: Player Perspective Mode. In action games, the player-controlled character serves as the protagonist. From the player's perspective, vibrotactile feedback should enhance the sense of control and agency. This mode emphasizes the player's actions, including light and heavy attacks, dodges, and skill executions (Fig. 2). By reinforcing these interactions, vibrotactile feedback improves action recognition, facilitates skill combination strategies, and enhances operational confirmation.

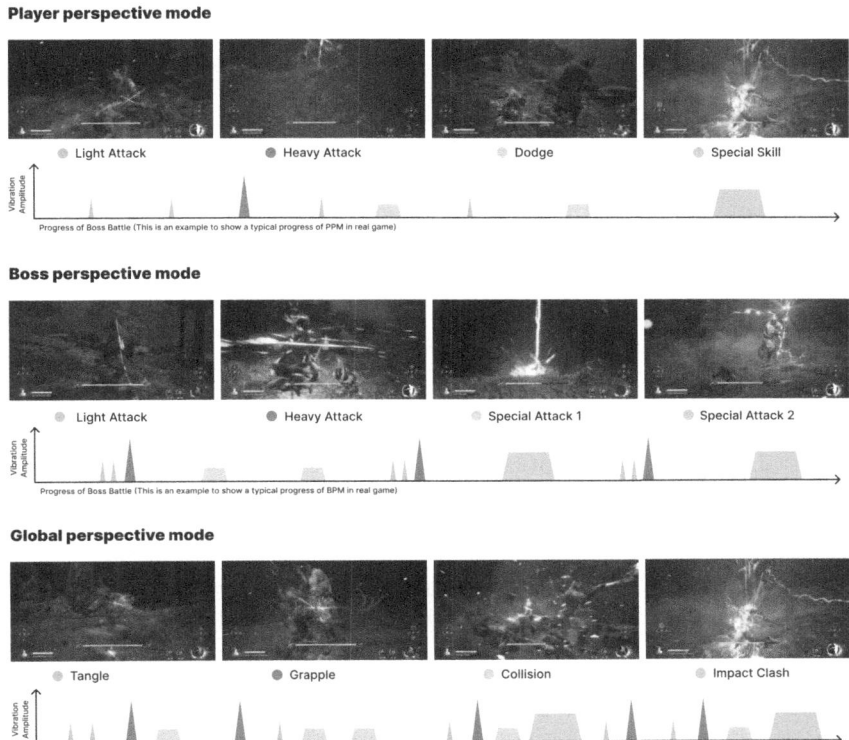

Fig. 2. Actions of Player and Boss in Battle. This figure shows the main actions of the player and boss in the game and the vibrotactile feedback to emphasize these actions. All vibrotactile feedback had a frequency of 210 Hz and an amplitude of either high (1.2g) or low (0.6g). The example waveforms in the figure show the types of vibration feedback (instantaneous or consistant) and their amplitudes (high or low), but do not represent the actual waveforms.

BPM: Boss Perspective Mode. The boss, as the player's opponent, is a focal point of combat design. From this perspective, vibrotactile feedback should amplify the boss's expressiveness, enabling players to perceive its movements and behaviors more clearly. Corresponding feedback is applied to the boss's light attacks, heavy attacks, special moves, and unique actions (Fig. 2). This approach increases player awareness of the boss's attacks, making encounters more immersive and intensifying the perceived challenge.

GPM: Global Perspective Mode. Beyond direct player control, game spectatorship offers another perspective. Streaming media plays a crucial role in modern game dissemination, and certain platforms have begun integrating vibrotactile feedback to enhance viewer engagement. In this mode, the audience experiences combat from a global third-person perspective, observing through the game camera rather than directly controlling the character. Key impactful moments–such as powerful attacks and dramatic movements by the player and boss–are emphasized through vibration feedback.

Given the need to compare player experiences with audience perceptions, creating a high-fidelity prototype that fully replicates real gameplay remains a challenge due to the dynamic nature of action games. Additionally, the stimuli must accommodate both players and spectators. To address this, we developed unified tactile videos as stimuli for both groups. We selected a boss battle from Black Myth: Wukong to generate haptic media clips (Fig. 2), leveraging the game's large player base to ensure adequate participant recruitment.

3.2   Participants

We recruited 52 participants aged between 18 and 35, all with normal hearing and intact hand tactile perception. Participants were divided into two groups: players and audience. The players group included 36 participants who had played Black Myth: Wukong for over 20 h. All players used controllers and played with vibrotactile feedback enabled. Based on their gaming experience, players were further classified into two subgroups: experienced players and beginner players. The experienced players consisted of 21 participants with at least 500 h of ARPG experience, while the beginner players included 15 participants with less than 50 h of ARPG experience. The audience group comprised 16 participants who had no prior ARPG gameplay experience but had watched over 5 h of gaming live streams or related videos. This study was approved by the Ethics Committee of Shanghai Jiao Tong University (E2022741), and all participants were informed the informed consent form.

3.3   Apparatus

Considering development feasibility and the actual scenario, we selected the linear resonant actuator (LRA) in an iPhone 13 mini as the haptic device. Our measurements show that the device operates within a frequency range of 80-240 Hz, with a maximum intensity of 1.3 g at 210 Hz. The LRA is manufactured by AAC Technologies, and the haptic driver used is Apple CoreHaptics. The haptic media was developed using Unity, version 2022.3.25f1c1.

3.4   Environment

The experiment was conducted in a quiet, closed indoor environment to minimize potential noise or other disturbances. Participants sat comfortably at a desk with their arms resting on the table to stabilize the phone. They were instructed to hold the phone with both hands, ensuring good contact between their palms and fingers and the phone's back and frame, which facilitated the effective transmission of vibrotactile feedback (Fig. 3).

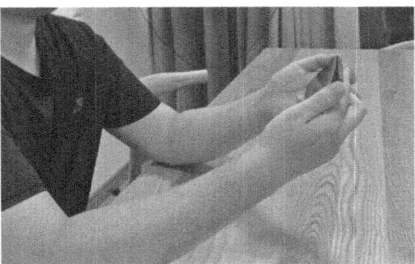

Fig. 3. Participant in experiment. Left figure shows the participant sitting in a stable posture during the experiment. Right figure shows the participant holding the phone with good contact.

3.5   Procedure

The experimenter first briefly introduced the background, purpose, and procedure of the experiment. Then, the participants were asked to hold the phone and watch the haptic media video. For players group, they were asked to imagine themselves actually controlling the character in the video. Specifically, we guided the players before playing the video: "Please imagine that you are controlling the character during the video". All articipants watched the tactile media of PPM, BPM, and GPM in a random order. Since the boss challenge result of gameplay may influence the player's evaluation [26], we ensured that each mode's video clip included two challenge failures and one challenge success to reduce the impact. After watching each mode's haptic video, the participants filled out the questionnaire. Between the two viewings, the participants took a 5-minute break to refresh their senses.

3.6   Questionnaire

We referenced the AttrakDiff scale [12], game experience questionnaire [16],haptic experience measurement [1,36] and Yun et al.'s questionnaire on vibrotactile effects [41]. Our questionnaire would not only focus on basic comfort and pleasure experiences but also examine the combination of vibration patterns and audio-visual effects, as well as whether the vibration patterns could provide continuous positive emotional stimulation to encourage players to continue playing or attract spectators to become players. Therefore, our questionnaire is divided into three aspects:

Table 1. Questionnaire.Using a 7-point Likert scale(1-7). 1 represents strong disagreement and 7 represents strong agreement.

Question	Description
GN1:Comfort	I think the vibration feels comfortable
GN2:Pleasure	I think the vibration is pleasant
PG1:Adequacy	I think the vibration matches the game's visual and auditory content perfectly
PG2:Harmony	I think the vibration is harmonious with the game's other elements
HQ1:Confidence	I think the vibration increases my confidence in winning the game
HQ2:Encouragement	I think the vibration encourages my interest in the game and motivates me to continue playing

General Experience. Questions focus on comfort(GE1) and pleasure(GE2). We ask players to evaluate whether the feedback mode feels comfortable overall and whether it makes them feel pleasant(Table 1).

Pragmatic Quality. Questions focus on the adequacy(PQ1) and harmony(PQ2) of vibrotactile feedback. Vibrotactile is often seen as an auxiliary modality to visual and auditory feedback, and it needs to match the visual and auditory content and be harmonious with them(Table 1).

Hedonic Quality. Questions focus on the confidence(HQ1) and encouragement(HQ2) of vibrotactile feedback for participants. Specifically, whether the mode enhances the participant's confidence in winning the game and whether it encourages players to continue challenging or attracts audience to start their first game(Table 1).

4   Result

Since the rating data did not conform to a normal distribution, as confirmed by the Shapiro-Wilk test ($p < .05$), we adopted non-parametric statistical methods for analysis. For the comparison among the three viewing modes, we used a within-subjects design and conducted a Friedman test. For the comparison among the three user groups (experienced players, beginner players, and audience members), we used a between-subjects design and conducted a Kruskal-Wallis test. Bonferroni correction was applied in both analyses to adjust for multiple comparisons.

4.1   Vibrotactile Modes Based on Different Perspectives

For GPM (Fig. 4a), There were no significant differences in comfort scores among all participant groups ($H(2) = 1.54, p > .05$). There were significant differences in pleasure scores among all participant groups ($H(2) = 18.92, p < .05$), experienced players' pleasure scores were significantly higher than other groups' ($p < .05$). There were significant differences in adequacy scores ($H(2) = 13.23, p < .05$) and harmony scores ($H(2) = 13.14, p < .05$) among all participant groups, audiences' adequacy and harmony scores were significantly lower than other

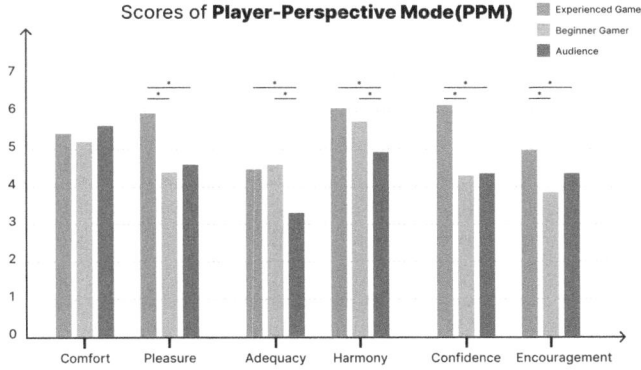

(a) Player-perspective mode.

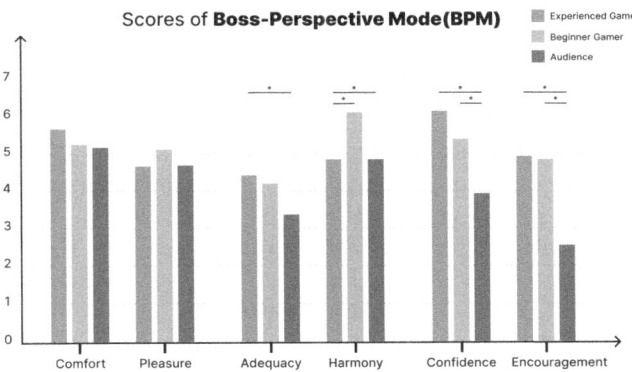

(b) Boss-perspective mode.

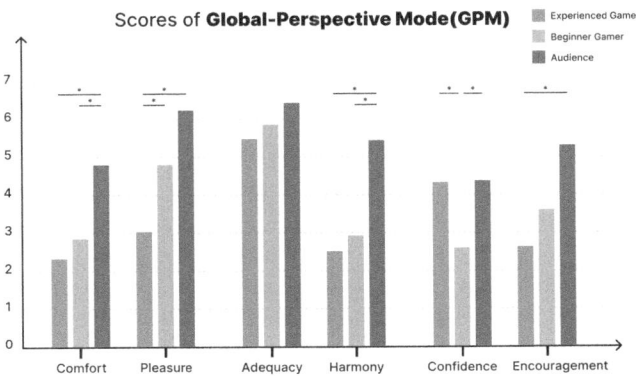

(c) Global-perspective mode.

Fig. 4. Result of Perspective-based modes. This figure shows the questionnaire scores for all three perspective modes, with significant differences between groups marked with *.

groups' ($p < .05$). There were significant differences in confidence scores (H(2) = 26.06, $p < .05$) and encouragement scores (H(2) = 11.70, $p < .05$) among all participant groups, experienced players' confidence and encouragement scores were significantly higher than other groups'($p < .05$).

For BPM (Fig. 4b),There was no significant difference in comfort (H(2) = 1.74, $p > .05$) and pleasure scores among all participant groups(H(2) = 2.35, $p > .05$). There were significant differences in adequacy scores (H(2) = 9.34, $p < .05$) and harmony scores (H(2) = 12.01, $p < .05$) among all participant groups, experienced players' adequacy scores were significantly higher than audiences'($p < .05$), beginner players' harmony scores were significantly higher than other groups'($p < .05$). There were significant differences in confidence scores (H(2) = 19.54, $p < .05$) and encouragement scores (H(2) = 25.73, $p < .05$) among all participant groups, Audiences' confidence and encouragement scores were significantly lower than other groups'($p < .05$).

For GPM (Fig. 4c), There were significant differences in comfort (H(2) = 28.88, $p < .05$) and pleasure (H(2) = 32.63, $p < .05$) scores among all participant groups, audiences' comfort scores were significantly higher than other groups'($p < .05$), and audiences' pleasure scores were higher than beginner players'($p < .05$), who in turn scored higher than experienced players($p < .05$). There was no significant difference in adequacy scores among all participant groups(H(2) = 5.72, $p > .05$). There were significant differences in harmony scores among all participant groups (H(2) = 24.83, $p > .05$), audiences' harmony scores were significantly higher than other groups'($p < .05$). There were significant differences in confidence scores (H(2) = 19.77, $p < .05$) and encouragement scores (H(2) = 20.72, $p < .05$) among all participant groups, beginner players' confidence scores were significantly lower than other groups'($p < .05$),and audiences' encouragement scores were significantly higher than other groups'($p < .05$).

4.2   Players and Audiences

For experienced players(Fig. 5a), there were significant differences in the comfort scores among the three modes($x^2(2) = 35.18$, $p < .05$), PPM and BPM had significantly higher comfort scores than GPM ($p < .05$). There were significant differences in the pleasure scores among the three modes($x^2(2) = 28.38$, $p < .05$), PPM had the highest pleasure(P<0.05), while GPM had the lowest($p < .05$). There were significant differences in the adequacy scores ($x^2(2) = 10.45$, $p < .05$) and harmony scores ($x^2(2) = 32.08$, $p < .05$) among the three modes, PPM had significantly higher adequacy scores than others'($p < .05$), but PPM had significantly higher harmony scores than others'($p < .05$). There were significant differences in the confidence scores ($x^2(2) = 29.34$, $p < .05$) and encouragement scores ($x^2(2) = 31.26$, $p < .05$) among the three modes. PPM and BPM had significantly higher confidence and encouragement scores than GPM($p < .05$).

For beginner players(Fig. 5b), there were significant differences in the comfort scores among the three modes($x^2(2) = 21.45$, $p < .05$), PPM and BPM had significantly higher comfort scores than GPM($p < .05$). There was no significant

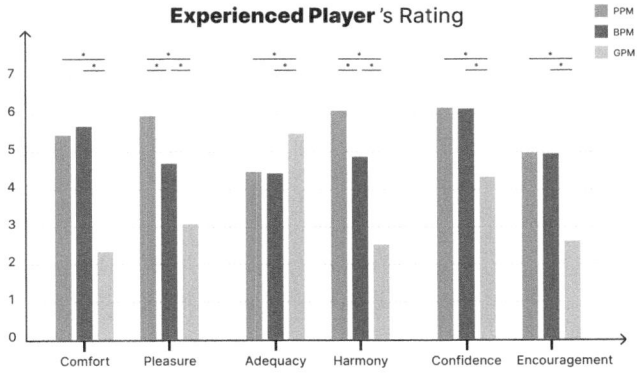

(a) Experienced Players' Rating

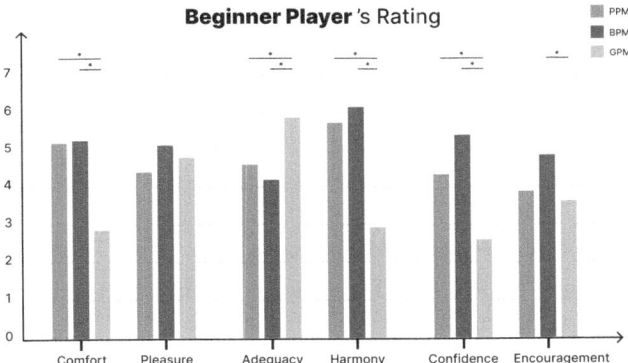

(b) Beginner Players' Rating

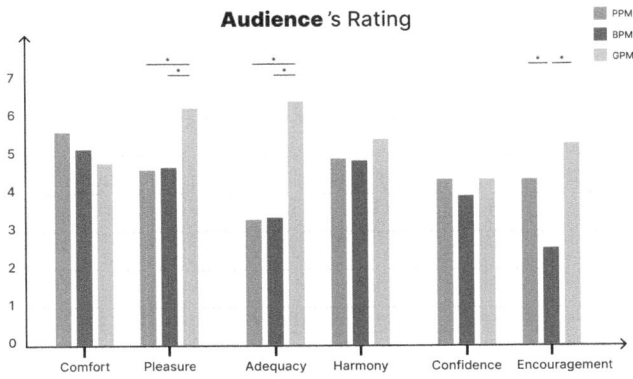

(c) Audiences'sRating

Fig. 5. Result of different types of participants. This figure shows the questionnaire scores for all three types of participants, with significant differences between groups marked with *.

difference in pleasure among all modes($\chi^2(2) = 5.54$, $p > .05$). There were significant differences in the adequacy scores ($\chi^2(2) = 16.75$, $p < .05$) and harmony scores ($\chi^2(2) = 23.31$, $p < .05$) among the three modes, PPM had significantly higher adequacy scores than others($p < .05$),and PPM had significantly better harmony than others'($p < .05$). There were significant differences in the confidence scores ($\chi^2(2) = 22.93$, $p < .05$) and encouragement scores ($\chi^2(2) = 10.18$, $p < .05$) among the three modes. BPM had higher confidence and encouragement scores, significantly better than GPM($p < .05$).

For audiences(Fig. 5c), There was no significant difference in comfort among all modes($\chi^2(2) = 4.25$, $p > .05$). There were significant differences in the pleasure scores among the three modes($\chi^2(2) = 19.02$, $p < .05$), GPM had significantly better pleasure than others'($p < .05$). There were significant differences in the pleasure scores among the three modes($\chi^2(2) = 27.43$, $p < .05$), GPM had significantly better adequacy than others'($p < .05$). There was no significant difference in harmony among all modes.($\chi^2(2) = 4.96$, $p > .05$). There was no significant difference in confidence among all modes($\chi^2(2) = 2.22$, $p > .05$). There were significant differences in the pleasure scores among the three modes($\chi^2(2) = 21.73$, $p < .05$), BPM had significantly lower encouragement than others'($p < .05$).

5   Discussion

5.1   Understanding Results with Interviews

Player-Perspective Mode Fits Experienced Players Better. The comfort scores showed no significant difference, indicating that PPM provides a comfortable experience with reasonable vibrotactile density. However, the audience rated adequacy significantly lower, desiring richer feedback to better match gameplay. One noted, "I feel like it's missing, like when I'm hit, there's no vibration."

In contrast, experienced players gave significantly higher harmony, pleasure, confidence, and encouragement scores, suggesting PPM aligns with familiar vibration patterns and enhances engagement. They reported a stronger sense of hitting and dodging, making gameplay more satisfying: "When I feel the vibration, I know my action is successful. It feels great." Another added, "If it were me, I would choose this mode."

PPM, though common, provides essential participation and control, which seems sufficient for experienced players. Kirginas et al. found that simple vibrotactile feedback is often the most effective, minimizing overstimulation risks [22].

Boss-Perspective Mode Is More Beginner Friendly. BPM provided a reasonable level of comfort, with no significant difference in pleasure scores, though beginner players showed a slight preference, reflected in their higher confidence and encouragement scores compared to GPM. BPM helped beginners focus on enemies by using vibrotactile cues to predict attacks, potentially improving performance: "If the game provides vibration cues for boss attacks, I may fail less."

Players emphasized BPM's functional benefits, particularly in ARPGs with complex action sequences, rich visuals, and sound effects. For beginners, this cognitive and sensory load can be overwhelming, and BPM helps mitigate this challenge. By enhancing enemy perception, BPM allows players to anticipate and respond more calmly to attacks.

BPM can be seen as a subtle difficulty adjustment, improving accessibility without explicit difficulty scaling, which can negatively impact immersion [35]. Its threat-warning feature reduces objective difficulty while maintaining engagement. Research by Rodriguez-Guerrero et al. [33] also supports the potential of haptic assistance in easing gameplay difficulty.

Keeping Audience-Perspective Mode for Videos and Cutscenes . Experienced players rated GPM significantly lower in comfort, indicating an aversion to excessive vibrotactile feedback. In ARPGs, frequent vibrations accompany every interaction, potentially leading to fatigue: "Because the game is difficult, it requires repeated challenges, and the vibration makes my hand tired easily." This aligns with Kao et al. [19], who found that amplified feedback can reduce positive experiences. While GPM's intensity may offer initial novelty, it can become overwhelming during repeated play.

In contrast, audiences gave significantly higher pleasure scores, appreciating GPM's richness. Both audiences and beginner players tolerated GPM better than experienced players. Players and audiences rated its adequacy highly, recognizing its role in reinforcing audiovisual cues, though experienced players rated it lower in harmony, confidence, and encouragement: "Although the vibration makes the battle feel more intense, the frequent vibration is annoying in this type of game (ARPG)." Meanwhile, audiences responded positively: "The vibration feels very impactful, very rich–I'm willing to try playing." Overall, experienced players preferred PPM, while beginners found both PPM and BPM acceptable, with BPM offering supportive feedback without overstimulation. Audiences, however, favored GPM for its immersive integration with visual and auditory elements, making it ideal for cutscenes and haptic media.

Contradictory findings exist–Ooms et al. [28] suggest that media without vibration may sometimes be preferable due to content-driven factors. Based on these results, we propose vibrotactile design strategies to guide game developers and haptic media creators.

5.2   Design Guidance of Game and Media's Haptic Experience

Video with Haptic Design Could Imporve Game Streaming Watching Experience. Our results indicate that integrating haptic feedback into game livestreams can significantly enhance audience preference. Currently, a considerable number of users watch game livestreams through mobile platforms, such as smartphones, which are among the most ubiquitous and commonly used haptic devices. Some streaming platforms, such as Bilibili and iQIYI, have already experimented with haptic feedback in select videos. We believe that incorporating real-time haptic feedback into highly expressive and interactive media, such as game livestreams, could be particularly effective. On one hand, haptic feedback can provide a more immersive experience; on the other, it can create a sense of active participation, making viewers feel as if they are playing the game themselves. Our findings suggest that this effect can encourage viewers to transition into actual players, benefiting both video platforms and game companies.

Different Haptic Modes for Streaming Medias and Games. We believe that players and audiences have different preferences for vibrotactile feedback modes, particularly in terms of tolerance for frequent feedback. Players are more focused on game performance, so they are more cautious about the need for vibrotactile feedback in games, some players even turn off haptic feedback in games to focus better. Therefore, for players, PPM and BPM are more suitable, as they cater to different types of players. Although GPM is not favored by players, it may be suitable for game cutscenes. Audiences are more concerned with the atmosphere of videos, so they are more tolerant of dense vibration feedback. Some streaming platforms have already provided haptic feedback in online videos to enhance the audience's multisensory experience. Videos and live streams are important touchpoints for game promotion and pre-purchase experience, and attractive feedback provided by GPM may have a positive effect.

Dynamic Vibrotactile for Different Player Skills. We propose that a multi-level or dynamic haptic feedback strategy could better accommodate the needs of players with varying skill levels. Experienced players are more confident in their victories and less affected by the feedback mode. They were more focused on their own performance, and PPM may be more suitable for them, which can enhance their sense of being the protagonist. PPM is a more universal method of enhancing game experience compared to BPM. However, for beginner players, they may become disoriented and make random movements during difficult game battles. Enhancing incorrect operations may have a negative impact. As a result, some games adopt a minimalist approach to haptic feedback, using it sparingly or even omitting it entirely. In many cases, games only provide a basic on/off toggle for haptic feedback, unlike audio and video settings, which often offer multiple levels of customization. This overly conservative strategy limits the potential benefits of haptic feedback in enhancing the gaming experience. We suggest that games explore multi-level haptic feedback options, allowing players to choose between progressively richer vibration effects. Additionally, haptic feedback could be dynamically adjusted based on in-game scenarios and player performance, further optimizing the tactile experience.

Using Vibrotactile Feedback for Game Difficulty Balancing. However, our research results suggest that using BPM may be helpful for balancing game difficulty. Typically, games offer different difficulty levels to accommodate players with varying skill levels and self-challenge preferences. However, these difficulty adjustments are often implemented through numerical changes, such as modifying the boss's health, attack, and defense values. Significant alterations to these parameters create distinct difficulty levels. Our BPM introduces a new way to tune game difficulty. For example, we can provide BPM after a certain number of failures, based on the player's challenge failure count, to enhance the player's understanding of the enemy's patterns and improve the gaming experience. According to the results, this may encourage players who frequently fail in difficult challenge. This new approach does not significantly alter the game's difficulty but preserves the intended challenge while subtly providing assistive functionality through haptic feedback. This can be particularly beneficial for novice players tackling high-difficulty games, such as Souls-like titles, by reducing frustration and enhancing the overall gaming experience.

6   Conclusion

In this study, we explore the application of juicy haptics in action games and their associated media. Excessive vibration in action games, when employing juicy haptics, may lead to confusion and discomfort. To address this, we propose a haptic feedback design framework based on three distinct perspectives. We evaluated these three modes with both players and media audiences. Our results indicate that media audiences prefer more expressive haptic feedback, whereas players tend to be more cautious in its use. Additionally, player skill level influences their preference: experienced players favor PPM, as it enhances operational confirmation, while novice players prefer BPM, as it provides additional guidance cues. We provide recommendations for integrating juicy haptics into both games and game-related media. Furthermore, we suggest implementing dynamic haptic feedback strategies that adapt to player skill levels, which could enhance both game media engagement and overall gameplay experience.

References

1. Anwar, A., Shi, T., Schneider, O.: Factors of haptic experience across multiple haptic modalities. In: Proceedings of the 2023 CHI Conference on Human Factors in Computing Systems. pp. 1–12 (2023)
2. Bavelier, D., Green, C.S.: Enhancing attentional control: lessons from action video games. Neuron **104**(1), 147–163 (2019)
3. Bourdin, P., Martini, M., Sanchez-Vives, M.V.: Altered visual feedback from an embodied avatar unconsciously influences movement amplitude and muscle activity. Sci. Rep. **9**(1), 19747 (2019)
4. Clement, J.: Lifetime unit sales generated by black myth: Wukong worldwide as of september 2024 (2024). https://www.statista.com/statistics/1488929/black-myth-wukong-games-sales-worldwide/
5. Danieau, F., Lécuyer, A., Guillotel, P., Fleureau, J., Mollet, N., Christie, M.: Enhancing audiovisual experience with haptic feedback: a survey on hav. IEEE Trans. Haptics **6**(2), 193–205 (2012)
6. Denisova, A., Cairns, P.: First person vs. third person perspective in digital games: do player preferences affect immersion? In: Proceedings of the 33rd Annual ACM Conference on Human Factors in Computing Systems. pp. 145–148 (2015)

7. Durmanova, K.: The Effects of Juicy Game Design on Exergames. Master's thesis, University of Waterloo (2022)
8. Dwivedi, A., Yu, S., Hao, C., Salvietti, G., Prattichizzo, D., Beckerle, P.: How positioning wearable haptic interfaces on limbs influences virtual embodiment. IEEE Trans. Haptics (2023)
9. Emmerich, K., Krekhov, A., Cmentowski, S., Krueger, J.: Streaming vr games to the broad audience: a comparison of the first-person and third-person perspectives. In: Proceedings of the 2021 CHI Conference on Human Factors in Computing Systems. pp. 1–14 (2021)
10. García, Á., Cerdán, V., Revuelta, P., Pena, J.M.S., Ortiz, T., Vergaz, R.: Vibrotactile stimulation for emotional elicitation during audiovisual events. IEEE Access (2023)
11. Gonzalez-Franco, M., Berger, C.C.: Avatar embodiment enhances haptic confidence on the out-of-body touch illusion. IEEE Trans. Haptics **12**(3), 319–326 (2019)
12. Hassenzahl, M.: The hedonic/pragmatic model of user experience. Towards a UX Manifesto **10**, 2007 (2007)
13. Hicks, K., Dickinson, P., Holopainen, J., Gerling, K.: Good game feel: an empirically grounded framework for juicy design. In: Proceedings of DiGRA 2018 Conference: The Game is the Message (2018)
14. Hicks, K., Gerling, K., Dickinson, P., Vanden Abeele, V.: Juicy game design: understanding the impact of visual embellishments on player experience. In: Proceedings of the Annual Symposium on Computer-Human Interaction in Play. pp. 185–197 (2019)
15. Hsu, S.H., Lee, F.L., Wu, M.C., et al.: Designing action games for appealing to buyers. CyberPsychol. Behav. **8**(6), 585–591 (2005)
16. Johnson, D., Gardner, M.J., Perry, R.: Validation of two game experience scales: the player experience of need satisfaction (pens) and game experience questionnaire (geq). Int. J. Hum Comput Stud. **118**, 38–46 (2018)
17. Jouybari, A.F., Franza, M., Kannape, O.A., Hara, M., Blanke, O.: Tactile spatial discrimination on the torso using vibrotactile and force stimulation. Exp. Brain Res. **239**(11), 3175–3188 (2021). https://doi.org/10.1007/s00221-021-06181-x
18. Ju, Y., Zheng, D., Hynds, D., Chernyshov, G., Kunze, K., Minamizawa, K.: Haptic empathy: Conveying emotional meaning through vibrotactile feedback. In: Extended Abstracts of the 2021 CHI Conference on Human Factors in Computing Systems. pp. 1–7 (2021)
19. Kao, D., Ballou, N., Gerling, K., Breitsohl, H., Deterding, S.: How does juicy game feedback motivate? testing curiosity, competence, and effectance. In: Proceedings of the CHI Conference on Human Factors in Computing Systems. pp. 1–16 (2024)
20. Kennedy, V.: Black myth: wukong prompts yet another steam record (2024). https://www.eurogamer.net/black-myth-wukong-prompts-yet-another-steam-record
21. Khalifa, A., de Mesentier Silva, F., Togelius, J.: Level design patterns in 2d games. In: 2019 IEEE Conference on Games (CoG). pp. 1–8. IEEE (2019)
22. Kirginas, S.: Exploring players' perceptions of the haptic feedback in haptic digital games. J. Digit. Media Int. **5**(13), 7–22 (2022)
23. Lee, Y., Lee, S., Lee, D.: Wearable haptic device for stiffness rendering of virtual objects in augmented reality. Appl. Sci. **11**(15), 6932 (2021)
24. Lin, Z., Duan, H., Wen, Z.A., Cai, W.: What features influence impact feel? a study of impact feedback in action games. In: 2022 IEEE Games, Entertainment, Media Conference (GEM). pp. 1–6. IEEE (2022)

25. McAnally, K., Wallis, G.: Visual-haptic integration, action and embodiment in virtual reality. Psychol. Res. **86**(6), 1847–1857 (2022)
26. Nakamura, T., Miyata, K.: Influence of audiovisual feedback on player behavior and performance in response to video game failure. In: International Workshop on Advanced Imaging Technology (IWAIT) 2021. vol. 11766, pp. 318–323. SPIE (2021)
27. Normand, E., Pacchierotti, C., Marchand, E., Marchal, M.: How different is the perception of vibrotactile texture roughness in augmented versus virtual reality? In: ACM Symposium on Virtual Reality Software and Technology, VRST 2024 (2024)
28. Ooms, S., Lee, M., Cesar, P., El Ali, A.: Feelthenews: Augmenting affective perceptions of news videos with thermal and vibrotactile stimulation. In: Extended Abstracts of the 2023 CHI Conference on Human Factors in Computing Systems. pp. 1–8 (2023)
29. Orozco, M., Silva, J., El Saddik, A., Petriu, E.: The role of haptics in games. Haptics Rendering and Applications pp. 217–234 (2012)
30. Palmquist, A., Jedel, I., Goethe, O.: Assistive technologies for attainable gaming experiences. In: Universal Design in Video Games: Active Participation Through Accessible Play, pp. 101–129. Springer (2024)
31. Pichlmair, M., Johansen, M.: Designing game feel: a survey. IEEE Trans. Games **14**(2), 138–152 (2021)
32. Richard, G., Pietrzak, T., Argelaguet, F., Lécuyer, A., Casiez, G.: Studying the role of haptic feedback on virtual embodiment in a drawing task. Front. Virtual Real. **1**, 573167 (2021)
33. Rodriguez-Guerrero, C., Knaepen, K., Fraile-Marinero, J.C., Perez-Turiel, J., Gonzalez-de Garibay, V., Lefeber, D.: Improving challenge/skill ratio in a multimodal interface by simultaneously adapting game difficulty and haptic assistance through psychophysiological and performance feedback. Front. Neurosci. **11**, 242 (2017)
34. Saint-Louis, C., Hamam, A.: Survey of haptic technology and entertainment applications. In: SoutheastCon 2021. pp. 01–07. IEEE (2021)
35. Sakaue, S., Kimura, T., Nishino, H.: Reducing objective difficulty without influencing subjective difficulty in a video game. In: Proceedings of the 5th ACM International Conference on Multimedia in Asia. pp. 1–5 (2023)
36. Sathiyamurthy, S., Lui, M., Kim, E., Schneider, O.: Measuring haptic experience: Elaborating the hx model with scale development. In: 2021 IEEE World Haptics Conference (WHC). pp. 979–984. IEEE (2021)
37. Schneider, O., MacLean, K., Swindells, C., Booth, K.: Haptic experience design: what hapticians do and where they need help. Int. J. Hum. Comput. Stud. **107**, 5–21 (2017)
38. Singhal, T., Schneider, O.: Juicy haptic design: vibrotactile embellishments can improve player experience in games. In: Proceedings of the 2021 Chi Conference on Human Factors in Computing Systems. pp. 1–11 (2021)
39. Smets, J.H., Van der Spek, E.D.: That sound's juicy! exploring juicy audio effects in video games. In: Entertainment Computing–ICEC 2021: 20th IFIP TC 14 International Conference, ICEC 2021, Coimbra, Portugal, November 2–5, 2021, Proceedings 20. pp. 319–335. Springer (2021)
40. Young, G.W., O'Dwyer, N., Vargas, M.F., Donnell, R.M., Smolic, A.: Feel the music!–audience experiences of audio–tactile feedback in a novel virtual reality volumetric music video. In: Arts. vol. 12, p. 156. MDPI (2023)

41. Yun, G., Mun, M., Lee, J., Kim, D.G., Tan, H.Z., Choi, S.: Generating real-time, selective, and multimodal haptic effects from sound for gaming experience enhancement. In: Proceedings of the 2023 CHI Conference on Human Factors in Computing Systems. pp. 1–17 (2023)
42. Zenner, A., Krüger, A.: Shifty: a weight-shifting dynamic passive haptic proxy to enhance object perception in virtual reality. IEEE Trans. Visual Comput. Graph. **23**(4), 1285–1294 (2017)

Exploring Cultural Heritage with AR: The TAM Case Study of Nvshu

Yejuan Xie[1,2], Xinrui Wu[1], Yichen Zhang[1], Rongrong Chen[3], Tulika Saha[2], Yuehan Dou[1], and Chengtao Ji[1(✉)]

[1] Xi'an Jiaotong-Liverpool University, Suzhou 215123, Jiangsu, China
{Yejuan.Xie21,Xinrui.Wu21,Yichen.Zhang2202}@student.xjtlu.edu.cn,
{Yuehan.Dou,Chengtao.Ji}@xjtlu.edu.cn
[2] University of Liverpool, Liverpool L69 3BX, UK
Tulika.Saha@liverpool.ac.uk
[3] Beijing Normal-Hong Kong Baptist University, Zhuhai 519087, China
rainerrchen@uic.edu.cn

Abstract. Preservation of intangible cultural heritage (ICH), such as Nvshu, faces considerable challenges in engaging younger generations in the digital era. This study presents an augmented reality (AR)-based Nvshu application and evaluates its user experience among 97 participants, primarily younger users. A research model based on the Technology Acceptance Model (TAM), enriched with interactivity, enjoyment, and information quality as external variables, was employed to assess user acceptance. Structural Equation Modeling (SEM) revealed that interactivity significantly enhances perceived usefulness (PU), while enjoyment positively influences perceived ease of use (PEOU). Surprisingly, information quality did not have a significant impact, highlighting younger users' preference for experiential and interactive elements over purely informational content. PEOU and PU emerged as critical determinants of behavioural intention, underscoring the enduring relevance of TAM in AR applications. These findings demonstrate how mobile AR can be effectively applied to the preservation and promotion of lesser-known ICH like Nvshu, by delivering culturally immersive experiences that resonate with younger, digitally native audiences.

Keywords: AR · Cultural Heritage · Technology Acceptance Model

1 Introduction

Digital transformation has reshaped cultural heritage conservation, with augmented reality (AR) emerging as a powerful tool for multimodal engagement. AR applications have been widely adopted for 3D reconstruction, virtual museums, and gamified learning, demonstrating their potential to enhance user engagement, learning, and cultural awareness [2,4]. To explore factors influencing user acceptance of AR in this domain, many studies have employed the Technology Acceptance Model (TAM), which examines how perceived usefulness (PU)

C. Mousas et al. (Eds.): CASA 2025, LNCS 15915, pp. 39–54, 2026.
https://doi.org/10.1007/978-981-95-0100-7_3

and perceived ease of use (PEOU) shape user behavior [5]. Recent research has extended TAM by incorporating external variables such as immersion, interactivity, and enjoyment, highlighting the need to design AR applications that balance educational value with engaging, interactive experiences [15,25]. This balance has been shown to enhance AR adoption for heritage dissemination.

Intangible cultural heritage (ICH) faces unique challenges in preservation, particularly when compared to tangible heritage. Nvshu[1], the world's only known female-specific script [28], exemplifies these challenges. With the loss of its last natural inheritors, Nvshu is at risk of fading away, leading to declining awareness and weakened transmission mechanisms. While previous efforts have used VR to reconstruct Nvshu's cultural context and enhance experiential learning [29], VR's high equipment and environmental requirements limit its accessibility. In contrast, mobile AR provides a more practical and widely accessible platform for engaging audiences in the preservation and dissemination of Nvshu.

This study contributes to the digital preservation of ICH in two key ways. First, it presents an AR-based application centered on Nvshu, combining visual elements, cultural storytelling, and interactive features such as a spelling game to support user engagement with the script and its heritage. Second, it extends the TAM by incorporating interactivity, enjoyment, and information quality as external variables, using Structural Equation Modeling (SEM) to examine their influence on user acceptance among younger audiences. While Nvshu is a specific case, the approach demonstrates potential for engaging users with other lesser-known cultural traditions, offering both practical and theoretical insights for the broader application of AR in cultural heritage contexts.

2   Related Work

2.1   AR in Cultural Heritage

AR technology has proven to be highly effective in preserving intangible cultural heritage by enriching cultural presentations and enhancing public engagement. Several studies have highlighted its role in heritage education, interactive experiences, and immersive storytelling. For instance, mobile AR applications have facilitated learning about traditional Chinese lanterns, enhancing both user interest and engagement [14,15]. Similarly, AR-enhanced heritage site tours have improved visitor experiences by offering immersive visualizations and interactive content [8,13]. AR has also been used to reenact historical scenes with actors in traditional attire, creating highly immersive learning environments [9]. Additionally, AR gamification has been explored to engage younger audiences, such as an AR game introducing children to the intangible heritage of the Ovahimba tribe through interactive storytelling and physical interactions [20]. These studies collectively demonstrate AR's effectiveness in enhancing ICH dissemination and providing engaging, accessible heritage experiences.

---

[1] https://www.ihchina.cn/art/detail/id/15067.html.

2.2   Theoretical Foundations

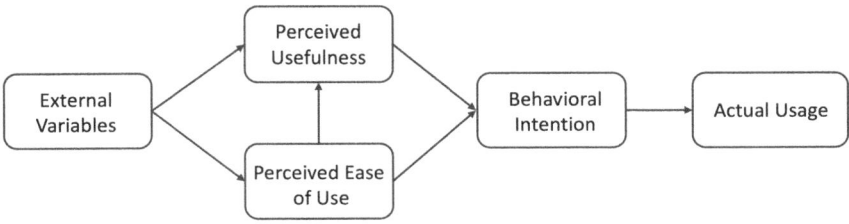

Fig. 1. The technology acceptance model (TAM).

The TAM [5] explains user acceptance through perceived usefulness (PU) and perceived ease of use (PEOU), which influence attitude (AT) and behavioral intention (BI). As shown in Fig. 1, TAM has been extended to include external variables that affect PU and PEOU, thereby influencing technology adoption [24]. Due to its adaptability, TAM has been widely applied in various domains, including e-learning, AR, and cultural heritage. In e-learning, researchers have identified self-efficacy, subjective norms, and enjoyment as key external factors influencing technology acceptance [1]. In the context of AR, studies have explored additional variables based on the specific application. For example, Papakostas et al. [18] examined playfulness and quality output in educational settings, while Li et al. [15] focused on AR-based heritage tourism and Generic Learning Outcomes. Wang et al. [25] analyzed immersion, interactivity, and aesthetic quality as determinants of AR adoption in cultural heritage. These studies demonstrate TAM's versatility in assessing user acceptance across various technological applications, particularly in AR-driven cultural heritage preservation.

3   System Design

3.1   Preliminary Survey Analysis

To understand user interests and needs for an AR-based Nvshu application, we conducted an online survey with 61 valid responses. Most participants (80.33%) were aged 20–30, and 57.38% held a bachelor's degree. While 55.74% had no prior knowledge of Nvshu, 78.7% expressed strong interest in using AR for CH preservation, and 59% believed AR could enhance the understanding and transmission of Nvshu. Smartphones were the preferred platform (88.52%), and 65.6% showed interest in simulating Nvshu script writing. Interactive engagement with the environment was considered the most appealing aspect of AR by 86.89% of respondents. These findings highlight the potential of AR to engage younger users and support immersive cultural heritage experiences.

3.2   The Nvshu AR System

We selected mobile marker-based AR for its portability, affordability, and accessibility, particularly for younger audiences. Unlike traditional mobile apps or head-mounted displays, our choice of online AR eliminates the need for app downloads, making it more convenient and accessible. Compared to head-mounted displays or traditional mobile apps, mobile AR offers a more intuitive, interactive form of engagement, making it a highly effective medium for cultural heritage preservation and dissemination. This decision aligns with the preferences indicated in our preliminary survey, where users favored mobile platforms for interacting with cultural content. As shown in Fig. 2, our AR system consists of four modules: *Information Display, Nvshu Model, Spelling Game, and Script Tracing,* each designed to support different stages of cultural understanding, from initial awareness to hands-on participation. The Nvshu scripts used in the system are sourced from the Unicode Standard[2] for Nvshu script, ensuring authenticity.

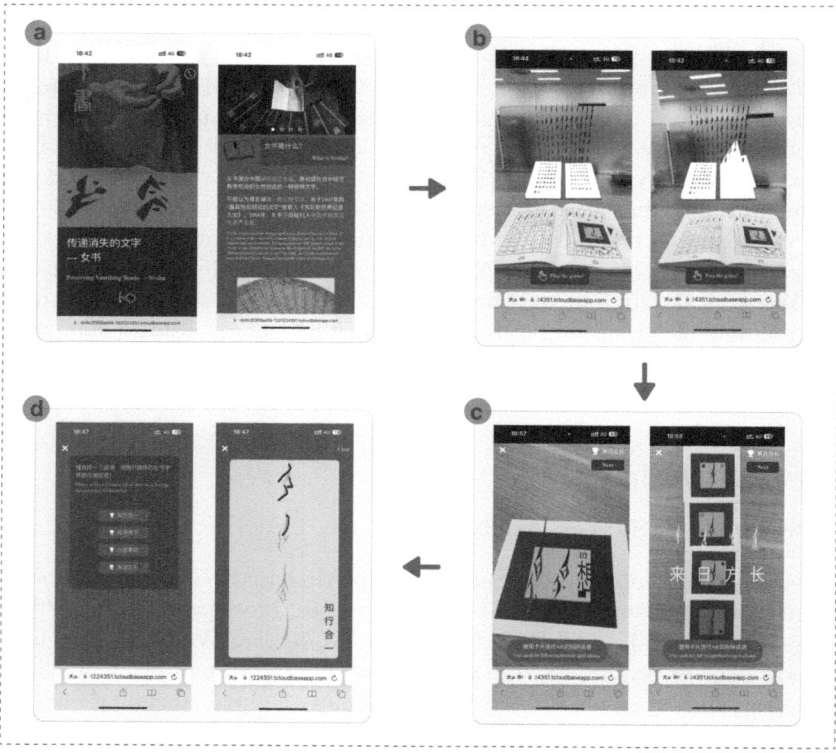

Fig. 2. Main interfaces of the Nvshu-AR application. (a) Introduction to the basic information of Nvshu. (b) AR presentation of Nvshu script. (c) Spelling game with interactive AR and physical cards. (d) Nvshu script tracing with templates.

---

[2] https://nushuscript.org/unicode/.

Given that Nvshu's transmission relies on both reading and writing but is constrained by regional dialects, our system prioritizes improving recognition and script tracing.

Information Display (Fig. 2a): This module introduces the origins, history, and cultural significance of Nvshu, serving as a contextual entry point for users unfamiliar with the tradition. It integrates illustrations, digital archives from the Nvshu Digital Museum, and traditional Nvshu chant music to create a multisensory foundation before users begin interactive tasks.

Nvshu Model (Fig. 2b): This module features an animated 3D book where Nvshu scripts dynamically emerge and arrange into poetic phrases, accompanied by their Chinese meanings. The scripts are sourced from authentic folk manuscripts, ensuring cultural accuracy. By integrating animated visualization within an AR environment, this design highlights the aesthetic and structural uniqueness of Nvshu, fostering a deeper appreciation of its literary heritage.

Spelling Game (Fig. 2c): This module uses printed Nvshu script cards as tangible markers to enrich user interaction and support a physical spelling experience. When users scan these cards, the corresponding 3D representations of the Nvshu script appear in AR, and participants arrange them into traditional four-character idioms. This integrated physical-virtual gameplay deepens engagement by combining hands-on manipulation of cultural artifacts with dynamic virtual feedback, motivating continued exploration and appreciation of the script.

Script Tracing (Fig. 2d): In this module, users select idioms they formed in the Spelling Game and engage in tracing Nvshu scripts. By comparing the scripts with those on the physical cards, users can further explore the distinctive features of Nvshu. This hands-on practice may reinforce memory retention and enhances familiarity with the script.

Following system deployment and testing, we introduce a TAM-based framework with new external variables to assess user engagement. This study evaluates how AR facilitates meaningful cultural interaction and technology acceptance, using Nvshu as a case of lesser-known heritage.

4   Research Model and Hypotheses

In the TAM, PEOU is defined as "the degree to which a person believes that using a particular system would be free of effort", while PU refers to "the degree to which a person believes that using a particular system would enhance their job performance" [5]. BI, a key component of TAM, describes an individual's likelihood of adopting a system in the future [26]. We propose an extended model (Fig. 3) that incorporates *information quality, interactivity, and enjoyment* as external variables within the TAM framework, specifically tailored to evaluate user acceptance of a mobile AR system for presenting cultural heritage (Nvshu).

Information Quality. Information quality is a multidimensional concept often defined in terms of accuracy and reliability [12]. In mobile AR applications, it

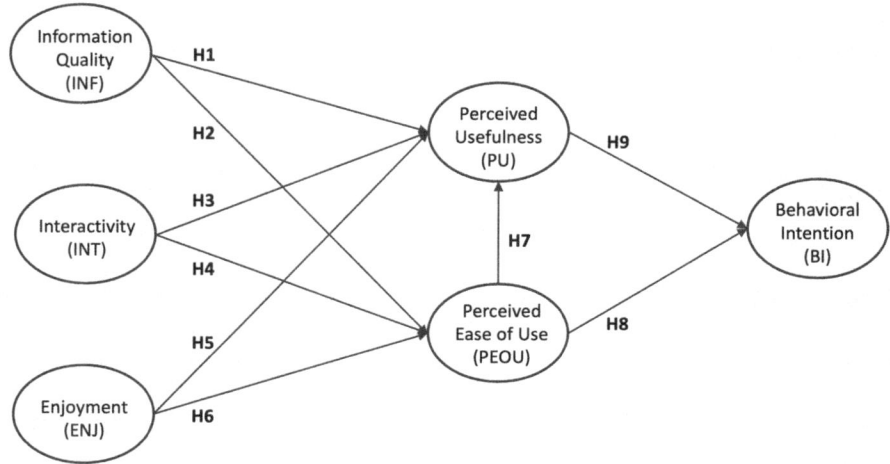

Fig. 3. TAM-based research model for Nvshu AR system with external variables and hypotheses (H1–H9).

plays a crucial role in delivering accurate, context-relevant content and ensuring that virtual elements are properly aligned with the real environment [3,11]. In this study, information quality refers to the Nvshu AR system's ability to track markers accurately and generate correct virtual content in real time. Previous research suggests that visual and informational accuracy in AR positively impacts perceived usefulness and user experience [11]. Therefore, we propose the following hypotheses:

H1: *Information quality (INF) of the AR application positively influences users' perceived usefulness (PU).*
H2: *Information quality (INF) of the AR application positively influences users' perceived ease of use (PEOU).*

Interactivity. Interactivity refers to the degree to which users can modify content or structure in real time [21]. In AR smartphone applications, it primarily entails users' ability to manipulate virtual elements and engage with their augmented environment [11]. Prior studies suggest that interaction mechanisms significantly shape user perceptions. For example, Wojciechowski and Cellary [27] found that AR interaction via cardboard markers enhanced perceived ease of use. Such findings indicate that greater interactivity can improve both perceived usefulness and usability by fostering a more intuitive and engaging experience. Therefore, we propose the following hypotheses:

H3: *Interactivity (INT) of the AR application positively influences users' perceived usefulness (PU).*
H4: *Interactivity (INT) of the AR application positively influences users' perceived ease of use (PEOU).*

Enjoyment. As early as 1992, Davis et al. [6] investigated the role of enjoyment in technology acceptance, defining it as "the extent to which using a computer is perceived as enjoyable in its own right, independent of any anticipated performance outcomes." Their findings suggested that a lack of enjoyment could hinder adoption, even when a system is functionally effective. Venkatesh [22] later expanded TAM by introducing "perceived enjoyment" as an external variable, emphasizing that users are motivated by both functional benefits and the pleasure derived from use. This aligns with the concept of hedonic motivation, where enjoyment enhances user engagement and system adoption. Building on previous research [1,16], we incorporate enjoyment as an external variable in TAM and propose the following hypotheses:

> **H5:** *Enjoyment (ENJ) of the AR application positively influences users' perceived usefulness (PU).*
> **H6:** *Enjoyment (ENJ) of the AR application positively influences users' perceived ease of use (PEOU).*

In the TAM, key constructs such as PEOU, PU, and BI are crucial in determining user acceptance of technology [5]. BI serves as the indicator of system acceptance, with PU being influenced by PEOU. This suggests that the ease of use significantly impacts users' perception of a system's usefulness. Both PU and PEOU are recognized as key determinants of technology acceptance [23]. Previous studies on TAM in AR contexts show that PEOU and PU affect BI, which in turn influences actual usage behavior [19,25,27]. Based on these findings, we propose the following hypotheses:

> **H7:** *Perceived ease of use (PEOU) positively influences users' perceived usefulness (PU).*
> **H8:** *Perceived Ease of Use (PEOU) positively influences users' behavioral intention to use (BI).*
> **H9:** *Perceived usefulness (PU) positively influences users' behavioral intention to use (BI).*

5 Methods

5.1 Questionnaire Design

Given the perceptual nature of the data, a questionnaire survey is the most suitable method to capture users' views and attitudes, as seen in previous TAM-based studies [25]. Drawing from relevant literature, the questionnaire was carefully designed to assess the impact of AR technology on users' willingness to engage with and learn about Nvshu. The survey, detailed in Table 1, consists of six sections aligned with the proposed research model (Fig. 3), each containing three items, for a total of 18. All items were rated using a seven-point Likert scale, ranging from "strongly disagree" to "strongly agree," ensuring a nuanced measurement of users' perceptions. This structured approach allows for a comprehensive analysis of user engagement and their interactions with the AR-enhanced presentation of Nvshu.

Table 1. Measurement of the variables

Construct	Items	Descriptions	References
Information Quality	INF1	The information provided by the AR application is clear and understandable	Kim et al. [11]
	INF2	The virtual image overlays with my real surroundings exactly well	
	INF3	The AR application provides accurate tracking	
Interactivity	INT1	I am in control of my navigation through the AR technology	Kim et al. [11]
	INT2	I have control over the content of the AR technology that I want to see	
	INT3	The AR application allows me to interact with virtual objects to obtain knowledge about Nvshu	
Enjoyment	ENJ1	I find using the system to be enjoyable	Venkatesh et al. [22]
	ENJ2	The actual process of using the system is pleasant	
	ENJ3	I have fun using the system	
Perceived Usefulness	U1	Using the system improves my performance in studying intangible cultural heritage (Nvshu)	Davis [5]
	U2	Using the system enables me to accomplish tasks more quickly in learning about intangible cultural heritage (Nvshu)	
	U3	Using the system enhances my effectiveness in understanding and learning about intangible cultural heritage (Nvshu)	
Perceived Ease of Use	E1	Using the system is easy for me	Davis [5]; Venkatesh and Davis [23]
	E2	My interactions with the system are clear and understandable	
	E3	Interacting with the system does not require a lot of my mental effort	
Behavioral Intention	I1	I intend to use the system in the future	Davis [5]; Papakostas et al. [17]
	I2	I will recommend others to use Nvshu-AR	
	I3	I would like to see AR embedded in more cultural heritage education domains	

5.2   Data Collection

A total of 97 valid questionnaires were collected over a two-week period from participants who used the Nvshu AR application. Participation was voluntary and free of charge, with participants receiving postcards featuring elements of Nvshu culture as a token of appreciation. The application was hosted on a server, allowing participants to access it on their personal mobile devices. During the experience, participants learned about Nvshu culture, with a focus on the distinctive features of the script during the card recognition phase. The participant group included 63 females and 34 males, with 61.86% aged between 18 and 25, and 25.77% aged 26 to 30. Most participants were university students (70.1%), 20.62% were master's students, and the remainder were in other professions. This demographic composition provided a representative sample of young adults.

5.3   Research Methodology

To test the proposed research model, we employed the *SmartPLS* 4, leveraging the partial least squares structural equation modeling (PLS-SEM) approach. This method was chosen for its ability to handle complex models with multiple constructs, indicators, and structural paths while avoiding strict assumptions about data distribution. As noted by Hair et al. [10], PLS-SEM is particularly effective for exploratory research aimed at expanding theoretical frameworks and addressing intricate relationships. Furthermore, its robustness with small sample sizes makes it a practical choice for studies involving numerous constructs and measurement items. The analysis followed standard PLS-SEM procedures, including constructing the measurement model, assessing indicator reliability and validity, and estimating the structural model to evaluate hypothesized relationships.

6   Results

6.1   Descriptive Statistics and Correlations

Table 2 provides the descriptive statistics and the Pearson correlation matrix for the latent variables in the proposed research model. The mean values for the constructs range from 5.27 (INF and INT) to 5.84 (BI), suggesting overall positive perceptions from participants regarding the AR-Nvshu system. Standard deviations range from 0.79 (PU) to 0.99 (INT), indicating moderate variability in responses. The Pearson correlation coefficients reveal statistically significant positive relationships among all latent variables. For instance, BI demonstrates

Table 2. Descriptive Statistics and Latent Variable Correlation Matrix

	Mean	SD	INF	INT	ENJ	PU	PEOU	BI
INF	5.27	0.94	-					
INT	5.27	0.99	0.82**	-				
ENJ	5.49	0.96	0.77**	0.74*	-			
PU	5.66	0.79	0.66**	0.71**	0.66**	-		
PEOU	5.54	0.81	0.71**	0.69**	0.71**	0.67**	-	
BI	5.84	0.82	0.68**	0.69**	0.67**	0.73**	0.66**	-

Note: * p < 0.05, ** p < 0.01.

strong correlations with PU (r = 0.73, p < 0.01) and PEOU (r = 0.66, p < 0.01), highlighting their crucial roles in predicting users' intentions to adopt the AR-Nvshu system. All correlation coefficients are statistically significant at either p < 0.05 or p < 0.01 levels, supporting the robustness of the measured relationships. As a Pearson correlation matrix, these findings provide an initial validation of the hypothesized associations and offer a basis for further structural equation modeling analysis.

6.2   Measurement Model

The measurement model assessment results, summarized in Table 3, demonstrate strong reliability and validity across all constructs. Factor loadings, which indicate how well each item represents its underlying construct, all exceed the recommended threshold of 0.7 [10], ranging from 0.821 (U3) to 0.907 (I2), confirming adequate indicator reliability. Cronbach's alpha (CA) values range from 0.797 (PU, PEOU) to 0.869 (ENJ), exceeding the acceptable cutoff of 0.7 and indicating consistent internal reliability. Composite reliability (CR) further supports this, with values between 0.882 (PU) and 0.920 (ENJ), well above the 0.7 threshold [10], reflecting strong internal consistency while accounting for measurement error.

Table 3. Construct Reliability and Validity

Construct	Items	Factor Loadings	CA	CR	AVE
Information Quality	INF1	0.844	0.837	0.902	0.754
	INF2	0.873			
	INF3	0.887			
Interactivity	INT1	0.865	0.838	0.902	0.755
	INT2	0.870			
	INT3	0.871			
Enjoyment	ENJ1	0.902	0.869	0.920	0.793
	ENJ2	0.887			
	ENJ3	0.882			
Perceived Usefulness	U1	0.884	0.799	0.882	0.714
	U2	0.828			
	U3	0.821			
Perceived Ease of Use	E1	0.861	0.797	0.881	0.711
	E2	0.833			
	E3	0.835			
Behavioral Intention	I1	0.834	0.838	0.903	0.756
	I2	0.907			
	I3	0.866			

Table 4. Discriminant Validity

	INF	INT	ENJ	PU	PEOU	BI
INF	**0.868**					
INT	0.821	**0.869**				
ENJ	0.773	0.742	**0.890**			
PU	0.662	0.713	0.658	**0.845**		
PEOU	0.714	0.694	0.712	0.679	**0.843**	
BI	0.678	0.696	0.670	0.729	0.664	**0.870**

Note: Bold values are the square root of the AVEs.

Convergent validity is confirmed by average variance extracted (AVE) values, which range from 0.711 (PEOU) to 0.793 (ENJ), all above the minimum criterion of 0.5 [7]. These values indicate that each construct captures a substantial proportion of variance from its indicators. For example, the AVE for BI (0.756) indicates that approximately 75.6% of the variance in its observed indicators is accounted for by the latent construct.

Discriminant validity was verified using the Fornell-Larcker criterion (Table 4). For each construct, the square root of its AVE (shown in bold on the diagonal) exceeds its correlations with other constructs, confirming that each construct is empirically distinct. For example, the square root of AVE for BI (0.870) is greater than its correlations with PU (0.729), while the value for ENJ (0.890) surpasses its correlations with INF (0.773) and INT (0.742). These results, together with the evidence of reliability and convergent validity, affirm that the model's constructs are both robust and conceptually distinct, establishing a foundation for subsequent structural model analysis and hypothesis testing.

6.3 Structural Model

The structural model was evaluated to test the hypothesized relationships between constructs, with results shown in Fig. 4 and Table 5. To ensure robustness and rule out multicollinearity, Variance Inflation Factors (VIFs) for all paths were examined and found to be below the threshold of 5, indicating no multicollinearity concerns [10]. The significance of path coefficients was assessed using a bootstrapping procedure with 5,000 resamples via the Bias-Corrected and Accelerated (BCa) method. A two-tailed test was conducted, and hypotheses were evaluated at the 5% significance level ($p < 0.05$). The analysis revealed that five out of nine hypotheses were supported. Notably, H3, which examines the effect of INT on PU, was supported with a significant path coefficient ($\beta = 0.377$, $p = 0.010$), underscoring the importance of interactive features in shaping users' perceptions of utility. H6, linking ENJ to PEOU, was also supported ($\beta = 0.341$, $p = 0.002$), suggesting that hedonic factors enhance usability. Additionally, H7, which posits the influence of PEOU on PU, reached significance

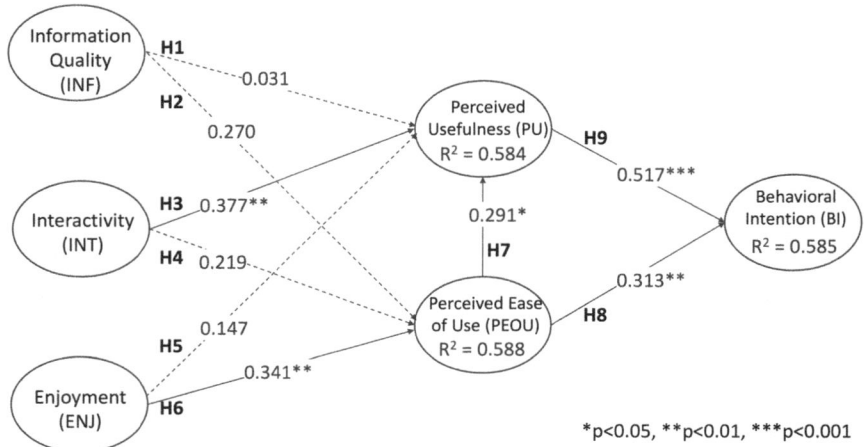

Fig. 4. Path model and PLS-SEM estimates.

Table 5. Results of the Structural Model

H.	Path	β	t	p	Result
H1	INF → PU	0.031	0.195	0.846	Not Supported
H2	INF → PEOU	0.270	1.879	0.060	Not Supported
H3	INT → PU	0.377	2.561	0.010	Supported
H4	INT → PEOU	0.219	1.849	0.065	Not Supported
H5	ENJ → PU	0.147	1.116	0.264	Not Supported
H6	ENJ → PEOU	0.341	3.066	0.002	Supported
H7	PEOU → PU	0.291	2.071	0.038	Supported
H8	PEOU → BI	0.313	3.148	0.002	Supported
H9	PU → BI	0.517	5.510	0.000	Supported

Note: β = Path Coefficient; t = t-statistic; p = p-value.

($\beta = 0.291$, p = 0.038), highlighting the role of usability in shaping perceived usefulness. Finally, both PEOU and PU had significant direct effects on behavioral intention (BI), with H8 ($\beta = 0.313$, p = 0.002) and H9 ($\beta = 0.517$, p = 0.000), respectively, reinforcing the central role these constructs play in driving user acceptance.

However, other hypotheses reveal non-significant relationships, which merit further discussion. For instance, H1 and H2 suggest that INF has no significant effect on PU ($\beta = 0.031$, p = 0.846) and a marginal effect on PEOU ($\beta = 0.270$, p = 0.060), indicating that users may not perceive information quality as a critical determinant of usability or usefulness in this context. Another possible explanation is that our operationalization of information quality may have been influenced by technical aspects such as AR marker tracking stability, which could have overshadowed the perceived value of the content itself. Additionally, H4, the link between INT and PEOU, is not statistically significant ($\beta = 0.219$, p = 0.065), suggesting that while interactivity strongly influences PU, it has limited impact on users' ease of interaction. Notably, H5, which investigates the relationship between ENJ and PU, is also unsupported ($\beta = 0.147$, p = 0.264), implying that enjoyment does not directly enhance perceived usefulness. These findings underscore the complexity of user acceptance in AR applications for intangible cultural heritage, suggesting that while certain external variables, such as interactivity and enjoyment, play pivotal roles, their influence may vary depending on whether they target perceived usefulness or usability.

The coefficient of determination (R^2) values provide an assessment of the model's explanatory power for the endogenous latent variables, reflecting its prediction accuracy. As shown in Fig. 4, the R^2 values for PU, PEOU, and BI are 0.584, 0.588, and 0.585, respectively, indicating that the model explains a moderate proportion of variance in these constructs. Specifically, the R^2 for PU demonstrates that 58.4% of the variance in users' perceptions of the application's usefulness is explained by external variables such as Information Quality, Interactivity, Enjoyment, and PEOU. Similarly, the R^2 for PEOU indicates that 58.8% of the variance in ease of use is accounted for by the external variables, underscoring the significance of the application's design features in shaping usability perceptions. For BI, the R^2 of 58.5% reflects the extent to which PU and PEOU collectively influence users' intentions to adopt the AR application. These results confirm the model's ability to capture key factors that shape user acceptance.

7   Discussion

7.1   External Variables

Among the external variables, interactivity significantly influenced perceived usefulness (PU) but had no significant effect on perceived ease of use (PEOU). This suggests that interactive features enhance the perceived value of AR applications but do not necessarily reduce their complexity. While interactive elements, such as gamified learning experiences, improve engagement, they may also introduce cognitive load, requiring careful design to balance engagement with usability.

Enjoyment positively affected PEOU but did not significantly impact PU, indicating that hedonic factors facilitate ease of use but do not necessarily enhance perceptions of utility. For young users, this may reflect a preference for entertaining and intuitive applications that simplify their engagement with cultural content. Developers should consider how to leverage enjoyment to reduce barriers to adoption without compromising the educational and cultural depth of the experience.

Surprisingly, information quality did not emerge as a strong predictor of user perceptions. This may reflect a shift in how younger users engage with cultural content, prioritizing interaction and experience over informational depth. Alternatively, aspects of technical performance—such as AR marker tracking—may have unintentionally influenced users' evaluation of information quality, highlighting the need to distinguish between content clarity and system stability in future assessments.

7.2 Limitations and Future Work

This study has several limitations. First, because our evaluation focuses on Nvshu—a relatively obscure form of ICH—our findings may not be directly transferable to other ICH domains. However, the core interaction mechanisms we propose—marker-based AR storytelling, card-driven gamification—form a flexible design framework that can be adapted to different heritage contexts with appropriate content customization. Furthermore, AR's capacity to make lesser-known traditions more accessible and engaging offers promising potential for raising public interest in other underrepresented cultural practices. Second, our participant sample comprised predominantly younger, digitally literate users, which may constrain generalizability; future research should examine how generational differences affect AR adoption for cultural heritage experiences. Third, our study was limited to three external variables (interactivity, enjoyment, and information quality). We acknowledge that perceptions of information quality in our study may have been influenced by both the clarity of cultural content and the technical performance of the AR system, which could benefit from more apparent separation in future evaluations. Finally, as we examined initial user acceptance only, longitudinal studies are necessary to assess sustained engagement and its impact on cultural learning and heritage transmission.

8 Conclusion

This study developed an AR system for Nvshu and explored its effectiveness in the dissemination of intangible cultural heritage using an extended TAM model. By integrating interactivity, enjoyment, and information quality as external variables, the findings reveal that interactivity enhances perceived usefulness, while enjoyment improves perceived ease of use. However, information quality did not significantly influence user perceptions, suggesting that younger users may prioritize interactive and engaging experiences over textual content. These results provide insights for designing AR applications that balance engagement with cultural authenticity. Future research could examine long-term user engagement, generational differences, and additional factors influencing AR adoption in cultural heritage contexts.

References

1. Abdullah, F., Ward, R.: Developing a general extended technology acceptance model for e-learning (getamel) by analysing commonly used external factors. Comput. Hum. Behav. **56**, 238–256 (2016)
2. Billinghurst, M., Kato, H., Poupyrev, I.: The magicbook-moving seamlessly between reality and virtuality. IEEE Comput. Graphics Appl. **21**(3), 6–8 (2001)
3. Bimber, O.: Spatial augmented reality: merging real and virtual worlds. AK Peters (2005)
4. Boboc, R.G., Băutu, E., Gîrbacia, F., Popovici, N., Popovici, D.M.: Augmented reality in cultural heritage: an overview of the last decade of applications. Appl. Sci. **12**(19), 9859 (2022)
5. Davis, F.D.: Perceived usefulness, perceived ease of use, and user acceptance of information technology. MIS Q. 319–340 (1989)
6. Davis, F.D., Bagozzi, R.P., Warshaw, P.R.: Extrinsic and intrinsic motivation to use computers in the workplace 1. J. Appl. Soc. Psychol. **22**(14), 1111–1132 (1992)
7. Fornell, C.: Structural equation models with unobservable variables and measurement error: algebra and statistics. Publications Sage (1981)
8. Galani, S., Vosinakis, S.: An augmented reality approach for communicating intangible and architectural heritage through digital characters and scale models. Pers. Ubiquit. Comput. 1–20 (2024)
9. Gheorghiu, D., tefan, L.: Immersing into the past: an augmented reality method to link tangible and intangible heritage. PLURAL. Hist. Cult. Soc. (2), 91–102 (2020)
10. Hair, J.F., Risher, J.J., Sarstedt, M., Ringle, C.M.: When to use and how to report the results of PLS-SEM. Eur. Bus. Rev. **31**(1), 2–24 (2019)
11. Kim, K., Hwang, J., Zo, H., Lee, H.: Understanding users' continuance intention toward smartphone augmented reality applications. Inf. Dev. **32**(2), 161–174 (2016)
12. Knight, S., Burn, J.: Developing a framework for assessing information quality on the world wide web. Informing Sci. **8** (2005)
13. Lang, Y., Deng, X., Zhang, K., Wang, Y.: Construction of intangible cultural heritage spot based on AR technology—taking the intangible cultural heritage of the li nationality in the areca valley as an example. In: IOP Conference Series: Earth and Environmental Science, vol. 234, p. 012119. IOP Publishing (2019)
14. Li, X.Z., Chen, C.C., Kang, X.: Research on intangible cultural heritage education inheritance based on augmented reality technology. In: 2022 IEEE International Conference on Consumer Electronics-Taiwan, pp. 49–50. IEEE (2022)
15. Li, X.Z., Chen, C.C., Kang, X., Kang, J.: Research on relevant dimensions of tourism experience of intangible cultural heritage lantern festival: integrating generic learning outcomes with the technology acceptance model. Front. Psychol. **13**, 943277 (2022)
16. Liu, Y., Sun, J., Chen, S.K.: Comparing technology acceptance of AR-based and 3d map-based mobile library applications: a multigroup sem analysis. Interact. Learn. Environ. **31**(7), 4156–4170 (2023)
17. Papakostas, C., Troussas, C., Krouska, A., Sgouropoulou, C.: Measuring user experience, usability and interactivity of a personalized mobile augmented reality training system. Sensors **21**(11), 3888 (2021)
18. Papakostas, C., Troussas, C., Krouska, A., Sgouropoulou, C.: Exploring users' behavioral intention to adopt mobile augmented reality in education through an extended technology acceptance model. Int. J. Hum.-Comput. Interact. **39**(6), 1294–1302 (2023)

19. Park, S., Yun, H.: Relationships between students' affective experiences and technology acceptance in augmented reality design training in higher education. Educ. Tech. Res. Dev. **72**(2), 479–501 (2024)
20. Peter, K., Auala, S., Winschiers-Theophilus, H.: An AR game for primary learners to safeguard intangible cultural heritage of the ovahimba tribe. In: Proceedings of the 2023 ACM International Conference on Interactive Media Experiences, pp. 359–361 (2023)
21. Steuer, J.: Defining virtual reality: dimensions determining telepresence. Communication in the age of virtual reality/Lawrence Erlbaum and Associates (1995)
22. Venkatesh, V.: Determinants of perceived ease of use: integrating control, intrinsic motivation, and emotion into the technology acceptance model. Inf. Syst. Res. **11**(4), 342–365 (2000)
23. Venkatesh, V., Davis, F.D.: A theoretical extension of the technology acceptance model: Four longitudinal field studies. Manag. Sci. **46**(2), 186–204 (2000)
24. Wang, S., Chen, S., Nah, K.: Exploring the mechanisms influencing users' willingness to pay for green real estate projects in Asia based on technology acceptance modeling theory. Buildings **14**(2), 349 (2024)
25. Wang, S., Sun, W., Liu, J., Nah, K., Yan, W., Tan, S.: The influence of AR on purchase intentions of cultural heritage products: the tam and flow-based study. Appl. Sci. **14**(16), 7169 (2024)
26. Warshaw, P.R., Davis, F.D.: Disentangling behavioral intention and behavioral expectation. J. Exp. Soc. Psychol. **21**(3), 213–228 (1985)
27. Wojciechowski, R., Cellary, W.: Evaluation of learners' attitude toward learning in Aries augmented reality environments. Comput. Educ. **68**, 570–585 (2013)
28. Zhang, M.: Promoting, regulating, and guiding the subjectivity of the inheritance of nvshu culture-fieldwork on the inheritors and the way of inheritance. Trans. Soc. Sci. Educ. Hum. Res. **5**, 162–168 (2024)
29. Zhang, X., Sun, L., Yan, S.: Nvshu: virtual reality design and narrative popularization for intangible cultural heritage characters. In: SIGGRAPH Asia 2023 XR, pp. 1–2 (2023)

Motion Style Transfer: Methods, Challenges, and Future Directions

Siyao Du, Boyuan Cheng, Yi Wen, Zixuan Zhou, and Xiaosong Yang[✉]

National Center for Computer Animation, Bournemouth University, Poole, UK
{bcheng,s5721301,xyang}@bournemouth.ac.uk

Abstract. Motion Style Transfer (MST) is a key research area in computer graphics, enabling motion sequences to acquire stylistic attributes while preserving semantic consistency. Recent advancements have significantly improved MST's flexibility and scalability, facilitating high-quality motion adaptation across various applications. This paper presents a comprehensive survey of MST research, categorizing existing approaches into generative models, content-target combination methods, and text-semantics-driven techniques. We further review commonly used MST datasets and evaluation metrics, highlighting inconsistencies in benchmarking methodologies. We highlight the need for scalable dataset generation and standardized evaluation protocols to advance MST research.

Keywords: Motion Style Transfer · literature survey · Computer Animation · Generative Model

1 Introduction

Motion Style Transfer (MST) modifies the stylistic attributes of character animations while preserving original motion content. It finds applications in animation, gaming, VR/AR, and robotics, where it automates motion stylization, reducing manual workload while enhancing expressiveness and realism.

Recent advancements have explored novel representations and learning paradigms to improve MST adaptability and robustness. Multimodal learning integrates motion with other inputs, such as music [1–4], enhancing contextual synthesis. Self-supervised [5–7] and few-shot learning [8] reduce dependency on large-scale labeled datasets, enabling style adaptation with minimal supervision. Improved motion style representation through high-dimensional embeddings and contrastive learning has facilitated better disentanglement of style and content. Additionally, text-driven motion generation allows natural language descriptions to guide motion synthesis, expanding interactive content creation.

MST has also begun integrating semantic reasoning mechanisms, such as Large Language Models (LLMs), bridging linguistic descriptions and motion synthesis [9]. These models improve interpretability and control, shifting MST toward more intuitive, human-centered frameworks.

C. Mousas et al. (Eds.): CASA 2025, LNCS 15915, pp. 55–76, 2026.
https://doi.org/10.1007/978-981-95-0100-7_4

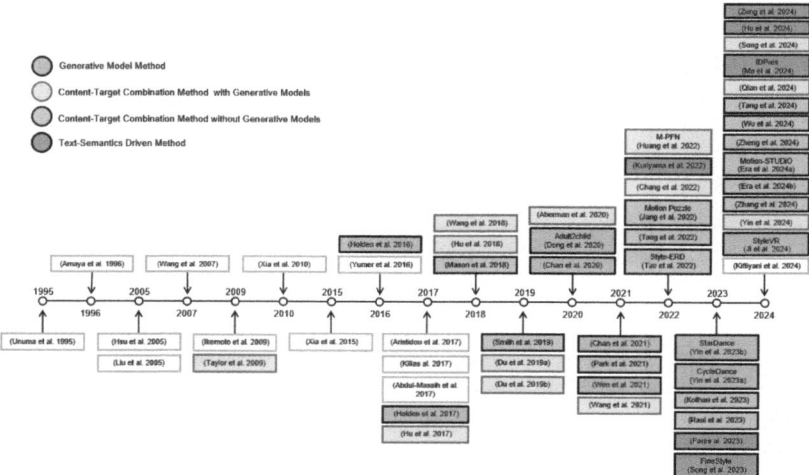

Fig. 1. Evolution of Motion Style Transfer Methods (1995–2024)

While significant progress has been made, MST still lacks a unified framework for defining, transferring, and evaluating motion styles, limiting its practical adoption. With the rise of multi-modal and text-driven motion generation and increasing large-scale datasets, a systematic review is needed to consolidate these developments.

Previous surveys, such as Syed Muhammad Abrar Akber et al. [10], have provided valuable overviews of MST methodologies and skeleton-based motion datasets. However, they lack a structured categorization of motion styles, making it difficult to define stylistic attributes. Additionally, existing surveys have not comprehensively reviewed evaluation metrics, particularly their role in benchmarking and real-world applicability.

To bridge these gaps, this survey provides a structured review of MST research, focusing on three key aspects: a comprehensive taxonomy of motion styles, a systematic review of evaluation protocols, and an analysis of emerging methodologies such as multi-modal learning and text-driven motion generation. This review spans MST research conducted from 1995 to 2024 as shown in Fig. 1, offering a historical and technical perspective across nearly three decades. By addressing these areas, this paper serves as a foundational reference for researchers and industry practitioners.

Literature Collection Methodology. To ensure a rigorous and systematic survey, we adopted a structured literature collection methodology. We first prioritized recent papers published in high-impact conferences and journals relevant to motion modeling and animation, including CVPR, ICCV, ECCV, ICLR, NeurIPS, AAAI, SIGGRAPH, Eurographics, and ACM Multimedia (MM), as well as journals such as TOG, CGF, TPAMI, and TVCG. We then extended our search using Google Scholar and arXiv with keywords such as "motion style transfer", "stylized motion generation", "motion style modeling", and "style-content disentanglement". From an initial pool of approximately 80 publications, we selected 56 papers based on their relevance to motion style modeling techniques, evaluation metrics, and datasets, with an emphasis on studies published within the past five years.

2 Motion Style Categories

A well-defined taxonomy of motion styles is essential for standardizing MST methodologies, improving reproducibility, and enabling systematic benchmarking. Our taxonomy is informed by established frameworks such as Laban Movement Analysis (LMA) [11] for detailed categorization of expressive movement features (e.g., posture, rhythm, amplitude, energy) and Dodge et al. [12], who proposed a structured approach for classifying movement patterns using primitive parameters and compound spatio-temporal characteristics. By leveraging these frameworks, we ensure clarity and consistency in defining motion styles.

2.1 Emotion-Based Styles

Emotion-driven styles significantly influence motion characteristics such as velocity, amplitude, posture, and rhythm, making them essential for expressive animation. For example, *Angry* motion is marked by forceful movements, heavy footfalls, a stiff posture, and abrupt gestures, reflecting heightened energy and frustration. *Happy* styles feature energetic, rhythmic motion with increased arm swing and light, quick steps, conveying enthusiasm and dynamism. In contrast, *Sad* motion is characterized by slow, sluggish movements, minimal arm motion, and a hunched posture, indicating low energy and motivation. *Fearful* styles exhibit erratic pacing, sudden hesitations, and a contracted body posture, signaling nervousness or avoidance. *Surprised* motion features sudden limb expansion followed by rapid contraction. Aristidou et al. [13] classified emotions using Russell's Circumplex Model (RCM), mapping them into four quadrants based on arousal and valence. MST enhances the synthesis of these styles, enabling realistic emotional expression in animation and interactive storytelling.

2.2 Personality and Behavioral Styles

Personality-driven motion styles reflect individual behavioral tendencies and are widely used in NPC animation and robotic motion design. For example, *Confident* movement is defined by a steady, controlled gait with wide strides and an upright posture, exuding assurance and stability. *Casual* motion is relaxed and natural, with moderate arm swings and a steady pace, simulating everyday human locomotion. *Strutting* is characterized by deliberate, rhythmic steps with pronounced hip and shoulder motion, conveying assertiveness and self-assurance. Gender-based variations also exist, where *Masculine* movements tend to have broader, angular strides, while *Feminine* styles emphasize fluid, circular gestures. MST enables adaptive personality modeling, allowing virtual agents to exhibit individualized behaviors in dynamic storytelling and human-computer interaction.

2.3   Biomechanical and Age-Related Styles

Biomechanical factors such as age, weight, and physical condition significantly impact movement characteristics. For example, *Elderly* motion typically includes slower steps, shorter strides, reduced arm swing, and frequent balance adjustments, reflecting age-related motor decline. *Childlike* styles, in contrast, are bouncy and energetic, with higher limb elevation and irregular step timing, often associated with playfulness [14]. *Fatigued* motion shows sluggish movement and increased impact forces, common in elderly or burdened individuals. On the other hand, *Light* movement styles exhibit agile, high-centered movements, often conveying elegance and nimbleness. MST facilitates biomechanically accurate adaptation, supporting applications in rehabilitation, sports training, and humanoid robotics.

2.4   Cultural and Context-Driven Styles

Motion styles are also shaped by cultural, environmental, and professional contexts, influencing animation and robotic applications. For example, *Military* motion is highly structured, featuring rigid, synchronized movements with strict step timing, often used in formations and disciplined behaviors. *Sneaky* or *Crouched* styles involve small, controlled steps with minimal arm motion, commonly seen in stealth-based movements. *Dancing* styles are highly rhythmic and fluid, incorporating coordinated arm and leg gestures synchronized with music, making them prevalent in performance-based applications. *Drunk* motion is recognized by unstable, exaggerated sways, sudden stops, and inconsistent pacing, simulating impaired motor control. MST enhances the synthesis of culturally and contextually adaptive animations, enabling realistic interactions in VR, film, and social robotics.

2.5   Stylized and Non-Human Motion

Some motion styles deviate from natural human movement, either due to extreme stylization or non-human anatomy. For example, *Mechanical* or *Robot-Like* motion is characterized by rigid joint angles, uniform stride lengths, and minimal variation, often seen in humanoid robots or synthetic characters. *Exaggerated Animation Styles* emphasize extreme squash-and-stretch dynamics, common in highly stylized cinematics. Additionally, *Non-Human Creature* [15] motion involves adaptive retargeting techniques for quadrupeds, fantasy creatures, and alien forms, requiring MST to handle unique anatomical constraints. By leveraging MST, these stylized motions can be effectively synthesized across diverse character archetypes, enhancing animation realism and artistic expression.

2.6   Dance Styles

Dance represents one of the most complex and expressive forms of human movement, making it a crucial domain for motion style analysis. Different dance genres exhibit distinctive movement characteristics that can be analyzed through Laban Movement Analysis [11]. *Ballet* emphasizes Light Weight and Sustained Time, creating its characteristic floating quality, while *hip-hop* employs Strong Weight and Sudden Time for percussive movements. *Contemporary dance* explores the full range of Effort qualities, allowing for greater expressive variety.

The spatial aspects of dance are equally significant. Classical forms like *ballet* maintain vertical alignment and precise positioning, while modern dance explores more fluid spatial patterns. *Folk dances* often feature group formations with synchronized movements that reflect cultural traditions. *Social dances* like ballroom and Latin styles develop partner-specific interaction patterns. By combining LMA principles with quantitative metrics such as beat alignment, path complexity, and energy expenditure, we can systematically analyze and categorize dance styles for more effective motion style transfer applications.

3   Methods of Motion Style Transfer

MST methods can be categorized into four main groups: Traditional Methods, Generative Models, Content-Target Combination Methods, and Text-Semantics Driven Methods. This classification is based on the underlying techniques used for motion transformation and their ability to capture and apply stylistic variations. Traditional methods rely on rule-based transformations and signal processing, making them computationally efficient but limited in stylistic flexibility. Generative models leverage deep learning to learn complex, non-linear style variations, enabling more diverse motion synthesis, particularly for dance, gesture, and personality-driven styles. Content-target combination methods blend source and target motion, offering finer control over gait, emotions, and biomechanical adaptations while preserving content integrity. Text-semantics-driven approaches expand MST by mapping linguistic descriptions to motion styles, enhancing interpretability and user control. A summary of these techniques is provided in Table 1.

3.1   Traditional Methods

Traditional methods primarily handle gait and emotion-based styles, relying on mathematical transformations such as Fourier Transform and Gaussian Process Regression, as illustrated in the Fig. 2. Generative models excel in dance, gesture, and personality-driven styles by leveraging deep learning for non-linear stylization. Early frequency-based methods, such as Fourier analysis [16] and intensity adjustments [17], enabled basic emotion-driven gait transfer but lacked generalization. Linear [18] and nonlinear transformations [19] improved flexibility, while probabilistic models [21,22] ensured smooth transitions in emotion-based gait adaptation.

Table 1. Methods, Approches, Models and Styles in MST Researches

Methods of MST	Approach of MST	Generative Model	Style	Paper
Traditional Methods	Fourier Transform		Walk Styles	[16]
	Signal Processing		Walk Styles	[17]
	LTI + IMW		Walk Styles for Real-time MST	[18]
	NIO		Walk Styles	[19]
	MF-GP		Walk Styles	[20]
	GPR		Walk Styles	[21]
	BN		Walk Styles	[22]
	MAR		Walk Styles for Real-time MST	[23]
	Spectral Style Transfer		Walk Styles	[24]
	LMA + RBF		Walk Styles in RCM Emotion-based Categories	[13]
	Statistical Style Difference. ΔStyle		Walk Styles	[25]
	SDV + Linear Transformation		Walk Styles	[15]
	Constraint Optimization + GBPs		Emotion-based Styles, Giar Styles and Personality-based Styles	[26]
Generative Model Methods	CAE + Gram Matrix + FNN	Autoencoder	Walk Styles for Game	[27]
	CNN + CAE + Gram + F-FCN	Autoencoder	Walk Styles in Zombie, Old, Injured, Depressed and Confident for Real-time MST	[28]
	CycleGAN	GAN	Child Action Styles and Adult Action Styles	[14]
	StarGAN	GAN	Hand Movement Emotional-based Styles	[29]
	StarGAN	Normalising Flow	Emotion-based Styles, Hand Gesture Styles, Giar Styles and Content-Specific Styles	[30]
	Generative Flow + Transformer	GAN	Emotion-based Styles, Giar Styles, Personality-based Styles and Content-Specific Styles	[31]
	CycleGAN + MTE + GN	GAN	Dance Styles, Motion Trajectory and Multimodal Integration with Music	[2]
	CycleGAN + MTE	Normalising Flow	Dance Styles, Motion Trajectory and Multimodal Integration with Music	[1]
	FlowSMM	Normalising Flow	Emotion-based Styles and Personality-based Styles in VR Scene	[32]
Content-Target Combination Methods	[FCRBM] + Style Variables	FCRBM	Walk Styles	[33]
	Autoencoder + RBM + Gram Matrix	Autoencoder	Walk Styles	[34]
	Adversarial Autoencoder (AAE) + SAAE	GAN-based	Emotion-based Styles, Giar Styles, Personality-based Styles and Content-specific Styles	[35]
	c-GAN + ConvLSTM + Gram Loss	GAN	Walk Styles, Run Styles, Gesture Styles and Emotion-Based Styles	[36]
	CA + CVAE	VAE	Walk Styles	[37]
	CA + CVAE	VAE	Walk Styles	[38]
	TCNNs + AdaIN	GAN	Emotion-based Styles, Giar Styles, Personality-based Styles and Content-specific Styles	[39]
	CCycle4GAN	GAN	Emotion-based Styles, Giar Styles, Personality-based Styles, Content-specific Styles and KC	[40]
	Flow Network+ Transformer + AdaIN	Normalising Flow	Emotion-based Styles, Giar Styles, Personality-based Styles and Content-specific Styles	[41]
	DDPM + MTA + AT + PR	Diffusion	Emotion-based Styles, Giar Styles, Personality-based Styles and Content-specific Styles	[3]
	MCM-LDM + M-c Denoiser	Diffusion & VAE	Emotion-based Styles, Giar Styles, Personality-based Styles and Trajectory-aware Style Transfer	[42]
	Diffusion Model + Mamba	Diffusion	Emotion-based Styles, Giar Styles, Personality-based Styles and Trajectory-aware Style Transfer	[43]
	KMCGs	Diffusion	Locomotion Styles, Dance Styles and Artistic Styles	[44]
	PFNN + Residual Adapters		Emotion-based Walk Styles and Personality-based Walk Styles	[8]
	Pose Network + TN + One-Hot Vector		Walk Styles	[45]
	ST-GCN + GAN		Emotion-based Styles, Giar Styles, Personality-based Styles and Content-specific Styles	[46]
	BPStyleNet(BP-AdaIN + BP-ATN)		Per-body-part Styles, Emotion-based Styles, Giar Styles, Personality-based Styles and Dynamic Motion Styles	[47]
	MTCN + MOE + IN		Character Personality Styles, Emotion-based Styles, Gait Styles and Content-specific Styles for Online Control	[6]
	ERD + FT-Att Discriminator		Emotion-based Styles, Giar Styles, Personality-based Styles, Content-specific Styles	[7]
	MoSA + P-ETL		Social Norms of Motion Styles in a Specific Environment or Agent Type	[48]
	TD3 RL + AE for feature extraction		Robot's Emotion Movement in Emotion-based Styles	[49]
	Transformer Decoder, Motion Decomposing		Walk Styles, Contact Timing and Trajectory	[50]
	Contrastive Learning + SS-D		Emotion-based Styles, Gait Styles and Action-based Styles	[5]
	TCN + SPAdaIN		Emotion-based Styles, Personality-based Styles and Action-based Styles	[51]
	Pretrained Style & Dance Encoders + Adversarial Training		Emotion-based Dance Styles and Personality-based Dance Style	[52]
	Metadata-independent Learning		Emotion-based Styles, Giar Styles and Personality-based Styles	[53]
	MST + GCN		Emotion-driven Styles, Action-based Styles and Personality-based Styles	[54]
Text-Semantics-Driven Methods	Token-based Style Transfer + Transformer	Transformer-based	Gesture Styles and Context-Aware Styles	[55]
	TransFTVler + Transformer	Transformer-based	Multimodal Facial Expression Styles, Gesture Styles, Personality-based Styles and Emotion-based styles	[4]
	SGSE + Semantic Tokenizer + DI-FG	GAN	Emotion-based Styles, Giar Styles, Personality-based Styles, Content-specific Styles	[56]
	GAN-based Gesture Style Transfer + LLM for Style Selection	GAN	Co-speech Gesture Manner Styles	[9]
	Disentanglement Block + Generator Block	GAN	Individualized Motion Styles and Human Structure Styles	[57]
	CLIP + Diffusion Model Reverse Process	Diffusion	Personalized styles, Emotion-driven Styles, Locomotion Styles and Artistic Styles	[58]

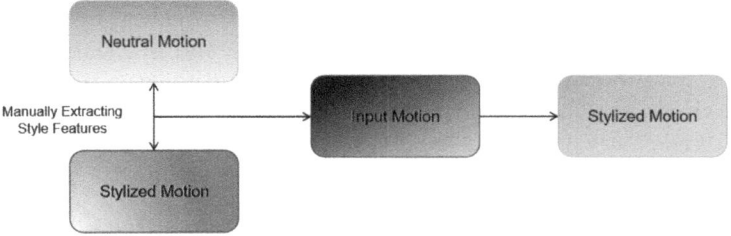

Fig. 2. Flow Chart of Traditional Methods

Real-time MST advanced with local mixture autoregressive models [23], allowing immediate style adjustments. Statistical methods [15,25] enhanced motion retargeting, adapting emotional gait styles to different body structures. Recently, ΔStyle [26] improved fine-grained emotional gait control while minimizing content distortion.

Despite their efficiency, traditional methods struggle with high-dimensional motion spaces and diverse stylistic expressions, making them less effective beyond structured patterns like walking. This limitation has driven the shift toward deep learning-based generative models for greater flexibility and scalability.

3.2 Generative Model Methods

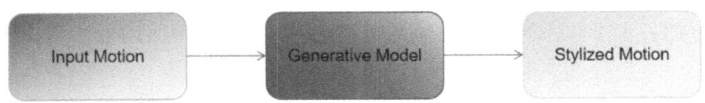

Fig. 3. Flow Chart of Generative Model Methods

As shown in Fig. 3, Generative models leverage deep learning architectures such as GANs and diffusion models to automate motion transformation, capturing complex, non-linear style variations. These models primarily use supervised and weakly-supervised learning, excelling in capturing styles such as dance, gesture, and personality-driven motions through fine-grained stylization.

Supervised methods train on labeled datasets to explicitly map content motions to stylized counterparts. Holden et al. [27] introduced a convolutional autoencoder (CAE) for structured motion representations, later refined with more efficient architectures [28]. However, these models are constrained primarily to predefined locomotion styles, like walking, and thus struggle with adapting to broader, diverse motion styles.

Weakly-supervised methods, using adversarial learning and probabilistic constraints, have improved scalability and style flexibility. Dong et al. [14] developed

Adult2Child, a CycleGAN-based model specifically targeting age-related style adaptations. Yin et al. [1, 2] introduced CycleDance and StarDance, leveraging CycleGAN and StarGAN architectures for culturally-contextualized dance styles aligned with music. Chan et al. [29, 30] employed StarGAN for emotion-driven gestures, significantly enhancing expressive body language. Wen et al. [31] and Ji et al. [32] utilized normalizing flows and transformer architectures for emotion-based and personality-driven styles, effectively disentangling complex stylistic nuances from content motions.

Despite their effectiveness, generative models struggle with fine-grained control and often fail to generalize to unseen motion styles without fine-tuning. This limitation motivated the development of content-target combination methods for greater stylistic flexibility.

3.3   Content-Target Combination Methods

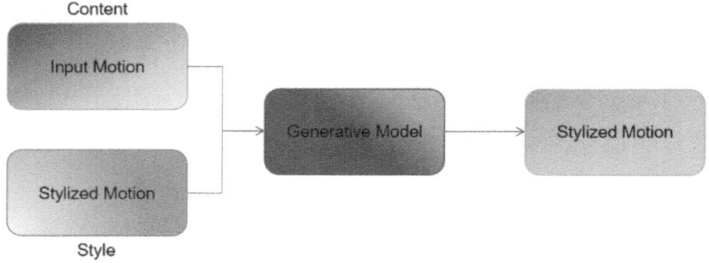

Fig. 4. Flow Chart of Content-Target Combination Methods

As shown in Fig. 4, Content-target combination methods explicitly merge stylistic attributes such as rhythm, amplitude, posture, and dynamics from target motions into source content, offering fine-grained control. These methods are widely effective in emotion-driven gestures, biomechanical adaptations, and personality-driven locomotion styles.

Several approaches incorporate generative architectures like adversarial learning, diffusion models, and latent transformations. Huang et al. [41] proposed M-PFN, utilizing a Transformer-based architecture that encodes personality-driven and emotion-based styles into shared latent spaces, employing Adaptive Instance Normalization (AdaIN) for detailed style adjustments. Du et al. [37] developed a CVAE-based method specifically optimized for biomechanical adaptations, ensuring stylistic fidelity across diverse body structures. Hu et al. [34] developed an autoencoder model facilitating smooth transitions specifically for emotional styles, improving realism in interactive applications.

Diffusion models have particularly advanced MST's ability to ensure consistency across complex and dynamic styles. Song et al. [42] introduced MCM-LDM to enhance realism and coherence in complex dance movements. Qian et al. [43] developed SMCD, excelling in capturing long-term dependencies critical for personality-driven motion synthesis. Chang et al. [3] proposed DDPM to manage subtle emotional and personality transitions, ensuring natural and coherent style adaptations.

Other techniques avoid generative model complexities by focusing on feature disentanglement, parameter adaptation, and temporal modeling. Tang et al. [50] developed methods to accurately adapt biomechanical styles through motion manifold representations. Era et al. [52] utilized unlabeled data to synthesize diverse dance and gesture styles effectively.

Few-shot and self-supervised learning have reduced data reliance significantly. Mason et al. [8] introduced residual adapters for efficient few-shot style learning, targeting personality-driven gait variations. Kothari et al. [48] proposed modular low-rank adaptation for quick style adaptation with minimal training, especially useful in emotion-based and biomechanical scenarios. Zheng et al. [51] leveraged semi-supervised ST-GCN for localized personality-based and emotional style modifications, ensuring precise content preservation.

These methods collectively address scalability and fine-grained style control, enhancing MST applicability across diverse stylistic contexts.

3.4 Text-Semantics Driven Methods

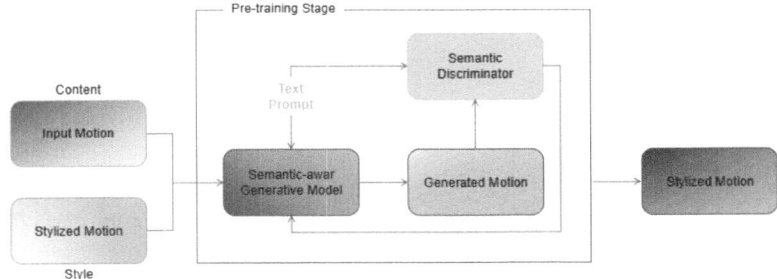

Fig. 5. Flow Chart of Text-Semantics Driven Methods

As shown in Fig. 5, Text-semantics driven methods incorporate linguistic context into MST, allowing flexible, interpretable, and controllable motion synthesis. This makes them particularly useful for emotion-based animation, personality-driven transformations, and multimodal human-computer interactions.

Hu et al. [58] introduced a diffusion-based MST framework, leveraging semantic-guided learning in CLIP's space. The model first trains a text-to-motion diffusion prior, then fine-tunes it on a single style example using few-shot learning. While enabling style transfer from minimal data, it requires full-sequence motion input, limiting real-time applications and increasing computational demands. Fares et al. [4] developed TranSTYLer, a transformer-based multimodal style transfer model integrating facial expressions, gestures, and full-body animations. By learning style-content disentanglement through adversarial learning, it supports zero-shot adaptation, making it ideal for real-time virtual assistants and AI-driven avatar animation. Kuriyama et al. [55] proposed a context-aware gesture style transfer model that segments gestures into tokenized motion units using a vision transformer, ensuring natural style transitions in interactive storytelling and AI-driven animation. Song et al. [56] introduced FineStyle, a GAN-based framework integrating dual interactive-flow fusion (DIFF) for fine-grained text-to-motion stylization. While it improves adaptability, it struggles when semantic labels misalign with target motion, requiring dataset-specific retraining. Ma et al. [57] developed IDPres, an identity-preserving MST framework that integrates gait recognition-based motion disentanglement. By ensuring motion characteristics remain unique to the target identity, it is particularly useful for biomechanical applications and personalized animation. However, identity-specific training increases computational overhead, limiting generalization.

Recent advancements in Large Language Models (LLMs) have further expanded MST capabilities, enhancing semantic understanding and user control. Zeng et al. [9] integrated an LLM-based style selection system into a GAN-driven gesture MST model, mapping impression words to motion styles. This bridges motion perception and linguistic descriptors, enabling natural language-driven MST. By combining LLMs with generative models, researchers are moving toward more intuitive and flexible MST frameworks, where text inputs guide style adaptation in text-to-animation pipelines, AI-driven motion synthesis, and real-time interactive applications.

4   Datasets for MST

MST datasets capture how movements are performed rather than just which actions occur, emphasizing stylistic variations influenced by personality, emotion, biomechanics, and culture. High-quality, well-annotated datasets are essential for training MST models that generate realistic and expressive motion. A detailed summary of previously used MST datasets can be found in Table 2.

Different datasets define motion style in distinct ways. Some, like 100STYLE [60], explicitly categorize styles (e.g., naturalistic, exaggerated, robotic), while others, such as CMU MoCap [68], contain unlabeled stylistic variations requiring additional processing. Some datasets emphasize physical constraints (e.g., aging, fatigue in Du Dataset [37]), while others focus on emotional variations (e.g., happiness, sadness in Emilya Dataset [66]).

A key challenge in MST datasets is balancing style diversity and dataset scale. Some datasets, like Holden Dataset [27] and Mason Dataset [8], offer diverse styles but few samples per style, limiting fine-grained modeling. Others, such as HumanML3D [59] and UTD-MHAD [65], provide deep motion data but with limited stylistic variation. 100STYLE strikes a balance by combining large-scale motion sequences with explicit style labels.

Table 2. Used Datasets in Motion Style Transfer Researches

Dataset name	Year	Collection	Body	Subjects	Sequence	Frame	Length	Label	Other
Dancer99 [57]	2024	Video collection	Body	99	3,168	-	0.5 mins per dance	Identity & Motion Style (Dance)	Individuals performing complex and identical dance routines
MUCS [9]	2024	YouTube Video Collection	Upper body	225	225	25 fps	32 h	Identity (Speaker)	Diverse natural gesture variations from different speakers and cultures.
Dancer101 [57]	2024	Video collection	Body	101	8181	64 fps	3.5 mins per dance	Identity & Motion Style (Dance)	Individuals performing complex and identical dance routines
HumanML3D [59]	2022	From HumanAct12 and AMASS datasets	Body	144	14616	-	0.03 -0.16 mins per motion	Content Motion Only	Covers multiple sports style categories, especially daily, sports, acrobatic and artistic performance styles.
100STYLE [60]	2022	Motion capture	Body	1	10,000+	60 fps	18.5+ h	Style & Action (Walk)	100 different styles of locomotion
PATS [61]	2022	Motion capture	Upper body	25	-	25 fps	251 h	Identity (Speaker)	Pose sequences of 25 speakers
Kuriyame Dataset [55]	2022	Motion Capture	Upper body	1	-	60 fps	-	Style (Speaker)	Focuses on expressive gestures and style transfer using tokenized gestures.
Tang Dataset [6]	2022	Motion Capture	Body	-	16	-	-	Style & Action (Game)	Includes 8 styles: Zombie, Gun-holding, Female, gait labels, action type annotations
AIST++ [62]	2021	Motion capture	Body	30	1,408	≈256.4 fps	≈10.85 h	Style (Dance)	Includes 10 dance styles
The Body Movement Library [30]	2021	Motion capture	Body & Hands	30	4,080	120 fps	-	Style & Action (Daily)	Each motion type (include hand motion) with at least four different emotion status: Neutral, Angry, Happy, and Sad.
PATS 2.0 Corpus [4]	2020+	From Video	Upper body	25	84000	64 fps	251 h	Identity (Speaker)	Includes speech features, contains dialog act labels and emphasizes gesture diversity
Aberman Dataset [39]	2020	Motion capture	Body	1	10500	120 fps	5–6 min per style	Style (Walk)	16 distinct motion styles, specifically captured for this research.
Adult2ChildCycle-GAN [14]	2020	Motion capture	Body	17	-	120 fps	-	Identity & Action (Daily)	3 types of motions: discrete actions, cyclic locomotion, anddynamic combinations.
Chan Dataset [29]	2020	Motion capture	Hands	-	35	-	-	Style & Action (Daily)	7 different types of hand motion. 5 'different types of emotions
Du Dataset [37]	2019	Motion capture	Body	3	-	-	0.6 h of walking	Style (Walk)	6 styles (anger, depression, pride, child, feminine, old age)
Mason Dataset [8]	2018	Motion capture	Body	1	-	120 fps	-	Style (Walk)	8 styles (angry, childlike, depressed, neutral, old, proud, sexy, strutting)
Mixamo [63]	2017	Animation software	Body	-	2500+	-	-	Action with style	High-quality 3D character animations
Aristidou Dataset [13]	2017	Motion capture	Body	9	108	480fps	-	Style (Dance)	Total of 12 emotion categories.
Liberated Pixel Cup [64]	2017	2D Animation	Body	672	13440	-	-	Identity & Action (Game)	Characters with different attributes has 5 predefined animation types from 4 viewpoints
Kilias Dataset [25]	2017	Motion Capture	Body	1	-	-	-	Style (Walk)	Includes styles: happy, angry, sad, proud, sneaky, cat walk, crab walk, lame walk
Holden Dataset [27]	2016	Motion capture	Body	-	300	120fps	0.3 h	Style & Action (Basic)	Includes locomotion styles and motion types like run, punch and kick.
UTD-MHAD [65]	2015	Motion capture and sensors	Body	8	261	-	1–4 seconds per action	Content Motion Only	27 action classes included
Xia et al. Dataset [23]	2015	Motion capture	Body	10	1500	120fps	0.15 h	Style & Action (Basic)	Includes 8 distinct motion styles and 5 motion contents.
Emilya Dataset [66]	2014	Motion Capture	Body	11	36	-	0.5 ± 0.3 mins per action	Style & Action (Daily)	Includes 8 emotions, 7 daily actions, synchronized video & motion capture
Xia Dataset [22]	2010	Motion capture	Body	25	-	-	-	Style & Action (Walk)	three behaviors in database: sideways stepping, walking and running.
HDM05 [67]	2007	Motion capture	Body	5	2337	120 fps	-	Content Motion Only	Movement categories include everyday actions such as walking, running, jumping, striking.etc.
Liu Dataset [19]	2005	Motion capture	Body	-	-	120 fps	-	Style (Walk)	Data contains multiple movement patterns such as gait and running
Hsu Dataset [18]	2005	Motion capture	Body	-	-	120 fps	1–2 mins per style	Style (Walk)	Locomotion data set included several styles: normal, catwalk, crouch, limp, and sideways.
CMU [68]	2003	Motion capture	Body	144	2605	120 fps	-	Style & Action (Daily)	Includes different categories such as walking, running, jumping, dancing, and fighting.

The choice of dataset depends on the application. Game animation and inter-active AI require broad stylistic diversity, whereas film production and high-fidelity simulation demand extensive intra-style variations. However, few datasets achieve both, limiting MST models' generalization.

MST datasets also vary in suitability for real-time vs. offline applications. Real-time MST requires smooth motion transitions and structured style informa-tion for seamless blending, as seen in 100STYLE [60] and The Body Movement Library [30]. Offline MST, used in animation and post-production, prioritizes detailed style variations, such as Emilya Dataset [66] and PATS [61].

Despite their value, current datasets exhibit key limitations. Most focus on locomotion styles (e.g., walking, running, dancing), while dynamic styles (e.g., martial arts, sports, group interactions) remain underrepresented. Additionally, inconsistent labeling complicates cross-dataset learning—100STYLE explicitly categorizes styles, whereas CMU MoCap lacks predefined labels.

Another limitation is the discrete treatment of motion style, despite real-world motion existing on a continuous spectrum. Few datasets support smooth interpolation between styles, such as transitioning from neutral walking to exag-gerated strutting. Future MST datasets should expand motion categories, stan-dardize annotations, and support progressive style variations.

5   Evaluation Metrics of Motion Style Transfer

Evaluating MST methods requires a comprehensive framework that captures various aspects of generated motion, including fidelity, realism, consistency, and diversity.

Based on a thorough literature review, we categorize evaluation metrics into several key groups. **Distribution Similarity** measures how closely generated motions align with real-world motion distributions. **Spatial Accuracy** evaluates joint positions and overall movement correctness. **Dynamic Metrics** capture temporal consistency, motion smoothness, and biomechanical plausibility. **Vari-ety** ensures diversity in generated motions, preventing mode collapse. **Accuracy** includes style and content recognition accuracy to assess how well models retain both intended style and content. **Style Alignment** examines the consistency of transferred motion styles, while **Content Alignment** ensures that essential motion attributes remain intact. **Other** covers computational efficiency, scala-bility, and data privacy concerns. **User Study** provides qualitative insights into the perceptual quality and naturalness of generated motions. Table 3 summa-rizes the evaluation metrics used in MST research, organized according to these categories.

Table 3. Summary of Evaluation Metrics for MST

Classification of Evaluation Metrics	Evaluation Metrics	Paper
Distribution Similarity	Fréchet Motion Distance (FMD)	[1, 2, 5, 7, 26, 42, 44, 46, 47, 50, 51, 56–58]
	Fréchet Pose Distance (FPD)	[1, 2, 44]
	Fréchet inception distance (FID)	[3, 43, 53]
	G2T Criterion (Generated to True)	[35]
	T2G Criterion (Ture to Generated)	[35]
	Similarity Distance Between Motion Primitives and Style Examples (Eq. 12)	[37]
	Kernel Inception Distance (KID)	[5, 43]
Spatial Accuracy	Joint Location Error	[24]
	Average Displacement Error (ADE)	[48]
	Final Displacement Error (FDE)	[48]
	Mean Squared Displacement (MSD)	[47]
	Mean Square Error (MSE)	[6, 36, 57]
	Mean Average Error (MAE)	[57]
	RMS Prediction Error	[33]
	Minkowski Distance	[4]
Dynamic Metrics	Style Distance	[5]
	Variance Evaluation of Walk Left Stance (Pose$_S$D, V$_S$D, Step$_S$D)	[37]
	Motion Continuity Loss (Lcon)	[32]
	Contact Precision	[42, 50]
	Temporal Consistency	[7]
	Velocity, Acceleration, Jerk	[4]
Varity	Diversity	[5, 43]
	Silhouette Coefficient (SCoeff)	[31, 32, 41]
	Calinski-Harabaz Index (CHI)	[31, 41, 53]
Accuracy	Content Recognition Accuracy (CRA)	[26, 42, 47, 56, 58]
	Style Recognition Accuracy (SRA)	[26, 42, 47, 50, 56, 58]
	Transfer Strength Accuracy	[4]
Style Alignment	Style Consistency (SC)	[32]
	Identity Score (ID-Score)	[57]
Content Alignment	Beat Alignment Score (BeatAlign)	[52]
	Content Preservation	[4, 5, 7]
	Content Errors	[55]
	Content Distance	[5]
	Cycle Consistency	[44]
	Trajectory Similarity Index (TSI)	[42]
Other	IC weighted score	[9]
	The Concordance Correlation Coefficient (CCC)	[9]
	Scalability and Data Privacy	[44]
User Study	User Study	[1, 2, 5, 7, 13–15, 24, 30, 32, 39, 42–46, 50, 51, 56]

5.1   Objective Evaluation Metrics

While various metrics have been proposed, this study focuses on five key evaluation measures that are particularly crucial for assessing motion style transfer in terms of style-content separation and generation quality.

Fréchet Motion Distance (FMD) is a widely used distribution-based metric adapted from FID to measure the similarity between generated and real motions, specifically evaluating the overall realism of synthesized motion. Following Maiorca et al. [69], FMD employs a pre-trained motion feature encoder to extract feature embeddings, using their mean and covariance. It is defined as:

$$FMD = ||\mu_g - \mu_t||^2 + Tr(\Sigma_g + \Sigma_t - 2(\Sigma_g \Sigma_t)^{1/2}) \tag{1}$$

where μ_g, Σ_g and μ_t, Σ_t represent the mean and covariance of the generated and target motion distributions, respectively. This metric effectively captures overall distribution similarity and is crucial for assessing motion style fidelity.

Style Recognition Accuracy (SRA) assesses the accuracy of generated motion in reflecting intended styles. It compares generated samples against predefined style labels using independently trained style classifiers, which may differ across studies in terms of datasets, architectures, and training details. The formula for SRA is:

$$SRA = \frac{N_c}{N_t} \tag{2}$$

where N_c is the number of generated samples correctly classified as the target style and N_t is the total number of generated samples. This metric provides a clear and interpretable measure of how well the generated motions match the desired style, making it an essential component in evaluating the performance of motion style transfer systems. Due to variations in pre-trained classifiers, explicit documentation of classifier specifics (training dataset, architecture, parameters) is essential to interpret results clearly.

Content Recognition Accuracy (CRA) evaluates how effectively the generated motion retains the original content semantics post-style transfer. Similar to SRA, CRA utilizes independently trained content classifiers, whose variations across implementations (e.g., training data, model structures, parameters) significantly influence results. CRA is defined as:

$$CRA = \frac{N_c}{N_t}, \tag{3}$$

where N_c is the number of correctly recognized content labels, and N_t is the total number of samples. Due to these variations, precise details of the pre-trained classifiers used should be explicitly described to ensure reproducibility and comparability.

Diversity measures the variation in generated motion sequences, assessing whether the model produces a wide range of outputs rather than converging to a limited set of patterns. It evaluates how well the generated motions capture stylistic variability across different samples.

$$Diversity = \frac{1}{N} \sum_{i=1}^{N} ||x_i - \mu||^2 \tag{4}$$

where x_i represents an individual generated motion sequence, and μ is the mean of all generated sequences. Higher diversity values indicate a broader range of generated motion styles, reflecting the model's ability to generalize across different motion variations. This metric is crucial for ensuring that motion style transfer models generate a rich variety of motions rather than repetitive or overly similar sequences.

Content Preservation assesses how well the generated behaviors maintain the original motion structure and meaning after style transfer. Content Preservation ensures that the key features of the source motion are maintained in the generated output. It is often quantified using feature similarity or reconstruction loss.

These metrics collectively evaluate both *style accuracy and content preservation*, which are fundamental challenges in motion style transfer.

5.2   Other Evaluation Metrics

Certain evaluation metrics are tailored for specific contexts and are challenging to generalize: **IC weighted score** assesses information content similarity between generated and target motions, focusing on complexity and density within motion sequences. **Concordance Correlation Coefficient (CCC)** measures agreement between predicted and actual motions, capturing correlation and systematic differences, emphasizing accuracy. **Scalability and Data Privacy** [44] evaluates model efficiency and privacy protection, critical for practical deployment scenarios.

5.3   User Study

User studies are essential for evaluating the perceptual quality and naturalness of generated motions in MST. While objective metrics provide quantitative assessments, user studies capture subjective qualities such as expressiveness, realism, and contextual appropriateness, which are critical in gaming, animation, and VR.

User study evaluations can be classified into two main categories: **preference-based evaluations** and **rating-based evaluations**. Preference-based studies require participants to choose between alternatives, such as selecting the more natural motion from pairs of animations. Rating-based studies ask participants to score individual motions on various criteria using numerical scales. These studies often involve animators, motion experts, or general users, depending on the application. For example, Ma et al. [57] used user studies to assess motion identity and realism in their IDPres framework, while Yin et al. [44] employed professional dancers to evaluate transfer strength and content preservation in dance style transfer.

Despite their value, challenges remain, including participant recruitment, evaluation standardization, and study consistency. Addressing these issues is crucial for improving the reliability and comparability of user studies in MST research.

5.4   Limitations in Cross-Method Comparisons

Direct quantitative comparisons among existing MST methods are inherently challenging due to differences in selected datasets and evaluation metrics. Furthermore, even when identical methods are evaluated on the same datasets using the same metrics, significant discrepancies in reported results often occur. For example, substantial variations in reported FMD, CRA, and SRA values for methods such as MotionPuzzle can be observed between studies (e.g., Jang et al. [47] vs. Song et al. [56] and Hu et al. [58]). Importantly, these differences primarily stem from variations in independently trained content/style recognition classifiers rather than issues with method reproduction or dataset splits. Given that classifier implementations—including training data, architectures, and parameter settings—typically differ across studies and are rarely thoroughly documented, direct comparisons of these metrics become unreliable. Thus, this survey underscores the necessity for standardized evaluation protocols and detailed, transparent experimental documentation in future MST research.

6   Challenge, Future Direction and Ethical Issues

Despite recent advances, MST still faces several key challenges that limit its broader adoption. One fundamental issue is style-content disentanglement, as existing methods often struggle to fully separate stylistic attributes from motion semantics, leading to undesired content distortion or incomplete style transfer. Future research should explore self-supervised learning and improved disentanglement techniques to enhance generalization and enable more robust style adaptation.

Another challenge is the lack of standardized evaluation frameworks. While metrics such as Fréchet Motion Distance (FMD) and Content Recognition Accuracy (CRA) provide insights into motion realism and content preservation, they fail to fully capture temporal coherence and stylistic diversity. Additionally, user studies, although valuable, suffer from subjectivity and inconsistencies in evaluation criteria. Future research should develop comprehensive, standardized evaluation protocols that integrate both quantitative metrics and structured user studies. Multi-modal evaluation approaches incorporating audio, linguistic, and visual feedback could improve assessment, particularly in applications such as dance and gesture synthesis.

Computational efficiency remains a bottleneck, particularly for real-time applications in gaming, animation, and VR. Many existing MST models rely on resource-intensive architectures, limiting their practical deployment. Future work should focus on designing lightweight models through model compression, pruning, and efficient inference techniques to achieve real-time MST without compromising quality.

One promising direction is the integration of Large Language Models (LLMs) into MST. LLMs offer new opportunities for text-driven MST, enabling more intuitive and controllable style adaptation. Future research should investigate how LLMs can be leveraged to generate more semantically rich motion representations, facilitating natural language-based motion customization. Combining LLM-driven descriptions with generative motion synthesis could enhance interpretability and user control, benefiting interactive applications.

Additionally, dataset diversity remains a critical limitation. While existing datasets capture various motion styles, they often lack sufficient representation of cultural variations, environmental contexts, and fine-grained stylistic nuances. Expanding MST datasets to include broader motion categories or leveraging synthetic data generation techniques could improve model generalization and applicability.

Beyond technical challenges, MST research must also address ethical considerations. Privacy concerns arise as many motion datasets involve human subjects, necessitating stricter data anonymization and informed consent protocols. The ownership and attribution of generated motion remain unresolved, requiring clearer guidelines for fair use and intellectual property rights. Additionally, biases in motion style transfer could lead to misrepresentations of cultural and emotional styles, reinforcing stereotypes or social misalignment. Ensuring ethically responsible motion synthesis should be a priority, with safeguards to mitigate these risks.

To advance MST research, future efforts should focus on: (1) Developing self-supervised and weakly-supervised learning frameworks to improve adaptability and style-content disentanglement. (2) Enhancing real-time MST by optimizing model architectures for efficient inference in gaming, animation, and robotics. (3) Advancing multi-modal MST by integrating text, speech, and environmental cues for more intuitive motion synthesis. (4) Expanding dataset diversity and annotation standards to support broader motion categories and realistic style representations. (5) Addressing ethical concerns and bias mitigation strategies to ensure responsible MST deployment in creative and interactive applications.

By tackling these challenges, MST research can move toward more scalable, interpretable, and application-driven solutions, fostering innovations in character animation, virtual reality, and human-computer interaction.

7 Conclusion

MST has progressed from traditional mathematical models to deep learning-based generative and text-semantics-driven approaches. This survey provides a structured review of MST methodologies, highlighting the growing influence of generative models and the emerging role of semantic-driven techniques. While significant advancements have been made, challenges remain in feature disentanglement, computational efficiency, dataset diversity, and evaluation standardization. Future research should focus on bridging generative modeling with semantic motion editing, developing efficient architectures, and establishing standardized evaluation frameworks. The continued integration of AI-driven evaluation and real-time MST solutions will further expand its applications in gaming, animation, and virtual reality.

Disclosure of Interests. The authors have no competing interests to declare that are relevant to the content of this article.

References

1. Yin, W., et al.: Multimodal dance style transfer. Mach. Vis. Appl. **34**(4), 48 (2023)
2. Yin, W., et al.: Dance style transfer with cross-modal transformer. In: Proceedings of the IEEE/CVF Winter Conference on Applications of Computer Vision (WACV), pp. 5058–5067 (2023)
3. Chang, Z., et al.: Unifying human motion synthesis and style transfer with denoising diffusion probabilistic models. arXiv preprint arXiv:2212.08526 (2022)
4. Fares, M., Pelachaud, C., Obin, N.: TranSTYLer: multimodal behavioral style transfer for facial and body gestures generation. arXiv preprint arXiv:2308.10843 (2023)
5. Wu, Z., et al.: Contrastive disentanglement for self-supervised motion style transfer. Multimed. Tools Appl. **83**(27), 70523–70544 (2024). https://doi.org/10.1007/s11042-024-18238-4
6. Tang, Y., et al.: Online motion style transfer for interactive character control. arXiv preprint arXiv:2203.16393 (2022)
7. Tao, T., et al.: Style-ERD: responsive and coherent online motion style transfer. In: Proceedings of the IEEE/CVF Conference on Computer Vision and Pattern Recognition (CVPR), pp. 6593–6603 (2022)
8. Mason, I., et al.: Few-shot learning of homogeneous human locomotion styles. Comput. Graph. Forum **37**(7), 143–153 (2018). https://doi.org/10.1111/cgf.13555. https://onlinelibrary.wiley.com/doi/pdf/10.1111/cgf.13555
9. Zeng, J., et al.: Modifying gesture style with impression words. In: Proceedings of the 24th ACM International Conference on Intelligent Virtual Agents, IVA 2024. GLASGOW, UK. Association for Computing Machinery (2024). https://doi.org/10.1145/3652988.3673931. ISBN 9798400706257
10. Akber, S.M.A., et al.: Deep learning-based motion style transfer tools, techniques and future challenges. Sensors **23**(5) (2023). https://doi.org/10.3390/s23052597. https://www.mdpi.com/1424-8220/23/5/2597. ISSN 1424-8220
11. Laban, R., Ullmann, L.: The mastery of movement (1971)
12. Dodge, S., Weibel, R., Lautenschütz, A.-K.: Towards a taxonomy of movement patterns. Inf. Vis. **7**(3–4), 240–252 (2008)
13. Aristidou, A., et al.: Emotion control of unstructured dance movements. In: Proceedings of the ACM SIGGRAPH/Eurographics Symposium on Computer Animation, SCA 2017, Los Angeles, California. Association for Computing Machinery (2017). https://doi.org/10.1145/3099564.3099566. ISBN 9781450350914
14. Dong, Y., et al.: Adult2child: motion style transfer using CycleGANs. In: Proceedings of the 13th ACM SIGGRAPH Conference on Motion, Interaction and Games, MIG 2020. Virtual Event, SC, USA. Association for Computing Machinery (2020). https://doi.org/10.1145/3424636.3426909. ISBN 9781450381710
15. Abdul-Massih, M., Yoo, I., Benes, B.: Motion style retargeting to characters with different morphologies. Comput. Graph. Forum **36**(6), 86–99 (2017). https://doi.org/10.1111/cgf.12860. https://onlinelibrary.wiley.com/doi/pdf/10.1111/cgf.12860

16. Unuma, M., Anjyo, K., Takeuchi, R.: Fourier principles for emotion-based human figure animation. In: Proceedings of the 22nd Annual Conference on Computer Graphics and Interactive Techniques, SIGGRAPH 1995, pp. 91–96. Association for Computing Machinery, New York (1995). https://doi.org/10.1145/218380.218419. ISBN 0897917014

17. Amaya, K., Bruderlin, A., Calvert, T.: Emotion from motion. In: Graphics Interface, Toronto, Canada, vol. 96, pp. 222–229 (1996)

18. Hsu, E., Pulli, K., Popović, J.: Style translation for human motion. In: ACM SIGGRAPH 2005 Papers, SIGGRAPH 2005, Los Angeles, California, pp. 1082–1089. Association for Computing Machinery (2005). https://doi.org/10.1145/1186822. 1073315. ISBN 9781450378253

19. Karen Liu, C., Hertzmann, A., Popović, Z.: Learning physicsbased motion style with nonlinear inverse optimization. ACM Trans. Graph. **24**(3), 1071–1081 (2005). https://doi.org/10.1145/1073204.1073314. ISSN 0730-0301

20. Wang, J.M., Fleet, D.J., Hertzmann, A.: Multifactor Gaussian process models for style-content separation. In: Proceedings of the 24th International Conference on Machine Learning, ICML 2007, Corvalis, Oregon, USA, pp. 975–982. Association for Computing Machinery (2007). https://doi.org/10.1145/1273496.1273619. ISBN 9781595937933

21. Ikemoto, L., Arikan, O., Forsyth, D.: Generalizing motion edits with Gaussian processes. ACM Trans. Graph. **28**(1) (2009). https://doi.org/10.1145/1477926. 1477927. ISSN 0730-0301

22. Xia, S.: Modeling style and variation in human motion. In: 2010 4th International Universal Communication Symposium, p. 207 (2010). https://doi.org/10. 1109/IUCS.2010.5666642

23. Xia, S., et al.: Realtime style transfer for unlabeled heterogeneous human motion. ACM Trans. Graph. **34**(4) (2015). https://doi.org/10.1145/2766999. ISSN 0730-0301

24. Ersin Yumer, M., Mitra, N.J.: Spectral style transfer for human motion between independent actions. ACM Trans. Graph. **35**(4) (2016). https://doi.org/10.1145/2897824.2925955. ISSN 0730-0301

25. Kilias, A., Mousas, C.: Motion style transfer in correlated motion spaces. In: De Paolis, L.T., Bourdot, P., Mongelli, A. (eds.) AVR 2017. LNCS, vol. 10324, pp. 242–252. Springer, Cham (2017). https://doi.org/10.1007/978-3-319-60922-5_18

26. Kiftiyani, U., Lee, S.: Controlling cross-content motion style transfer via statistical style difference. In: SIGGRAPH Asia 2024 Posters, SA 2024. Association for Computing Machinery (2024). https://doi.org/10.1145/3681756.3697968. ISBN 9798400711381

27. Holden, D., Saito, J., Komura, T.: A deep learning framework for character motion synthesis and editing. ACM Trans. Graph. **35**(4) (2016). https://doi.org/10.1145/2897824.2925975. ISSN 0730-0301

28. Holden, D., et al.: Fast neural style transfer for motion data. IEEE Comput. Graph. Appl. **37**(4), 42–49 (2017). https://doi.org/10.1109/MCG.2017.3271464

29. Chan, J.C.P., Irimia, A.-S., Ho, E.S.L.: Emotion transfer for 3D hand motion using StarGAN. In: Ritsos, P.D., Xu, K. (eds.) Computer Graphics and Visual Computing (CGVC). The Eurographics Association (2020). https://doi.org/10. 2312/cgvc.20201146. ISBN 978-3-03868-122-9

30. Chan, J.C.P., Ho, E.S.L.: Emotion transfer for 3D hand and full body motion using StarGAN. Computers **10**(3) (2021). https://doi.org/10.3390/computers10030038. https://www.mdpi.com/2073-431X/10/3/38. ISSN 2073-431X

31. Wen, Y.-H., et al.: Autoregressive stylized motion synthesis with generative flow. In: Proceedings of the IEEE/CVF Conference on Computer Vision and Pattern Recognition (CVPR), pp. 13612–13621 (2021)
32. Ji, B., et al.: StyleVR: stylizing character animations with normalizing flows. IEEE Trans. Vis. Comput. Graph. **30**(7), 4183–4196 (2024). https://doi.org/10.1109/TVCG.2023.3259183
33. Taylor, G.W., Hinton, G.E.: Factored conditional restricted Boltzmann machines for modeling motion style. In: Proceedings of the 26th Annual International Conference on Machine Learning, ICML 2009, Montreal, Quebec, Canada, pp. 1025–1032. Association for Computing Machinery (2009). https://doi.org/10.1145/1553374.1553505. ISBN 9781605585161
34. Hu, D., Liu, X., Peng, S., Zhong, B., Du, J.: Automatic character motion style transfer via autoencoder generative model and spatio-temporal correlation mining. In: Yang, J., et al. (eds.) CCCV 2017. CCIS, vol. 771, pp. 705–716. Springer, Singapore (2017). https://doi.org/10.1007/978-981-10-7299-4_59
35. Wang, Q., et al.: Transferring style in motion capture sequences with adversarial learning. In: ESANN, Bruges, Belgium (2018).https://hal.science/hal-02100672
36. Hu, D., Peng, S.-J., Liu, X.: Pixel-level character motion style transfer using conditional adversarial networks. In: Proceedings of Computer Graphics International, pp. 129–138 (2018)
37. Du, H., et al.: Stylistic locomotion modeling and synthesis using variational generative models. In: Proceedings of the 12th ACM SIGGRAPH Conference on Motion, Interaction and Games, MIG 2019, Newcastle upon Tyne, UK. Association for Computing Machinery (2019). https://doi.org/10.1145/3359566.3360083. ISBN 9781450369947
38. Du, H., et al.: Stylistic locomotion modeling with conditional variational autoencoder. In: Eurographics (Short Papers), pp. 9–12 (2019)
39. Aberman, K., et al.: Unpaired motion style transfer from video to animation. ACM Trans. Graph. (TOG) **39**(4), 64 (2020)
40. Wang, H., et al.: A cyclic consistency motion style transfer method combined with kinematic constraints. J. Sens. **2021**(1), 5548614 (2021). https://doi.org/10.1155/2021/5548614. https://onlinelibrary.wiley.com/doi/pdf/10.1155/2021/5548614
41. Huang, Y., et al.: Unpaired motion style transfer with motion-oriented projection flow network. In: 2022 IEEE International Conference on Multimedia and Expo (ICME), pp. 1–6 (2022). https://doi.org/10.1109/ICME52920.2022.9859776
42. Song, W., et al.: Arbitrary motion style transfer with multi-condition motion latent diffusion model. In: 2024 IEEE/CVF Conference on Computer Vision and Pattern Recognition (CVPR), pp. 821–830 (2024). https://doi.org/10.1109/CVPR52733.2024.00084
43. Qian, Z., et al.: SMCD: high realism motion style transfer via mambabased diffusion. arXiv preprint arXiv:2405.02844 (2024)
44. Yin, W., et al.: Scalable motion style transfer with constrained diffusion generation. In: Proceedings of the AAAI Conference on Artificial Intelligence, vol. 38, no. 9, pp. 10234–10242 (2024). https://doi.org/10.1609/aaai.v38i9.28889. https://ojs.aaai.org/index.php/AAAI/article/view/28889
45. Smith, H.J., et al.: Efficient neural networks for real-time motion style transfer. Proc. ACM Comput. Graph. Interact. Tech. **2**(2) (2019). https://doi.org/10.1145/3340254
46. Park, S., Jang, D.-K., Lee, S.-H.: Diverse motion stylization for multiple style domains via spatial-temporal graph-based generative model. Proc. ACM Comput. Graph. Interact. Tech. **4**(3) (2021). https://doi.org/10.1145/3480145

47. Jang, D.-K., Park, S., Lee, S.-H.: Motion puzzle: arbitrary motion style transfer by body part. ACM Trans. Graph. **41**(3), (2022). https://doi.org/10.1145/3516429. ISSN 0730-0301

48. Kothari, P., et al.: Motion style transfer: modular low-rank adaptation for deep motion forecasting. In: Liu, K., Kulic, D., Ichnowski, J. (eds.) Proceedings of The 6th Conference on Robot Learning, vol. 205. Proceedings of Machine Learning Research. PMLR, 14–18 December 2023, pp. 774–784 (2023). https://proceedings.mlr.press/v205/kothari23a.html

49. Fernandez-Fernandez, R., et al.: Transferring human emotions to robot motions using Neural Policy Style Transfer. Cogn. Syst. Res. **82**, 101121 (2023). https://doi.org/10.1016/j.cogsys.2023.05.010. https://www.sciencedirect.com/science/article/pii/S1389041723000499. ISSN 1389-0417

50. Tang, X., et al.: Decoupling contact for fine-grained motion style transfer. In: SIGGRAPH Asia 2024 Conference Papers, SA 2024. Association for Computing Machinery (2024). https://doi.org/10.1145/3680528.3687609. ISBN 9798400711312

51. Zheng, R., Liu, G., Hu, R.: Semi-supervised character motion style transfer. J. Comput.-Aided Des. Comput. Graph. (2024). https://doi.org/10.3724/SP.J.1089.2023-00385. https://www.jcad.cn/en/article/doi/10.3724/SP.J.1089.2023-00385

52. Era, Y., et al.: Motion-STUDiO: motion style transfer utilized for dancing operation by considering both style and dance features. In: 2024 International Conference on Consumer Electronics - Taiwan (ICCETaiwan), pp. 127–128 (2024). https://doi.org/10.1109/ICCE-Taiwan62264.2024.10674583

53. Era, Y., et al.: Generalizing human motion style transfer method based on metadata-independent learning. In: SIGGRAPH Asia 2024 Posters, SA 2024. Association for Computing Machinery (2024). https://doi.org/10.1145/3681756.3697890. ISBN 9798400711381

54. Zhang, F., Li, P., Lei, J.: A spatially adaptive motion style transfer method with temporal convolutional network. J. Comput.-Aided Des. Comput. Graph. **36**(10), 1653–1662 (2024). https://doi.org/10.3724/SP.J.1089.2024.20083. https://www.jcad.cn/en/article/doi/10.3724/SP.J.1089.2024.20083. ISSN 1003-9775

55. Kuriyama, S., et al.: Context-based style transfer of tokenized gestures. Comput. Graph. Forum **41**(8), 305–315 (2022). https://doi.org/10.1111/cgf.14645. https://onlinelibrary.wiley.com/doi/pdf/10.1111/cgf.14645

56. Song, W., et al.: FineStyle: semantic-aware fine-grained motion style transfer with dual interactive-flow fusion. IEEE Trans. Vis. Comput. Graph. **29**(11), 4361–4371 (2023). https://doi.org/10.1109/TVCG.2023.3320216

57. Ma, J., Zhang, X., Shiqi, Yu.: An identity-preserved framework for human motion transfer. IEEE Trans. Inf. Forensics Secur. **19**, 3495–3509 (2024). https://doi.org/10.1109/TIFS.2024.3364018

58. Hu, L., et al.: Diffusion-based human motion style transfer with semantic guidance. Comput. Graph. Forum **43**(8), e15169 (2024). https://doi.org/10.1111/cgf.15169. https://onlinelibrary.wiley.com/doi/pdf/10.1111/cgf.15169

59. Guo, C., et al.: Generating diverse and natural 3d human motions from text. In: Proceedings of the IEEE/CVF Conference on Computer Vision and Pattern Recognition, pp. 5152–5161 (2022)

60. Mason, I., Starke, S., Komura, T.: Real-time style modelling of human locomotion via feature-wise transformations and local motion phases. Proc. ACM Comput. Graph. Interact. Tech. **5**(1), 1–18 (2022)

61. Ahuja, C., Lee, D.W., Morency, L.-P.: Lowresource adaptation for personalized co-speech gesture generation. In: Proceedings of the IEEE/CVF Conference on Computer Vision and Pattern Recognition, pp. 20566–20576 (2022)
62. Li, R., et al.: AI choreographer: music conditioned 3D dance generation with AIST++. In: Proceedings of the IEEE/CVF International Conference on Computer Vision, pp. 13401–13412 (2021)
63. Adobe Mixamo. Adobe's Mixamo (2017). https://www.mixamo.com. Accessed 28 Sept 2017
64. Liberated Pixel Cup. Liberated Pixel Cup (2017). http://lpc.opengameart.org/. Accessed 27 Nov 2017
65. Chen, C., Jafari, R., Kehtarnavaz, N.: UTD-MHAD: a multimodal dataset for human action recognition utilizing a depth camera and a wearable inertial sensor. In: 2015 IEEE International conference on image processing (ICIP), pp. 168–172. IEEE (2015)
66. Fourati, N., Pelachaud, C.: Emilya: emotional body expression in daily actions database. In: LREC, pp. 3486–3493 (2014)
67. Müller, M., et al.: Mocap database hdm05. In: Institut für Informatik II, Universität Bonn, vol. 2, no. 7 (2007)
68. Carnegie Mellon University Motion Capture Database. CMU Motion Capture Database (2003). http://mocap.cs.cmu.edu. Accessed 13 Feb 2025
69. Maiorca, A., Yoon, Y., Dutoit, T.: Evaluating the quality of a synthesized motion with the fréchet motion distance. In: ACM SIGGRAPH 2022 Posters, pp. 1–2 (2022)

ReDACT: Reconstructing Detailed Avatar with Controllable Texture

Zezheng Chen, Huizhi Zhu, Fei Luo[✉], and Chunxia Xiao[✉]

School of Computer Science, Wuhan University, Wuhan, China
{chenzezheng,zhuhuizhi,luofei,cxxiao}@whu.edu.cn

Abstract. Generating high-quality, detailed 3D avatars from monocular video presents a significant challenge in digital human community. Recent methods have shown the potential to recover 3D geometry from monocular video, but they typically suffer from pose variability, geometric inaccuracies and insufficient texture realism. To address these challenges, we propose ReDACT, a novel framework designed for the reconstruction of high-fidelity 3D avatars from monocular video. To improve geometric accuracy, ReDACT first proposes a cycle-deforming field ensuring consistent geometry across frames during NeRF-based 3D reconstruction for the generation of high-fidelity avatars. To further enhance texture quality, we introduce a cascaded diffusion structure that emphasizes fine-grained details, such as skin and fabric patterns, allowing for controllable texture generation. Finally, the reconstructed avatars are animated via pose-driven deformation and rendered photo-realistically using volume rendering. Qualitative and quantitative results demonstrate that our method achieves high-quality reconstruction shapes, good texture realism, and robust generalization compared to prior methods.

Keywords: Avatar Reconstruction · Human NeRF · Diffusion Model

1 Introduction

Reconstructing realistic 3D avatars has become an essential aspect of applications in VR, AR, and the rapidly expanding metaverse. These digital human representations enhance immersive experiences and enable rich interactions within virtual environments. However, due to the depth ambiguity within monocular videos and the wide diversity of human motions, generating true-to-life 3D avatars from monocular video is still a challenging task.

Recently, advancements in neural rendering [1] and volumetric modeling techniques [2,3] have driven substantial progress in the field. Neural Radiance Fields (NeRF) [4] have emerged as a powerful solution for 3D scene reconstruction, employing volumetric rendering and neural networks to represent complex scenes

Supplementary Information The online version contains supplementary material available at https://doi.org/10.1007/978-981-95-0100-7_5.

with remarkable geometric and visual fidelity. Existing methods [4–7] have been successfully applied to static scenes, where they produce highly detailed reconstructions by modeling the volumetric radiance and density fields.

Despite the remarkable progress has been achieved by the NeRF-based methods, two notable challenges still persist in high-fidelity animatable avatar reconstruction. (1) **Inaccurate deformation from varying poses.** NeRF is commonly trained solely on static objects [4]. As a result, for efficient NeRF training, it is necessary to accurately warp the observation poses into a canonical pose, which aligns different posed frames into a consistent static pose, i.e., mapping to canonical space. (2) **Low-quality rendered appearance from varying poses.** Existing methods encounter limitations in capturing high-frequency texture details [8,9] and generating dynamic textures animated by novel poses [8,10–12]. They are unable to restore detailed and dynamic textures such as creases or wrinkles of clothes. Therefore, high-fidelity appearance generation needs more attention in the avatar reconstruction task.

To address these challenges, we propose ReDACT, a framework for reconstructing detailed animatable avatars with controllable texture generation from monocular video input. Firstly, we introduce the Cycle Deformation module to improve the accuracy of pose deformation. Specifically, connecting the forward and backward skinning deformations, we can train a more accurate transformation from observation space to canonical space based on the cycle consistency loss. This helps to achieve a better appearance in NeRF-based rendering for the human body. Secondly, we propose an integration of NeRF with a diffusion-based Texture Generation module for high-fidelity and dynamic appearance rendering. This combination not only enhances the visual quality of the avatars but also introduces a novel mechanism for texture generating, highly benefiting the dynamic appearance on unseen poses. Finally, we validate the effectiveness of ReDACT through extensive experiments, demonstrating significant improvements in both reconstruction accuracy and texture realism under novel poses compared to existing methods.

In summary, ReDACT advances the state-of-the-art in 3D avatar reconstruction by addressing the dual challenges of accurate appearance rendering and dynamic texture generation. Our main contributions are as follows:

- Introduce the Cycle Deformation module based on the cycle consistency loss to achieve accurate deformation, which can reconstruct a clearer appearance.
- Design a cascaded diffusion structure that exploits the generative potentials of diffusion models, which can enhance the visual reality and generalization for novel poses.

2   Related Work

2.1   Avatar from a Single Image

Traditional works focus on reconstructing human body geometry from multi-view videos [13] or depth cameras [14,15]. To overcome the limitation of multi-view constraints, many methods have explored reconstructing digital humans from a single image. Zhou et al. [16] focus on parametric human reconstruction, where a digital human model is reconstructed by estimating the body parameters and texture maps from an image. The limitation of parametric reconstruction methods is their inability to represent accurate geometry, as they only provide an approximation of the human shape. PiFu [17] employs a pixel-level implicit representation by training a pixel-aligned occupancy function to enhance geometry accuracy. PiFuHD [18] further improves the resolution and quality with a coarse-to-fine strategy. For better regularization on different poses, PaMIR [19] conditions the implicit function on a voxelized SMPL [20] mesh for robustness to pose variation. ICON [21] achieves better performance in challenging poses and loose clothing by estimating the normal map of both front and back views of the human. Recently, Diffusion-FOF [22] introduces a novel approach for single-view human reconstruction by employing a wavelet-domain diffusion model to predict a Fourier Occupancy Field, enabling detailed geometry and texture synthesis.

2.2   Avatar from Monocular Video

To model human dynamics, DeepCap [23] aims to deform pre-scanned human models from monocular video. With a monocular self-rotation video, Alldieck et al. [24] reconstruct the human body by optimizing the displacements of the SMPL model. Recently, SelfRecon [25] improves reconstruction quality by representing body motion as learnable non-rigid deformations combined with predefined SMPL skinning weights. DLCA-Recon [26] proposes a dynamic deformation field based on physical connection information between consecutive frames, enhancing performance in dynamic human reconstruction, particularly for loose clothing.

To take advantage of NeRF to address data accessibility, researchers are exploring its adaptation for monocular video. Nerfies [27] employs deformable NeRF in conjunction with deformation or hybrid networks to model dynamic humans, where the network maps light from the current motion space to the canonical space. However, challenges such as depth ambiguities and limited pose observations in monocular videos lead to overfitting of the deformation fields to the training data, resulting in artifacts when rendering from novel viewpoints.

To address these issues, HumanNeRF [10] introduces motion priors to regularize the deformation process. It decouples the deformation field into a skeletal motion field and a non-rigid motion field. NeuMan [8] further divides the NeRF into human and scene NeRF. By introducing more optimizations in human-NeRF, NeuMan achieves superior abilities of animation than HumanNeRF.

2.3   Avatar Animation

After reconstructing an avatar, the subsequent task is to animate it with different poses. Neural Actor [28] proposes a deformable NeRF conditioned on the posed SMPL model and texture map, optimizing details through predicted texture maps. MonoHuman [11], based on HumanNeRF [10], introduces the Shared

Bidirectional Deformation Module and Forward Correspondence Search Module to enhance the model's robustness in unseen poses. Although NeRF has achieved impressive results in digital human animation tasks, its model size and training time present inevitable challenges. Compared to the several dozen hours of training required by previous methods [8,10,11], InstantAvatar [29] reduces training time to the minute level by incorporating InstantNGP [30] and other space skipping strategies. Furthermore, HumanNeRF-SE [12] significantly reduces the model size and training time of the deformation network by fully leveraging the skinning prior of SMPL. More recently, some methods [31,32] introduce 3D Gaussian Splatting (3DGS) [33] for head avatar reconstruction with more accurate appearance and real-time rendering. In addition to head avatars, both GauHuman [9] and Gaussian Avatar [34] achieve highly efficient full-body avatar reconstruction using 3DGS. However, visual results show that NeRF-based methods offer superior rendering performance on high-frequency textures.

3   Method

We present ReDACT, a comprehensive framework designed to reconstruct detailed 3D avatars from monocular video with controllable texture generation. We focus on key challenges in high-fidelity avatar reconstruction, including the complexities of normalizing human poses and generating detailed appearance with dynamic texture on various unseen poses.

In this section, we illustrate the framework of our method (Fig. 1). Given a monocular video of a moving human, an animatable avatar is represented by NeRF in the canonical space through the Cycle Deformation module (Sect. 3.1). To reconstruct fine-grained appearance details, we also introduce the Texture Generation module (Sect. 3.2), which leverages cascaded diffusion models. Finally, the avatar can be animated in novel poses and rendered into images (Sect. 3.3).

3.1   Cycle Deformation

We define the deformation from the canonical pose to any arbitrary pose as the forward deformation. For an input video frame (a subject in the observation space), the transformation to the canonical space is defined as the backward deformation. We decompose a single deformation into two steps: rigid and non-rigid deformations following [10]. The backward deformation first performs the rigid deformation, followed by the non-rigid deformation, whereas the forward deformation follows the opposite order. The rigid deformation utilizes linear blend skinning, intending to transform the human body from the observation pose to an approximate canonical pose. LBS (Linear Blend Skinning) [35] for point position $\mathbf{x}$ and pose $\mathbf{p}$ in SMPL is represented by the following formula:

$$T_{LBS}(\mathbf{x}, \mathbf{p}) = \sum_{i=1}^{K} w^i(\mathbf{x}) T_{\mathbf{p}}^i(\mathbf{x}), \tag{1}$$

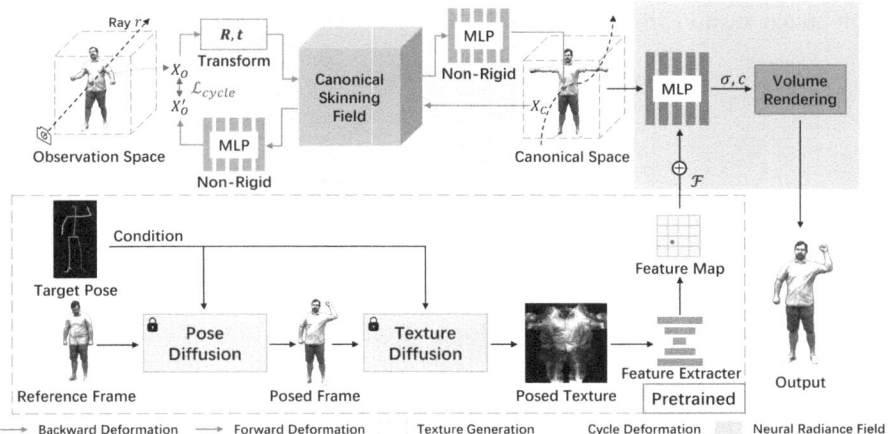

Fig. 1. Overview of ReDACT. Our method reconstructs a detailed avatar from monocular video. First, the human pose of each frame is deformed into a canonical pose to ensure consistent geometry for reconstruction via the Cycle Deformation module. After that, the NeRF is applied to reconstruct a high-fidelity avatar in canonical space. Besides, we pre-train a Texture Generation module to generate texture maps under the condition of target poses. Then the feature of texture map is extracted and fed into the NeRF to enhance the texture realism further and capture dynamic appearance. Finally, we render the pose-driven avatar photo realistically by volume rendering.

where w^i is the blend weight for the i-th joint influence. $T_{\mathbf{p}}^i$ is the transformation matrix of the i-th bone computed from pose $\mathbf{p}$, applied to the point $\mathbf{x}$. The non-rigid deformation aims to capture and complement the non-rigid geometric details, represented by an MLP. The MLP refines the deformation by accounting for flexible, pose-dependent variations that are not captured by the rigid transformation alone.

However previous methods [8,10] apply just a single backward deformation network to transform the human body from the observation space to the canonical space. This approach may lead to deformation errors, as the network can be only constrained by the reconstruction loss and lacks additional regularization. Inspired by SCANimate [36], we additionally introduce the cycle consistency to guide the deformation network and improve the accuracy.

To achieve this, we redesign the deformation process into a cyclic structure, incorporating both backward and forward deformations, similar to [11]. Since both the backward and forward deformations depend on the current pose in observation space, directly adopting a Siamese network structure may lead to overfitting issues. As illustrated in Fig. 1, we present a parameter-shared canonical skinning field and two independent MLPs with identical structures, which are employed for rigid and non-rigid deformations respectively.

For an input video frame, we always apply the backward deformation, sequentially performing the rigid and non-rigid deformation. For point position in observation space $\mathbf{x_o}$ and target pose $\mathbf{p}$:

$$T^b(\mathbf{x_o}, \mathbf{p}) = T_R^b(\mathbf{x_o}, \mathbf{p}) + T_{NR}^b(T_R^b(\mathbf{x_o}, \mathbf{p}), \mathbf{p}), \tag{2}$$

$$T_R^b(\mathbf{x_o}, \mathbf{p}) = \sum_{i=1}^{K} w_o^i(\mathbf{x_o})(\mathbf{R_i}\mathbf{x_o} + \mathbf{t_i}), \tag{3}$$

$$w_o^i(\mathbf{x}) = \frac{w_c^i(\mathbf{R_i}\mathbf{x} + \mathbf{t_i})}{\sum_{k=1}^{K} w_c^k(\mathbf{R_k}\mathbf{x} + \mathbf{t_k})}, \tag{4}$$

where T_R^b is a kind of inverse LBS (Eq. 1) from observation to canonical space. w_o^i is the blend weight for the i-th bone, and K is the number of keypoints ($K = 24$). $\mathbf{R_i}, \mathbf{t_i}$ are the rotation and translation that map the bone's coordinates from observation to canonical space, computed from pose $\mathbf{p}$. The blend weights in observation space w_o can be derived from canonical blend weight w_c.

Compared to computing different sets of weight volumes $\{w_o^i(\mathbf{x})\}$ for each frame in observation space, directly computing a single set $\{w_c^i(\mathbf{x})\}$ in canonical space leads to better generalization. So we design a canonical skinning field to represent the blend weights volume in canonical space $W_c(\mathbf{x}) = \{w_c^i(\mathbf{x})\}$, optimized by CNN network with initially random latent code $\mathbf{z}$, following [10]:

$$W_c(\mathbf{x}) = \mathrm{CNN}(\mathbf{x}, \mathbf{z}). \tag{5}$$

After rigid deformation, non-rigid deformation $T_{NR} : (\mathbf{x}, \mathbf{p}) \mapsto \Delta\mathbf{x}$ focus on deforming error correction for non-rigid human parts like clothes. We utilize MLP network to estimate this compensation:

$$T_{NR}(\mathbf{x}, \mathbf{p}) = \mathrm{MLP}(T_R(\mathbf{x}, \mathbf{p}), \mathbf{p}). \tag{6}$$

Forward deformation for point $\mathbf{x_c}$ in canonical space is similar to the backward (Eq. 2), but the blend weight can be directly queried from the shared canonical skinning field. Since the skinning field is defined within the canonical space, there is not any form of rotation or translation for the canonical points $\mathbf{x_c}$, i.e. $\mathbf{R_i} = 1, \mathbf{t_i} = 0$:

$$T_R^f(\mathbf{x_c}, \mathbf{p}) = \sum_{i=1}^{K} w_c^i(\mathbf{x_c})\mathbf{x_c}. \tag{7}$$

Finally, we introduce the cycle consistency loss $\mathcal{L}_{cycle}$ to constrain the network for better deformation accuracy:

$$\mathbf{x}_o' = T^f(T^b(\mathbf{x_o}, \mathbf{p}), \mathbf{p}), \tag{8}$$

$$\mathcal{L}_{cycle} = ||\mathbf{x}_o' - \mathbf{x}_o||_2, \tag{9}$$

where $T^f(T^b(\mathbf{x_o}, \mathbf{p}))$ denotes the cycle deformation, resulting in a reference point $\mathbf{x}_o'$ that differs from the original $\mathbf{x}_o$ point.

3.2   Controllable Texture Generation

The visual realism of a 3D avatar depends heavily on the quality and customization of its textures. High-quality textures not only enhance the appearance of the avatar, but also ensure consistency across various poses and viewpoints [11,28]. However, producing detailed and dynamic textures from monocular video input is challenging. Some previous methods either rely on simple texture mapping techniques [17,18] or require complex multiview setups [28,37]. In ReDACT, we design a cascaded diffusion model for controllable texture generation.

Preliminaries of Diffusion Models. Diffusion models [38–40] are a class of generative models that learn to produce high-quality images by reversing a gradual noising process. Specifically, they model a Markovian forward process that incrementally adds Gaussian noise to data, and a neural network is trained to approximate the reverse denoising process, enabling the generation of realistic samples from random noise. Stable Diffusion [39] is a powerful latent diffusion model for high-quality image generation. It produces detailed and realistic images by denoising latent representations of data instead of working directly in pixel space, making it both efficient and scalable. Stable Diffusion consists of an autoencoder VQ-VAE [41] and a time-conditioned U-Net for noise estimation. Following Stable Diffusion, ControlNet [40] manipulates the input to the intermediate layers of the U-Net for better controllable generation.

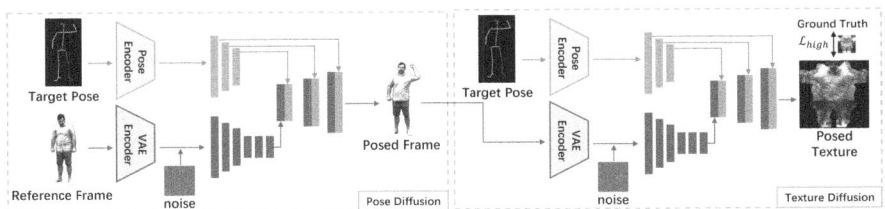

Fig. 2. Texture Generation Module. Following ControlNet [40], we design Pose Diffusion and Texture Diffusion for controllable texture generation under the constraint of target poses and reference subjects. The main difference between the two diffusion models lies in the generated data. Therefore, they can be trained separately on different datasets first, and then jointly trained.

Pose-Conditioned Texture Generation. Inspired by [28], we propose a Pose-Conditioned Texture Generation module illustrated in Fig. 2, which focuses on generating the corresponding texture maps under the control of the reference frame I_r and target pose $\mathbf{p}$. We design a cascaded architecture consisting of two distinct diffusion models based on ControlNet [40] network structure, namely Pose Diffusion G_p and Texture Diffusion G_t. The cascaded architecture is designed to leverage various datasets without ground truth (GT) of textures and mitigate the risk of overfitting. In summary, our generating procedure for posed texture map I_t can be represented by the following equation:

$$I_t = G_p(G_t(I_r, \mathbf{p}), \mathbf{p}). \tag{10}$$

In addition to loss functions for the noise-diffusing process, we introduce a generating loss function in the high-frequency domain with a Gaussian high-pass filter $H(I)$:

$$\mathcal{L}_{high} = ||H(I_t) - H(\tilde{I}_t)||_2, \tag{11}$$

where $\tilde{I}_t$ is the GT of texture map. $\mathcal{L}_{high}$ imposes additional constraints in the high-frequency domain, which guides the model in generating more detailed texture maps.

3.3 Avatar Animating and Rendering

From a monocular video clip, our method reconstructs a NeRF-based animatable avatar in the canonical space. The crucial final step is to enable animating and rendering the avatar from different viewpoints. This process involves leveraging the reconstructed NeRF representation and adapting it to dynamic and pose-driven animation, where different poses can be synthesized based on the reconstructed canonical avatar. The volume rendering techniques used in NeRF allow for realistic viewpoint synthesis, enhancing the quality and immersion of the rendered avatars.

Pose-Driven Texture Feature. We can take any frame as reference frame I_r and generate texture map I_t with the condition of target pose $\mathbf{p}$ in the Texture Generation module (Eq. 10). Meanwhile, the corresponding point $\mathbf{x_{UV}}$ in UV coordinates can be derived from the UV mapping of the dataset [28]. Therefore, the texture feature $\mathcal{F}$ used for refining NeRF's training is represented as:

$$\mathcal{F}(\mathbf{x_{UV}}) = \text{UNet}(I_t, \mathbf{x_{UV}}), \tag{12}$$

where a U-Net is used as a feature extractor on texture I_t.

Volume Rendering. In the observation space, we can define a NeRF model F_o with a driven pose $\mathbf{p}$ and texture feature $\mathcal{F}$:

$$F_o(\gamma(\mathbf{x}), \mathbf{p}, \mathcal{F}) = (\sigma(\mathbf{x}), \mathbf{c}(\mathbf{x})), \tag{13}$$

where γ is a sinusoidal positional encoding [4] of $\mathbf{x}$. For each sampled point $\mathbf{x}$, the NeRF model calculates density $\sigma(\mathbf{x})$ and color values $\mathbf{c}(\mathbf{x})$. In our method, F_o can be computed by warping the canonical NeRF volume F_c:

$$F_o(\gamma(\mathbf{x}), \mathbf{p}, \mathcal{F}) = F_c(\gamma(T^b(\mathbf{x}, \mathbf{p})), \mathcal{F}), \tag{14}$$

so that we can render an animated avatar in the canonical space by backward deformation.

NeRF's volume rendering capabilities enable photorealistic rendering by simulating light as it travels through the avatar's geometric structure. For a given viewpoint, we cast rays from the virtual camera's center through the avatar, sampling points along each ray path. According to the volume rendering formula [4], the color $C(r)$ of a ray r with D samples can be calculated like:

$$C(r) = \sum_{i=1}^{D} (\prod_{j=1}^{i-1} (1 - \alpha_j) \alpha_i \mathbf{c}(\mathbf{x_i}), \tag{15}$$

where $\alpha_i = 1 - exp(-\sigma(\mathbf{x_i})\Delta t_i)$, Δt_i is the interval between sample i and $i + 1$.

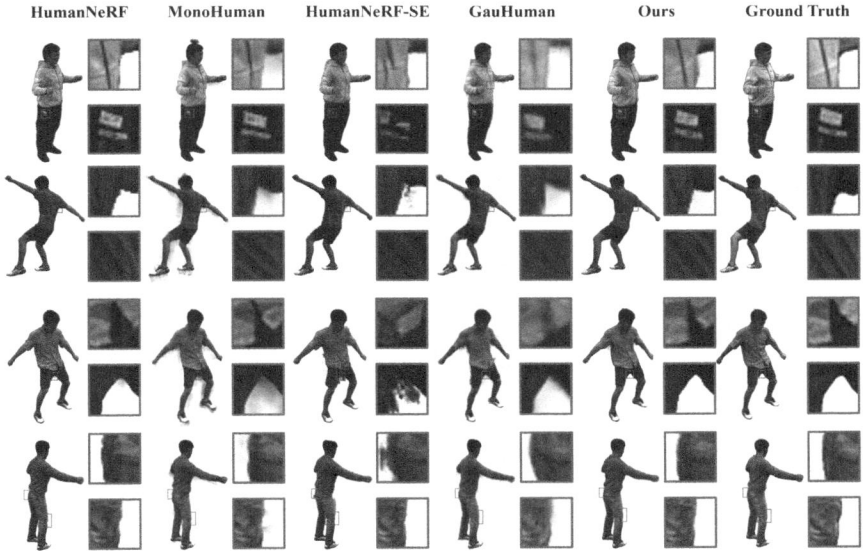

Fig. 3. Qualitative comparison for reconstruction task on ZJU-MoCap dataset. We enlarge certain detailed regions in the results to facilitate a more comprehensive visual comparison. The magnified areas are marked with red rectangles. (Color figure online)

3.4 Network Training

The network training is divided into two stages. In the first stage, we pre-train the Texture Generation module with the NeuralActor dataset [28]. The NeuralActor dataset provides dense multiview images from dozens of cameras for each subject. These multiview images are then used to synthesize ground truth texture maps. Based on the multiview images and ground truth texture maps, our Texture Generation module can be pretrained. Initially, the Pose Diffusion and Texture Diffusion models are trained independently, followed by joint training of both components. To enhance generalization, any front-facing frame can be randomly selected as a reference frame. In the second stage, the Cycle Deformation module and NeRF are trained on the input monocular video, while the parameters of the Texture Generation module remain frozen. During this process, the following loss functions are optimized:

$$\mathcal{L}_{MSE} = \sum_{\mathbf{r} \in R} (||C(\mathbf{r}) - \hat{C}(\mathbf{r})||_2^2), \tag{16}$$

where R is the set of sampling rays and $C(\mathbf{r}), \hat{C}(\mathbf{r})$ are rendered color and ground truth color of camera ray $\mathbf{r}$ respectively. Besides, we introduce LPIPS [42] loss $\mathcal{L}_{LPIPS}$ for better visual perception. Combining the loss functions mentioned above, the total loss can be expressed as:

$$\mathcal{L}_{total} = \mathcal{L}_{cycle} + \mathcal{L}_{MSE} + \lambda \mathcal{L}_{LPIPS}. \tag{17}$$

4 Experiments

4.1 Experimental Settings

During the experiments, a single RTX 3090 is used for training and rendering.

Dataset. We use the ZJU-MoCAP [37] dataset to evaluate our method. We follow previous work [11,12] to evaluate our results with the same six subjects from the ZJU-MoCAP dataset. Besides, we partition the datasets into a training set and a test set, following a 4:1 ratio. So we can animate reconstructed avatars in novel poses from the test set and evaluate the performance with ground truth.

Evaluation Tasks. Since our method supports both avatar reconstruction and animation, we evaluate its performance separately on the reconstructing and animating tasks.

Evaluation Metrics. We use three metrics: peak signal-to-noise ratio (PSNR), structural similarity index (SSIM), and learned perceptual image patch similarity (LPIPS) [42]. It should be noted that LPIPS is the most human-perceptually aligned metric among these indicators, while PSNR prefers smooth results but may have bad visual quality [42]. Metrics are computed from the average results of the same six subjects in ZJU-MoCAP dataset as previous works [11,12].

4.2 Quantitative Evaluation

To evaluate the performance of reconstruction and animation, we use only the Camera 1 data from the ZJU-MoCap dataset for training. The frames from Camera 1 are further divided into a seen-pose training set and an unseen-pose test set in a 4:1 ratio. We compare our method with baseline approaches across two tasks:

Reconstruction. As shown in Table 1a, we train using only the frames from the training set and evaluate performance against the ground truth.

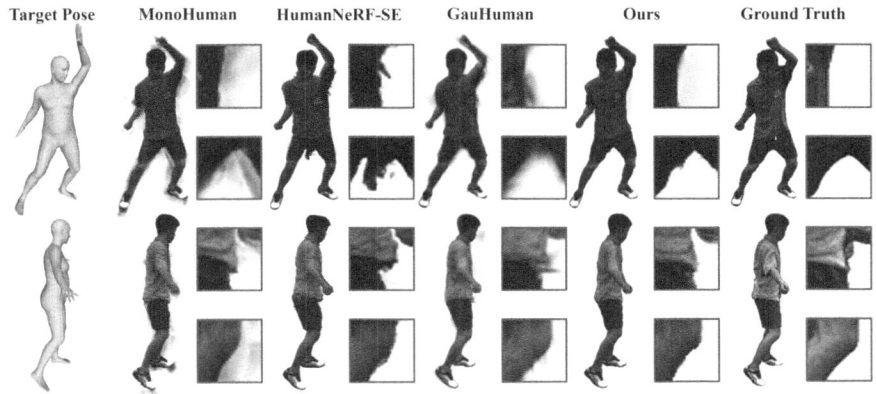

Target Pose   MonoHuman   HumanNeRF-SE   GauHuman   Ours   Ground Truth

Fig. 4. Qualitative comparison for animation task on ZJU-MoCap dataset. For more comparative results, please refer to the supplementary materials.

Animation. As shown in Table 1b, we train using the frames from the training set and evaluate on the frames from the test set along with their SMPL pose parameters.

There is only one LPIPS metric in the reconstruction task, in which our method is slightly worse than HumanNeRF-SE [12]. HumanNeRF-SE combines NeRF with voxel representation and achieves better generalization and visualization than our method. However, it still suffers from the lack of information in the task of animation with unseen poses, which our Texture Generation module aims to alleviate. Therefore, our method outperforms the latest methods in the animation task shown in Table 1b. Overall, the quantitative results demonstrate that our method delivers state-of-the-art performance in both reconstruction and animation tasks, excelling in geometric accuracy and texture realism.

4.3 Qualitative Evaluation

To compare the rendered results, we visualize the reconstruction and animation outputs on the ZJU-MoCap dataset for HumanNeRF [10], MonoHuman [11], HumanNeRF-SE [12], GauHuman [9] and our method. The comparison is separately illustrated in Fig. 3 and Fig. 4.

Reconstruction. In Fig. 3, our method exhibits more detail in textures and better accuracy of geometry compared to the baseline methods. Benefiting from the Texture Generation module, our textures appear more realistic and natural, with better alignment between the textures and poses. HumanNeRF achieves commendable reconstruction accuracy by being fully trained on each video frame with a non-rigid motion network [10]. However, this approach limits its ability to generalize to novel poses. Both MonoHuman and HumanNeRF-SE suffer from the issue of floating artifacts and noises on the surface. Since HumanNeRF-SE introduces voxel representation [12], its artifacts even appear sharper in the edge

88   Z. Chen et al.

Table 1. Quantitative comparison on the ZJU-MoCap dataset. We compute the average results on the six subjects following the baseline methods. LPIPS* = LPIPS $\times 10^3$.

(a) Reconstruction task

Methods	PSNR ↑	SSIM ↑	LPIPS* ↓
HumanNeRF [10]	30.61	0.9625	38.45
MonoHuman [11]	29.96	0.9683	31.74
HumanNeRF-SE [12]	<u>31.09</u>	<u>0.9707</u>	**24.09**
GauHuman [9]	30.92	0.9662	32.2
Ours	**31.12**	**0.9724**	<u>29.31</u>

(b) Animation task

Methods	PSNR ↑	SSIM ↑	LPIPS* ↓
MonoHuman [11]	29.85	0.9671	32.51
HumanNeRF-SE [12]	30.09	<u>0.9679</u>	<u>31.09</u>
GauHuman [9]	<u>30.19</u>	0.9645	33.1
Ours	**30.25**	**0.9687**	**30.93**

w/o $\mathcal{L}_{cycle}$ w/o feature   w/o cascaded   Full Model   Ground Truth

Fig. 5. Qualitative comparison of ablation study on ZJU-MoCap dataset. Experiments show that the proposed components can effectively reduce floating artifacts and enhance texture details.

Table 2. Ablation study on the ZJU-MoCap dataset.

Settings	PSNR ↑	SSIM ↑	LPIPS* ↓
(a) Reconstruction task			
w/o $\mathcal{L}_{cycle}$	30.43	0.9682	31.74
w/o feature	30.71	0.9685	30.73
w/o cascaded	30.74	0.9689	30.59
Full Model	**31.12**	**0.9724**	**29.31**
(b) Animation task			
w/o $\mathcal{L}_{cycle}$	29.89	0.9679	32.35
w/o feature	30.07	0.9682	31.36
w/o cascaded	30.13	0.9684	31.14
Full Model	**30.25**	**0.9687**	**30.93**

regions. The rendering results of GauHuman are blurry, with texture details lost and artifacts caused by errors in 3DGS parameter estimation [33] (Fig. 5).

Animation. In Fig. 4, our method preserves detailed texture while maintaining high accuracy in the motion-driving process. Since HumanNeRF does not originally support animation, it is not included in the comparison for this task. Mono-Human exhibits significant floating artifact issues, and the accuracy of motion deformation is suboptimal. While HumanNeRF-SE demonstrates improved accuracy in motion deformation, the problem of floating artifacts persists. And GauHuman exhibits more severe blurry texture and edge artifacts during animating. For more comparative results, please refer to our supplementary materials.

Fig. 6. Failure cases. Artifacts may appear along the edges of the human in challenging poses during animating.

Table 3. Training and rendering time.

Methods	Training	Rendering
HumanNeRF [10]	57 h	0.41 FPS
MonoHuman [11]	72 h	0.17 FPS
HumanNeRF-SE [12]	3 h	6.25 FPS
GauHuman [9]	**5 min**	**201.65 FPS**
Ours	68 h	0.16 FPS

4.4 Ablation Study

To validate the effectiveness of the key components of the ReDACT framework, we perform an ablation study that evaluates the contributions of various parts of the model in both reconstruction and animation tasks, which contains the cycle consistency loss $\mathcal{L}_{cycle}$, the texture feature from Texture Generation module and the cascaded structure of Diffusion model in Texture Generation module. This helps to understand how each module affects the final results, and the results are shown in Table 2.

In each of the ablation experiments, we compare both quantitative metrics and qualitative assessments. The results consistently support the effectiveness of each individual component in our method.

4.5 Limitation

While ReDACT achieves high-fidelity avatar reconstruction, it has two primary limitations:

(1) Although our method incorporates mechanisms, artifacts still appear along the edges of the human in challenging poses (Fig. 6).
(2) The training and rendering process is relatively slow compared to 3DGS-based methods (Table 3). This makes our approach less suitable for applications requiring real-time or rapid avatar generation.

5 Conclusion

In this paper, we propose ReDACT, a novel framework for reconstructing high-fidelity 3D avatars from monocular video input, combining NeRF with a diffusion-based Texture Generation module. Our approach introduces a canonical pose normalization, NeRF-based volumetric rendering, and a controllable texture generation process that leverages a high-frequency loss to enhance texture details. The result is avatars with accurate geometry and detailed textures, suitable for VR, AR, and gaming applications. Our experiments show that ReDACT outperforms existing methods with better geometric accuracy and texture realism in both reconstruction and animation tasks. However, our work still faces limitations in generalizing to challenging poses and in the efficiency of training and rendering. Although 3DGS offers advantages in efficiency, we still use NeRF to better capture detailed appearances, to achieve high-fidelity avatar reconstruction. In future work, we aim to extend the method to handle more complex scenes and optimize computational efficiency to enable real-time rendering applications.

Acknowledgments. This work is partially supported by the National Natural Science Foundation of China (No. 61972298 and No. 62372336).

References

1. Yariv, L., Gu, J., Kasten, Y., Lipman, Y.: Volume rendering of neural implicit surfaces. Adv. Neural. Inf. Process. Syst. **34**, 4805–4815 (2021)
2. Jackson, A.S., Manafas, C., Tzimiropoulos, G.: 3D human body reconstruction from a single image via volumetric regression. In: Proceedings of the European Conference on Computer Vision (ECCV) Workshops (2018)
3. Sitzmann, V., Thies, J., Heide, F., Nießner, M., Wetzstein, G., Zollhofer, M.: DeepVoxels: learning persistent 3d feature embeddings. In: Proceedings of the IEEE/CVF Conference on Computer Vision and Pattern Recognition, pp. 2437–2446 (2019)
4. Mildenhall, B., Srinivasan, P.P., Tancik, M., Barron, J.T., Ramamoorthi, R., Ng, R.: NeRF: representing scenes as neural radiance fields for view synthesis. In: European Conference on Computer Vision, pp. 405–421 (2020)
5. Wang, Y., et al.: NeuralRoom: geometry-constrained neural implicit surfaces for indoor scene reconstruction. arXiv preprint arXiv:2210.06853 (2022)
6. Wang, Y., Zhou, K., Zhang, W., Xiao, C.: MegaSurf: scalable large scene neural surface reconstruction. In: Proceedings of the 32nd ACM International Conference on Multimedia, pp. 6414–6423 (2024)
7. Qin, J., Luo, F., Cao, T., Xu, W., Xiao, C.: HS-Surf: a novel high-frequency surface shell radiance field to improve large-scale scene rendering. In: Proceedings of the 32nd ACM International Conference on Multimedia, pp. 6006–6014 (2024)
8. Jiang, W., Yi, K.M., Samei, G., Tuzel, O., Ranjan, A.: Neuman: neural human radiance field from a single video. In: European Conference on Computer Vision, pp. 402–418. Springer (2022)
9. Hu, S., Hu, T., Liu, Z.: GauHuman: articulated gaussian splatting from monocular human videos. In: Proceedings of the IEEE/CVF Conference on Computer Vision and Pattern Recognition, pp. 20418–20431 (2024)
10. Weng, C.Y., Curless, B., Srinivasan, P.P., Barron, J.T., Kemelmacher-Shlizerman, I.: HumanNerf: free-viewpoint rendering of moving people from monocular video. In: Proceedings of the IEEE/CVF Conference on Computer Vision and Pattern Recognition, pp. 16210–16220 (2022)
11. Yu, Z., Cheng, W., Liu, X., Wu, W., Lin, K.Y.: MonoHuman: animatable human neural field from monocular video. In: Proceedings of the IEEE/CVF Conference on Computer Vision and Pattern Recognition, pp. 16943–16953 (2023)

12. Ma, C., Liu, Y.L., Wang, Z., Liu, W., Liu, X., Wang, Z.: HumanNeRF-SE: a simple yet effective approach to animate HumanNeRF with diverse poses. In: Proceedings of the IEEE/CVF Conference on Computer Vision and Pattern Recognition, pp. 1460–1470 (2024)

13. de Aguiar, E., Stoll, C., Theobalt, C., Ahmed, N., Seidel, H.P., Thrun, S.: Performance capture from sparse multi-view video. ACM Trans. Graph. 1–10 (2008). https://doi.org/10.1145/1360612.1360697

14. Newcombe, R.A., Fox, D., Seitz, S.M.: DynamicFusion: reconstruction and tracking of non-rigid scenes in real-time. In: 2015 IEEE Conference on Computer Vision and Pattern Recognition (CVPR) (2015). https://doi.org/10.1109/cvpr.2015.7298631

15. Luo, F., Zhu, Y., Fu, Y., Zhou, H., Chen, Z., Xiao, C.: Sparse RGB-D images create a real thing: a flexible voxel based 3D reconstruction pipeline for single object. Vis.Inform. **7**(1), 66–76 (2023)

16. Zhou, Y., Habermann, M., Habibie, I., Tewari, A., Theobalt, C., Xu, F.: Monocular real-time full body capture with inter-part correlations. In: Proceedings of the IEEE/CVF Conference on Computer Vision and Pattern Recognition, pp. 4811–4822 (2021)

17. Saito, S., Huang, Z., Natsume, R., Morishima, S., Kanazawa, A., Li, H.: PIFu: pixel-aligned implicit function for high-resolution clothed human digitization. In: Proceedings of the IEEE/CVF International Conference on Computer Vision, pp. 2304–2314 (2019)

18. Saito, S., Simon, T., Saragih, J., Joo, H.: PIFuHD: multi-level pixel-aligned implicit function for high-resolution 3D human digitization. In: Proceedings of the IEEE/CVF Conference on Computer Vision and Pattern Recognition, pp. 84–93 (2020)

19. Zheng, Z., Yu, T., Liu, Y., Dai, Q.: PaMIR: parametric model-conditioned implicit representation for image-based human reconstruction. IEEE Trans. Pattern Anal. Mach. Intell. **44**(6), 3170–3184 (2021)

20. Loper, M., Mahmood, N., Romero, J., Pons-Moll, G., Black, M.J.: SMPL: a skinned multi-person linear model. ACM Trans. Graphics (Proc. SIGGRAPH Asia) **34**(6), 248:1–248:16 (2015)

21. Xiu, Y., Yang, J., Tzionas, D., Black, M.J.: ICON: implicit clothed humans obtained from normals. In: 2022 IEEE/CVF Conference on Computer Vision and Pattern Recognition (CVPR), pp. 13286–13296. IEEE (2022)

22. Li, Y., Luo, F., Xiao, C.: Diffusion-FOF: single-view clothed human reconstruction via diffusion-based Fourier occupancy field. In: Proceedings of the IEEE/CVF Conference on Computer Vision and Pattern Recognition, pp. 9525–9534 (2024)

23. Habermann, M., Xu, W., Zollhofer, M., Pons-Moll, G., Theobalt, C.: DeepCap: monocular human performance capture using weak supervision. In: Proceedings of the IEEE/CVF Conference on Computer Vision and Pattern Recognition, pp. 5052–5063 (2020)

24. Alldieck, T., Magnor, M., Xu, W., Theobalt, C., Pons-Moll, G.: Video based reconstruction of 3D people models. arXiv Computer Vision and Pattern Recognition (2018)

25. Jiang, B., Hong, Y., Bao, H., Zhang, J.: SelfRecon: self reconstruction your digital avatar from monocular video. In: Proceedings of the IEEE/CVF Conference on Computer Vision and Pattern Recognition, pp. 5605–5615 (2022)

26. Luo, C., Luo, F., Wang, Y., Zhao, E., Xiao, C.: DLCA-Recon: dynamic loose clothing avatar reconstruction from monocular videos. In: Proceedings of the AAAI Conference on Artificial Intelligence, vol. 38, pp. 3963–3971 (2024)

27. Park, K., et al.: NeRFies: deformable neural radiance fields. In: 2021 IEEE/CVF International Conference on Computer Vision (ICCV) (2021). https://doi.org/10.1109/iccv48922.2021.00581

28. Liu, L., Habermann, M., Rudnev, V., Sarkar, K., Gu, J., Theobalt, C.: Neural actor: neural free-view synthesis of human actors with pose control. ACM trans. graph. (TOG) **40**(6), 1–16 (2021)

29. Jiang, T., Chen, X., Song, J., Hilliges, O.: InstantAvatar: learning avatars from monocular video in 60 seconds. In: Proceedings of the IEEE/CVF Conference on Computer Vision and Pattern Recognition, pp. 16922–16932 (2023)

30. Müller, T., Evans, A., Schied, C., Keller, A.: Instant neural graphics primitives with a multiresolution hash encoding. ACM Trans. Graph. (TOG) **41**(4), 1–15 (2022)

31. Xiang, J., Gao, X., Guo, Y., Zhang, J.: FlashAvatar: high-fidelity head avatar with efficient gaussian embedding. In: Proceedings of the IEEE/CVF Conference on Computer Vision and Pattern Recognition (CVPR), pp. 1802–1812 (2024)

32. Xu, Y., Chen, B., Li, Z., Zhang, H., Wang, L., Zheng, Z., Liu, Y.: Gaussian head avatar: Ultra high-fidelity head avatar via dynamic gaussians. In: Proceedings of the IEEE/CVF Conference on Computer Vision and Pattern Recognition (CVPR), pp. 1931–1941 (2024)

33. Kerbl, B., Kopanas, G., Leimkühler, T., Drettakis, G.: 3D Gaussian splatting for real-time radiance field rendering. ACM Trans. Graph. **42**(4) (2023). https://repo-sam.inria.fr/fungraph/3d-gaussian-splatting/

34. Hu, L., et al.: GaussianAvatar: towards realistic human avatar modeling from a single video via animatable 3D Gaussians. In: Proceedings of the IEEE/CVF Conference on Computer Vision and Pattern Recognition (CVPR), pp. 634–644 (2024)

35. Magnenat, T., Laperrière, R., Thalmann, D.: Joint-dependent local deformations for hand animation and object grasping. In: Proceedings of Graphics Interface 1988, pp. 26–33. Canadian Information Processing Society (1988)

36. Saito, S., Yang, J., Ma, Q., Black, M.J.: SCANimate: weakly supervised learning of skinned clothed avatar networks. In: Proceedings of the IEEE/CVF Conference on Computer Vision and Pattern Recognition, pp. 2886–2897 (2021)

37. Peng, S., et al.: Neural body: implicit neural representations with structured latent codes for novel view synthesis of dynamic humans. In: Proceedings of the IEEE/CVF Conference on Computer Vision and Pattern Recognition, pp. 9054–9063 (2021)

38. Ho, J., Jain, A., Abbeel, P.: Denoising diffusion probabilistic models. Adv. Neural. Inf. Process. Syst. **33**, 6840–6851 (2020)

39. Rombach, R., Blattmann, A., Lorenz, D., Esser, P., Ommer, B.: High-resolution image synthesis with latent diffusion models. In: Proceedings of the IEEE/CVF Conference on Computer Vision and Pattern Recognition, pp. 10684–10695 (2022)

40. Zhang, L., Rao, A., Agrawala, M.: Adding conditional control to text-to-image diffusion models. In: Proceedings of the IEEE/CVF International Conference on Computer Vision, pp. 3836–3847 (2023)

41. Van Den Oord, A., Vinyals, O., et al.: Neural discrete representation learning. Adv. Neural. Inf. Process. Syst. **30** (2017)

42. Zhang, R., Isola, P., Efros, A.A., Shechtman, E., Wang, O.: The unreasonable effectiveness of deep features as a perceptual metric. In: Proceedings of the IEEE Conference on Computer Vision and Pattern Recognition, pp. 586–595 (2018)

ShadowCraft-NeRF: Occlusion and Shadow Mitigation via SAM-Guided NeRF

Xun Chen[1], Yushi Li[1(✉)], Yunyao Shen[2], Rong Chen[3], Chao Xu[4], Xiaobo Jin[1], Along Jin[1], and Yu Han[5(✉)]

[1] Xi'an Jiaotong-Liverpool University, Suzhou, China
`xun.chen23@student.xjtlu.edu.cn`,
`{yushi.li,xiaobo.jin,along.jin}@xjtlu.edu.cn`
[2] Monash University, Melbourne, Australia
`yshe0089@student.monash.edu`
[3] Dalian Maritime University, Dalian, China
`rchen@dlmu.edu.cn`
[4] Tianjin University, Tianjin, China
`xuchao@tju.edu.cn`
[5] Shenzhen University, Shenzhen, China
`hany@szu.edu.cn`

Abstract. While NeRF is a groundbreaking method in the field of scene reconstruction, it faces challenges when dealing with the data characterized by varying occlusions and shadows. To overcome the limitations of NeRFs in occlusion removal and shadow mitigation, we propose a shadow-casting object removal framework based on the Segment Anything Model (SAM) and associate it with NeRF. Specifically, we first introduce a prompt fusion method to effectively mix point and text prompts, guiding the vanilla SAM to better capture the masking edges. Another fine-tuned SAM incorporates with an enhanced edge extraction that leverages consistency in texture and color across the same material to improve the removal of shadows cast by objects within the scene. By combining the refined object mask with shadow-insensitive masks, our model significantly enhance the scene rendering quality, particularly when handling occluded objects. Comprehensive quantitative and qualitative results demonstrate that the proposed framework effectively addresses geometric alignment, color consistency, and texture fidelity, achieving superior performance in object removal and shadow mitigation tasks for NeRFs.

Keywords: 3D scene editing · NeRF · multiview segmentation · shadow mitigation

1 Introduction

Neural Radiance Fields (NeRF) [1] have demonstrated exceptional performance in 3D scene reconstruction [2], generating realistic and captivating environments.

C. Mousas et al. (Eds.): CASA 2025, LNCS 15915, pp. 93–108, 2026.
https://doi.org/10.1007/978-981-95-0100-7_6

Recently, the application of NeRF has broadened to encompass object editing tasks [3] such as object addition, deletion, geometric deformation [4], and stylization. Among these, obstruction and shadow removal presents a fundamental and challenging problem. In other words, achieving seamless shadow-casting occlusion removal without disrupting the overall integrity of the scene remains a significant obstacle.

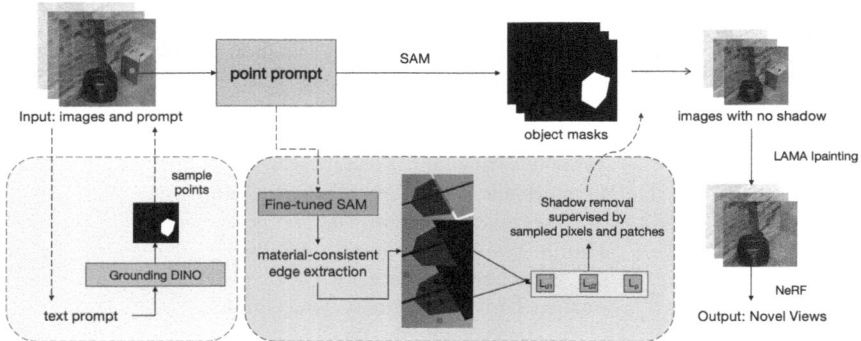

Fig. 1. Framework Overview. The proposed framework builds upon NeRF by incorporating multi-view occlusion and shadow removal, enhancing NeRF to generate consistent 3D scenes. The system first employs Grounding DINO to associate text prompt with the initial point prompt of SAM for accurately identifying occlusion edges. In addition, a fine-tuned SAM is incorporated with material-consistent edge extraction to encourage shadow-insensitive segmentation. At last, LaMa inpainting is applied to restore regions affected by occlusion and shadow removal.

To address this issue, various approaches have been proposed. One common method involves segmenting the object to be removed using masks, followed by its elimination from multi-view images. NeRF is then employed to reconstruct the scene from these adjusted images. For instance, NeRF-ObjectRemoval [5] and SPIn-NeRF [6] rely on 2D inpainting techniques such as LaMa [7] to generate color and depth priors, which are subsequently used to improve NeRF reconstruction. However, NeRF-ObjectRemoval [5] suffers from limitations in mask refinement, while SPIn-NeRF [6] requires a multi-view segmentation pipeline that cannot effectively handle the residual shadows after object removal. Differently, OR-NeRF [8] tackles object removal by introducing more precise region localization and applying region-level lighting consistency constraints. Although this model shows some improvement in blending the removed area with its surrounding regions, visual inconsistency problems like lingering artifacts and incomplete shadow removal remain.

Unlike purely appearance-based methods, SAM-based segmentation can encode high-level semantics. Specifically, SAM's prompt integrates semantic cues (identify what to segment) with visual adaptability (how to segment), making it suitable for removal tasks where understanding context and intent is important.

By integrating promptable multi-view segmentation with visibility consistency refinement, we propose a framework to solve the occlusion and shadow issue caused by objects blocking parts of the scene from certain viewpoints. Different from previous methods that improve object segmentation through point and text prompts separately, we present a prompt fusion approach that combines manually selected points with predefined text and use its output as the prompt for the subsequent SAM [9] segmentation to accurately identify objects for removal. At first, we leverage Grounding DINO [10] which takes text as prompt to generate object identification boxes. Then, we select the points from the masks produced by the SAM prompted by these boxes and combine them with the initial prompt points for this SAM in a weighted manner to better guide the SAM segmentation. With this fusion method, our model is allowed to better recognize the occlusion edges.

As an accompanying problem arises from occlusion, shadows also negatively affect the appearance of 3D scenes generated by NeRF, especially when viewing from different perspectives [11]. Existing shadow removal methods often depend on shadow mask ground truth datasets, like SRRMSE [12], which are incompatible with commonly used datasets in our domain. To address this, we fine-tune another SAM with texture and color consistency edge extraction to reduce the mask's sensitivity to shadows. In the shadow mitigation phase, we compare object masks produced by LaMa [7] with the shadow-insensitive masks to extract consistent boundaries. Finally, we employ multi-view loss functions to ensure that object restoration and shadow removal maintain consistency across different viewpoints, preserving both geometric structures and appearance. To demonstrate the effectiveness of our model in dealing with occlusion and shadows for NeRF, we conduct comprehensive experiments based on various datasets. In comparison with state-of-the-art methods, our approach successfully addresses the unnatural scene reconstruction artifacts and significantly improve the performance of NeRF. Overall, our contributions are as follows:

– We propose a framework that integrates promptable multi-view segmentation with visibility consistency refinement to address occlusion and shadow issues caused by scene obstructions. By improving object segmentation accuracy and refining visibility across views, our model ensures consistent scene reconstruction.
– We introduce a prompt fusion approach that combines points with text to guide SAM segmentation, improving the accuracy of object identification for removal, especially in occluded regions. This fusion enables better recognition of occlusion edges by leveraging both point and text prompts in a weighted manner.
– We propose an effective method to mitigate shadow issues by integrating a fine-tuned SAM with consistent edge extraction and inpainting, which also enhances texture and color consistency in shadow removal regions. It not only improves shadow removal but also enhances texture and color consistency in recovered regions.

2   Related Work

2.1   NeRF

NeRF [1] represent a 3D scene as a continuous function $f_\Theta : (\mathbf{x}, \mathbf{d}) \rightarrow (\mathbf{c}, \sigma)$, where $\mathbf{x} = (x, y, z)$ is a 3D spatial location, $\mathbf{d} = (\theta, \phi)$ is a 2D viewing direction, $\mathbf{c} = (r, g, b)$ denotes the emitted color, and σ is the volume density. The model employs a multi-layer perceptron (MLP) to map each input 5D coordinate to the corresponding output, optimizing the parameters Θ.

Using principles of volumetric rendering, the color of a ray $\mathbf{r}(t) = \mathbf{o} + t\mathbf{d}$ is computed as:

$$
\begin{aligned}
C(\mathbf{r}) &= \int_{t_n}^{t_f} T(t)\sigma(\mathbf{r}(t))\mathbf{c}(\mathbf{r}(t), \mathbf{d})\, dt \\
T(t) &= \exp\left(-\int_{t_n}^{t} \sigma(\mathbf{r}(s))\, ds \right)
\end{aligned}
\tag{1}
$$

where $\mathbf{r}(t) = \mathbf{o} + t\mathbf{d}$ represents the parameterized ray equation, $\sigma(\mathbf{r}(t))$ denotes the density at position $\mathbf{r}(t)$, and $\mathbf{c}(\mathbf{r}(t), \mathbf{d})$ is the color value conditioned on the viewing direction $\mathbf{d}$. $T(t)$ is the accumulated transmittance from the ray origin to t.

2.2   Scene Object Removal with NeRF

Neural Radiance Fields (NeRF) [1] have advanced the field of 3D scene editing by providing a framework for rendering complex scenes with high fidelity from novel viewpoints. Significant research efforts have been directed towards enabling flexible manipulations within 3D environments, as demonstrated in various studies aiming to enhance NeRF's capabilities in geometric editing, appearance editing, and object deletion [13–15].

In terms of geometric and appearance editing, studies like those by [16–18] have explored modifying object properties and appearances within scenes [17, 19], though these modifications often focus on simpler scene complexities. Furthermore, the challenge of deleting objects seamlessly from 3D scenes has been addressed by recent efforts [5, 6] which incorporate 2D inpainting models like LaMa [7] to infer color and depth information necessary for filling in the gaps left by removed objects. These methods leverage multi-view consistency to maintain the integrity of the scene, yet they still struggle with occluded areas and complex textures.

The introduction of OR-NeRF [8] marks a progression in rendering quality and operational efficiency by refining how scenes are synthesized. However, this model still does not fully consider the shadow effects caused by object removal, which remains a critical aspect of achieving realistic scene recompositions.

Overall, while these advancements in NeRF technology have pushed the boundaries of what's possible in 3D scene manipulation, balancing the improvements in rendering quality with editing efficiency continues to be a key challenge. Further research is necessary to optimize NeRF's capabilities for handling complex edits while maintaining the natural aesthetics of 3D environments.

2.3   Image Inpainting and Shadow Mitigation

Shadow mitigation is a crucial area in computer graphics and vision, significantly advancing in 2D image domains like inpainting and shadow removal. Initial methods focused on texture synthesis and diffusive filling [20], evolving to utilize convolutional neural networks for content generation from contextual image cues [21–25]. However, traditional 2D methods face limitations when applied to complex scenes, as they often rely on simpler shadow datasets [24, 26] with clear boundaries and uniform materials.

Expanding these techniques to 3D datasets like NeRF introduces significant challenges due to the complexity of multi-view 3D scene modeling, which involves intricate details like point clouds, camera poses, and depth information. NeRF scenes often feature complex backgrounds and heterogeneous materials, making it difficult to accurately mitigate shadows with existing 2D techniques. This necessitates the development of advanced methods and more comprehensive datasets to effectively handle shadow removal in diverse and complex 3D environments.

3   Method

Neural Radiance Fields (NeRF) excel at photorealistic 3D scene reconstruction but struggle with occlusions and shadows caused by objects blocking light or geometry in multi-view images. Existing methods for occlusion removal in NeRF face the limitations including inaccurate segmentation and shadow artifacts. For instance, Traditional mask generation (e.g., point/text prompts alone) fails to precisely delineate occlusion boundaries, especially for complex or partially hidden objects. In addition, after object removal, residual shadows often persist, breaking visual consistency across viewpoints due to inadequate material-aware shadow mitigation. To address these issues, we integrates SAM prompt fusion and material consistency extraction with Nerf for improving prior segmentation and boundary identification.

As shown in Fig. 1, the proposed framework combines promptable multi-view segmentation with visibility consistency enhancement to resolve occlusion and shadow issues in NeRF-generated 3D scenes. In the occlusion identification branch, unlike previous methods that separately process different types of prompt, we merge spatial points with predefined text into a unified prompt, guiding SAM (Segment Anything Model) to more effectively detect occlusion edges. To mitigate shadows, which distort 3D scene appearance from different viewpoints, we fine-tune an additional SAM and incorporate it with material-consistent edge extraction to reduce shadow sensitivity in segmentation by emphasizing texture and color consistency in background. Next, we follow NeRF-In [27] and OR-NeRF [8] to obtain color priors for removal region through LaMa [7] and then reconstruct the scene by filling in the occlusion and shadow removal regions.

3.1   Prompt Fusion for SAM Segmentation

Different from separately taking point and text prompts into account, which overlook their combined potential, we integrate both types of prompts to further refine segmentation accuracy. In particular, we associate the text prompt information with points in the corresponding image regions and combine these points with the initial point prompts incorporated into SAM.

Let the original point prompts provided to the model be denoted as $P_{\mathrm{orig}} = \{p_1, p_2, \ldots, p_n\}$, where each $p_i \in \mathbb{R}^2$ represents the 2D coordinates of the point prompts in the view space. In parallel, T_{text} is a text prompt processed by Grounding DINO, which generates a corresponding set of point-based prompts. More specifically, T_{text} is first input into Grounding DINO to a bounding box that roughly defines the region of the object described by the text prompt. This box prompt is then used as input for SAM, yielding a corresponding segmentation mask. Points are subsequently sampled from this mask to form the point-based prompts for later use, represented as $P_{\mathrm{text}} = \{p_{t1}, p_{t2}, \ldots, p_{tn}\}$, where $p_{ti} \in \mathbb{R}^2$ are the locations of the points derived from the given text description. After this, we combine the two sets of point prompts as follows:

$$P_{\mathrm{combined}} = \mathcal{R}_\alpha(P_{\mathrm{orig}}) \cup \mathcal{R}_\beta(P_{\mathrm{text}}) \tag{2}$$

where $\mathcal{R}$ denotes random sampling. Meanwhile, α and β are sampling ratio parameters.

SAM then uses the refined point prompts P_{combined} to perform segmentation across multi-view images. Let the multi-view images be represented as $\{I_1, I_2, \ldots, I_k\}$, with each I_i being a color image from a distinct viewpoint. The segmentation output for each image I_i is given by

$$S_i = SAM(I_i, P_{\mathrm{combined}}) \tag{3}$$

where S_i represents the segmentation masks for the i-th view.

3.2   Occlusion and Shadow Removal

For effectively eliminating shadow-casting occlusion and improve appearance consistency across views, we integrate material-consistent segmentation into the occlusion and shadow removal pipeline. Fortunately, the SAM with fused prompt as outlined in Sect. 3.1 allows our model to achieve accurate occlusion segmentation. To mitigate shadow affect, we fine-tune the SAM model and introduce edge extraction based on material consistency. This enables our model to accurately segment different material regions and provide a foundation for effective shadow handling during object removal.

Since the intractable shadow regions are typically cast along object edges in most scenes, enhancing shadow removal requires restoration on both sides of these edges. We employ the LaMa design methodology by first extracting image features and performing inpainting, and then using these features to generate a larger target object mask, the LaMa mask $\mathcal{M}$, enabling precise identification and processing of the target region. To ensure that subsequent pixel and patch sampling accurately targets areas inside or outside the object edges, as shown in Fig. 2, we first match $\mathcal{M}$ and the material-consistent mask $\mathcal{M}_c$, resulting in a new mask $\mathcal{M}_p$ that represents the region within the same material. As $\mathcal{M}_p$ covers regions that do not overlap with $\mathcal{M}_c$, these areas are defined as the regions requiring further processing. To control the dilation and erosion of the mask, we set the scale to 5 to extract the regions inside and outside the object edges. First, a larger dilated mask $\mathcal{M}_p^{\mathrm{dl}}$ is created by expanding $\mathcal{M}_p$, while a smaller dilated mask $\mathcal{M}_p^{\mathrm{ds}}$ is produced by applying dilation at a smaller scale. The regions outside the edges are then obtained by subtracting the smaller dilated mask from the larger one:

$$\mathcal{M}_{\mathrm{outside}} = \mathcal{M}_p^{\mathrm{dl}} - \mathcal{M}_p^{\mathrm{ds}} \tag{4}$$

The regions $\mathcal{M}_{\mathrm{inside}}$ are obtained using a similar approach.

3.3 Training Objective and Consistency Constraints

To ensure consistency in color and material properties at the boundary of $\mathcal{M}_p$, three losses are used: RGB distance loss, RGB distribution loss, and LPIPS (Learned Perceptual Image Patch Similarity) loss. These losses address different aspects of consistency: pixel-level color matching, overall color distribution, and perceived texture similarity. Together, they guide the inpainting model to generate results that maintain realistic transitions between the inpainted area and its surroundings while effectively achieving shadow removal.

– **RGB Distance Loss** (L_{d1}): In this loss, we minimize the color difference between pixels inside and outside the $\mathcal{M}_p$. Initially, the pixels from the $\mathcal{M}_{\mathrm{inside}}$ are denoted as $A_{in} = \{s_1, \ldots, s_i, \ldots, s_M\}$, where $i \in [1, M]$, representing the sampled pixels inside the $\mathcal{M}_p$. Similarly, the pixels from the $\mathcal{M}_{\mathrm{outside}}$ edge are presented as $A_{out} = \{t_1, \ldots, t_j, \ldots, t_N\}$, where $j \in [1, N]$, corresponding to the sampled pixels outside $\mathcal{M}_p$. This loss is then defined as:

$$L_{\mathrm{d1}} = \frac{1}{M} \sum_{i=1}^{M} \min_{j \in [1, N]} d(s_i, t_j) \tag{5}$$

where $s_i \in \mathcal{A}_{in}$ and $t_j \in \mathcal{A}_{out}$ are the pixel values in the RGB space. This loss is applied to ensure that the inpainted region aligns with the material color of its surroundings.
– **RGB Distribution Loss** (L_{d2}): This loss calculates the Earth Mover's Distance (EMD) between the color histograms of A_{in} and A_{out} to ensure the overall consistency of color distribution. It is defined as:

$$L_{\mathrm{d2}} = \mathrm{EMD}(\mathrm{Hist}(A_{\mathrm{in}}), \mathrm{Hist}(A_{\mathrm{out}})) \tag{6}$$

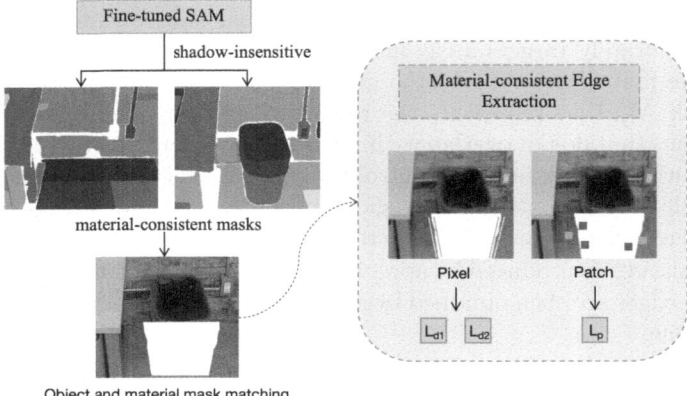

Fig. 2. SAM with material consistent edge extraction. We combines a fine-tuned SAM (for shadow-insensitive, material-aware segmentation) and LaMa Mask (for precise edge refinement) to extract consistent object boundaries. These edges guide pixel/block-level sampling, optimized via three losses: pixel-wise distance loss (L_{d1}), RGB distribution loss (L_{d2}), and perceptual loss (L_p).

– **LPIPS Loss** (L_{p}): To capture perceptual consistency, this loss compares patches inside and outside $\mathcal{M}_p$. It guarantees similarity in texture and detail across regions with shared material properties. The formula is expressed as:

$$L_{\mathrm{p}} = \frac{1}{M} \sum_{i=1}^{M} \min_{j \in [1,N]} \mathrm{LPIPS}(p_i, q_j) \tag{7}$$

where $p_i \in P_{a_{in}}$, and $P_{a_{in}}$ is the set of patches sampled from inside the edge of M_p, while $q_i \in P_{a_{out}}$, where $P_{a_{out}}$ represents the set of patches sampled from outside the edge of M_p.

In the aforementioned **color loss**, we primarily focus on restoring object edges, particularly removing shadows and recovering details at object boundaries. However, color loss mainly optimizes local details and has limitations in enhancing the overall spatial structure and visual quality of the image. To address this, we introduce two additional loss functions: **depth loss** (L_{dp}) and **perceptual loss** (L_{lp}). These losses aim to improve the overall image generation quality and ensure geometric consistency across multiple views.

$$\mathcal{L}_{\mathrm{dp}} = \sum_{r \in \mathcal{R}} \|\hat{D}(r) - D(r)\|_2^2 \tag{8}$$

$$\mathcal{L}_{\mathrm{lp}} = \frac{1}{B} \sum_{i \in B} LPIPS(\hat{I}(r), I(r)) \tag{9}$$

$D(r)$ represents the depth value obtained through volume rendering, and $\hat{D}(r)$ is the corresponding ground truth depth. $I(r)$ and $\hat{I}$ are the rendered pixel patch and corresponding ground truth respectively. The total loss ($\mathcal{L}_{total}$) combines the three loss components, weighted by hyperparameters $\lambda_1, \lambda_2, \lambda_3, \lambda_4, \lambda_5$:

$$L_{\text{total}} = \lambda_1 L_{d1} + \lambda_2 L_{d2} + \lambda_3 L_p + \lambda_4 L_{dp} + \lambda_5 L_{lp} \tag{10}$$

In our experiments, we set all these weighting parameters to 1. This comprehensive loss formulation balances geometric, perceptual, and color fidelity, enabling the model to achieve photorealistic results in both shadow removal and object removal tasks.

Table 1. Comparison between our method with SoTA methods using text-only or point-only prompts, denoted as O-N-t (**OR-NeRF-t**), O-N-P (**OR-NeRF-p**) and S-N-tp (**SPIn-NeRF-tp**).

Scenes(Our-NeRF-tp)								Mean	O-N-t [8]	O-N-p [8]	S-N-tp [6]
4	9	10	book	trash	qq13	fortress	statue				
Acc	99.87	99.88	99.91	99.89	99.92	99.87	99.90	99.88	**99.89**↑	99.71	99.71	98.91
IoU	98.68	98.50	97.43	96.29	95.47	91.73	98.04	98.90	**96.88**↑	95.38	95.42	91.66

4   Experiments

4.1   Datasets

We evaluate the performance of our method using four publicly available datasets, which provide a diverse range of scenes and settings for object removal and shadow mitigation tasks. The SPIn-NeRF dataset [28], consisting of synthetic scenes, is widely used for benchmarking object removal and 3D scene reconstruction. Additionally, we utilize synthetic data from the IBR-Net dataset [29] to assess the effectiveness of our method in handling complex scenes, with a focus on multi-view segmentation and material-consistent recovery. For real-world scenarios, we employ datasets such as NeRF LLFF and LLFF Real [30], which serve as benchmarks for occlusion and shadow removal under realistic conditions. We conduct both qualitative and quantitative evaluations across 20 scenes to comprehensively validate our approach.

4.2   Implementation and Evaluation Metrics

All experiments in this study were conducted on a server equipped with an RTX 4090 GPU. During the material-consistent segmentation stage, we freeze SAM's image encoder and prompt encoder, fine-tuning only the mask decoder for 10 epochs. The dataset is randomly split into 80% training and 20% validation sets. Each image is resized using longest side, then processed with 32 uniformly sampled sparse prompts alongside dense prompts. These prompts are fed into the mask decoder of SAM to generate candidate masks. For training, we optimize the model using Adam (learning rate = 0.0001, weight decay = 0.0005) with a batch size of 1. After each epoch, we log the average validation loss and save training/validation curves. Finally, the fine-tuned decoder weights are exported for material-consistent mask generation.

To evaluate the performance of multi-view segmentation algorithms, we use standard segmentation metrics, including pixel accuracy (Acc) and intersection over union (IoU). For assessing the scene object removal module, we employ peak signal-to-noise ratio (PSNR), a widely adopted metric for 3D reconstruction quality. Additionally, we incorporate Learned Perceptual Image Patch Similarity (LPIPS), which better reflects human perceptual quality. These metrics enable a comprehensive comparison between the ground truth data and the rendered output generated by our method.

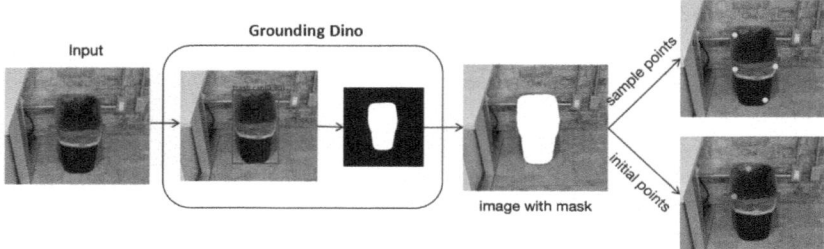

Fig. 3. Prompt fusion and point selection.

4.3   Prompt Fusion for SAM Segmentation

Our framework enhances the segmentation process by converting text prompts into point prompts and integrating them with the original point prompts, providing more comprehensive guidance for segmentation. This combined hinting approach leverages the strengths of both hinting types. During multi-view segmentation, COLMAP [31] is used to map hint points from a single image to other views. However, this mapping process can introduce projection errors due to the complexity of multi-view geometry.

Hence, we indirectly provide additional supervision for the segmentation task by converting text hints into point hints, alleviating these mapping errors and improving segmentation quality across multiple views. We begin by generating an initial mask from the input image using Grounding DINO, conditioned on the text prompt. From this mask, we extract four key points: the top-left corner, bottom-right corner, and the midpoints of the left and right edges. These text-derived point prompts are then fused with manually provided initial points using weighted averaging ($\alpha = 0.6$ for manual points, $\beta = 0.4$ for text-derived points). The higher weight for manual points reflects their greater precision and stability. The resulting combined prompt set is then used for SAM segmentation. Our prompt point selection is further indicated in Fig. 3.

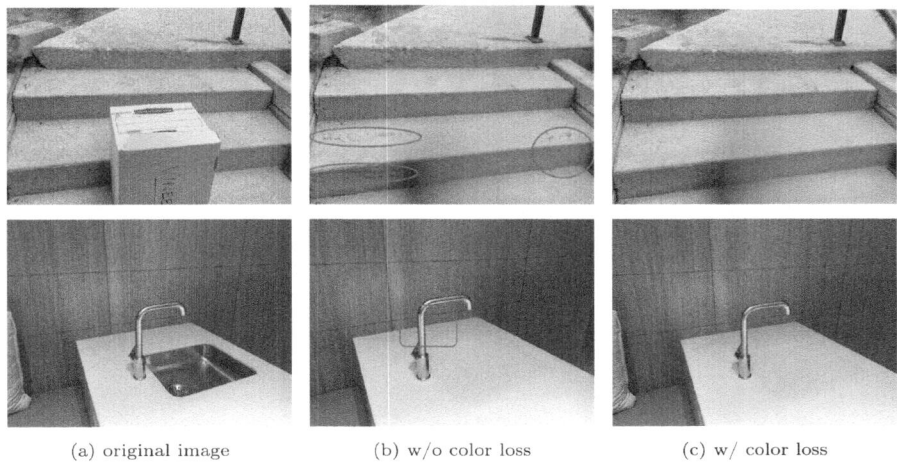

(a) original image   (b) w/o color loss   (c) w/ color loss

Fig. 4. Comparison of the object removal results with and without color loss. Subfigure (a) shows the original image, while (b) and (c) present the results with color loss and without color loss, respectively. The result with color loss (b) demonstrates enhanced color consistency and fewer artifacts around the object boundaries, as highlighted in the marked region, compared to the result without color loss (c).

Table 1 shows the mask generation comparison results between our method and OR-NeRF [8]. Quantitative results in this table show a mean IoU of 99.89%, outperforming OR-NeRF text-only (95.38%) and point-only (95.42%) variants. The proposed model with combined prompts mitigate missegmentation in occluded regions (e.g., objects partially hidden behind others), as evidenced by the 99.89% mean pixel accuracy. These quantitative results underscores the effectiveness of our combined hinting approach in generating accurate and consistent segmentation masks, particularly in complex scenes.

Table 2. Experimental results of scene object removal. **da** indicates the use of LaMa prior and all depth information, **lpips** represents the use of perceptual loss, and **rgb** denotes the use of color loss.

	Ours			OR-NeRF [8]		
	da	lpips	rgb	da	lpips	rgb
PSNR↑	14.84	14.96	**14.99**	14.85	14.82	14.83
LPIPS↓	0.6834	0.7022	**0.6273**	0.6810	0.6752	0.6506

4.4   Occlusion and Shadow Removal in Scene Object Removal

Our research provides a comprehensive evaluation of the effectiveness of the Our-NeRF method in object removal tasks, combining both quantitative and quali-

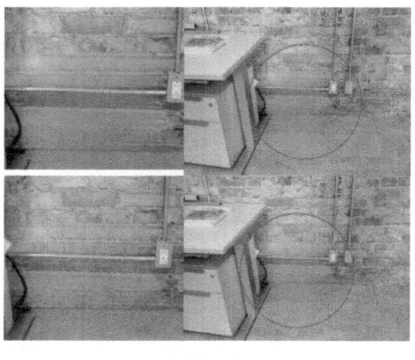

(a) trash   (b) fortress

Fig. 5. The results of the region marked in Our-NeRF after applying perceptual loss, showing significant differences. The perceptual loss enriches the texture details, improving the overall visual quality.

tative analyses. Table 2 presents experimental results focusing on PSNR (Peak Signal-to-Noise Ratio) and LPIPS (Learned Perceptual Image Patch Similarity), with targeted experiments conducted to analyze performance variations. We also performed ablation studies to further examine the impact of specific adjustments on the method's performance. As shown in Table 2, our method outperforms state-of-the-art approaches in both PSNR and LPIPS. Notably, the inclusion of color loss improves PSNR, indicating enhanced overall image quality. Table 2 highlights a PSNR of 14.99 dB and LPIPS of 0.6273 when using color loss, outperforming OR-NeRF (14.83 dB, 0.6506), which illustrates better texture consistency in the regions recovered by our method. The inclusion of all losses (Eq. 10) is critical; omitting perceptual loss (LPIPS: 0.7022) or depth supervision (PSNR: 14.84) degrades results.

In the scene object removal, we introduce color loss, which effectively improves the consistency of color and material after object removal, addressing shadow residue issues. As illustrated in Fig. 4, the inclusion of color loss significantly reduces visual artifacts in shadowed regions, leading to a reduction in shadow intensity. From a generation quality perspective, we further enhance the results through depth supervision and perceptual loss. As shown in Fig. 6, our method adjusts the depth map concurrently when removing objects, ensuring that newly generated regions maintain consistent geometric structure. This mechanism prevents inconsistencies caused by depth information distortion after object removal, enhancing overall visual coherence and ensuring stable rendering quality. Furthermore, the perceptual loss enhances texture details, as illustrated in Fig. 5. Experimental results in Fig. 7 show that, compared to OR-NeRF, our method produces clearer edges and more natural textures after object removal, significantly improving overall visual quality.

(a) original image	(b) Our-NeRF	(c) OurNeRF+da

Fig. 6. The figure compares the original image, the depth map of the original image, and the depth map generated by Our-NeRF with depth supervision. When an object in the image is removed, corresponding adjustments should also be reflected in the depth map. These adjustments play a crucial role in ensuring the consistency of the final scene synthesis, contributing to improved geometric alignment and rendering quality.

Fig. 7. The comparison of rendering quality between OR-NeRF and Our-NeRF is shown, and the circled areas have obvious differences in sentiment.

5 Conclusion

In this paper, we introduce a new pipeline tailored for object removal and shadow mitigation in Neural Radiance Fields (NeRF). Our approach incorporates a series of innovations that collectively enhance segmentation accuracy and scene reconstruction quality. The method demonstrates superior performance compared to baseline techniques, achieving higher scores in quantitative metrics and delivering improved qualitative outcomes, including sharper object boundaries, more consistent color distribution, and greater visual coherence. Future research will aim to optimize computational efficiency, tackle more intricate shadow scenarios, and further advance the application of NeRF in object removal and shadow mitigation.

While ShadowCraft-NeRF advances occlusion/shadow removal, addressing its limitations—prompt sensitivity, shadow complexity, The method relies heavily on the accuracy of input prompts (text/points). Ambiguous text or sparse point selections can lead to over or under-segmentation. It also struggles with soft shadows (e.g., diffuse lighting), and high memory costs (due to SAM-based mask inference). An potential improvement for this method is integrating a lightweight SAM to generate precise masks in real-time with progressive NeRF updates focus on the vase region.

References

1. Mildenhall, B., Srinivasan, P.P., Tancik, M., Barron, J.T., Ramamoorthi, R., Ng, R.: NeRF: representing scenes as neural radiance fields for view synthesis. Commun. ACM **65**(1), 99–106 (2021)
2. Tewari, A., et al.: Advances in neural rendering. In: Computer Graphics Forum, vol. 41, pp. 703–735. Wiley Online Library (2022)
3. Bao, C., et al.: SINE: semantic-driven image-based nerf editing with prior-guided editing field. In: Proceedings of the IEEE/CVF Conference on Computer Vision and Pattern Recognition, pp. 20919–20929 (2023)
4. Yuan, Y.-J., Sun, Y.-T., Lai, Y.-K., Ma, Y., Jia, R., Gao, L.: NeRF-editing: geometry editing of neural radiance fields. In: Proceedings of the IEEE/CVF Conference on Computer Vision and Pattern Recognition, pp. 18353–18364 (2022)
5. Weder, S., et al.: Removing objects from neural radiance fields. In: CVPR (2023)
6. Mirzaei, A., et al.: Spin-NeRF: multiview segmentation and perceptual inpainting with neural radiance fields. In: Proceedings of the IEEE/CVF Conference on Computer Vision and Pattern Recognition, pp. 20669–20679 (2023)
7. Suvorov, R., et al.: Resolution-robust large mask inpainting with fourier convolutions. arXiv preprint arXiv:2109.07161 (2021)
8. Yin, Y., Fu, Z., Yang, F., Lin, G.: OR-NeRF: object removing from 3D scenes guided by multiview segmentation with neural radiance fields. arXiv preprint arXiv:2305.10503 (2023)
9. Kirillov, A., et al.: Segment anything. In: Proceedings of the IEEE/CVF International Conference on Computer Vision, pp. 4015–4026 (2023)
10. Liu, S., et al.: Grounding DINO: marrying DINO with grounded pre-training for open-set object detection. In: European Conference on Computer Vision, pp. 38–55. Springer (2025)

11. Yang, W., Chen, G., Chen, C., Chen, Z., Wong, K.-Y.K.: S^3-nerf: neural reflectance field from shading and shadow under a single viewpoint. In: Advances in Neural Information Processing Systems, vol. 35, pp. 1568–1582 (2022)
12. Hu, S., Le, H., Athar, S., Das, S., Samaras, D.: Shadow removal refinement via material-consistent shadow edges. arXiv preprint arXiv:2409.06848 (2024)
13. Gao, K., Gao, Y., He, H., Lu, D., Xu, L., Li, J.: NeRF: neural radiance field in 3d vision, a comprehensive review. arXiv preprint arXiv:2210.00379 (2022)
14. Kosiorek, A.R., et al.: NeRF-VAE: a geometry aware 3D scene generative model. In: International Conference on Machine Learning, pp. 5742–5752. PMLR (2021)
15. Nguyen, T.-A.-Q., Bourki, A., Macudzinski, M., Brunel, A., Bennamoun, M.: Semantically-aware neural radiance fields for visual scene understanding: a comprehensive review. arXiv preprint arXiv:2402.11141 (2024)
16. Liu, S., Zhang, X., Zhang, Z., Zhang, R., Zhu, J.-Y., Russell, B.: Editing conditional radiance fields. In: Proceedings of the IEEE/CVF International Conference on Computer Vision, pp. 5773–5783 (2021)
17. Wang, C., Chai, M., He, M., Chen, D., Liao, J.: CLIP-NeRF: text-and-image driven manipulation of neural radiance fields. In: Proceedings of the IEEE/CVF Conference on Computer Vision and Pattern Recognition, pp. 3835–3844 (2022)
18. Yang, B., et al.: Learning object-compositional neural radiance field for editable scene rendering. In: Proceedings of the IEEE/CVF International Conference on Computer Vision, pp. 13779–13788 (2021)
19. Huang, Y.-H., He, Y., Yuan, Y.-J., Lai, Y.-K., Gao, L.: StylizedNeRF: consistent 3D scene stylization as stylized nerf via 2D-3D mutual learning. In: Proceedings of the IEEE/CVF Conference on Computer Vision and Pattern Recognition, pp. 18342–18352 (2022)
20. Finlayson, G.D., Hordley, S.D., Lu, C., Drew, M.S.: On the removal of shadows from images. IEEE Trans. Pattern Anal. Mach. Intell. **28**(1), 59–68 (2005)
21. Chen, Z., Long, C., Zhang, L., Xiao, C.: CANet: a context-aware network for shadow removal. In: Proceedings of the IEEE/CVF International Conference on Computer Vision, pp. 4743–4752 (2021)
22. Ding, B., Long, C., Zhang, L., Xiao, C.: ARGAN: attentive recurrent generative adversarial network for shadow detection and removal. In: Proceedings of the IEEE/CVF International Conference on Computer Vision, pp. 10213–10222 (2019)
23. Fu, L., et al.: Auto-exposure fusion for single-image shadow removal. In: Proceedings of the IEEE/CVF Conference on Computer Vision and Pattern Recognition, pp. 10571–10580 (2021)
24. Qu, L., Tian, J., He, S., Tang, Y., Lau, R.W.H.: DeshadowNet: a multi-context embedding deep network for shadow removal. In: Proceedings of the IEEE Conference on Computer Vision and Pattern Recognition, pp. 4067–4075 (2017)
25. Jam, J., Kendrick, C., Walker, K., Drouard, V., Hsu, J.G.-S., Yap, M.H.: A comprehensive review of past and present image inpainting methods. Comput. Vision Image Underst. **203**, 103147 (2021)
26. Wang, J., Li, X., Yang, J.: Stacked conditional generative adversarial networks for jointly learning shadow detection and shadow removal. In: Proceedings of the IEEE Conference on Computer Vision and Pattern Recognition, pp. 1788–1797 (2018)
27. Liu, H.-K., Shen, I., Chen, B.-Y., et al.: NeRF-in: free-form nerf inpainting with RGB-D priors. arXiv preprint arXiv:2206.04901 (2022)
28. Mirzaei, A., et al.: SPIn-NeRF: multiview segmentation and perceptual inpainting with neural radiance fields. In: CVPR (2023)
29. Wang, Q., et al.: IBRNet: learning multi-view image-based rendering. In CVPR (2021)

30. Mildenhall, B., et al.: Local light field fusion: practical view synthesis with prescriptive sampling guidelines. ACM Trans. Graph. (ToG) **38**(4), 1–14 (2019)
31. Schönberger, J.L., Price, T., Sattler, T., Frahm, J.-M., Pollefeys, M.: A vote-and-verify strategy for fast spatial verification in image retrieval. In: Computer Vision–ACCV 2016: 13th Asian Conference on Computer Vision, Taipei, Taiwan, 20–24 November 2016, Revised Selected Papers, Part I 13, pp. 321–337. Springer (2017)

Hybrid-Granularity Image-Music Retrieval Using Contrastive Learning Between Images and Music

Xudong He[1], Li Wang[1(✉)], Zhao Wang[2], and Jun Xiao[1]

[1] Zhejiang University, Hangzhou, Zhejiang, China
{22360396,li.wang,junx}@zju.edu.cn
[2] Ningbo Innovation Center, Zhejiang University, Ningbo, Zhejiang, China
zhao_wang@zju.edu.cn

Abstract. Cross-modal music retrieval is still a challenging task for current search engines. Existing search engines conduct music tracks matching via coarse-granularity retrieval of metadata, such as natural language queries including pre-defined tags and genres. However, such retrieval methods often encounter difficulties while handling fine-granularity queries on contexts. We aim to address fine-granularity music retrieval issue in this work. We construct a dataset with 66,048 image-music pairs for cross-modal music retrieval task. A modality-joint embedding space is learned, where hybrid-granularity context-alignment between images and music is considered via contrastive learning. Additionally, contrastive learning losses on hybrid-granularity contexts are designed to ensure image-music alignment in both inter-modal and intra-modal scenarios. The proposed approach is evaluated through experiments, which demonstrate that our method successfully aligns images and music, and outperforms previous methods in terms of cross-modal music retrieval tasks (image-to-music and music-to-image). Codes (https://blossomers.github.io/) will be available for public.

Keywords: Multimodal Learning · Cross-Modal Retrieval · Contrastive Learning · Image-Music Alignment

1 Introduction

Large-scale music websites, such as SoundCloud[1] and Audiomack[2], facilitate search engines based on cross-modal retrieval methods, which fetches music tracks by matching their metadata (e.g., song titles, artists' names, and music genres) with natural language queries. Though some offer more personalized query options (i.e., mood and theme), these retrieval methods still often fail to find soundtracks with implicit context aligned with films and their derivative works. And this is critical for creators to choose appropriate soundtracks (Fig. 1).

---

[1] https://soundcloud.com/.
[2] https://audiomack.com/.

C. Mousas et al. (Eds.): CASA 2025, LNCS 15915, pp. 109–123, 2026.
https://doi.org/10.1007/978-981-95-0100-7_7

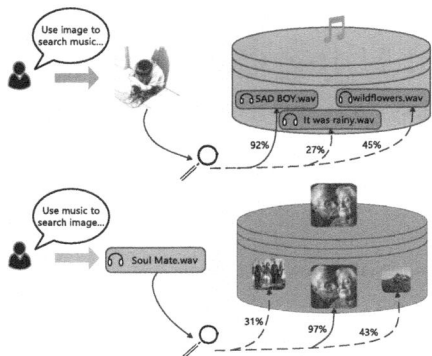

Fig. 1. An example that shows retrieval between image and music in searching engine.

Researchers dedicate to improve the cross-modal music retrieval systems. Manco *et al.* [21] and Doh *et al.* [7] make the attempts to bridge audio and text in music domain by learning a multimodal embedding to facilitate text-based music retrieval task on both tag-level and sentence-level. However, the increasing need to find soundtracks based on contexts is not yet considered, as such text-based music retrieval methods mainly focus on the metadata but not the contexts. To meet these needs, video-based music retrieval methods are developed recently. Yi et al. [32] and Cheng *et al.* [2] propose micro-video based music retrieval systems from perspectives of cross-modal generation mechanism and labels noises reduction in datasets, respectively. These micro-videos (less than 10 s) usually display consecutive frames in a similar scene, which can be effectively compressed to one single key frame. Thus such video-based music retrieval can be simplified to image-base music retrieval.

Image-music retrieval has addressed lots of attention, since the images express the context information more effectively than text-based ones while holding retrieval efficiency than video-based approaches. In addition, image-based music retrieval are more preferred by users than text-based ones in terms of user experience and usability [25]. Nakatsuka *et al.* [24] utilize contrastive learning technique to learn a joint embedding space to align images and music based on the music genres and their cover art. Stewart *et al.* [27] further propose a cross-modal version of SupCon loss to better align images and music on emotion labels.

Aforementioned image-music retrieval methods are able to handle **coarse-granularity** retrieval as they align images and music based on explicit information like image classes and emotions. However, such methods probably match music with context unrelated images. As shown in the left of Fig. 2, a music clip about happiness moment of couples is matched with an image of a dog smiling (same tender emotion), and an epic music clip of films is matched with images of team gathering as they share content-similarity with superheros gathering. We refer these retrieval tasks on context information contained implicitly in queries as **fine-granularity** retrieval, which are not considered by methods [24,27].

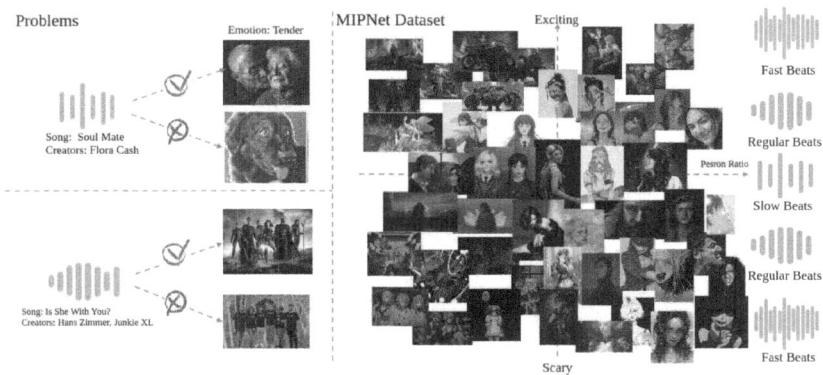

Fig. 2. Prior image-based music retrieval methods [24,27] will mismatch music and images with unrelated contexts. The proposed MIPNet dataset contains over 66k image-music pairs, which share similar contexts, aligning with general human intuition.

To achieve such fine-granularity retrieval, this work leverages a cross-modal version of Barlow Twins loss [34] to capture the implicit context information. Then we combine it with coarse-granularity retrieval to form a framework HG-CLIM for **H**ybrid-**G**ranularity Context Alignment **C**ontrastive **L**earning between **I**mages and **M**usic. It is capable of capturing context information in a hybrid manner. To conduct context-alignment on both coarse-granularity and fine-granularity, we construct a dataset consists of 66,048 image-music pairs, where both coarse-granularity (including the explicit contents in images, beats and rhythm with emotions in music) and fine-granularity (including the implicit context connections between images and music) are considered. As shown in Fig. 2, music clips with slow beat tunes and emotional rhythm are paired with images containing raining weather, desolation landscapes and cold colors. Furthermore, to align these hybrid context information effectively, we propose hybrid-granularity contrastive learning losses for both inter-modal and intra-modal scenarios. Our work follows the modality-symmetric feature as [27] that is capable of image-to-music and music-to-image retrieval. The key contributions are summarised as follows:

- To the best of our knowledge, HG-CLIM is the first framework that performs image-music retrieval on queries about contexts which learns a hybrid context alignment between two modalities, which could benefit current metadata based music searching paradigm.
- To address the lack of datasets in the area of image-based music retrieval, we construct a private dataset termed MIPNet. It contains 66,048 image-music pairs with alignment of hybrid context information, which is essential for further research in the area of image-based music retrieval.
- To capture the implicit contexts, we leverage a cross-modal version of Barlow Twins loss to propose fine-granularity contrastive learning losses for both

inter- and intra-modal scenarios. Experimental results has demonstrated the effectiveness of our hybrid-granularity design.

2   Related Works

Cross-modal music retrieval methods [6,30] utilize triplet loss to find items that close to the anchor queries by distance metrics. With the recent success of contrastive learning on cross-modal alignment [9,14,26,35], it is naturally applied to align music modality with another modality (e.g., texts, videos and images) [7,11,12,21,32]. Intuitively, researchers connect text modality with music by learning a multi-modal embeddings [7,21] to perform text-based music retrieval task. However, these methods limit the queries to pre-defined tags and sentences. To retrieve music with more personalized queries, video-based music retrieval approaches are developed rapidly as the micro-video platforms (e.g., Tiktok and Reels) show increasing needs for searching matched background music for micro-videos. And several methods(e.g., [17,22,32,33] put efforts to learn an effective embedding space by leveraging extra information (e.g., optical flow and text) to perform music retrieval. There is a recent method [28] pioneer Control-MVR, which integrates both paradigms via semi-supervised contrastive and dynamically balance audiovisual alignment and genre-specific semantics during inference. More recently, several methods [5,8,23] attempt to integrate Large Language Models (LLM) into the frameworks, which involves interactive chat to further refine users' queries and preferences. However, these video-based approaches are not practical for many music websites (e.g., SoundCloud). Furthermore, it can be simplified to music retrieval based on single key frame, as the mirco-videos usually show consecutive frames of one similar scene.

In contrast, image-based music retrieval approaches are more straightforward and practical since the images express more accurate and complex contexts than tags, and they are more effective than micro-videos on key context deliverance. With such advantages, Nakatsuka *et al.* [24] learn a joint embedding space to align images and music based on the music genres and their cover art. Stewart *et al.* [27] further propose to align images and music on emotion labels. However, these methods only perform image-based music retrieval as classification task (aka coarse-granularity retrieval) but not contexts alignment (aka fine-granularity retrieval). To address this problem, we propose a hybrid-granularity image-based music retrieval framework which takes both coarse-granularity retrieval and fine-granularity retrieval into account.

Large Language Models (LLMs) and diffusion models have advanced content generation across modalities. For example, liu *et al.* [19] leverages latent diffusion models for open-ended visual storytelling, demonstrating LLMs' capability to generate narrative text from images. However, such generative approaches prioritize creative content synthesis over precise cross-modal alignment required for retrieval tasks. Wang *et al.* [29] highlight challenges in AI-generated content (e.g., hallucination, consistency), underscoring the need for retrieval systems to complement generative paradigms.

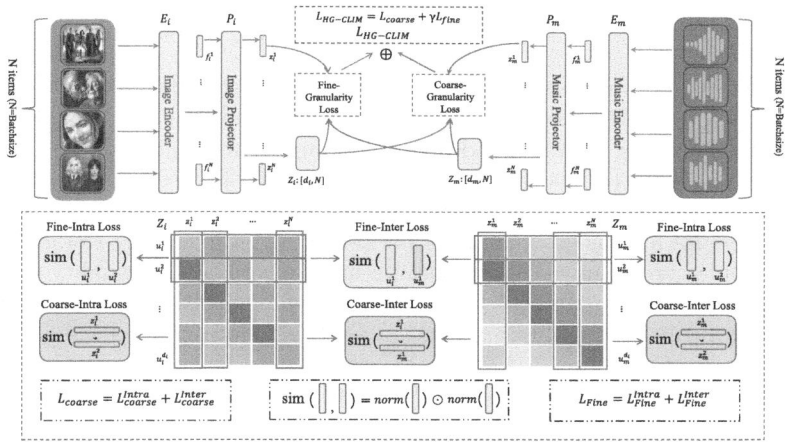

Fig. 3. The overview framework of HG-CLIM. The proposed loss term $\mathcal{L}_{HG-CLIM}$ is constructed with two losses: coarse-granularity $\mathcal{L}_{coarse}$ and fine-granularity $\mathcal{L}_{fine}$, which compute contrastive loss along the batch(u_i, u_m) and feature dimensions(z_i, z_m), respectively. u_i and u_m are the normalized vectors along with the batch dimension, and z_i and z_m are the normalized vectors along with the feature dimension. The sim() function computes cosine similarity which is employed by inter-modal loss and intra-modal loss.

3   Methodology

3.1   The MIPNet Dataset

To the best of our knowledge, there is no existing dataset that considers alignment of music and images on context information. Thus we construct a **M**usic-**I**mage **P**airing from **Net**s Dataset, termed MIPNet. The MIPNet dataset consisting of 66,048 image-music pairs, which contains music clips (10 s per clip), images, and their emotional labels (in text format). There are seven emotion labels for both modalities: "Exciting", "Funny", "Happy", "Tender", "Sad", "Angry", "Scary" as [10]. The image-music pairs are collected by downloading music clips and thumbnails of music videos from online Social Media platforms Youtube[3] and Bilibili[4], and the emotion labels are pre-annotated by a LLM (e.g.,Qwen-VL [1]) and refined by human annotations. In addition, the music clips and images are carefully paired which considers implicit context connections. For example, the images presenting story moments in films are paired with their background music clips, and the images presenting happy moments of couples are paired with music clips containing slow beats with chorus of male and female vocals with happy emotion. The images in the dataset are saved in JPG format, while the music clips are saved with a sampling rate of 32 kHz in

---

[3] https://www.youtube.com/.
[4] https://www.bilibili.com/.

WAV format. The dataset is randomly split into train, valid, and test subsets in an 8:1:1 ratio.

To reduce the noise in image domain, several filtering methods are applied, for example, duplication removal (based on MD5 hashes and CNN-based model [13]), quality filtering (CNN-based model [18] and human judgement for image quality assessment), textual filtering in images (crop out textual contents), and ratio filtering that filters out abnormal aspect ratio (e.g., greater than 4:1). To reduce the noise in music domain, we perform filtering based on sound quality. The audio files are removed if it contains unclear vocals, low quality of music instruments and concert lives. For the openness of our dataset, we will make the dataset **available** through an application process following Creative Commons Attribution-NonCommercial (CC BY-NC 4.0) license.

Compared to other datasets, our dataset offers more accurate and rigorous image-music matching logic, aligning with our research focus: fine-grained one-to-one image-music matching. The advantages of our dataset lie in its fine-grained alignment between image and music modalities across multiple levels, coupled with its substantial scale. For further details, please refer to the table below:

Table 1. Comparison of Different Datasets

	Emotion Match	Scene Match	Rhythm Match	Style Match	Key Segment	Over 50k
MIPNet	✓	✓	✓	✓	✓	✓
EMO	✓	×	×	×	×	×
MCA [24]	×	✓	×	✓	×	✓
IMSA [31]	✓	×	×	×	×	✓

3.2 The Proposed HG-CLIM Framework

As shown in Fig. 3, the HG-CLIM framework consists of three main components: encoders for feature extraction, projectors for feature projection into a joint embedding space, and the proposed contrastive learning loss term: $\mathcal{L}_{HG-CLIM}$. Given an image x_i and a music clip x_m, HG-CLIM computes an image feature z_i and an music feature z_m as follows:

$$z_i = \mathbf{P_i}(\mathbf{E_i}(x_i)); z_m = \mathbf{P_m}(\mathbf{E_m}(x_m))$$

Feature Extraction. In this work, ConvNext [20] is employed as the image feature encoder, which is shown with both superior efficiency and effectiveness of image classification on ImageNet [4]. The music encoder utilizes PaSST (Patchout Spectrogram Transformer) Hear21 model [16], which performs state-of-the-arts performances of music classification on Audioset [10]. These encoders are capable of capturing robust and informative representations for cross-modal alignment due to their effective extraction of global and local patterns for images and audios.

Projectors for Joint Embedding Space. To project extracted features of image and music into a joint embedding space, we employ a projector for one modality to follow each encoder. Each projector is a multi-layer perception (MLP) network. To be specific, the image projector consists of two linear layers, each followed by one BatchNorm and one ReLU activation layer, and one single linear projector. Similarly, the music projector has the same structure as the image projector, and their output dimensions are set to 8192, which is crucial for reconciling the substantial differences between the music and image modalities [34].

3.3   Loss Terms for Aligning Modalities

In this paper, $z_i \in \mathbb{R}^{d_i}$ and $z_m \in \mathbb{R}^{d_m}$ denote the **normalized embedding vector** from image and music projectors, where d_i and d_m denote their dimensions. And $Z_i \in \mathbb{R}^{d_i \times N}$ and $Z_m \in \mathbb{R}^{d_m \times N}$ denote the matrix formed by z_i and z_m in a training batch, where N is the batch size. Also, $u_i \in \mathbb{R}^N$ and $u_m \in \mathbb{R}^N$ indicate the normalized embedding vector extracted along with the batch dimension of Z_i and Z_m, and ω_p indicates the modalities of p, with $p \in \{1, 2\}$.

Coarse-Granularity Contrastive Learning Loss for Inter-Intra Modality. The coarse-granularity contrastive loss along the batch dimension for cross-modal is defined as :

$$\mathcal{L}_{\text{coarse}}^{\omega_1 \to 2} = -\frac{1}{N} \sum_{k=1}^{N} \log \frac{\text{sim}\left(z_{\omega_1}^k, z_{\omega_2}^k\right)}{\lambda_c \sum_{\substack{j=1 \\ j \neq k}}^{N} \text{sim}(z_{\omega_1}^k, z_{\omega_2}^j)} \tag{1}$$

where $\text{sim}(\boldsymbol{u}, \boldsymbol{v}) = \exp(\frac{\boldsymbol{u}^\top \boldsymbol{v}/\|\boldsymbol{u}\|\|\boldsymbol{v}\|}{\tau})$. $z_{\omega_1}^k$ is defined as the k-th embedding vector of modality ω_1. τ is the temperature factor that adjusts the distribution of the logits. We define intra-modal loss as $\mathcal{L}_{\text{coarse}}^{Intra}$ and inter-modal as $\mathcal{L}_{\text{coarse}}^{Inter}$. The coarse-granularity contrastive learning loss is defined as the weighted sum of both inter-modal and intra-modal losses:

$$\mathcal{L}_{\text{coarse}}^{Intra} = \mathcal{L}_{\text{coarse}}^{I} + \lambda^M \mathcal{L}_{\text{coarse}}^{M} \tag{2}$$

$$\mathcal{L}_{\text{coarse}}^{Inter} = \mathcal{L}_{\text{coarse}}^{I \to M} + \lambda^{M \to I} \mathcal{L}_{\text{coarse}}^{M \to I} \tag{3}$$

$$\mathcal{L}_{\text{coarse}} = \mathcal{L}_{\text{coarse}}^{Inter} + \alpha \mathcal{L}_{\text{coarse}}^{Intra} \tag{4}$$

where we set $\alpha = 1$, $\lambda^M = 1$, and $\lambda^{M \to I} = 1$ empirically.

Fine-Granularity Contrastive Learning Loss for Inter-Intra Modality.
Inspired by Barlow Twins loss [34], the fine-granularity contrastive learning loss
for cross-modal is formulated as:

$$\mathcal{L}_{fine}^{\omega_1 \to 2} = \sum_k \left(1 - C_{k,k}^{\omega_1 \to 2}\right)^2 \tag{5}$$

$$+ \lambda_f \sum_k \sum_{j \neq k} (C_{k,j}^{\omega_1 \to 2})^2$$

$$\mathcal{L}_{fine} = \mathcal{L}_{fine}^{Inter} + \beta \mathcal{L}_{fine}^{Intra} \tag{6}$$

where λ_f is introduced as a balance factor, $\beta = 1$ empirically, and $C_{k,j}^{\omega_1 \to \omega_2}$ is the
cross-correlation matrix computed between the embeddings $u_{\omega_1}^k$ and $u_{\omega_2}^j$, which
is defined as:

$$C_{k,j}^{\omega_1 \to 2} = \frac{u_{\omega_1}^k u_{\omega_2}^j}{\sqrt{\left(u_{\omega_1}^k\right)^2}\sqrt{\left(u_{\omega_2}^j\right)^2}} \tag{7}$$

Follow Eq. (4), we design two components: the inter-modal loss and the intra-
modal loss, while the fine-granularity contrastive learning loss contains these two
parts.

The proposed HG-CLIM loss is a weighted sum of Eq. (4) and Eq. (6), defined
as:

$$\mathcal{L}_{HG-CLIM} = \mathcal{L}_{coarse} + \gamma \mathcal{L}_{fine} \tag{8}$$

where γ denotes the weight factor between two loss terms. The loss term $\mathcal{L}_{coarse}$
"unite" embeddings with similar explicit information (e.g., emotions, rhythms in
audios and contents in images) and "separate" embeddings without such information. The loss term $\mathcal{L}_{fine}$ "unite" embeddings with same implicit contexts
(e.g., vocals in audios and styles in images) and "separate" embeddings with
different contexts.

The theoretical background behind the fine-granularity loss term lies on the
alignment between two **normalized vectors sharing a same dimension**.
Specifically, in a sharing embedding space, the distance metric for measuring two
vectors is using consine similarity, which calculates the angles between two vectors. However, since the values in vectors contain information on both the scale
and direction, thus the consine similarity only take the coarse-grained direction
into account but without fine-grained scale information. To address this issue,
the values of each element in the vectors should be considered. In this work,
we firstly normalize every vector into a unit vector, then calculate the cross-
correlation matrix between any two vectors, as the correlation matrix should be
close to the identity matrix when their values in each element are close enough.
In this way, each value in every element of vectors (presenting fine-grained information) are taken into account. By leveraging this with coarse-grained information on direction, we achieve more accurate alignment than regular contrastive
learning methods.

4   Experiments

4.1   Implementation Details

We use the Adam [15] optimizer with a learning rate of 8×10^{-5} and a weight decay of 0.1 with 400 training epochs. The dimensions of image features and music features extracted from their pre-trained encoders [16, 20] are fixed to 2048 and 768, respectively, then they are all projected to the same dimension 8192. During the training procedure, the image encoder and music encoder is frozen, and the projectors are trained from scratch. To balance the hyperparameters in Eq. (1), (6) and (8), we set temperature-scaling $\tau = 0.2, \lambda_c = 1, \lambda_f = 0.0061, \gamma = 0.01$.

4.2   Experimental Results

Since the proposed MIPNet dataset is composed of one-to-one pairs, evaluation on this dataset is a pair-wise retrieval task. In order to conduct further comparisons with other methods, we also apply our method to other type of retrieval tasks (e.g., emotion-based music retrieval) and assess the generalizability of our approach.

Table 2. Cross-modal Retrieval performance comparisons between methods on MIPNet Dataset. $I \rightarrow M$ and $M \rightarrow I$ denote image-to-music and music-to-image retrieval respectively

Method	$I \rightarrow M$			$M \rightarrow I$		
	MRR	R@10	P@1	MRR	R@10	P@1
EMO-CLIM	0.0804	0.1592	0.0831	0.0812	0.1633	0.0791
VM-NET	0.3279	0.6463	0.2001	0.3165	0.6258	0.2057
HG-CLIM (ours)	**0.5124**	**0.8080**	**0.2931**	**0.5104**	**0.8082**	**0.2910**

Results on MIPNet Dataset. To evaluate the effectiveness of our proposed method, we conduct cross-modal retrieval tasks on the proposed MIPNet dataset. Both image-to-music and music-to-image retrieval tasks are conducted. Inspired by [24] [27], evaluation metrics including Mean Reciprocal Rank (MRR [3]), Recall@10 ($R@10$), and Precision@1 ($P@1$) are employed to assess the performance of the retrieval tasks.

Since there are no previous methods available for direct comparison on the same task, we selected two models that have demonstrated strong performance in similar tasks. The EMO-CLIM [27] model matches images and music based on emotion labels, while VM-NET [11] pairs videos with music. We extracted the respective feature encoders from these models and reconstructed their loss functions to align with the task of pair-wise matching. We then train all three models: EMO-CLIM, VM-NET, and our method on the MIPNet dataset, and compare them with same evaluation metrics for fair comparisons. As shown in Table 2, our model consistently outperforms the others across all metrics.

Table 3. Cross-modal emotion-based music retrieval comparison among MMTS* [30], EMO-CLIM [27] and our method on MIPNet and EMO Dataset. * denotes MMTS is text-based music retrieval on emotion labels. MRR, R@10, P@1 represent the performance metrics for both I→ M (left side) and M→ I (right side). Best results are shown in underline

Dataset	Method	MRR	R@10	P@1
MIPNET	MMTS	0.4575/0.4807	0.6887/0.7123	0.4070/0.4188
	EMO-CLIM	0.4619/0.5072	0.8237/0.7986	0.4917/0.4935
	HG-CLIM	0.4765/0.5123	0.8215/0.7921	0.5033/0.5094
EMO	MMTS	0.6616/0.6843	0.6013/0.6125	0.3904/0.3988
	EMO-CLIM	0.7859/0.7400	0.6533/0.6238	0.4125/0.4234
	HG-CLIM	0.8012/0.7485	0.6908/0.6574	0.4577/0.4396

The table compares Top1 retrieval results of three methods (EMO-CLIM, VM-NET, and HG-CLIM) on bidirectional tasks: Music→Image and Image→Music retrieval. Our method (HG-CLIM) consistently achieves superior alignment accuracy by capturing both explicit and implicit contexts.

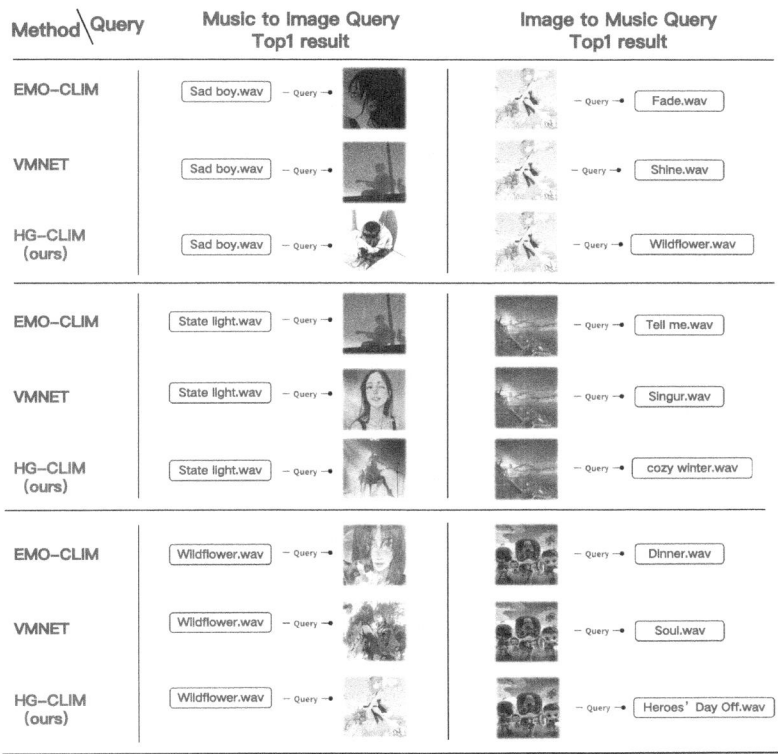

Fig. 4. Top1 retrieval results of HG-CLIM compared to baselines (EMO-CLIM, VM-NET) on bidirectional cross-modal retrieval tasks

Also, as illustrated in Fig. 4, the HG-CLIM model successfully aligns the song "sad boy.wav" with an image depicting a boy bowing his head in tears and accurately pairs the image of a girl holding flowers with the song "Wildflower.wav". In contrast, baseline methods (e.g., EMO-CLIM and VM-NET) exhibit mismatches in emotional or contextual alignment under the same queries. These results validate HG-CLIM's capability to capture fine-granularity semantic relationships (e.g., scene-specific textures and implicit stylistic cues), demonstrating its superiority in context-aware cross-modal retrieval tasks.

Results on Emotion-Aligned Music Retrieval. We recognize that the emotion-based music retrieval task is also a valuable research task. Thus we compare our method with the EMO-CLIM and the MMTS [30] framework in this context. Music and images with same emotion labels are regarded as positive pairs, while the others are treated as negative pairs. Besides, we identified a dataset designed for emotion-based matching. Following the EMO dataset construction approach for AudioSet described in [27], we constructed a dataset and performed comparative experiments, with the results presented in Table 1. Based on this matching criterion, we conduct experiments and report the same retrieval metrics on Table 3.

The results demonstrate that the proposed method (HG-CLIM) continues to perform strongly in this context, further validating the generalizability of the HG-CLIM approach.

4.3 Ablation Studies

We conduct in-depth ablation studies to systematically evaluate the effectiveness of different components in proposed HG-CLIM framework. The experimental results are shown in Table 4. The baseline method consists of only the coarse-granularity contrastive learning loss. We apply the fine-granularity loss term to the intra- and inter-modality repsectively to evaluate its impact on retrieval performance with MRR metric. In Table 4, it is noticeable that the fine-granularity loss on intra-modal (second row) contributes a slight improvement in task performance compared to the baseline. While applied on inter-modal (third row), the fine-granularity loss contributes significant improvement for model performance. This demonstrates that the fine-granularity loss enables the model to learn more robust and informative representations of images and music for retrieval tasks, which indicates contribution on learning implicit context-alignment information on MIPNet Dataset.

Table 4. Ablation studies on different losses under MRR$(I \to M)$ and MRR$(M \to I)$ metrics. Baseline method is trained only with loss $\mathcal{L}_{coarse}$, and next two following methods are trained with extra losses $\mathcal{L}_{fine}^{intra}$, and $\mathcal{L}_{fine}^{inter}$, respectively

Loss	MRR$(I \to M)$	MRR$(M \to I)$
Baseline	0.3164	0.2662
Baseline + $\mathcal{L}_{fine}^{intra}$	0.3272	0.3196
Baseline + $\mathcal{L}_{fine}^{inter}$	0.4793	0.4761
Baseline + $\mathcal{L}_{fine}^{intra}$ + $\mathcal{L}_{fine}^{inter}$	0.5124	0.5104

5 Conclusion

In this work, we propose HG-CLIM, a novel image-based music retrieval framework, which aims to align images and music on contexts. To address the lack of dataset for such purpose, we construct a private dataset MIPNet, which contains 66,048 image-music pairs and their emotion labels. With our proposed hybrid-granularity contrastive learning loss, HG-CLIM is capable of learning an image-music joint embedding space, which considers context alignment on both coarse-granularity and fine-granularity. Experiments on our MIPNet dataset demonstrate this embedding space is effective for cross-modal music retrieval task.

Our approach shows a promising direction for image-based music retrieval on context queries. Beyond cross-modal retrieval, our framework's ability to align implicit contexts between images and music has broader implications for AI-driven creative applications. For instance, in AI storytelling, dynamically matching music to narrative scenes (e.g., pairing suspenseful music with a thriller plot) can enhance emotional engagement. Similarly, in AI music generation, retrieval-based context alignment can guide models to synthesize music that aligns with visual themes (e.g., generating orchestral scores for fantasy landscapes). Our work bridges multimodal understanding and generative AI, offering a foundation for context-aware applications in virtual reality (VR), interactive media, and automated content creation.

Acknowledgments. This research has been supported by Natural Key Research and Development Project of Zhejiang Province (Grant No. 2023C01043), and in part by the Major Program of The National Social Science Fund of China (Grant No. 24&ZD070), Ningbo Natural Science Foundation (Grant No. 2024Z234).

References

1. Bai, J., et al.: Qwen-vl: a versatile vision-language model for understanding, localization, text reading, and beyond. arXiv preprint arXiv:2308.12966 (2023)
2. Cheng, X., Zhu, Z., Li, H., Li, Y., Zou, Y.: Ssvmr: saliency-based self-training for video-music retrieval. In: ICASSP 2023-2023 IEEE International Conference on Acoustics, Speech and Signal Processing (ICASSP), pp. 1–5. IEEE (2023)
3. Craswell, N.: Mean reciprocal rank. Encyclopedia of database systems, pp. 1703–1703 (2009)
4. Deng, J., Dong, W., Socher, R., Li, L.J., Li, K., Fei-Fei, L.: Imagenet: a large-scale hierarchical image database. In: 2009 IEEE Conference on Computer Vision and Pattern Recognition, pp. 248–255. IEEE (2009)
5. Doh, S., Lee, M., Jeong, D., Nam, J.: Enriching music descriptions with a finetuned-llm and metadata for text-to-music retrieval. In: ICASSP 2024-2024 IEEE International Conference on Acoustics, Speech and Signal Processing (ICASSP), pp. 826–830. IEEE (2024)
6. Doh, S., Won, M., Choi, K., Nam, J.: Textless speech-to-music retrieval using emotion similarity. In: ICASSP 2023-2023 IEEE International Conference on Acoustics, Speech and Signal Processing (ICASSP), pp. 1–5. IEEE (2023)
7. Doh, S., Won, M., Choi, K., Nam, J.: Toward universal text-to-music retrieval. In: ICASSP 2023-2023 IEEE International Conference on Acoustics, Speech and Signal Processing (ICASSP), pp. 1–5. IEEE (2023)
8. Dong, Z., Liu, X., Chen, B., Polak, P., Zhang, P.: Musechat: a conversational music recommendation system for videos. In: Proceedings of the IEEE/CVF Conference on Computer Vision and Pattern Recognition, pp. 12775–12785 (2024)
9. Elizalde, B., Deshmukh, S., Al Ismail, M., Wang, H.: Clap learning audio concepts from natural language supervision. In: ICASSP 2023-2023 IEEE International Conference on Acoustics, Speech and Signal Processing (ICASSP), pp. 1–5. IEEE (2023)

10. Gemmeke, J.F., et al.: Audio set: an ontology and human-labeled dataset for audio events. In: 2017 IEEE International Conference on Acoustics, Speech and Signal Processing (ICASSP), pp. 776–780. IEEE (2017)
11. Hong, S., Im, W., Yang, H.S.: CBVMR: content-based video-music retrieval using soft intra-modal structure constraint. In: Proceedings of the 2018 ACM on International Conference on Multimedia Retrieval, pp. 353–361 (2018)
12. Huang, Q., Jansen, A., Lee, J., Ganti, R., Li, J.Y., Ellis, D.P.: Mulan: a joint embedding of music audio and natural language. arXiv preprint arXiv:2208.12415 (2022)
13. Jain, T., Lennan, C., John, Z., Tran, D.: Imagededup (2019). https://github.com/idealo/imagededup
14. Khosla, P., et al.: Supervised contrastive learning. Adv. Neural. Inf. Process. Syst. **33**, 18661–18673 (2020)
15. Kingma, D.P., Ba, J.: Adam: a method for stochastic optimization. arXiv preprint arXiv:1412.6980 (2014)
16. Koutini, K., Schlüter, J., Eghbal-Zadeh, H., Widmer, G.: Efficient training of audio transformers with patchout. arXiv preprint arXiv:2110.05069 (2021)
17. Lee, Y.S., Tseng, W.C., Wang, F.E., Sun, M.: Vmcml: video and music matching via cross-modality lifting. In: Proceedings of the IEEE/CVF Conference on Computer Vision and Pattern Recognition, pp. 2060–2069 (2024)
18. Lennan, C., Nguyen, H., Tran, D.: Image quality assessment (2018). https://github.com/idealo/image-quality-assessment
19. Liu, C., Wu, H., Zhong, Y., Zhang, X., Wang, Y., Xie, W.: Intelligent grimm-open-ended visual storytelling via latent diffusion models. In: Proceedings of the IEEE/CVF Conference on Computer Vision and Pattern Recognition, pp. 6190–6200 (2024)
20. Liu, Z., Mao, H., Wu, C.Y., Feichtenhofer, C., Darrell, T., Xie, S.: A convnet for the 2020s. In: Proceedings of the IEEE/CVF Conference on Computer Vision and Pattern Recognition, pp. 11976–11986 (2022)
21. Manco, I., Benetos, E., Quinton, E., Fazekas, G.: Contrastive audio-language learning for music. arXiv preprint arXiv:2208.12208 (2022)
22. Mao, T., Liu, S., Zhang, Y., Li, D., Shan, Y.: Unified pretraining target based video-music retrieval with music rhythm and video optical flow information. In: ICASSP 2024-2024 IEEE International Conference on Acoustics, Speech and Signal Processing (ICASSP), pp. 7890–7894. IEEE (2024)
23. McKee, D., Salamon, J., Sivic, J., Russell, B.: Language-guided music recommendation for video via prompt analogies. In: Proceedings of the IEEE/CVF Conference on Computer Vision and Pattern Recognition, pp. 14784–14793 (2023)
24. Nakatsuka, T., Hamasaki, M., Goto, M.: Content-based music-image retrieval using self-and cross-modal feature embedding memory. In: Proceedings of the IEEE/CVF Winter Conference on Applications of Computer Vision, pp. 2174–2184 (2023)
25. Park, J., Shin, H., Oh, C., Kim, H.Y.: "is text-based music search enough to satisfy your needs?" a new way to discover music with images. In: Proceedings of the CHI Conference on Human Factors in Computing Systems, pp. 1–21 (2024)
26. Radford, A., et al.: Learning transferable visual models from natural language supervision. In: International Conference on Machine Learning, pp. 8748–8763. PMLR (2021)
27. Stewart, S., Avramidis, K., Feng, T., Narayanan, S.: Emotion-aligned contrastive learning between images and music. In: ICASSP 2024-2024 IEEE International Conference on Acoustics, Speech and Signal Processing (ICASSP), pp. 8135–8139. IEEE (2024)

28. Stewart, S., KV, G., Lu, L., Fanelli, A.: Semi-supervised contrastive learning for controllable video-to-music retrieval. arXiv preprint arXiv:2412.05831 (2024)
29. Wang, Y., Pan, Y., Yan, M., Su, Z., Luan, T.H.: A survey on ChatGPT: AI-generated contents, challenges, and solutions. IEEE Open J. Comput. Soc. **4**, 280–302 (2023)
30. Won, M., Salamon, J., Bryan, N.J., Mysore, G.J., Serra, X.: Emotion embedding spaces for matching music to stories. arXiv preprint arXiv:2111.13468 (2021)
31. Xing, B., Zhang, K., Zhang, L., Wu, X., Dou, J., Sun, S.: Image–music synesthesia-aware learning based on emotional similarity recognition. IEEE Access **7**, 136378–136390 (2019). https://doi.org/10.1109/ACCESS.2019.2942073
32. Yi, J., Zhu, Y., Xie, J., Chen, Z.: Cross-modal variational auto-encoder for content-based micro-video background music recommendation. IEEE Trans. Multimedia **25**, 515–528 (2021)
33. Yi, J., Zhu, Y., Xie, J., Chen, Z.: Cross-modal variational auto-encoder for content-based micro-video background music recommendation. IEEE Trans. Multimedia **25**, 515–528 (2023). https://doi.org/10.1109/TMM.2021.3128254
34. Zbontar, J., Jing, L., Misra, I., LeCun, Y., Deny, S.: Barlow twins: self-supervised learning via redundancy reduction. In: International Conference on Machine Learning, pp. 12310–12320. PMLR (2021)
35. Zheng, M., et al.: Weakly supervised contrastive learning. In: Proceedings of the IEEE/CVF International Conference on Computer Vision, pp. 10042–10051 (2021)

Text-Driven Tree Modeling
via CLIP-Based Optimization

Yudai Ichimura[1] and Syuhei Sato[1,2(✉)]

[1] Hosei University, 3-7-2 Kajino-cho, Koganei-shi, Tokyo 184-8584, Japan
ssato@hosei.ac.jp
[2] Prometech CG Research, 34-3, Hongo 3-chome, Bunkyo-ku, Tokyo 113-0033, Japan

Abstract. Creating tree 3D models is a complex task that requires significant effort. In order to make tree modeling easier, several methods have been proposed on reconstructing tree 3D models from images or sketches. However, users need to provide appropriate images to obtain satisfactory reconstructed results, and depicting various types of trees is difficult for users who are not accustomed to drawing. Therefore, we propose a novel method to obtain tree 3D models in a zero-shot manner using text as input, by leveraging CLIP (Contrastive Language-Image Pre-training), which has garnered attention in recent years. CLIP can compute semantic similarities between input texts and images. Utilizing this property, we formulate the modeling of trees through text as an optimization problem with the evaluation by CLIP as the objective function. We adopt a genetic algorithm for the optimization problem. Since CLIP is a pre-trained model, our system does not require learning processes. The tree models are generated using the Lindenmayer System (L-system), and our method determines the parameters of the L-system that result in tree models aligned with the input text. The efficacy of our method is demonstrated through various examples.

Keywords: modeling · tree model · CLIP · zero-shot generation · text-driven generation · L-system

1 Introduction

In computer graphics, the creation of intricate 3D models such as buildings and trees is indispensable for enhancing the reality of animations. However, to obtain complex 3D models, manual editing of numerous vertices and faces is required, involving intricate efforts and a significant amount of time. This problem becomes particularly pronounced when dealing with complex shapes, such as trees. To address this issue, procedural modeling techniques have been proposed to automatically generate intricate shapes from minimal rules. One widely-used method for modeling trees is the L-system [21]. In this approach,

Supplementary Information The online version contains supplementary material available at https://doi.org/10.1007/978-981-95-0100-7_8.

a recursive structure is described by replacing strings according to predefined rules. The L-system generates the shape of a tree by interpreting the final string as instructions for manipulating a virtual robot called a "turtle." However, the rules of the L-system lack intuitiveness, and obtaining the desired tree model often requires trial and error in editing the rules.

On the other hand, image-based method can easily create 3D models. While numerous approaches exist for 3D model creation, including reconstructions from real images or sketches, these methods face challenges when suitable visual references are unavailable or users lack proficient sketching skills. Textual inputs have recently emerged as a viable alternative, and several methods have been proposed for generating images or 3D models [4, 8, 11, 16, 19, 27]. Texts are convenient to prepare and have become popular inputs for generating 3D models due to their ease of use compared to images or sketches. However, previous methods of text-to-3D model generation cannot be simply applied to tree models due to their complexity: tree models are generally much more intricate than other models, such as those of humans, animals, and artificial objects. Figure 1 shows the results of creating tree models using CLIP-Mesh [16] and DreamFusion [19] in our preliminary experiments. In the CLIP-Mesh result (Fig. 1 left), the generated model appears as a simple shape with a tree image. In the DreamFusion result (Fig. 1 right), the overall appearance looks plausible, but the branches and leaves lack detail.

To address this, we propose a novel text-driven approach specialized for tree modeling. In image input, it is difficult to individually recognize branches and leaves, and it is labor-intensive to accurately draw all the branches and leaves in a sketch. On the other hand, with text input, it is sufficient to provide the tree's name and characteristics, without the need for high-precision recognition of branches and leaves from an image. This makes it possible for users without knowledge or skills in 3D modeling or L-Systems to intuitively create plausible trees, potentially greatly simplifying the creation of assets required for games, metaverse spaces, and more. We adopt L-system [21] for tree generation and optimize its parameters to align with user-input texts. Our method allows the use of three different L-systems, each generating trees with distinct characteristics, enabling the user to select the system that produces the desired tree. Our optimization process utilizes genetic algorithms (GA) and evaluates fitness through CLIP [22], which is a pre-training model adept at assessing the semantic similarity between texts and images. In our system, CLIP is used to calculate similarity between input texts and tree images obtained from L-system. Since we directly utilize the pre-trained CLIP model, no additional training is required. Ours is the first CLIP-based system specialized for generating tree models, which are more complex than 3D models treated in the existing deep learning-based systems. We demonstrate the effectiveness of our approach through various examples.

2   Related Work

2.1   Tree Modeling Using L-System

For modeling trees, Prusinkiewicz et al. developed a formal language which describes recursive structures by transforming strings according to rewriting

CLIP-Mesh   DreamFusion
[Khalid et al. 2022]   [Poole et al. 2022]

Fig. 1. The result of tree generation using CLIP-Mesh [16] and DreamFusion [19]. The input text is *"A photo of a wide tree, full shot, with green leaves.* (Color figure online)"

rules [21]. These rewritten strings are interpreted as control instructions of *Turtle Graphics*, and tree images are generated. Turtle Graphics can be extended to generate 3D shapes. We adopt L-system to generate tree 3D models. In the subsequent work, Prusinkiewicz et al. extended L-system for animating developmental processes of plants [20]. This integrates L-system-style productions and differential equations. Curry proposed an interactive method based on a genetic algorithm to generate user-desired plant models by optimizing L-system parameters [5]. This method optimizes the L-system parameters according to user's choices: several plant models are generated via L-system from genes (parameters), and the users choice desired ones among these models at each generation. While this method does not require extensive knowledge of L-system, the users must repeatedly choice plant models closest to their preference. These are tedious and time-consuming tasks. Palubicki's method [18] can generate complex trees, but with more complex L-systems, the number of parameters becomes too large, sometimes resulting in shapes that are not trees. Therefore, we adopt a simpler L-system.

Št'ava et al. achieved inverse procedural modeling by generating parametric context-free L-systems that represent an input 2D model [29]. This algorithm takes as input a 2D vector image. Guo et al. introduced an inverse procedural modeling that learns L-system representations of images with branching structures [7]. This model generates a set of textual rewriting rules and uses deep learning to discover structures such as line segments or branches. In contrast to these approaches, we construct a tree modeling system which takes as input the texts. Lee et al. introduced a new deep learning-based framework for generating tree 3D models represented as L-system strings [12]. A transformer of this method can encode hierarchical tree-like string structures. This deep neural model is trained to produce the output strings instead of writing the rules. This model can only generate tree models close to the learning data: non-learned tree types cannot be generated. Senn et al. proposed a neural network that learns rules from noisy L-system strings [1]. However, the results they showed are limited to the 2D "dragon curve," which can be represented by relatively simple rules. Jacob proposed a method to represent L-systems as genes in Genetic Programming (GP) [9]. Using this formulation, Chen et al. proposed a method to automatically evolve L-systems by employing a Convolutional Neural Network (CNN) as a fitness function to classify whether a shape is a tree or to classify tree species [3]. However, because these methods modify the rules themselves, they tend to generate non-tree-like shapes. In contrast, our method imposes stronger constraints on the L-system to facilitate the generation of plausible tree shapes.

2.2   Image-Based Tree Modeling

Various image-based methods for reconstructing tree models have been proposed. Neubert et al. introduced an approximate voxel-based tree volume estimated from input photographs with only limited user intervention [17]. A set of particles is generated according to the volume, and then the particles are traced downwards based on a 3D flow simulation. Tan et al. presented a method for generating tree 3D models from images with little user intervention [25]. This method reconstructs leaves from segmented source images. Obscured branches are predicted from the shape patterns of visible branches. In the subsequent work, Tan et al. proposed a 3D tree reconstruction method from a single image with user sketching [24]. In this method, the user draws at least two strokes in the tree image: the first stroke specifies the leaf region, the second stroke marks up the main trunk. Li et al. proposed a learning-based method from single photographs [13]. The reconstruction pipeline is defined based on three neural networks: masking out trees in input photographs, identifying a tree's species, and obtaining its 3D radial bounding volume. These methods can easily create tree models from images. However, image-based methods are sensitive for scenes in input images; when input images contain multiple trees or are difficult to decompose foreground and background, these methods might not be work well.

Chen et al. constructed a sketch-based tree modeling system [2]. This system selected the best matching model by comparing 2D projections of tree models and the input sketch. Then, branches are modeled via Markov random field, subject to the constraint of 3D projection to the sketch. While sketch-based methods do not face the problems like the image-based methods, detailed structures of branches and leaves are difficult to specify in the sketch-based methods.

2.3   Text-Based Generation Model

For evaluating similarities between images and texts, Radford et al. proposed a pre-trained model called CLIP, which predicts pairs of images and texts [22]. This model consists *Image Encoder* and *Text Encoder* which convert images/texts to feature embedding, respectively. The model is learned by jointly training Image Encoder and Text Encoder to maximize the cosine similarity of the image and text feature embedding. Our system adopts this CLIP for text-based modeling of trees. We obtain fitness between texts and tree models based on these pre-trained two encoders.

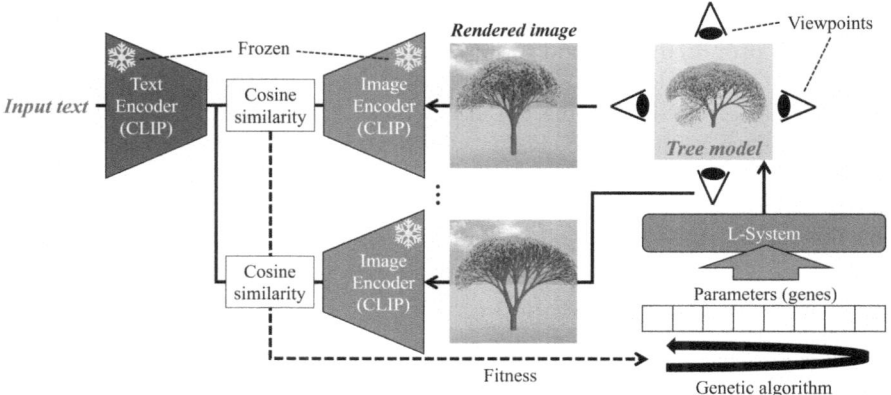

Fig. 2. Overview of our system.

Many text-based image generation methods have recently been developed. Frans et al. developed a text-driven method for generating drawings [6]. This method uses CLIP as an evaluation function and optimizes parameters of Bézier curves which represent drawings. Jiang et al. proposed a method for generating images of a human wearing clothes specified textual inputs [11]. Chen et al. proposed a text-driven framework to generate 4K+ resolution HDRIs [4]. Given a free-form text describing the scene, the corresponding HDRI is then synthesized.

Text-based methods for generating 3D models, textures, and motions have also developed. Jain et al. developed a 3D model generation from textual inputs by optimizing Neural Radiance Field(NeRF) with CLIP [10]. Poole et al. achieved synthesis from text to 3D without requiring a large-scale 3D dataset [19]. This was accomplished by utilizing a pretrained diffusion model that generates 2D images from text. However, this approach requires a significant amount of computation time. To address this issue, Lin et al. introduced a two-stage optimization framework [14]. Hong et al. proposed a text-driven framework for 3D avatar generation and animation [8]. This method adopts CLIP for supervising neural human generation, in terms of 3D geometry, texture and animation. Khalid et al. presented a technique for text-driven generation of a 3D model [16]. This method uses a pre-trained CLIP model and performs optimization on mesh parameters directly to generate shape, texture or both. Several methods have been proposed for generating 3D shapes as surfaces from texts using Diffusion models [26,28], but these methods need huge number of 3D data for learning. Sarafianos et al. generated 3D garments by deforming template meshes along to texts as a guide [23]. Zhang et al. proposed a method that enables non-rigid human generation with diverse appearance, full control over poses and viewpoints [27]. This method only requires 2D images for training. We also adopt CLIP in order to use texts as inputs, and our goal is to achieve text-driven tree modeling. In our experiments, we found that previous methods cannot generate models with complex shapes, such as trees, as shown in Fig. 1.

Tree models are more complex than the models targeted by the previous methods mentioned above, making it difficult to generate 3D models directly, as also discussed in Liu et al. [15]. Therefore, we propose a novel method for text-to-tree model generation by combining CLIP and L-system.

3 Our Method

Our objective is to obtain L-system parameters that generate a tree 3D model M_{tree} fit to the user-input text T_{usr}. We define this as an optimization problem to maximize the following evaluation function O:

$$\arg \max_{\mathbf{g}} O(T_{usr}, M_{tree}(\mathbf{g})), \qquad (1)$$

where, $\mathbf{g}$ is a vector comprising all the L-system parameters to be optimized, and a tree 3D model M_{tree} is generated from these parameters through the L-system. O is an evaluation function that assesses the similarity between the input text T_{usr} and the tree 3D model M_{tree} generated by the L-system.

However, directly evaluating the similarity between a tree model and text is difficult. Therefore, we adopt CLIP, which can assess the similarity between text and images. This leads to the rewriting of Eq. 1 as follows:

$$\arg \max_{\mathbf{g}} \sum_i O'(T_{usr}, I(M_{tree}(\mathbf{g}), i)), \qquad (2)$$

where, I is an image rendered from the generated tree model M_{tree}, i is the index of the viewpoint on rendering, and the total number of viewpoints is N_v. We set $N_v = 4$ for all our experiments. We adopt GA to solve our maximization problem, utilizing similarities obtained from CLIP as fitness values.

An overview of our system is illustrated in Fig. 2. First, the user inputs text representing the desired tree. Next, several individuals encoding L-system parameters are randomly generated as a gene cluster of the initial generation. Tree models are generated from these genes through L-system, and multiple images are obtained by rendering these tree models. Our method allows the user to select one from three different L-systems, each with distinct tree characteristics. Then, similarities between these images and the input text are calculated through CLIP and these are as fitness of each individual. Repeating these processes, our system detects the individual with the maximum similarity for the input text. Details of each part of our system are described in the following subsections.

3.1 Generating Tree Model Using L-System

We adopt the parametric L-system [5] to generate tree 3D models. Our system utilizes three different L-systems, each generating trees with distinct characteristics: Sympodial, Monopodial, and Ternary models (Fig. 3). Sympodial model

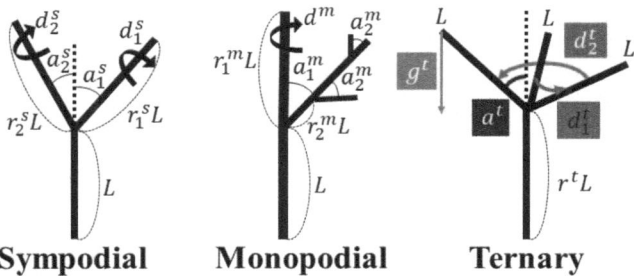

Sympodial   Monopodial   Ternary

Fig. 3. Correspondence between each tree generation model and parameters. L is length of the parent branch.

Table 1. L-system parameters for the tree model. Superscript characters represent the model types: s is Sympodial, m is Monopodial, and t is Ternary

a_1^s, a_2^s	rotation angle of branches in yaw direction
d_1^s, d_2^s	rotation angle of branches in roll direction
r_1^s, r_2^s	attenuation rate for length of branches
a_0^m	angle between trunk and lateral branches
a_2^m	rotation angle of branch
d^m	rotation angle of trunk in roll direction
r_1^m, r_2^m	attenuation rate for length of trunk and branch
d_1^t, d_2^t	rotation angle of branches in roll direction
a^t	angle from parent branch
r^t	elongation rate for length of branch
g^t	strength of gravity

generates trees with complex branching structures without a dominant central axis, making it suitable for broadleaf trees such as beeches and maples. Monopodial model produces trees with a single, upright trunk and alternating lateral branches, making it ideal for coniferous trees like pines and cedars. Compared to the other models, it offers a greater variety of heights and branch spreads, allowing it to be used for non-coniferous trees as well. Ternary model is similar to the Sympodial model but incorporates the effect of gravity, enabling the representation of weeping trees. Users select one of these three tree generation models based on their desired tree characteristics. Sympodial model follows the method of Curry [5], while Monopodial and Ternary models are based on those mentioned in [21], extended using the same scaling approach as Curry's Sympodial model. The parameters optimized for each model are shown in Table 1.

L-system comprises an initial string, rewriting rules, and parameters. We optimize only the parameters, because L-system can sufficiently represent diverse trees even if the initial string and rewriting rules are fixed. Tree generation is executed according to the following process. First, an initial string is transformed

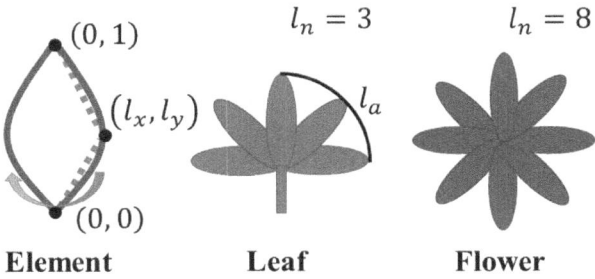

Fig. 4. Definitions of leaf and flower models.

Table 2. Parameters of our leaf and flower models.

l_x, l_y	control point of a base element
l_a	The range of angles for element placement (leaves only).
l_n	number of elements
l_s	scale of leaves and flowers
l_r, l_g, l_b	r, g, b values of leaves and flowers

iteratively based on predefined rewriting rules (see Prusinkiewicz's book [21] and Curry's thesis [5] for further details). In our experiments, a number of the transformation iterations is set to 8 for Ternary model and 14 for the other models. Subsequently, the system interprets the transformed string as control instructions for a virtual robot, termed Turtle, situated in three-dimensional space. The turtle follows the given instructions to generate a cylindrical mesh while creating branches from the lower part of the main trunk upward. The meshes are then smoothly connected, and bark material is applied to obtain the final tree model. If any branches, such as drooping ones, penetrate the ground, the corresponding meshes are removed.

Leaves and flowers are generated separately from the L-system. In our method, the shapes of leaves and flowers are defined using a procedural approach, and several parameters representing their shape and color are included in our leaf and flower models (Table 2). Since leaf shapes can be intuitively edited, users create leaves in advance to match the desired tree. During the optimization of the tree model, the pre-created leaves are attached to the branch tips, allowing them to be evaluated in the rendered images. Only the size and color of the leaves are optimized along with the L-system parameters.

The shapes of leaves and flowers are represented using one or more single elements (referred to as LF elements) defined by curves (Fig. 4, left). Half of an LF element is defined by two line segments connecting three coordinate points: $(0,0)$, (l_x, l_y) and $(0,1)$. This half is then subdivided to form a smooth curve, which is mirrored to create the complete shape of the LF element. For leaves (Fig. 4, center), l_n elements are arranged by incrementally varying their angles by l_a/l_n within the range of l_a on both sides from the top. Finally, a petiole is attached. Flowers (Fig. 4, right) are created by arranging l_n elements within a $360°$ range, rotating each element by $360/l_n$ degrees.

3.2   Optimizing Parameters Using GA

We optimize L-system parameters to obtain tree models aligned with the given textual inputs. We utilize GA for the optimization. The reason is that gradient-based approaches are not suitable for our problem, because resultant tree models might largely vary for small changes of L-system parameters. In fact, in our preliminary experiments, we have observed that the evaluation function values obtained using CLIP fluctuate significantly even for similar parameters. In this system, we handle real-valued parameters, but employ an algorithm similar to that used in conventional genetic algorithms, which handle binary values.

First, a vector with the same dimension as the number of the L-system parameters is initialized using uniform random values, forming the initial population. The optimal parameters are determined through selection, crossover, and mutation. Specifically, the two individuals with the highest similarity from the parent generation are selected first. Next, two-point crossover is repeatedly applied to these individuals to generate a new set of offspring equal in size to the parent generation. Finally, each element of all offspring is modified by adding a value obtained by multiplying a uniform random number by a mutation factor that controls the mutation strength. We found that applying mutations to all offspring, rather than probabilistically, tended to yield better results. In our experiments, each generation consisted of 20 individuals, with 50 iterations. The range of random values for initialization and mutation was set to -0.5 to 0.5, and the mutation factor was set to 0.33.

3.3   Evaluating Similarities Using CLIP

Fitness evaluation within GA adopts CLIP [22] to assess the similarity between input texts and output tree models. Tree models, derived from L-system parameters (gene), are rendered based on a local illumination model and multiple images are generated from diverse viewpoints. We utilize four viewpoints differing by $90°$ centered on the tree model. Additionally, to prevent the tree's shape from collapsing outside the image frame, the camera is adjusted forward or backward for each rendering to ensure the entire tree fits within the screen. Then, the textual input and resultant images are converted into feature vectors through Text and Image Encoders (refer to Fig. 2). Cosine similarities between these feature vectors are calculated, and then a minimum similarity value across viewpoints forms the fitness metric for each individual. By adopting the minimum value, we ensure that a model consistent with the text is generated even for the view with the lowest similarity.

Sympodial

A photo of a wide tree, full shot, with green leaves   *A photo of a wide tree, full shot, with Autumn leaves*   *A photo of a wide tree, full shot, with cobalt blue leaves*   *A photo of a red maple tree, full shot*   *A photo of an American elm tree, full shot*   *A photo of a cherry tree, full shot*

Fig. 5. Various results created using Sympodial model. Each example shows the result of running the same input with the same parameter settings multiple times.

4 Results

Figures 5, 6 show tree models generated through our system, accompanied by respective input texts. These resultant images are rendered using a physically-based renderer implemented in Houdini which is different from the renderer used in our optimization. Tree textures are used only for rendering these resultant images; textures are not contained in our optimization. The CLIP module in Python is used, and the CLIP model is ViT-B/32. We used a desktop PC with an Intel Core i9-13900K CPU, NVIDIA RTX A6000 GPU and 64 GB of memory to compute the examples. For all the examples, input texts are shown under each image. The leaf and flower models (Fig. 7) were selected based on the tree name specified in the input text. If a matching model was not available, "normal" was used instead. Additionally, "weeping willow" used "coniferous" leaves. Supplementary material includes videos demonstrating the rendered models.

In the three examples on the left of Fig. 5, only the leaf colors were varied. In all cases, the generated leaves match the specified colors. Notably, even for "cobalt blue," which does not exist in reality, the system successfully generated the specified color. In the three examples on the right of Fig. 5 and in Fig. 6, the input text specifies the names of actual tree species. The results demonstrate that the generated tree models resemble the actual appearance of the specified tree types. Notably, comparing "coniferous" and "acacia" in Fig. 6, "coniferous" exhibits a tall, slender form characteristic of coniferous trees, while "acacia" appears shorter and more spread out. Ternary model successfully represents weeping trees in all cases. However, since our system employs a genetic algorithm (GA), the generated tree shape may vary between executions, even when the

Fig. 6. Results created using Monopodial (left 3 column) and Ternary (right 3 column) models. Each example shows the result of running the same input with the same parameter settings multiple times.

same input text is used except for leaf color. The execution time for each run was approximately 30–40 minutes for Sympodial and Monopodial, and 20–30 minutes for Ternary. However, for "acacia", the execution time was 88 min, which is longer than the other examples. This is likely due to the increased number of mesh copies resulting from the large number of polygons composing the flowers.

The transition of the maximum similarity at each generation of the genetic algorithm is shown in Fig. 8. For clarity, one example from each model is presented. The number following the tree name corresponds to the column number in Figs. 5 and 6. In many cases, the similarity increases significantly in the first few generations, and after about 20 generations, the change becomes similar to a random walk. However, in the case of "red maple (2)", the similarity remained low for the first few generations and gradually increased over several dozen generations. This suggests that a certain number of optimization iterations are necessary for our system. In multiple trials for the same inputs, the similarity curve for "coniferous" remained relatively consistent, whereas for "red maple" and "weeping cherry", there were greater variations between trials. Specifically, the evaluation value for "weeping cherry" fluctuated significantly, indicating that the Ternary model is more sensitive to parameter changes in its evaluation.

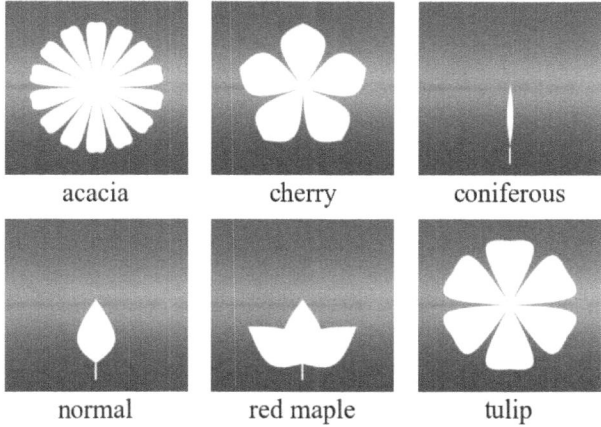

Fig. 7. Leaf and flower models used in our experiments.

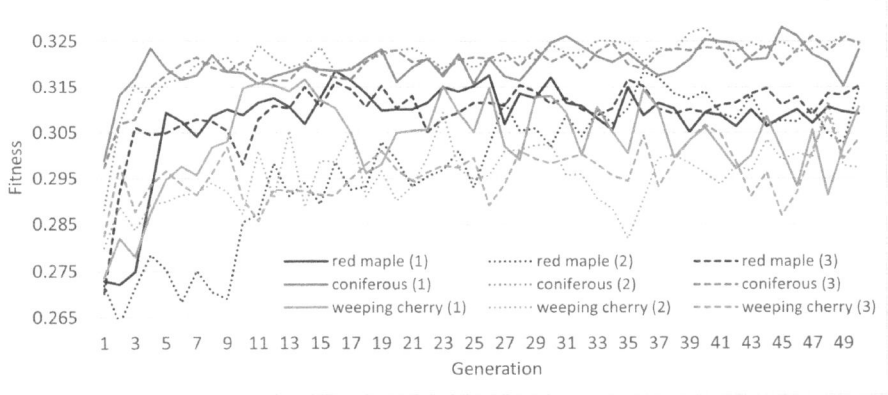

Fig. 8. The graph of similarity over iterations. (Color figure online)

5   Conclusions

This paper proposed a novel tree modeling system based on user-specified textual inputs. Leveraging L-system and optimizing its parameters through GA, and CLIP is utilized for calculating fitness values in GA. Our approach can generate tree models aligned with the given textual inputs.

However, there are cases where the generated tree differs from the actual one due to convergence to a local optimum. As a result, multiple executions of the system may be required in some cases. Further improvements in the optimization method will be a future challenge. In this method, the shapes of leaves and flowers, as well as tree textures, are not included in the optimization and need to be edited and prepared by the user. In the future, we plan to improve the method to include these elements in the optimization process. Furthermore, we confirmed that our method does not successfully generate unrealistic tree shapes such as "tree like a house" or "tree with a hole." While this paper focuses on the generation of plausible trees, we anticipate that extending our approach in the future to also represent such non-photorealistic shapes could enable a broader range of expressions.

References

1. Neural Lindenmayer Systems, Artificial Life Conference Proceedings, vol. ALIFE 2024: Proceedings of the 2024 Artificial Life Conference (2024). https://doi.org/10.1162/isal_a_00784,
2. Chen, X., Neubert, B., Xu, Y.Q., Deussen, O., Kang, S.B.: Sketch-based tree modeling using markov random field. ACM Trans. Graph. **27**(5) (2008). https://doi.org/10.1145/1409060.1409062,
3. Chen, X.E., Ross, B.J.: Deep neural network guided evolution of l-system trees. In: 2021 IEEE Congress on Evolutionary Computation (CEC), pp. 2507–2514 (2021). https://doi.org/10.1109/CEC45853.2021.9504827
4. Chen, Z., Wang, G., Liu, Z.: Text2light: zero-shot text-driven HDR panorama generation. ACM Trans. Graph. **41**(6) (2022). https://doi.org/10.1145/3550454.3555447
5. Curry, R.: On the evolution of parametric L-systems. University of Calgary, Department of Computer Science (1999)
6. Frans, K., Soros, L., Witkowski, O.: Clipdraw: exploring text-to-drawing synthesis through language-image encoders. In: Advances in Neural Information Processing Systems, vol. 35, pp. 5207–5218 (2022)
7. Guo, J., et al.: Inverse procedural modeling of branching structures by inferring L-systems. ACM Trans. Graph. **39**(5) (2020). https://doi.org/10.1145/3394105
8. Hong, F., Zhang, M., Pan, L., Cai, Z., Yang, L., Liu, Z.: Avatarclip: zero-shot text-driven generation and animation of 3d avatars. ACM Trans. Graph. **41**(4) (2022)
9. Jacob, C.: Genetic l-system programming. In: Davidor, Y., Schwefel, H.P., Männer, R. (eds.) Parallel Problem Solving from Nature – PPSN III, pp. 333–343. Springer, Heidelberg (1994)
10. Jain, A., Mildenhall, B., Barron, J.T., Abbeel, P., Poole, B.: Zero-shot text-guided object generation with dream fields . In: 2022 IEEE/CVF Conference on Computer Vision and Pattern Recognition, pp. 857–866 (2022). https://doi.org/10.1109/CVPR52688.2022.00094,
11. Jiang, Y., Yang, S., Qiu, H., Wu, W., Loy, C.C., Liu, Z.: Text2human: text-driven controllable human image generation. ACM Trans. Graph. **41**(4) (2022)
12. Lee, J.J., Li, B., Benes, B.: Latent L-systems: transformer-based tree generator. ACM Trans. Graph. **43**(1) (2023). https://doi.org/10.1145/3627101
13. Li, B., et al.: Learning to reconstruct botanical trees from single images. ACM Trans. Graph. **40**(6) (2021). https://doi.org/10.1145/3478513.3480525,
14. Lin, C.H., et al.: Magic3d: high-resolution text-to-3d content creation. In: IEEE Conference on Computer Vision and Pattern Recognition (CVPR) (2023)
15. Liu, Z., Wu, K., Guo, J., Wang, Y., Deussen, O., Cheng, Z.: Single image tree reconstruction via adversarial network. Graph. Models **117**, 101115 (2021). https://doi.org/10.1016/j.gmod.2021.101115

16. Mohammad Khalid, N., Xie, T., Belilovsky, E., Popa, T.: Clip-mesh: generating textured meshes from text using pretrained image-text models. In: SIGGRAPH Asia 2022 Conference Papers (2022). https://doi.org/10.1145/3550469.3555392
17. Neubert, B., Franken, T., Deussen, O.: Approximate image-based tree-modeling using particle flows. ACM Trans. Graph. **26**(3), 88es (2007). https://doi.org/10.1145/1276377.1276487,
18. Palubicki, W., et al.: Self-organizing tree models for image synthesis. ACM Trans. Graph. **28**(3) (2009). https://doi.org/10.1145/1531326.1531364,
19. Poole, B., Jain, A., Barron, J.T., Mildenhall, B.: Dreamfusion: text-to-3d using 2d diffusion. arXiv (2022)
20. Prusinkiewicz, P., Hammel, M.S., Mjolsness, E.: Animation of plant development. In: Proceedings of the 20th Annual Conference on Computer Graphics and Interactive Techniques, pp. 351–360 (1993). https://doi.org/10.1145/166117.166161,
21. Prusinkiewicz, P., Lindenmayer, A.: The Algorithmic Beauty of Plants. Springer, Cham (1990)
22. Radford, A., et al.: Learning transferable visual models from natural language supervision. In: International Conference on Machine Learning, pp. 8748–8763 (2021)
23. Sarafianos, N., Stuyck, T., Xiang, X., Li, Y., Popovic, J., Ranjan, R.: Garment3dgen: 3d garment stylization and texture generation (2024). https://arxiv.org/abs/2403.18816
24. Tan, P., Fang, T., Xiao, J., Zhao, P., Quan, L.: Single image tree modeling. ACM Trans. Graph. **27**(5) (2008). https://doi.org/10.1145/1409060.1409061
25. Tan, P., Zeng, G., Wang, J., Kang, S.B., Quan, L.: Image-based tree modeling. ACM Trans. Graph. **26**(3), 87es (2007). https://doi.org/10.1145/1276377.1276486
26. Yu, Z., et al.: Surf-d: high-quality surface generation for arbitrary topologies using diffusion models. arXiv preprint arXiv:2311.17050 (2023)
27. Zhang, J., et al.: Avatargen: a 3d generative model for animatable human avatars. In: Computer Vision – ECCV 2022 Workshops, pp. 668–685 (2023)
28. Zhou, J., Zhang, W., Ma, B., Shi, K., Liu, Y.S., Han, Z.: Udiff: generating conditional unsigned distance fields with optimal wavelet diffusion. In: Proceedings of the IEEE/CVF Conference on Computer Vision and Pattern Recognition (2024)
29. Šťava, O., Beneš, B., Měch, R., Aliaga, D.G., Krištof, P.: Inverse procedural modeling by automatic generation of L-systems. Comput. Graph. Forum **29**(2), 665–674 (2010). https://doi.org/10.1111/j.1467-8659.2009.01636.x

Virtual Guides and Crowd Behaviors: Understanding Evacuation Decision-Making in Virtual Reality

Ruochen Cao, Ziyuan Feng, Changyue Ma, Xin Wen, Yanrong Hao, Chenchen Zhang, Zequn Liang, Ziarmal Hussain, and Rui Cao[✉]

School of Software, Taiyuan University of Technology, Taiyuan, China
caorui@tyut.edu.cn

Abstract. Achieving realistic crowd simulation in Virtual Reality (VR) is crucial for applications such as training, emergency preparedness, and AI - driven crowd modeling. A key aspect of these simulations is understanding how individuals make decisions under various conditions. This work focuses on emergency scenarios. Specifically, this study investigates the influence of virtual guides (artificial agents), environmental familiarity, and crowd patterns on evacuation decision-making. Findings reveal that evacuees do not blindly follow artificial agents but integrate spatial and social cues when selecting routes. Compliance is influenced by the alignment between guide instructions, crowd movement, and prior spatial knowledge, with uneven crowd distributions exerting a stronger effect than familiarity. These insights contribute to the development of adaptive virtual agents, AI-enhanced crowd simulations, and VR-based evacuation training, supporting data-driven emergency response systems.

Keywords: Artificial Agents · Crowd Simulation · Evacuation Decision-Making

1 Introduction

Virtual crowd simulation is critical for urban planning, public safety, and AI-driven behavioral modeling, providing insights into human-agent interaction and group dynamics. In immersive Virtual Reality (VR) simulations, realistic decision-making enhances the credibility of artificial agents and improves predictive crowd behavior models. A key challenge lies in understanding how individuals process virtual guidance, integrate environmental familiarity, and respond to social cues such as crowd movement patterns, which collectively shape evacuation dynamics and route selection.

Research on evacuation behavior provides a structured framework for analyzing decision-making under uncertainty, particularly regarding guidance, environmental familiarity, and crowd distributions [34]. However, most studies focus on aggregate crowd movement rather than individual decision-making in VR environments, often assuming visible exit locations, which biases navigation choices.

This raises key questions such as how do individuals respond to virtual guidance when exits are obscured and how do environmental familiarity and crowd behavior shape compliance with artificial agents.

Decision-making in virtual crowds is influenced by environmental and social factors [21]. Environmental familiarity allows individuals to navigate independently of artificial agents, while crowd patterns shape route selection through herding behaviors or congestion avoidance [22]. However, the interplay between virtual guidance, spatial knowledge, and social cues remains underexplored, necessitating further VR-based crowd simulation research.

VR simulations offer an ecologically valid, controlled environment for studying human decision-making in virtual crowds. Unlike rule-based or physics-driven computational models, VR enables researchers to systematically analyze individual interactions with artificial agents and crowd behavior. While prior studies have examined neighbor behaviors, spatial awareness, and virtual signage effects [20,22], limited research has explored the combined effects of virtual agents, crowd patterns, and environmental familiarity in large-scale simulations.

This study investigates how virtual guides (artificial agents), environmental familiarity, and crowd patterns collectively influence route selection in VR-based crowd simulations. Specifically, we address 1) How do crowd patterns and environmental familiarity affect compliance with virtual guides? and 2) How do these three factors shape navigation when exits are not visible? Our contributions are twofold:

(1) We demonstrate how crowd patterns and environmental familiarity moderate the effectiveness of virtual guides, showing that evacuees do not follow artificial agents unquestioningly.
(2) We highlight the dominant influence of uneven crowd distributions over environmental familiarity in shaping navigation decisions, contributing to more realistic virtual crowd simulations.

The remainder of this paper is structured as follows: Sect. 2 reviews related work. Section 3 describes the methodology, including the experimental design, virtual environment, and data collection process. Section 4 presents the results on participant responses to virtual agents, crowd patterns, and environmental familiarity. Section 5 discusses the implications of these findings, while Sect. 6 outlines the studys limitations. Finally, Sect. 7 concludes with key findings and directions for future research.

2   Related Work

This section reviews human crowd simulation research, with a focus on key factors influencing individual decision-making in virtual environments. Additionally, it examines the role of virtual agents (e.g., virtual guides) and immersive VR simulations in advancing realistic crowd behavior modeling.

2.1 Crowd Simulation and Individual Decision-Making in Evacuations

Crowd simulation is essential for public safety, training, and virtual environments, offering insights into human movement dynamics and decision-making under constrained conditions. Traditional evacuation research is broadly classified into macroscopic models, which examine collective crowd behaviors, and microscopic models, which focus on individual decision-making processes. Computational approaches such as Reciprocal Velocity Obstacles (RVO) [19], cellular automata [10], and social force models [26] have been widely employed to simulate large-scale evacuations, evaluating evacuation time, route optimization, and herding effects.

At the individual level, decision-making is shaped by factors such as personality traits [9], stress levels [34], panic responses [29], neighbor behaviors [8], and environmental familiarity [11]. Among these, virtual guides (artificial agents) play a critical role in evacuees navigation choices. However, their effectiveness depends on interaction design, user trust, and their alignment with environmental and social cues.

2.2 Virtual Guides and Artificial Agents in Evacuations

In emergency evacuations, individuals are strongly influenced by the behavior of those around them [18]. These surrounding agents include both fellow evacuees and guiding figures [24,25]. Virtual guides serve as key decision-making aids in both real-world evacuations and VR-based crowd simulations [14]. Research has explored the impact of guide placement, number, and interaction strategies [30, 34]. While well-positioned virtual guides enhance evacuation efficiency, studies indicate that simply increasing the number of guides does not always improve decision-making [7,31].

Although prior studies have examined the macro-level effects of virtual guidance, individual responses to artificial agents remain underexplored. In immersive VR environments, evacuees must interpret and react to virtual agents dynamically, balancing competing inputs such as crowd movement and spatial familiarity [2,3]. Three primary factors influence compliance with virtual guidance:

- **Crowd patterns:** High-density groups influence route selection, leading to herding behaviors, though some evacuees actively avoid congestion [4,5,22].
- **Environmental familiarity:** Familiarity with an environment allows individuals to navigate without solely relying on artificial agents [11].
- **Guide reliability:** Virtual guides may be trusted or disregarded depending on their alignment with other environmental cues [16,34].

While these factors have been studied independently, their combined effects on virtual guide compliance remain largely unexplored, highlighting the need for a more integrated approach to artificial agent design.

2.3   Virtual Reality for Crowd Simulation and Evacuation Research

VR has emerged as a powerful tool for simulating human behavior in immersive environments, enabling researchers to create controlled yet highly realistic crowd interactions. Compared to real-world evacuation drills, VR simulations offer greater ecological validity, enhanced safety, and improved scalability. Prior research has validated VR-based evacuation training, demonstrating that VR scenarios accurately replicate real-world behaviors [1,6,23].

VR has been extensively used to study factors influencing crowd navigation, including neighbor behaviors [22], spatial knowledge and cognitive mapping [20], emergency signage effects [27], and route complexity [32]. However, limited research has systematically examined the interplay between virtual guides, crowd behavior, and environmental familiarity in VR-based simulations. Understanding these interactions is crucial for designing adaptive artificial agents and enhancing VR-based evacuation training and predictive crowd modeling.

3   Methodology

This study investigates the influence of virtual guides (artificial agents), crowd patterns, and environmental familiarity on evacuation decision-making. By systematically analyzing path selection behavior, the findings contribute to realistic agent-based modeling and AI-driven virtual human behavior simulation.

A virtual building evacuation scenario was developed with two routes of differing lengths. Non-Player Characters (NPCs) simulate crowd agents, while virtual guides provide directional cues. The study explores 1) The impact of virtual agents on real-time decision-making; 2) The interaction between crowd distributions, environmental familiarity, and artificial guidance; and 3) The combined effects of guides, crowds, and prior knowledge on evacuation behavior in VR.

3.1   Experimental Variables

This study examines three independent variables—guidance behavior, crowd patterns, and environmental familiarity—and two dependent variables—route selection and guide compliance.

Independent Variables:

1. Guidance Behavior (Virtual Agents as Artificial Guides)
   – No guide (baseline).
   – Virtual guide pointing left.
   – Virtual guide pointing right.
2. Crowd Patterns (Pre-Animated NPC Movement) NPCs were pre-animated to simulate evacuees moving towards the exits. Five predefined crowd distribution conditions were designed [20,33]:
   – 0:0: No evacuees visible.
   – 2:8: Two NPCs on the left, eight on the right.

- 8:2: Eight NPCs on the left, two on the right.
- 2:2: Two NPCs on both routes.
- 8:8: Eight NPCs on both routes.
3. Environmental Familiarity (Prior Spatial Knowledge)
    - Familiar: Participants explored the environment before the experiment.
    - Unfamiliar: No prior exploration.

Dependent Variable:

- Route Selection (Decision Outcome): Left (shorter) or right (longer) route.
- Guide Compliance: Guide Compliance Percentage

3.2   Virtual Representation

Map Design. The floor plan of the virtual environment is shown in Fig. 1. The experimental setup consists of one entrance, two exits, and three rooms, featuring two evacuation routes—a left route and a right route (illustrated by green arrows in the figure). The left route is shorter, while the right route is longer, introducing variability in escape distance. Fire hazard zones are marked with red rectangles, and blue solid dots denote decision points where participants make route choices.

To simulate realistic navigation uncertainty, each route includes both visible and non-visible sections. As illustrated in Fig. 1, yellow rectangles highlight the visible portions, while hidden sections require participants to rely on virtual guides (artificial agents) or crowd behavior for navigation. Specifically, the evacuation scenario included two routesleft and rightmarked with green arrows, with the left route being shorter in total length. Each route was divided into a visible and a non-visible section from the participant's viewpoint at the decision point (marked as a blue dot). Yellow rectangles indicated the visible sections, which were equidistant across both routes to prevent visual bias. The remaining sections were non-visible and differed in length, potentially affecting evacuation time. This visibility distinction was explicitly based on what participants could see before making a choice.

Virtual Scene Construction. The VR environment was developed in Unity3D with predefined experimental conditions, incorporating artificial agents (virtual guides) and NPCs (crowd animation) to create a controlled yet immersive evacuation scenario. The construction process comprised two stages: base environment construction and atmospheric enhancements, ensuring realism and ecological validity.

In the base environment construction phase, the building layout was designed based on real-world fire evacuation scenarios, with Unitys physics-based rendering applied to achieve lighting and textures. NPCs were pre-animated with predefined movement paths, simulating various crowd patterns.

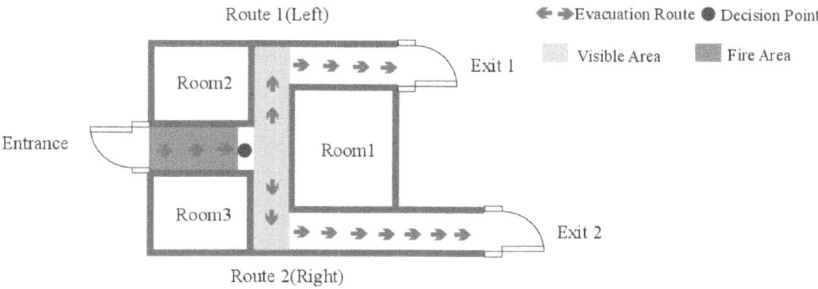

Fig. 1. Floor plan of the experimental scene.

The appearance, animations, and movement paths of the NPCs were implemented using the Population System PRO Unity asset. Specifically, the evacuation speed of crowd agents was set to 3.5 m/s, following the empirical work reported by Zhang et al. [33]. The guide character was implemented using the same base model system as other NPCs. To ensure a clear visual distinction, the guide was designed to resemble a security guard, which made it visually distinguishable from surrounding NPCs. Directional guidance was conveyed through a waving animation of the guide's arm to indicate the recommended route. The guide was positioned near the decision point, placed at the left or right corner of the front wall depending on the intended direction. Specifically, if the guide pointed to the left path, it was placed at the left corner; otherwise, it was placed at the right. Since the study focused solely on visual guidance, the guide provided no auditory cues. Since all NPCs moved at the same speed and followed consistent directional paths within each route, their collective movement did not introduce additional directional information beyond the explicitly provided guide's gestures.

To enhance immersion, fire and smoke effects heightened urgency, while real-time reflections and dynamic lighting contributed to a visually convincing fire scenario. Spatialized audio (fire crackling, alarms, and panic calls) reinforced the emergency atmosphere. A 5-second countdown timer introduced time pressure, simulating real-world constraints. After each trial, dynamic text-based feedback provided real-time progress updates to participants (i.e. after participants made a route decision, their choice was immediately displayed as text on the wall, as illustrated in Fig. 2 (c).

Figure 2 illustrates the virtual scene, depicting the virtual guide directing right and the NPC crowd distribution, with two NPCs on the left and eight on the right.

3.3   Experimental Design

This section provides a detailed description of the participants, experimental equipment, and procedure.

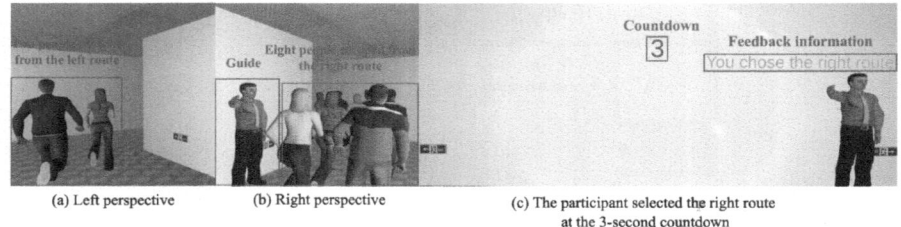

(a) Left perspective   (b) Right perspective   (c) The participant selected the right route at the 3-second countdown

Fig. 2. Experimental scene display.

Participants. A total of 40 participants (26 males, 14 females) were recruited from a university. Participants had an average age of 22.35 years (SD $= 2.479$, range: 18–27). Eligibility criteria required normal or corrected-to-normal vision, with no history of motion sickness in VR or any cardiovascular or neurological conditions that could affect participation. All participants provided informed consent prior to the experiment. This study was approved by the Ethics Committee under protocol number (TYUT2023111001).

Experimental Equipment. The experiment utilized an HTC Vive Pro headset (2880 × 1600 resolution) for immersive VR interaction. The virtual environment was rendered on a high-performance computer equipped with an Intel Core i7 processor and an NVIDIA RTX 4090 GPU. VR scenarios and NPC animations were developed in Unity 2018.3.6f1.

Experimental Procedure. The experiment employed a within-subject design with two counterbalanced sequences (P1 and P2) to control for potential order effects related to environment familiarity. In sequence P1, participants completed the unfamiliar-environment condition first, followed by the familiar-environment condition. Sequence P2 reversed this order. In the familiar-environment condition, participants completed an additional exploration phase, during which they used the controllers touchpad to freely navigate the building until they fully understood the layout (e.g., which route was shorter). This phase was omitted in the unfamiliar-environment condition. To ensure that participants—especially in sequence P2—did not recognize the identical layout across conditions and thereby bias results, we introduced a confounding map strategy. Before the experiment, participants were explicitly informed that the two experimental conditions would employ different layouts randomly selected from a pool of visually similar maps, differing only in the non-visible sections. In reality, the same layout was consistently used. This method effectively minimized potential interference from participants' spatial memory and enhanced experimental validity. Participants were assigned to these sequences in alternating order (P1-P2-P1-P2) to balance exposure.

The experimental process included three stages: pre-experiment briefing, training session, and formal experiment.

(1) Pre-experiment Briefing: Participants first signed an informed consent form. Experimenters then introduced the experimental scenario and task requirements through a standardized slide presentation. Participants were informed they would enter a virtual building, encounter a simulated fire event, and make route decisions at a bifurcation point based on available cues. They were also informed about the two experimental conditions (familiar and unfamiliar), and the confounding map strategy was clearly explained to them (i.e., each condition using a visually identical visible section with differences only in non-visible sections). Lastly, participants viewed a short demonstration video to familiarize themselves with the appearance and behaviors of NPCs and the virtual guide, ensuring recognition of these critical elements during the formal trials.

(2) Training Session: After the briefing, participants underwent a training session to familiarize themselves with VR equipment and experimental procedures. This session did not include experimental stimuli such as crowd agents, guides, fire visuals, or sound effects, to prevent procedural confusion or premature exposure. Participants repeated this training phase as needed until they confirmed familiarity and comfort with both equipment and trial processes.

(3) Formal Experiment: Participants proceeded to the formal experiment following their assigned sequence (P1 or P2). In formal trials, the experimental conditions manipulated three primary factors: environment familiarity, crowd flow patterns, and presence of directional guidance. Following completion of both experimental conditions, participants completed a questionnaire assessing perceived ecological validity and evaluating how experimental factors affected their route-choice decisions.

4   Results

This section presents the analysis of how environmental familiarity and crowd patterns influence the effectiveness of virtual guides (artificial agents) and how these three human-related factors interact to shape route selection behavior in immersive VR simulations. As the data in this study were categorical (e.g., route choice, compliance), we used Pearson chi-square tests and binary logistic regression [13,17]. These methods are common in evacuation studies. A significance level of $p < 0.05$ was adopted for all tests. Sections 4.1–4.3 address Research Question 1, and Sect. 4.4 addresses Research Question 2.

4.1   Effect of Environmental Familiarity on Artificial Agent Effectiveness

To examine how environmental familiarity impacts the effectiveness of virtual guides (artificial agents), we analyzed participant decision-making under the following conditions:

1. A virtual guide was present, functioning as an artificial agent providing directional cues.
2. Participants were categorized as either familiar or unfamiliar with the environment.
3. No crowd (0:0 pattern) was present to isolate the guides influence.

Figure 3 illustrates participant compliance rates when the artificial agent pointed to either the left or right route, segmented by environmental familiarity. A Pearson chi-square test revealed that when the guide pointed to the left route, compliance rates did not significantly differ between familiar and unfamiliar participants ($\chi^2 = 1.053$, $p = 0.305 > 0.05$). However, when the guide pointed to the right route, a significant difference was observed $\chi^2 = 13.867, p < 0.001$), indicating that environmental familiarity plays a moderating role in how individuals respond to virtual guidance in VR.

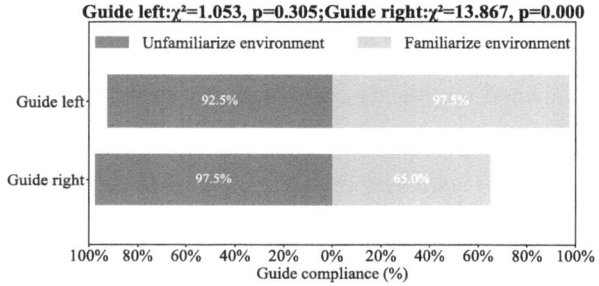

Fig. 3. Guide compliance graph with different levels of environment familiarity.

4.2   Effect of Crowd Simulation on Artificial Agent Effectiveness

To assess how pre-animated NPCs representing evacuees (crowd patterns) affect artificial agent effectiveness, we analyzed decision-making under the following conditions:

1. A virtual guide was present, directing participants toward one of the two routes.
2. Participants were unfamiliar with the environment, ensuring that decisions were not influenced by prior knowledge.
3. The crowd distribution varied across all predefined configurations.

Figure 4 presents compliance rates for different crowd patterns when the artificial agent pointed to either the left or right route. A Pearson chi-square test revealed that when the guide pointed left, compliance rates significantly differed across crowd conditions (($\chi^2 = 37.749, p < 0.001$). Similarly, when the guide pointed right, crowd patterns continued to have a significant effect (($\chi^2 = 18.767, p < 0.05$). These results indicate that individuals in immersive VR simulations are highly sensitive to virtual crowd behavior, which interacts with artificial agent guidance to influence evacuation decisions.

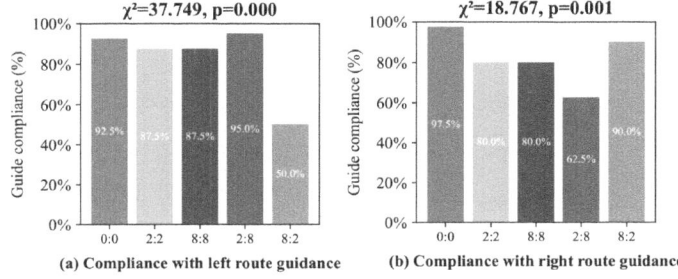

Fig. 4. Guidance compliance graph for different crowd patterns. (a) Left: Guide pointing to the left. (b) Right: Guide pointing to the right.

4.3 Interaction Between Environmental Familiarity and Crowd Simulation on Artificial Agent Effectiveness

To analyze how environmental familiarity and crowd behaviors jointly influence compliance with artificial agents, we examined four experimental conditions: Participants familiar with the virtual environment, two asymmetric crowd patterns (2:8 and 8:2), and presence of a virtual guide directing left or right These conditions were classified into four experimental groups:

- A1: Familiar environment, 2:8 crowd pattern, virtual guide pointing left.
- B1: Familiar environment, 8:2 crowd pattern, virtual guide pointing right.
- B2: Familiar environment, 8:2 crowd pattern, virtual guide pointing left.
- C1: Familiar environment, 2:8 crowd pattern, virtual guide pointing right.

Figure 5 illustrates compliance rates across these conditions. The results suggest that environmental familiarity reduces reliance on artificial agents, particularly when crowd distributions strongly favor one route. This supports the hypothesis that VR-based crowd dynamics significantly impact human decision-making in artificial agent-guided environments.

4.4 Influence of Virtual Guides, Crowd Patterns, and Environmental Familiarity on Route Selection

Table 1. Levels and values for guides behavior.

Participants' route choices	No guide	Guide left	Guide right	$\chi 2$	P-value
Left route	235	335	117		
Right route	165	65	283		
Left route selection rate	58.75%	83.75%	29.25%	243.275	<0.001

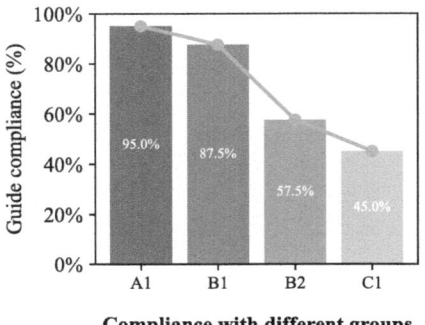

Fig. 5. Guide compliance graph with different groups.

Table 2. Levels and values for crowd patterns.

Participants' route choices	0:0	2:2	8:8	2:8	8:2	$\chi2$	P-value
Left route	140	143	156	170	78		
Right route	100	97	84	70	162		
Left route selection rate	58.33%	59.58%	65.00%	70.83%	32.50%	84.70	<0.001

Table 3. Levels and values for environmental familiarity.

Participants' route choices	Unfamiliar	Familiar	$\chi2$	P-value
Left route	302	385		
Right route	298	215		
Left route selection rate	50.33%	64.17%	23.475	<0.001

To examine the combined effects of virtual guides (artificial agents), crowd distributions, and environmental familiarity on route selection, categorical data were analyzed using contingency tables. Results showed that virtual guide behavior significantly influenced route selection ($\chi^2 = 243.275, p < 0.001$, Table 1), while crowd patterns ($\chi^2 = 84.70, p < 0.001$, Table 2) and environmental familiarity ($\chi^2 = 23.475, p < 0.001$, Table 3) also played key roles. The proportion of participants selecting the left route varied significantly across conditions, highlighting the complex interplay of individual, social, and environmental factors in VR-based evacuations.

A binary logistic regression model further quantified these effects (Table 4). Virtual guides strongly influenced route selection: participants were 4.436 times more likely to choose a left route when the guide pointed to the left than when the guide did not ($p < 0.05, OR = 4.436, CI = [3.085, 6.379]$). In contrast, participants were 0.244 times more likely to choose the left route when the guide pointed to the right than without the guide ($p < 0.05, OR = 0.244, CI =$

Table 4. Results of the binary logistic model.

	B	S.E.	P	OR	95% CI	
					Lower	Upper
Constant	0.036	0.185	0.844	1.037		
Guides' Behavior						
No Guides (Control)			0.000			
Guide Left	1.490	0.185	0.000	4.436	3.085	6.379
Guide Right	−1.411	0.162	0.000	0.244	0.178	0.335
Crowd Models						
0:0 (Control)			0.000			
2:2	0.070	0.215	0.747	1.072	0.703	1.636
8:8	0.378	0.218	0.083	1.459	0.952	2.236
2:8	0.728	0.223	0.001	2.071	1.338	3.203
8:2	−1.443	0.224	0.000	0.236	0.152	0.367
Environmental Familiarity						
Unfamiliar (Control)			0.000			
Familiar	0.798	0.142	0.000	2.221	1.683	2.931

$[0.178, 0.335]$), indicating that guide directionality plays a critical role in decision-making under uncertainty.

Crowd patterns also strongly affected route selection. Compared to the no-crowd condition, uniform crowd distributions (2:2 and 8:8) had no significant impact ($p = 0.747, p = 0.083$). However, asymmetric population distributions (2:8 and 8:2) significantly influenced decision making compared to no-crowd condition. In the 2:8 condition, participants were 2.071 times more likely to choose the left route ($OR = 2.071, CI = [1.338, 3.203]$), while in the 8:2 condition, they were 0.236 times more likely to select the left route ($OR = 0.236, CI = [0.152, 0.367]$), suggesting that crowd distributions may override artificial agent guidance, particularly in high-density scenarios.

Finally, environmental familiarity reduced reliance on virtual guides and crowd behaviors, with familiar participants 2.221 times more likely to choose the left route than those unfamiliar with the layout ($p < 0.05, OR = 2.221, CI = [1.683, 2.931]$). This underscores the importance of spatial knowledge in emergency navigation and VR-based evacuation training.

5   Discussion

This section discusses the findings presented in Sect. 4, focusing on how environmental familiarity and crowd patterns influence the effectiveness of virtual guides (artificial agents) and their combined impact on route selection in immersive VR simulations.

5.1 Effect of Environmental Familiarity on Artificial Agent Effectiveness

As shown in Sect. 4.1, environmental familiarity did not significantly affect compliance rates when the artificial agent directed participants toward the left route. This can be attributed to two factors. First, unfamiliar participants relied heavily on the artificial agent, as they lacked prior spatial knowledge and treated the guides instructions as the primary decision-making cue. Second, familiar participants already recognized the left route as shorter, naturally aligning their decision with the agents recommendation.

Since most unfamiliar participants defaulted to following the artificial agent, the difference between familiar and unfamiliar groups was negligible. However, when the artificial agent directed participants to the right route, environmental familiarity significantly influenced compliance. Familiar participants recognized the left route as shorter, leading them to disregard the agents guidance. This suggests that virtual guides do not dictate behavior in VR evacuations, but rather interact with participants spatial awareness, reinforcing that evacuees integrate multiple cognitive factors when making decisions in VR-based crowd simulations [12].

5.2 Effect of Crowd Simulation on Artificial Agent Effectiveness

As demonstrated in Sect. 4.2, pre-animated NPCs significantly influenced compliance rates, particularly in asymmetric crowd patterns, where compliance dropped compared to uniform distributions. In balanced crowd distributions (e.g., 2:2, 8:8), participants perceived both routes as viable, leading to minimal compliance changes. However, in asymmetric conditions (e.g., 8:2, 2:8), individuals were more likely to deviate from artificial agent instructions, prioritizing social cues from the virtual crowd over guide recommendations.

For instance, when the artificial agent directed participants left, but the crowd distribution favored right (8:2), only 50% complied. Similarly, when the agent directed right, but the crowd favored left (2:8), compliance was only 62.5%. These findings suggest that participants in immersive VR evacuations integrate both agent guidance and perceived environmental conditions, highlighting a complex interaction between individual decision-making and social influences.

Two key factors explain this behavior. First, route ambiguity weakens reliance on virtual guides—when both routes contain visible evacuees and signage, participants view them as equally viable. Second, congestion and safety concerns influence route selection—when the artificial agent's direction aligns with a crowded route, participants may anticipate delays and risks, prompting some to strategically avoid congestion, even against the agents guidance.

These results emphasize the need for VR-based artificial agents to adapt to real-time crowd dynamics, improving guidance reliability in evacuation simulations. Designing adaptive virtual guides that dynamically respond to human behavior and environmental factors is essential for enhancing VR-based training and crowd modeling.

5.3   Interaction Between Environmental Familiarity and Crowd Simulation on Artificial Agent Effectiveness

Previous sections examined environmental familiarity and crowd behaviors separately, but their combined effects provide deeper insights into how evacuees navigate conflicting environmental and social cues in VR evacuations. As shown in Fig. 5, compliance with artificial agents varied significantly based on the alignment between environmental familiarity and crowd patterns. When both factors supported the agents guidance (Condition A1), compliance reached 95%, while in conflicting conditions (Condition C1), compliance dropped to 45%, demonstrating that contradictory cues significantly weakened agent influence.

When only one factor aligned with the artificial agent, compliance differed notably. In Condition B1 (crowd behavior aligned, environmental familiarity opposed), 87.5% followed the guide. However, in Condition B2 (environmental familiarity aligned, crowd behavior opposed), compliance fell to 57.5%, a 30% difference, suggesting that virtual crowd behaviors exert a stronger influence than environmental familiarity. This indicates that participants prioritize social cues over prior spatial knowledge when making real-time navigation choices in VR.

These findings challenge the assumption that environmental familiarity is the dominant factor in evacuation decision-making, emphasizing the importance of real-time crowd interactions in shaping behavior. To enhance effectiveness, AI-driven virtual guides in VR-based training and simulations must dynamically adapt to crowd variations, improving evacuation efficiency and realism in immersive environments.

5.4   Influence of Virtual Guides, Crowd Patterns, and Environmental Familiarity on Route Selection

Findings from Sect. 4.4 reveal three key takeaways regarding evacuation decision-making in VR environments. First, artificial agents significantly influence route selection—when the virtual guide exists, most individuals are willing to follow the instructions of the guide, which highlights the importance of human-agent interaction in VR evacuation. However, their effectiveness depends on environmental and social factors.

Second, asymmetric crowd distributions impact decisions more than uniform ones—In uniform conditions (e.g., 2:2, 8:8), participants showed no strong preference for a particular route. However, in asymmetric conditions (e.g., 8:2, 2:8), they favored the less crowded route, aligning with Haghani et al. [15] and Teng et al. [28], but contradicting Lin et al. [22]. This discrepancy may stem from spatial complexity in large VR environments, evacuees may follow the majority due to navigation uncertainty, while in simpler spaces, high-density areas are perceived as bottlenecks, leading individuals to actively avoid crowded routes.

Finally, environmental familiarity influences route selection Familiar participants were more likely to choose the shorter left route, supporting prior findings [17]. This suggests that prior spatial knowledge reduces reliance on virtual guides and crowd cues, enabling individuals to navigate based on learned environmental features rather than reactive decision-making.

These findings underscore the complex interplay between artificial agents, crowd behavior, and spatial familiarity, providing insights for VR-based evacuation training and AI-driven crowd simulations.

6   Limitations

This study has several limitations. First, NPCs followed predefined movement patterns rather than dynamically responding to participants, which may not fully capture real-time social interactions. However, since the study focused on perceptions of static crowd distributions, this design was sufficient for analyzing decision-making trends. Second, the virtual environment featured only two evacuation routes, which may limit generalizability to more complex architectural settings with multiple decision points. Finally, most participants were VR novices, and their first-time exposure to the technology may have impacted performance and decision-making.

7   Conclusion

Realistic crowd simulation is essential for virtual training, emergency preparedness, and AI-driven evacuation modeling. Understanding real-time decision-making in immersive VR environments provides valuable insights into human-agent interactions and group dynamics. This study examined how evacuees respond to artificial agents (virtual guides), environmental familiarity, and crowd patterns, contributing to predictive evacuation modeling and virtual agent design.

Findings reveal that evacuees integrate multiple information sources rather than relying solely on artificial agents, highlighting the interplay between guidance, spatial knowledge, and social influences in route selection. Decision-making is highly sensitive to the alignment between agent instructions and external cues, underscoring the need for strategically designed virtual agents that adapt to conflicting information sources. Additionally, uneven crowd distributions strongly impact route selection, as individuals prioritize less crowded pathways over following the majority, emphasizing the importance of nuanced social behavior modeling in VR-based crowd simulations.

These insights advance AI-driven crowd simulation, predictive evacuation modeling, and adaptive virtual agents. Future research should explore intelligent artificial guides that dynamically adjust to real-time human interactions, bridging the gap between virtual agent design and realistic emergency training in VR.

Acknowledgements. This study was supported by Shanxi Scholarship Council of China (2023-036), the Natural Science Foundation of Shanxi (202303021222020), the Open Project Program of State Key Laboratory of Virtual Reality Technology and Systems, Beihang University (No.VRLAB2024B06).

References

1. Arias, S., Mossberg, A., Nilsson, D., Wahlqvist, J.: A study on evacuation behavior in physical and virtual reality experiments. Fire Technol. **58**(2), 817–849 (2022)
2. Bode, N.W., Kemloh Wagoum, A.U., Codling, E.A.: Human responses to multiple sources of directional information in virtual crowd evacuations. J. R. Soc. Interface **11**(91), 20130904 (2014)
3. Bode, N.W., Kemloh Wagoum, A.U., Codling, E.A.: Information use by humans during dynamic route choice in virtual crowd evacuations. R. Soc. Open Sci. **2**(1), 140410 (2015)
4. Bönsch, A., Ehret, J., Rupp, D., Kuhlen, T.W.: Wayfinding in immersive virtual environments as social activity supported by virtual agents. Front. Virtual Real. **4**, 1334795 (2024)
5. Bönsch, A., Güths, K., Ehret, J., Kuhlen, T.W.: Indirect user guidance by pedestrians in virtual environments. In: ICAT-EGVE (Posters and Demos), pp. 7–8 (2021)
6. Bourhim, E.M., Cherkaoui, A.: Simulating pre-evacuation behavior in a virtual fire environment. In: 2018 9th International Conference on Computing, Communication and Networking Technologies (ICCCNT), pp. 1–7. IEEE (2018)
7. Cao, S., Song, W., Lv, W.: Modeling pedestrian evacuation with guiders based on a multi-grid model. Phys. Lett. A **380**(4), 540–547 (2016)
8. Chen, A., He, J., Liang, M., Su, G.: Crowd response considering herd effect and exit familiarity under emergent occasions: a case study of an evacuation drill experiment. XXPhys. A **556**, 124654 (2020)
9. Chen, N., Zhao, M., Gao, K., Zhao, J.: Experimental study on the evaluation and influencing factors on individual's emergency escape capability in subway fire. Int. J. Environ. Res. Public Health (2021)
10. Chen, Y.X., Song, Y.H., Huo, F.Z.: Simulation of crowd evacuation behaviours at subway stations under panic emotion. Int. J. Simul. Model. (IJSIMM) **22**(4) (2023)
11. Fu, M., Liu, R., Liu, Q.: How individuals sense environments during indoor emergency wayfinding: an eye-tracking investigation. J. Build. Eng. **79**, 107854 (2023)
12. Fu, M., Liu, R., Zhang, Y.: Do people follow neighbors? An immersive virtual reality experimental study of social influence on individual risky decisions during evacuations. Autom. Constr. **126** (2021)
13. Fu, M., Liu, R., Zhang, Y.: Why do people make risky decisions during a fire evacuation? Study on the effect of smoke level, individual risk preference, and neighbor behavior. Saf. Sci. **140**, 105245 (2021)
14. Gan, Q., Liu, Z., Liu, T., Chai, Y.: An indoor evacuation guidance system with an AR virtual agent. Procedia Comput. Sci. **213**, 636–642 (2022)
15. Haghani, M., Sarvi, M.: 'herding' in direction choice-making during collective escape of crowds: how likely is it and what moderates it? Saf. Sci. **115**, 362–375 (2019)
16. Huo, F., Li, C., Li, Y., Lv, W., Ma, Y.: An extended model for describing pedestrian evacuation considering the impact of obstacles on the visual view. XXPhys. A **604**, 127932 (2022)
17. Kinateder, M., Comunale, B., Warren, W.H.: Exit choice in an emergency evacuation scenario is influenced by exit familiarity and neighbor behavior. Saf. Sci. **106**, 170–175 (2018)
18. Kinateder, M., Warren, W.H.: Social influence on evacuation behavior in real and virtual environments. Front. Rob. AI **3**, 43 (2016)

19. Li, J., Zhang, H.: Crowd evacuation simulation research based on improved reciprocal velocity obstacles (rvo) model with path planning and emotion contagion.
Transp. Res. Rec. **2676**, 740–757 (2021)

20. Lin, J., Cao, L., Li, N.: How the completeness of spatial knowledge influences the
evacuation behavior of passengers in metro stations: a vr-based experimental study.
Autom. Constr. **113**, 103136 (2020)

21. Lin, J., Li, N., Rao, L.L., Lovreglio, R.: Individual wayfinding decisions under
stress in indoor emergency situations: a theoretical framework and meta-analysis.
Saf. Sci. **160**, 106063 (2023)

22. Lin, J., Zhu, R., Li, N., Becerik-Gerber, B.: Do people follow the crowd in building
emergency evacuation? A cross-cultural immersive virtual reality-based study. Adv.
Eng. Inf. **43**, 101040 (2020)

23. Liu, R., Becerik-Gerber, B., Lucas, G.M.: Effectiveness of VR-based training on
improving occupants' response and preparedness for active shooter incidents. Saf.
Sci. **164**, 106175 (2023)

24. Rıos, A., Mateu, D., Pelechano, N.: Follower behavior in a virtual environment. In:
Virtual Humans and Crowds for Immersive Environments (VHCIE), IEEE. IEEE
(2018)

25. Ríos, A., Pelechano, N.: Follower behavior under stress in immersive VR. Virtual
Real. **24**(4), 683–694 (2020)

26. Shao, X., Feng, J., Wang, J., Wang, Y.: Research on emergency evacuation behavior
rules of pedestrians under fire and explosion accidents in chemical parks considering
social relationships. J. Loss Prev. Process Ind. **87**, 105244 (2024)

27. Tang, C.H., Wu, W.T., Lin, C.Y.: Using virtual reality to determine how emergency
signs facilitate way-finding. Appl. Ergon. **40**(4), 722–730 (2009)

28. Teng, Q., Wang, X., He, W., Pan, G., Mao, Y.: An investigation into the influence of
context effects on crowd exit selection under gender difference in indoor evacuation.
Front. Psychol. (2024)

29. Wang, G., et al.: Heterogeneous crowd dynamics considering the impact of personality traits under a fire emergency: a questionnaire & simulation-based approach.
XXPhys. A **610**, 128411 (2023)

30. Yang, X., Dong, H., Wang, Q., Chen, Y., Hu, X.: Guided crowd dynamics via
modified social force model. XXPhys. A **411**, 63–73 (2014)

31. Yang, X., Dong, H., Yao, X., Sun, X.: Effects of quantity and position of guides on
pedestrian evacuation. In: 2015 IEEE 18th International Conference on Intelligent
Transportation Systems, pp. 1317–1322. IEEE (2015)

32. Zhang, M., Ke, J., Tong, L., Luo, X.: Investigating the influence of route turning
angle on compliance behaviors and evacuation performance in a virtual-reality-
based experiment. Adv. Eng. Inf. **48**, 101259 (2021)

33. Zhang, M., Xu, R., Siu, M., Luo, X.: Human decision change in crowd evacuation:
a virtual reality-based study. J. Build. Eng. **68**, 106041 (2023)

34. Zhang, P.: Experimental study on evacuation behavior with guidance under high
and low urgency conditions. Saf. Sci. **154**, 105865 (2022)

Visualizing the Invisible: An Efficient Framework for Microscopic Visualization

Haoran Jia[1], Baijun Chen[2], and Nan Xiang[1(✉)] (iD)

[1] Department of Computing, Xian Jiaotong-Liverpool Uiversity,
Suzhou 215123, China
nan.xiang@xjtlu.edu.cn
[2] School of Digital Media and Design Arts, University of Posts and
Telecommunications, Beijing 100876, China

Abstract. The growing focus on microscopic entities such as cells or viruses in medical education and public health has highlighted the need for better visualizations of microscopic life. Traditional methods like microscopy provide detailed images but are often hard for non-specialists to understand. Existing 3D models for visualization are mostly manually created and face issues with accuracy, time, and cost, limiting their applicability in large-scale educational and outreach efforts. This project presents an efficient and high-quality visualization framework that directly generates high-fidelity 3D models from real biological scanning data. The proposed approach integrates 3D reconstruction, texture mapping, coloring, and lighting, enabling the creation of detailed and accurate microscopic models with reduced labor and time costs. By overcoming the limitations of existing methods, this framework has the potential to enhance both medical education and public engagement with the microscopic world, offering an efficient, scalable, and accurate solution for visualizing complex biological structures.

Keywords: Virus Visualization · Scientific Illustration · Volumetric Rendering

1 Introduction

In recent years, the global impact of the COVID-19 pandemic [19] and the upgrading of global health strategies have significantly increased the focus on cells and viruses in both medical education and public health communication [6]. Scientific imagery is an important medium for vividly presenting microscopic biological structures and is widely used in related teaching and science popularization [23]. However, traditional hand-drawn scientific illustrations struggle to meet the growing public demand, and due to the specialised technical knowledge required in this field, the number of researchers and artists actively working on these topics remains relatively small, and biological samples are often limited. This has created a gap in accessible research materials for medical trainees and has restricted opportunities for the public to engage with and understand these microscopic entities [29]. At present, the primary methods for observing microscopic life forms involve light microscopy and transmission electron microscopy. While these methods provide high-resolution images of cell and virus morphology, they are fundamentally limited by their static 2D nature. These techniques fail to convey spatial relationships or internal structure dynamics, making them insufficient for interactive education and scientific storytelling [11]. Furthermore, hand-drawn illustrations, while useful for conceptual understanding, often introduce artistic bias and cannot ensure structural fidelity. Their lack of dimensional accuracy and consistency makes them unreliable for advanced educational or diagnostic purposes [8].

Highly realistic 3D modeling and visualization created using computer technologies has become an essential approach in addressing these challenges. Unlike traditional 2D visualizations, 3D models allow for more detailed, interactive, and intuitive representations of microscopic structures. Such models can significantly enhance both medical education and public engagement by providing dynamic, accurate visualizations of cells and viruses. Currently, most 3D models are manually created or edited by digital artists, with some relying on biological scanning images as references. However, these models often face challenges in terms of structural accuracy, as the manual creation process can introduce errors or oversimplifications. Furthermore, the labor and time costs associated with manually creating detailed 3D models make this approach inefficient and unsustainable for large-scale educational and outreach purposes. While some models are based on scanning data, they still suffer from issues related to resolution, textural accuracy, and completeness.Moreover, existing workflows often isolate the modeling, texturing, and rendering stages, resulting in fragmented pipelines that are difficult to standardize and optimize. A method that can efficiently and accurately generate 3D models of microscopic structures directly from biological scan data would offer significant potential, greatly improving the quality and accessibility of these visualizations with reduced labor and time costs.

However, there is currently a lack of a comprehensive end-to-end process available for efficiently transforming raw scan data into accurate, detailed 3D models for cells and viruses. Even though there are some methods of 3D reconstruction, they are often limited in various ways when used for microstructure modeling. For example, models generated from biological scans may require manual intervention to address structural inaccuracies or to apply realistic texturing and lighting, which limits their scalability and applicability in practical applications. Additionally, many approaches still require substantial post-processing work, such as refining textures or enhancing lighting effects, which can be both time-consuming and technically challenging. There remains an urgent need for a standardized pipeline that minimizes manual intervention, preserves structural integrity, and delivers high-quality visualizations tailored for both expert analysis and public understanding. In this paper, we propose a novel end-to-end pipeline that directly processes real scan data to create 3D models of microscopic structures. This process encompasses texture mapping, shading, and lighting, ensuring high-fidelity, accurate visualizations. The proposed approach aims to contribute significantly to the visualization of the microscopic world, offering a more efficient, scalable, and accurate solution for both medical education and public outreach.

2   Related Work

2.1   Microscopic Structure Visualization

The visualization of complex structures such as viruses has always been an important topic in scientific research at the microscopic scale. As early as 1930, transmission electron microscopy (TEM) was applied to project two-dimensional images using electron beams to penetrate ultrathin samples [2]. Subsequently, in the 1950s, X-ray Crystallography and Negative Staining were also applied to observe the structure of biomolecules [9]. However, the former requires viruses to form large binary crystals to be irradiated by X-ray and the latter requires viruses to be stained with heavy metal salts, which may damage the structure of the viruses. The latter requires the use of heavy metal salts to stain the virus, which may damage the structure of the virus itself, and the resolution of these three methods is relatively low. Cryo-EM was born.

Cryo-EM, as a cutting-edge technology in the field of structural biology, is capable of reconstructing the three-dimensional structures of viruses, proteins, and other microscopic samples at a resolution close to the atomic level (up to 7A). Compared with traditional X-ray crystallography, Cryo-EM has the advantages of simple preparation, no need for crystallization, and maintaining the in situ state of the samples, and is therefore widely used in virology research [27]. Public platforms such as the Electron Microscopy Database (EMDB) include a large number of viral 3D models obtained using cryo-EM. These high-precision data provide the basis for viral structure visualization, propagation mechanism research and drug target development.

In 2020, the School of Life Sciences at Tsinghua University obtained the 3D structure of a complete particle of Neocoronavirus with a resolution of up to 7.8 by cryo-electron microscopy. This study not only provides an important reference for the invasion mechanism and vaccine design of Neocoronavirus, but also lays a reliable structural foundation for the production of viral science images [27]. This project is based on similar data sources to construct a 3D model of viruses, and on this basis, rendering and science popularization visual design, so that the public can intuitively understand the morphology and structural characteristics of viruses.

2.2   Scan-Based Modeling and Volumetric Rendering

Scan data-driven 3D modeling (Scan-based Modeling) has been an important technological tool in recent years in the fields of medical imaging, materials science and biological visualization. With high-precision imaging devices such as CT (Computed Tomography), MRI (Magnetic Resonance Imaging) and Cryo-EM, researchers are able to acquire continuous slice data to reconstruct complex micro or internal structure models [22]. To transform these discrete 2D slice data into continuous, interactive 3D models, surface reconstruction techniques have traditionally been used. For example, the Marching Cubes algorithm (1987) is a classical method for iso-surface extraction, which generates polygonal meshes by finding regions of equal intensity values in voxel data, and is widely used in medical simulation and scientific visualization [21]. In addition, surface smoothing, mesh optimization, and multi-resolution reconstruction are also commonly used to improve the model quality and make it suitable for scenarios such as animation simulation, surgical navigation, or scientific display.

However, surface modeling methods still have limitations for representing highly complex, dense or translucent internal structures. In contrast, Volumetric Rendering does not require explicit extraction of surfaces, but directly simulates the illumination of 3D voxel data, which can realistically reproduce the visual characteristics of non-homogeneous materials and semi-transparent media by taking into account the optical properties of volumetric absorption, scattering, emission, and so on. This advantage makes volumetric rendering an important tool for medical visualization, virtual reality, film production, game development, and other fields. For example, the direct volume rendering algorithm proposed by Drebin et al. in 1988 breaks through the limitation of two-dimensional splicing reconstruction by simulating the process of light transmission within a volume, and realizes for the first time an efficient representation directly from data to three-dimensional images [3].

In recent years, visualization techniques based on volume rendering have benefited from the introduction of Physically Based Rendering models and neural networks to further improve the accuracy and performance. NeRF (Neural Radiance Fields) utilizes a multilayer perceptron (MLP) to encode the radiance fields of the scene and achieves high-fidelity rendering of complex volumes [13]; VolSDF improves the dynamic scene modeling capability by introducing the signed distance function (SDF) to separate the geometric and appearance features, and provides a New solutions [24]. Although volumetric rendering techniques have been widely used in medical visualization, their use for microscopic visualization is still relatively rare due to difficult data acquisition and technical and artistic challenges. Therefore, our work explore the possibility of applying 3D reconstruction and volume rendering technology in microscopic visualization, aiming to provide a high-quality visual presentation solution for virus science images by using the biological scanning data as direct input.

2.3   Comparison with Existing Visualization Platforms

Several platforms have been developed for molecular and microscopic structure visualization, including UCSF ChimeraX [12], Thermo Scientific$^T M$ Amira [18], and Visual Molecular Dynamics (VMD) [20]. These tools are widely used in structural biology and biomedical research but differ fundamentally from the goals and target audience of the pipeline presented in this work.

ChimeraX, developed by the University of California, San Francisco (UCSF), is a molecular visualization and analysis platform that supports cryo-EM, X-ray, and NMR structural data. It offers advanced volume rendering, surface manipulation, and scripting-based control for scientific analysis [12]. While ChimeraX is capable of basic 3D reconstruction and surface generation from volumetric data, it lacks the flexibility for downstream model editing and aesthetic refinement, it is also difficult to directly export digital assets for the development of interactive applications. In contrast to Blender-based workflows, ChimeraX does not support direct artistic customization or structural disassembly. This makes it more appropriate for structural biology analysis than for public science communication or educational visualization.

Amira is a commercial-grade 3D/4D biomedical and material science visualization suite that specializes in multi-modal image processing, segmentation, and quantitative analysis. It is widely used for CT, MRI, and EM data but presents a steep learning curve and high licensing costs [18], and it also lacks a user-friendly 3D art pipeline. The VMD is tailored toward simulation-driven workflows and is not optimized for aesthetic visualization or public engagement [20]. In contrast, the proposed pipeline emphasizes accessibility, visual clarity, and public usability. It enables non-specialists to generate high-fidelity and visually appealing virus illustrations through a low-barrier, end-to-end process using easy-to-access tools.

3   Method

3.1   Overview

We propose a visualization pipeline based on volume rendering combined with different artistic and technical detail optimizations, as shown in Fig. 1.

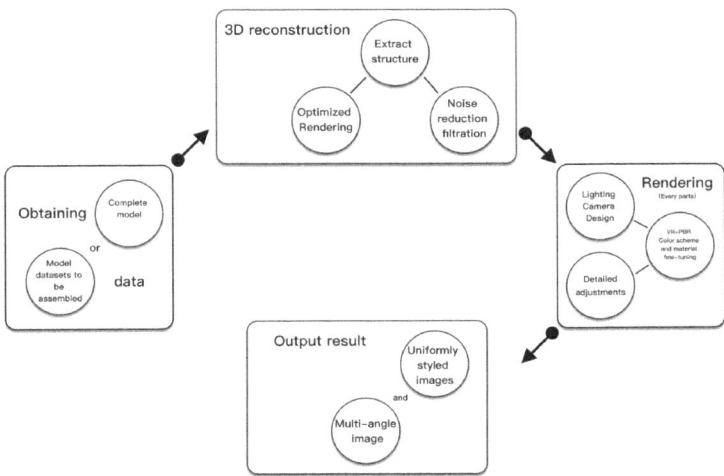

Fig. 1. Method overview.

The overall process includes 3D reconstruction, material and lighting settings, and scientific color matching and design, and the formation of standardized rendering templates ensures a unified visual style for different virus models and provides high-quality image materials for medical science popularization. Microscopy scanning data from public bioinformatics databases (such as EMDB) are selected. High-precision modeling and rendering are completed using the Blender platform, and finally output high-definition virus popular science images from multiple angles and under multiple lighting environments.

3.2 3D Model Acquisition

The 3D model acquisition for the virus relies on cryo-electron microscopy data with a resolution of about 3.6 from the EMDB database, including scans of complete viruses or partial virus structures. To address the large volume and heavy computational burden of cryo-EM data, the global size undergoes adjustment at the data import stage, which reduces volume resolution, minimizes memory consumption, and improves rendering efficiency.

In model processing, the density threshold adjustment node in Bioxel Nodes [5] extracts key structures, while density cropping and regional filtering remove background noise and abnormal low-density areas. Specifically, the *Threshold* node is used at this stage to eliminate voxels with low density values, which helps discard background artifacts and non-informative regions, allowing computational resources and visual attention to focus on the most relevant biological structures. The *Set Properties* node is employed to configure the visual and material properties of the model, including parameters such as model density, emission, specular intensity, roughness, and anisotropy, which collectively shape the visual quality and realism of the rendered virus model. Smoothing curve processing attenuates model surface noise and optimizes the visual effect. For viruses with more complex structures, such as the Hepatitis B virus, the process also requires importing the envelope, capsid, DNA, and other substructures, combining them, and then cutting or assembling virus components using the Sphere Cutter node (refer to Sect. 4 for more details on optimization for complex structures). Appropriately cutting local areas reveals the internal structure of the virus, providing an anatomical perspective for science popularization.

3.3 Rendering

The rendering of the virus model centers on the volumetric rendering capabilities of Bioxel Nodes [5], combined with PBR [16] for material adjustment and lighting design. In lighting design, a dual-light system enhances the visualization: a high-intensity white backlight (surface light, 90° diffusion angle) illuminates the overall silhouette, while a warm-toned point light simulates a shimmering environment and illuminates internal structures. The camera setup features a telephoto lens (typically with a focal length of 200 mm) with a black and gray background and "High Contrast" color management mode, ensuring a high-contrast visual style that mimics the micro-environment [5].

In terms of material settings, to simulate the semi-transparent optical properties of the virus envelope and the water environment in which the virus appears, parameters such as transparency, refractive index, subsurface scattering, and surface roughness undergo fine-tuning. These adjustments help restore the actual transmission and scattering behaviors of light rays within the microscopic structure. During the rendering process, initial outputs often suffered from visual issues such as depth blurring and loss of fine detail, particularly in overlapping semi-transparent structures. Solutions include repeated optimization of the refractive index and scattering coefficient, along with the introduction of local light attenuation and transparency fine-tuning in high-light areas (e.g., spiny proteins) to avoid overexposure while enhancing the sense of three-dimensionality and translucency.

3.4   Color Schemes

Since viruses do not naturally exhibit colors under visible light, direct restoration of their real-state appearance often lacks visual appeal and fails to meet the needs of easy recognition and aesthetics in science communication. Therefore, this project adopts a color scheme that balances scientific accuracy with artistic expression, enhancing both the scientific value and visual effect of the images.

The color scheme draws inspiration from the concept of "impression color" in micrography and the empirical basis of early biological staining experiments [7,14] . These approaches demonstrate that artificial coloring or optical processing effectively distinguishes different structures and highlights the layers and morphological features in microscopic visualization. Following this principle, this project applies partitioned color schemes to different structural areas of the virus model, helping viewers quickly understand the function and positional relationships of each part.

In terms of color layout, the external structural areas of the virus (e.g., attachment proteins, envelope) adopt a gradient color transition design to reflect the complexity and continuity of surface details. This approach enables viewers to clearly perceive morphological undulations and structural boundaries while enhancing the overall sense of hierarchy. In contrast, the internal structures of the virus (e.g., capsid, genetic material) utilize relatively stable and less varied color configurations to maintain simplicity and focus in the core areas, preventing visual clutter that may interfere with structural recognition. This "external richness, internal restraint" color logic highlights the overall hierarchical relationships while maintaining the visual center of gravity, guiding the audiences attention from the outside inward for an in-depth observation [4]. As shown in the Fig. 2, the visualization results of two viruses generated using our proposed method are presented, showing rich details.

4   Experiments and Results

As a preliminary experiment to verify the validity of the rendering pipeline, the complete 3D structural model of inactivated SARS-CoV-2 released by the

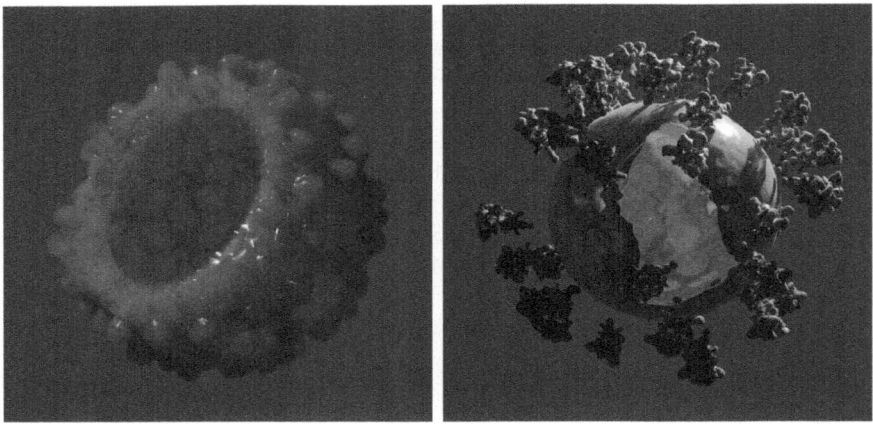

Fig. 2. Rendering results of HBV's and SARS-Cov-2's viral envelope and attachment protein, which can show a rich hierarchical structure.

School of Life Sciences of Tsinghua University was firstly used in this preliminary experiment. The model is based on cryo-electron microscopy technology and reaches a resolution of 7.8 , which has a high degree of structural integrity and scientific reliability. After verifying that the rendering pipeline works try to work on rendering other virus models and show the results.

4.1 Hardware Environment and Experimental Design

The experiment was done on a regular personal computer with the following hardware configuration:

- CPU: AMD Ryzen 9 5900HX with Radeon Graphics 3.30 GHz
- GPU: NVIDIA RTX 3080
- Memory: 64 GB
- Software: Blender 4.3.2, Bioxel Nodes

A total of 6 sets of virus rendering experiments were completed in this study, mainly involving the following datasets showed in Table 1:

Table 1. Virus Model Dataset

Virus Type	Data Source	Data Format	File Size	Voxel Count
SARS-CoV-2 [25]	EMDB	.map	512 MB	$2.720 \times 2.720 \times 2.720$ Å
HBV Envelope [17]	EMDB	.map	64 MB	$1.120 \times 1.120 \times 1.120$ Å
HBV HBsAg [15]	EMDB	.map	823 MB	$1.010 \times 1.010 \times 1.010$ Å
HBV Capsid [28]	EMDB	.map	30 MB	$1.938 \times 1.938 \times 1.938$ Å
HBV DNA and Polymerase [10]	EMDB	.map	301 MB	$1.063 \times 1.063 \times 1.063$ Å

4.2   Experiment on SARS-Cov-2

The complete SARS-CoV-2 dataset released by Tsinghua University was first imported into the pipeline. To balance visual quality and computational efficiency, the Bioxel Size parameter in the Bioxel Nodes plug-in was set to 5, which helped reduce volume resolution, memory consumption, and rendering time without significantly impacting visual detail.

At the initial stage of processing, a Threshold node was configured to remove voxels with a density value lower than 0.065. This operation helps focus computational resources and visual analysis on the most relevant structural regions by filtering out background noise and uninformative areas. After loading the data, the model was first centered using the Recenter node for subsequent editing, and then the realistic micro-surface effect was adjusted using the Set Properties node to enhance the material appearance by configuring the specular value to 0.5, the surface roughness to 0.2 and the model density to 0.3. Subsequently, a four-color gradient was applied using the Set Color by Ramp 4 node to enhance the models visual hierarchy, representing the transition from outer layers to the core density. The colors were set to E1D0FC (Alpha 1.0), FFE42D (Alpha 0.5), 3793FF (Alpha 0.5), and FFF8EC (Alpha 0.1), from the outside to the inside, to reflect the density transition from the virus surface to its core.

In the model detailing, considering the density overlap between the ribonucleoprotein (RNP) and the viral envelope, the Sphere Cutter node was used to spatially cut the RNP region. By adjusting the position and scaling of the Sphere Cutter, the RNP structure inside the virus is extracted independently, and the Set Color node is used to set an independent color (FFDDFE, Alpha 0.5) for it, so as to realize the differentiation of each key structure of the virus. Finally, the Join Component node is used to merge different components to form a complete hierarchical coloring model.

In terms of lighting and camera arrangement, this experiment adopts a dual light source design to simulate the light propagation effect in the microscopic environment. A white surface light source with an intensity of 500W and a diffusion angle of 90° is arranged at the back of the virus to illuminate the overall structural contour; a warm-colored point light source (FFD08D) with an intensity of 5W is placed inside the virus to increase the light transmission and shadow levels in the core area. A telephoto lens with a focal length of 200 mm was selected for the camera, the background color was pure black and gray, and the Look setting for color management was set to High Contrast to enhance the contrast and visual focusing effect.

For the optical properties of the viral membrane structure, the material is adjusted using the PBR (Physically Based Rendering) method. The transparency is set to 0.4 and the refractive index to 1.33 to simulate the optical behavior in the water environment, the sub-surface scattering coefficient is adjusted to 0.1, and the surface roughness is lowered to 0.2 to ensure that the light transmittance and scattering effects in the membrane are close to the natural state. During the experimental process, the initial rendering of the image appeared to have the problem of blurred levels and lack of details. In response to this phenomenon, the refractive index and scattering parameters were fine-tuned several times with reference to the optical properties of microphotography, and the local light attenuation control was increased in the area of spiny proteins, which effectively avoided the phenomenon of overexposure, and at the same time strengthened the sense of structural three-dimensionality and permeability.

In the rendering output, the image resolution was set to 1920×1080, and several sets of high-definition renderings were completed at different angles. The whole experiment took about 12 h from data import, modeling, material adjustment to the final rendering output, of which the rendering time was about 5 h. The final results show that this method can clearly present the typical microstructural features of the new coronavirus, and the distribution of spiny proteins, the envelope and the internal RNP arrangement have been effectively reproduced. The color gradient scheme increases the visual attractiveness and ensures the recognition degree in the science scene, which provides an important reference for the optimization of parameters and process specification of the subsequent formal experiments. The process is shown in the Fig. 3. In contrast, as shown in Fig. 4, the scanned raw image [26] lacks rich details and color representation, offering no advantage for public science outreach.

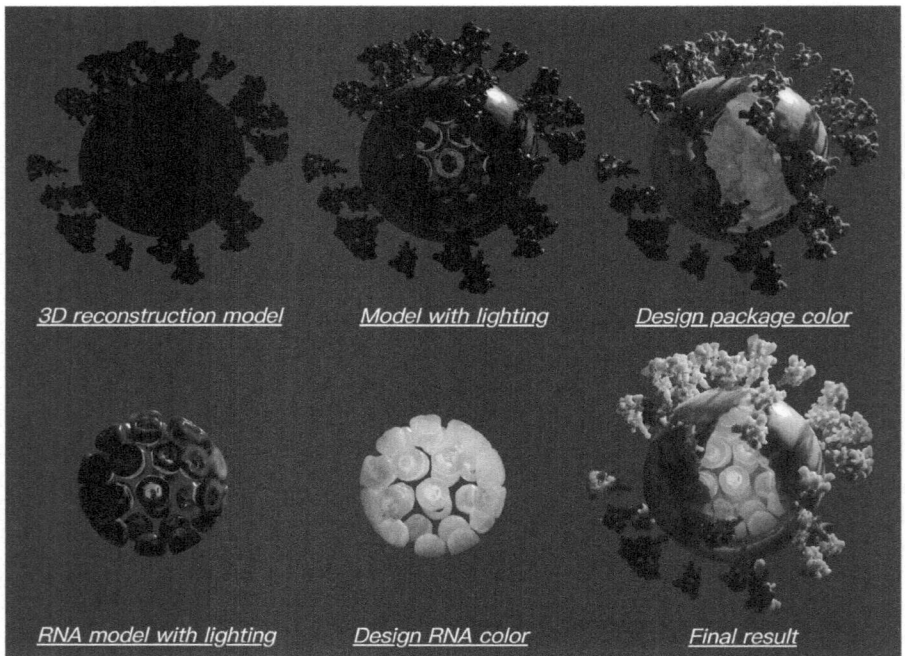

Fig. 3. The rendering process and results of the SARS-Cov-2 model. From left to right, extrusion of the model, setting up the light effect camera, and staining.

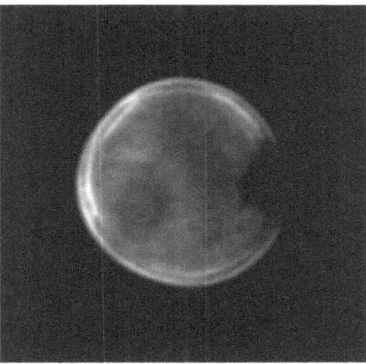

Fig. 4. A raw image of the SARS-CoV-2 virus obtained through low-temperature electron microscope scanning, which is orthogonally projected along the Y-axis. The structure corresponds to EMDB entry EMD-30430 [26].

4.3   Optimization for Complex Structures

For more complex microstructures, the proposed visualization framework can also produce promising results. Here, we present a case study and presentation of a hepatitis B virus experiment. Import the datasets of each part of the hepatitis B virus (envelope, capsid, DNA and polymerase) into Blender separately, and set the Bioxel Size parameter in the Bioxel Nodes plug-in to 5 for all of them. After the data is loaded, use the Threshold node to adjust the density range, and set the minimum density threshold to 0.22 to filter out background noise and extract the main structure of the virus. Subsequently, the Set Properties node was used to configure the material parameters, setting the specular value to 0.5, surface roughness to 0.2 and the model density to 1.0, in order to simulate highlight and surface scattering effects. After obtaining a complete model of each part, use the Center, Transform, Transform Parent nodes to adjust the model to the correct size and center each model together to form a complete hepatitis B virus cell. Then use two Sphere Cutter circle nodes to cut one side of the virus model to reveal the internal structure of the capsid and DNA.

Subsequently, a four-color gradient scheme was designed using the Set Color by Ramp 4 node to give the envelope and outer layer of attached protein model a sense of visual hierarchy. The colors are set from the outside in, in the order 358FBF (Alpha 0.25), 0086CB (Alpha 0.33), 8CE700 (Alpha 0.66) and D9FCFF (Alpha 0.75), to express the transition from the density of the virus's shell to its core.

The capsid and DNA are then colored separately. The Set Color by Ramp 4 node is used to set their colors from outside to inside, which are 2691B8 (Alpha 0.25), 70B48B (Alpha 0.33), D2C574 (Alpha 0.66), and CF7546 (Alpha 0.75) in order, to achieve a differentiated representation of the key structures of the virus. Finally, the different components are combined using the Join Component node to form a complete layered shading model.

In terms of lighting and camera layout, this experiment uses a dual-light source design to simulate the light propagation effect in a microscopic environment. A white surface light source with an intensity of 700W and a diffusion angle of 90° is arranged on the back of the virus to illuminate the overall structure outline; a warm-colored point light source (FFFFFF) with an intensity of 30 W is placed inside the virus to increase the light transmission and shadow layers in the core area. The camera selected a standard lens with a focal length of 50 mm, the background colors were set to solid black and gray, and the color management Look was set to High Contrast to enhance the contrast and visual focus.

The optical properties of the virus membrane structure were adjusted using the PBR (physics-based rendering) method in the Material section. The transparency was set to 0.5, the refractive index to 1.33 to simulate the optical behavior in a water environment, the subsurface scattering coefficient was adjusted to 0.3, and the surface roughness was reduced to 0.4 to ensure that the transmission and scattering of light through the membrane layer were close to natural. During the experiment, the first rendering had problems with blurry image layers and insufficient detail. To address this phenomenon, the refractive index and scattering parameters were fine-tuned multiple times with reference to the optical properties of microscopic photography, and local light attenuation control was added to the spike protein region to effectively avoid overexposure while enhancing the structural three-dimensionality and translucency.

The rendering output was set to a resolution of 1920×1080, with several high-definition views generated better showcase the structural details. The entire experiment took about 12 h in total, from data import, modeling, material adjustment to final rendering and output, of which the rendering time was about 5 h. The final results show that this method can clearly show the typical microscopic structural characteristics of the new coronavirus, and the distribution of the spike protein, the envelope, and the internal RNP arrangement have all been effectively restored. The color gradient scheme increases visual appeal while ensuring recognition in science popularization scenarios, providing an important reference for subsequent formal experiment parameter optimization and process standardization. The process is shown in the Fig. 5. And Fig. 6 presents the original low-temperature EM scan of HBV.

4.4   Performance Analysis

The above Table 2 shows the rendering speed of two experimental virus models. This study evaluates the performance of the rendering process of different virus models under the hardware conditions of a general workstation. The experimental results show that the complete processing and rendering of the largest dataset does not exceed 13 h, and the average processing time of the two experiments is about 11.75 h, indicating that the framework runs stably in a regular hardware environment without serious performance bottlenecks. It has normal computational efficiency and can meet the application needs of medical science popularization, teaching, and scientific visualization.

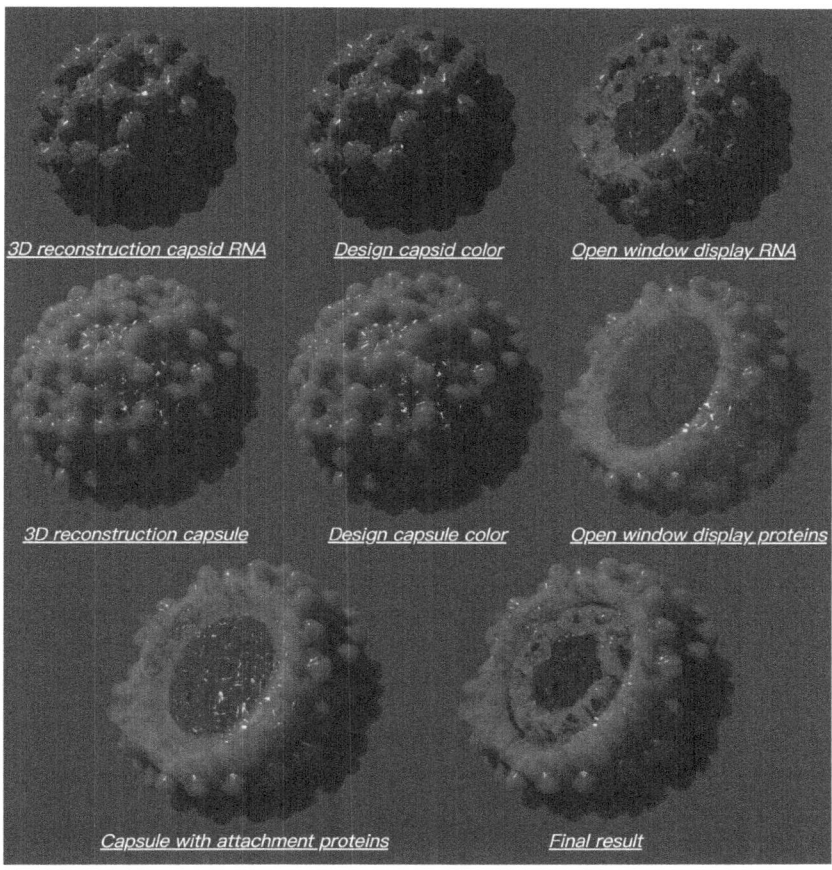

Fig. 5. The rendering process and results of the HBV model. From left to right, extrusion of the model, coloring, assembly and cutting of the model, and rendering.

Table 2. Processing Time for Virus Models

Processing Stage	COVID-19 Time (hh:mm)	HBV Time (hh:mm)
Data Loading and Preprocessing	1:04	1:06
Threshold Adjustment and 3D Reconstruction	2:13	2:09
Material and Lighting Configuration	2:49	2:43
High-Resolution Rendering	5:02	4:58
Total	**12:39**	**11:10**

Fig. 6. A raw image of the HBV obtained through low-temperature electron microscope scaning, which is orthogonally projected along the Y-axis. The structure corresponds to EMDB entry EMD-42824 [1].

Rendering Time Distribution and Influencing Factors. During the rendering of SARS-CoV-2 and hepatitis B virus models, high-definition rendering output is the most time-consuming part, accounting for more than 40% of the total time, followed by material and lighting configuration, which accounts for about 22%. The volume and complexity of cryo-EM data affect rendering efficiency. The SARS-CoV-2 data is intensive, 512 MB, and the hepatitis B virus data totals more than 1.2 GB. The larger data volume leads to longer loading times and consume a lot of computing resources. PBR material calculation is one of the main bottlenecks, especially the refraction and scattering calculation of the translucent virus envelope, which requires repeated optimization of transparency, refractive index and sub-surface scattering (SSS). Although it improves visual quality, it significantly increases rendering time. In addition, lighting calculations and camera settings also affect performance. The dual-light source system (high-intensity backlight + internal point light source) enhances the sense of depth, but increases the complexity of ray tracing calculations. The 200 mm telephoto lens improves the expression of detail while also increasing the computational burden, further prolonging rendering time.

Optimization Strategy. In order to reduce rendering time and maintain high-quality virus visualization, this study proposes a series of optimization strategies to improve computational efficiency and reduce resource consumption. First, in terms of rendering resolution and sampling rate, adaptive sampling can be used to reduce the sampling rate in low-detail areas, thereby reducing unnecessary computational overhead. In addition, the introduction of denoising algorithms (such as OptiX AI Denoiser) can maintain image clarity at lower sampling rates, thereby reducing the overall rendering time. For PBR material optimization, lookup tables (LUTs) for refractive index and scattering coefficient can be precalculated to reduce repeated calculations and thus reduce the time consumption of parameter adjustment. At the same time, an automated material optimization script has been developed to provide initial material parameter suggestions during data import, reducing the number of test renders and improving the efficiency of the overall workflow. In terms of optimizing lighting calculations, the cost of calculating subsurface scattering can be reduced. For virus envelopes with low transparency, a simple ray attenuation model is used to reduce the computational requirements. In addition, the arrangement of point light sources is optimized, or Global Illumination Approximation is used to reduce ray bounce calculations, thereby improving rendering speed. Through these optimization measures, the computational overhead can be effectively reduced while ensuring visual quality, and the rendering efficiency of the virus model can be improved.

5   Conclusion

This work focuses on the need for scientific visualization of microscopic viral structures and proposes a complete workflow for 3D modeling and rendering based on cryo-electron microscopy scan data. The pipeline integrates data import, thresholding, coloring, material tuning, and visualization into an accessible, reproducible process, specifically tailored for non-expert use in public science communication. Experiments demonstrate promising results in reconstructing and rendering the coronavirus and hepatitis B virus models, producing scientifically accurate and visually compelling illustrations. These outputs are achieved through the application of optimized PBR material settings, impression-based gradient coloring, and light simulation techniques, which collectively address issues such as structural complexity, lack of color, and loss of detail. The system performs reliably on standard hardware, efficiently handling 0.51.2 GB datasets without the need for advanced computing resources. This demonstrates the feasibility of creating high-quality scientific visuals at a low technical threshold. Overall, the proposed workflow offers a new, scalable pathway for bridging scientific accuracy with aesthetic clarity in both medical education and public engagement.

5.1   Limitations

Although the proposed visualization workflow demonstrates promising results, it still faces several challenges. First, it is currently optimized for biological scanning data with a resolution of approximately 3.6 , limiting its applicability to a narrow subset of virus samples with high-quality scans available in public databases. For most microbial or tissue-level structures, acquiring such high-resolution data is difficult, restricting the workflows generalizability across diverse microscopic structures. Second, the method is heavily dependent on the availability of cryo-electron microscopy (Cryo-EM) data. Since most researchers lack direct access to this specialized imaging technique, the workflow is not easily applicable for modeling novel or custom structures. Third, the rendering process remains computationally intensive. The current implementation using the

Bioxel Nodes does not support GPU acceleration, and models derived from scanning data often contain extremely high polygon counts, leading to low rendering efficiency. This poses challenges for high-resolution image or animation generation and limits the workflows suitability for real-time or large-scale applications. Lastly, while the generated images are scientifically accurate and detailed, it is unclear whether non-expert users can effectively interpret them. Future work should involve user testing to evaluate the clarity of these visualizations and investigate potential improvements in style, annotation, or simplification to enhance their effectiveness for educational and public outreach purposes.

5.2   Future Work

The ultimate goal is to design popular science posters or develop online display platforms to broaden the application of virus images in medical teaching and public science outreach. Building upon the current results, further improvements will focus on enhancing the workflows versatility and efficiency. We aim to extend its applicability to lower-resolution and diverse biological data types, broadening its use across various structural scales. Additionally, efforts will be made to reduce dependency on cryo-EM data by incorporating alternative imaging techniques and methods for approximating structural details. Rendering performance can be optimized through GPU integration and model simplification to enable faster processing. User studies will be conducted to assess the effectiveness of the visualizations for non-expert audiences, with the goal of refining their clarity, style, and educational impact. On this basis, further exploration can be conducted on the feasibility of developing interactive popular science applications on the Unity platform. Such applications would allow users to freely adjust lighting, camera position, and angle, as well as interactively disassemble virus models to observe their fine internal structures. This approach seeks to enhance the immersive understanding of microscopic knowledge and ultimately establish a virus popular science visualization solution that integrates scientific accuracy, visual appeal, and interactive engagement.

Acknowledgments. We thank the reviewers for the valuable comments. This study was supported by Research Development Fund, Xian Jiaotong-Liverpool Uiversity (No. RDF-21-02-065) and the Open Project Program of State Key Laboratory of Virtual Reality Technology and Systems, Beihang University (No.VRLAB2024B01).

References

1. Bianchini, E.N., Wang, J., Hu, J.: Hbv t=4 3a mutant capsid from hek-293t cells. Electron Microscopy Data Bank (EMDB) (2024). https://www.ebi.ac.uk/emdb/EMD-42824, eMD-42824
2. Blom, H., Brismar, H.: Sted microscopy: increased resolution for medical research? J. Int. Med. **276**(6), 560–578 (2014). https://doi.org/10.1111/joim.12278

3. Drebin, R.A., Carpenter, L., Hanrahan, P.: Volume rendering. In: Proceedings of the 15th Annual Conference on Computer Graphics and Interactive Techniques (SIGGRAPH '88), vol. 22, pp. 65–74. ACM (1988). https://doi.org/10.1145/378456.378484

4. Farin, G., Hamann, B., Hagen, H.: Hierarchical and Geometrical Methods in Scientific Visualization. Springer, Heidelberg (2003). https://doi.org/10.1007/978-3-642-19044-1

5. Feishu Wiki: Bioxel Nodes Handbook (2025). https://uj6xfhbzp0.feishu.cn/wiki/VEPiwpaGtiY3VvkTbdWca06QnDf. Accessed 06 Mar 2025

6. Ferrel, M.N., Ryan, J.J.: The impact of covid-19 on medical education. Cureus **12**(3), e7492 (2020). https://doi.org/10.7759/cureus.7492

7. Flynn, J.E., Spencer, T.J.: The effects of light source color on user impression and satisfaction. J. Illum. Eng. Soc. **6**(3), 167–179 (1977). https://doi.org/10.1080/00994480.1977.10747811

8. Gemtou, E.: Subjectivity in art history and art criticism. Rupkatha J. Interdisc. Stud. Humanities **2**(1) (2010). https://doi.org/10.21659/rupkatha.v2n1.02. http://rupkatha.com/V2/n1/SubjectivityinArtHistoryandArtCriticism.pdf

9. Klug, A.: From virus structure to chromatin: X-ray diffraction to three-dimensional electron microscopy. Ann. Rev. Biochem. **79**, 1–35 (2010). https://doi.org/10.1146/annurev.biochem.79.091407.093947

10. Makbul, C., Khayenko, V., Maric, M.H., Bottcher, B.: Hepatitis b core protein with bound geraniol (2023). https://www.ebi.ac.uk/emdb/EMD-17996. Accessed 06 Mar 2025

11. Meerbeek, B.V., et al.: Microscopy investigations. techniques, results, limitations. Am. J. Dentistry **13**(Special Issue), 3D–18D (2000). https://www.researchgate.net/publication/11593725_Microscopy_investigations_Techniques_results_limitations

12. Meng, E.C., et al.: Ucsf chimerax: tools for structure building and analysis. Protein Sci. **32**(11), e4792 (2023). https://doi.org/10.1002/pro.4792

13. Mildenhall, B., Srinivasan, P.P., Tancik, M., Barron, J.T., Ramamoorthi, R., Ng, R.: Nerf: representing scenes as neural radiance fields for view synthesis. Commun. ACM **65**(1), 99–106 (2022). https://doi.org/10.1145/3503250

14. Nordlund, J.J., Abdel-Malek, Z.A., Boissy, R.E., Rheins, L.A.: Pigment cell biology: an historical review. J. Investigat. Dermatol. **92**(4, Supplement), S53–S60 (1989). https://doi.org/10.1038/jid.1989.33

15. Petrova, E., Teixeira, A.I., Hallberg, B.M.: Hepatitis b virus core antigen (hbc) with insertion of spycatcher at mir (2024). https://www.ebi.ac.uk/emdb/EMD-19437. Accessed 06 Mar 2025

16. Pharr, M., Jakob, W., Humphreys, G.: Physically Based Rendering: From Theory to Implementation. MIT Press, Cambridge (2023)

17. Shahid, S., Liqun, J., Liu, Y., Hasan, S.S., Mariuzza, R.A.: Cryoem structure of neutralizing antibody hc84.26 in complex with hepatitis c virus envelope glycoprotein e2_new interface (2023). https://www.ebi.ac.uk/emdb/EMD-42041. Accessed 06 Mar 2025

18. Stalling, D., Westerhoff, M., Hege, H.C.: Amira: a highly interactive system for visual data analysis. In: The Visualization Handbook, pp. 749–767. zuse Institute Berlin (ZIB) (2005)

19. Sullivan, P., et al.: A data visualization and dissemination resource to support hiv prevention and care at the local level: analysis and uses of the aidsvu public data resource. J. Med. Internet Res. **22**(10), e23173 (2020). https://doi.org/10.2196/23173

20. Vieira, I.H.P., Botelho, E.B., de Souza Gomes, T.J., Kist, R., Caceres, R.A., Zanchi, F.B.: Visual dynamics: a web application for molecular dynamics simulation using gromacs. BMC Bioinf. **24**(1), 107 (2023). https://doi.org/10.1186/s12859-023-05234-y

21. Wang, X., Gao, S., Wang, M., Duan, Z.: A marching cube algorithm based on edge growth. Virtual Real. Intell. Hardware **3**(4), 336–349 (2021). https://doi.org/10.1016/j.vrih.2021.08.006

22. Wang, Z., Wan, X., Liu, Z., Fan, Q., Zhang, F., Tan, G.: A multi-gpu design for large size cryo-em 3d reconstruction. In: Proceedings of the 2021 IEEE International Parallel and Distributed Processing Symposium (IPDPS), pp. 847–858. IEEE, Portland (2021). https://doi.org/10.1109/IPDPS49936.2021.00094,

23. Wollmuth, E.M., et al.: Helping students see bacteria in 3d: cellular models increase student learning about cell size and diffusion. J. Microbiol. Biol. Educ. **24**(3) (2023). https://doi.org/10.1128/jmbe.00089-23

24. Wu, H., Graikos, A., Samaras, D.: S-volsdf: sparse multi-view stereo regularization of neural implicit surfaces. In: Proceedings of the IEEE/CVF International Conference on Computer Vision (ICCV), pp. 3556–3568. IEEE (2023)

25. Yao, H., et al.: The authentic sars-cov-2 virus (2020). https://www.ebi.ac.uk/emdb/EMD-30430. Accessed 06 Mar 2025

26. Yao, H., et al.: Molecular architecture of the sars-cov-2 virus. Cell **183**(3), 730-738.e13 (2020). https://doi.org/10.1016/j.cell.2020.09.018

27. Yao, H., et al.: Molecular architecture of the sars-cov-2 virus. Cell **183**(3), 730–738 (2020). https://doi.org/10.1016/j.cell.2020.09.018

28. Yip, R.P.H., Lai, L.T.F., Lau, W.C.Y., Ngo, J.C.K., Kwok, D.C.Y.: Hepatitis b virus capsid (hbv core protein) (2024). https://www.ebi.ac.uk/emdb/EMD-37631. Accessed 06 Mar 2025

29. Zhang, X., Yang, J., Chen, N., Zhang, S., Xu, Y., Tan, L.: Modeling and simulation of an anatomy teaching system. Visual Comput. Ind. Biomed. Art **2**(1), 1–8 (2019). https://doi.org/10.1186/s42492-019-0019-4

A Design Study on Contextual and Interactive Serious Games for Children's Learning of Chinese Character Culture

Lanqi Xu[1], Yifan Zhang[1], Xu Lang[2(✉)], Jianing Liu[3], Xianxuan Lin[1], Jing Zhang[1], Zheng Wang[1], Baiheng Liu[1], and Tianming Wu[4]

[1] Nanjing University of Information Science and Technology, Nanjing, China
[2] Zhejiang Gongshang University, Hangzhou, China
18693940096@163.com
[3] Lanzhou Resource and Environment Vocational and Technical University, Lanzhou, China
[4] Guangxi Institute of Meteorological Science, Nanning, China

Abstract. The complexity of Chinese characters and their cultural connotations pose challenges to children's cognitive development. Traditional teaching methods, often based on repetitive practice, fail to integrate cultural context and cognitive depth, limiting their effectiveness. This study introduces the "Situational Interactive Serious Game" paradigm, which incorporates a three-dimensional cognitive framework: the "Primitive, Constructive, and Cultural Layers." The developed system, WGIF, combines progressive tasks with the mental flow theory to enhance learning. Results show that the system significantly increased children's interest, retention rates, and cultural understanding, with experimental group scores 23.7% higher than the control group (p < 0.05). This research offers a targeted design for educational games that foster cross-cultural communication and improve Chinese character learning.

Keywords: Children's education · Chinese character culture · contextual interaction · game-based learning · serious games · situational interaction

1 Introduction

Chinese characters, as the cornerstone of Chinese culture, are not only the core of the writing system but also a multidimensional carrier of historical and philosophical values, playing a crucial role in conveying the culture of the Chinese nation [1]. However, the complexity and variety of Chinese character forms present a challenge in traditional teaching methods, which often fail to engage children's interest in learning them. Originating from pictographs, Chinese characters have undergone continuous abstraction and simplification [2]. Analyzing

C. Mousas et al. (Eds.): CASA 2025, LNCS 15915, pp. 173–186, 2026.
https://doi.org/10.1007/978-981-95-0100-7_11

the evolution of their forms can effectively promote children's cognitive abilities, creativity, and perceptual skills [3].

With the advancement of digital technology, educational innovations have accelerated. Research shows that game-based learning significantly stimulates children's interest, and digital serious games, with their high interactivity and engagement, better align with children's developmental psychology [4]. Serious games have revolutionized traditional education, transforming the learning process into a more engaging experience [5], and have provided a novel way to digitally transmit cultural heritage [6].

Cognitive development theory suggests that children aged 7 to 8 are in the concrete operational stage [7], where abstract concepts are learned through multimodal stimuli and interactive elements. Gamified learning fits children's natural play behavior, enhancing their interest and motivation [8], and contextual games positively impact language acquisition [9]. However, most existing serious games for teaching Chinese characters focus primarily on character structure rules and classroom learning, lacking integration with cultural context and developmental psychology.

Therefore, serious game design should focus on conveying the characteristics of Chinese character structure through situational interaction and the integration of cultural connotations.

This study proposes a three-dimensional cognitive framework, including the Primitive, Structural, and Cultural Layers, as the design architecture for the "Word Gets Its Fun" (WGIF) system. This framework bridges the gap between mechanical memorization and cultural literacy through the following elements:

1. **P**rimitive Layer: Strengthening the "form-sound-meaning" association;
2. **S**tructural Layer: Exploring the origin and evolution of Chinese characters;
3. **C**ultural Layer: Embedding symbolic meaning through task narratives.

This paper aims to enhance children's understanding of Chinese characters and culture through a hierarchical cognitive structure, while promoting active engagement in the learning process through situational interactions.

2   Related Work

Since the establishment of Chinese Language and Literature as an independent discipline in the twentieth century, Chinese character education has followed a 'decentralized literacy' model, focusing on isolated word recognition within a text-centered framework. Traditional methods rely on rote memorization and handwriting practice, with emphasis on teacher explanations and repetitive exercises. While this reinforces short-term memory, it fragments children's knowledge by lacking cultural context and disconnecting the 'form, sound, and meaning' of characters. Teaching materials, mainly classical texts like the Three Character Classic and the Analects of Confucius, impart knowledge through recitation and copying, but this detaches content from its context, limiting students' ability to apply characters in real life.

Serious Games, introduced by educator Clark C. Abt in 1970, are defined as games with well-defined educational purposes, not purely recreational [10]. Michael Zyda further elaborated on this in 2005, highlighting Serious Games as edutainment tools that integrate interactive, personalized experiences for educational purposes.

The rapid development of digital technology has expanded opportunities for language learning. Research shows growing interest in digital games for language acquisition [11]. Game-based learning enhances skills and knowledge through interactive content and gameplay in dynamic environments. This approach allows learners to internalize knowledge and refine skills while overcoming challenges [12]. In Chinese character education, engaging with character games has been shown to improve recognition, increase participation, and enhance academic performance. Evidence suggests educational games significantly outperform traditional methods in terms of learner engagement and outcomes [13].

For example, Jozua's study on the Scram Word application demonstrated its effectiveness in enhancing English vocabulary comprehension [14]. Hwang et al.'s computer game improved students' English listening skills and learning outcomes [15]. Wen's augmented reality-based game for learning Chinese characters revealed that while it helped second language learners, the lack of cultural context reduced motivation to master the characters [16]. This highlights the importance of incorporating cultural connotations to enhance motivation and learning effectiveness.

3   Game Concept and Implementation

This study aims to explore innovative methods for teaching Chinese characters and culture, enhancing children's engagement and fostering active participation. The WGIF Situational Interactive Chinese Character and Culture Serious Game System is introduced to address the challenges of fragmented cultural contexts and low motivation in traditional teaching, using narrative contextualization to improve learning.

3.1   Design Process

Gamification Knowledge Hierarchy. Chinese characters are traditionally taught through a 'decentralized method,' relying on repetitive exercises for memorization. While this can reinforce short-term memory, it fragments children's knowledge due to the lack of cultural context and the disconnection between the 'shape–sound–meaning' of characters. The reliance on rote memorization and writing makes learning monotonous, leading to low motivation. The framework includes three layers: the primitive layer, structural layer, and cultural layer as shown in Fig. 1.

A good learning experience relies on clear goals, appropriate challenges, and rewards tied to those challenges. The WGIF system effectively integrates this by balancing difficulty with skill, ensuring players can learn Chinese characters

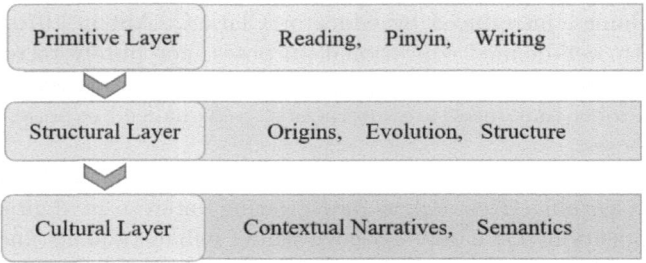

Fig. 1. Design of a framework for the game WGIF.

without frustration. According to Mihaly Csikszentmihalyi's flow theory, individuals engaged in activities that match their skill level enter a state of immersion [17]. Therefore, the game's difficulty is calibrated to be both achievable and stimulating.

The WGIF system uses a tiered approach, starting with basic Chinese character memorization and writing, before introducing more complex tasks as players advance. This ensures gradual skill development and encourages continued engagement [18]. The system also provides hints when players struggle, enhancing learning outcomes [19]. Gamification elements like badges and leaderboards boost motivation, especially for children [20]. The system offers fixed rewards (badges, virtual points) and random incentives (unknown rewards) to keep players engaged and motivated. Vygotsky's socio-cultural theory emphasizes collaborative learning to enhance motivation and learning outcomes [22]. The WGIF system incorporates this by allowing players to interact, share tasks, and earn 'friendship values' that can be exchanged for special items, enriching both social engagement and learning [23].

This approach ensures that the system is both motivating and educational, enhancing the overall learning experience. Here is the revised version, streamlined and divided into four distinct sections while maintaining the original content, references, and images:

Loop Feedback Interaction Design. This study introduces a three-stage learning cycle: Perception–Analysis–Reconstruction. Each Chinese character is learned through three steps: recognizing, learning, and reviewing. Abstract character concepts are transformed into engaging visual scenarios, enabling children to deeply understand Chinese characters in an interactive, fun environment [24]. The game emphasizes both input (listening and reading) and output (speaking and writing) skills. While players often focus on passive input, the game includes interactive tasks to encourage active output. For example, in the '鹿 (lú, 'deer')' module, as shown in Fig. 3, children interact with a symbolic deer, learning the character's morphology and cultural context.

The tasks include Recognizing the Character (Task 1: 'Recognizing Chinese Characters'), where children explore the character's evolution from oracle bone inscriptions to modern scripts, and Learning the Character (Task 2: 'Stroke Introduction'), where they practice writing '鹿' with tactile feedback. The Reviewing the Character phase includes Task 3: Character Riddle Challenge and Task 4: Timeline Puzzle, which consolidate learning, as shown in Fig. 4. Research shows that linking shape, sound, and physical objects enhances learning more effectively than phonics alone [25] (Fig. 2).

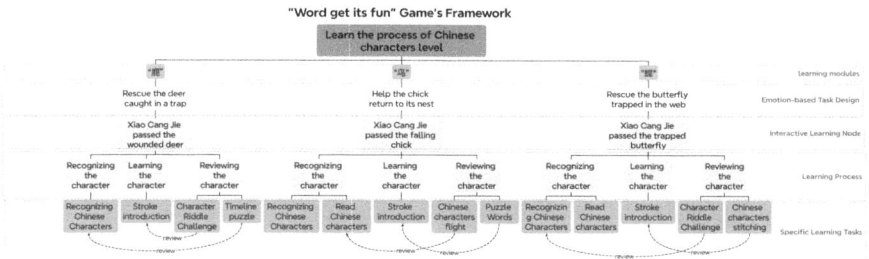

Fig. 2. Design of a framework for the game WGIF.

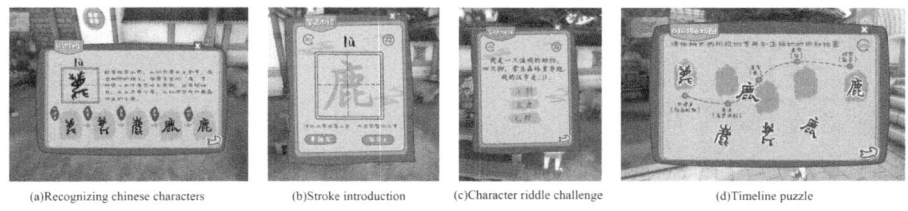

(a)Recognizing chinese characters   (b)Stroke introduction   (c)Character riddle challenge   (d)Timeline puzzle

Fig. 3. Interaction design task process.

UI Design. This study's design is inspired by traditional Chinese calligraphy, utilizing metaphors such as 'unfolding Chinese character culture books' to shape the user interface. Elements like ink textures and brush strokes are used to replicate calligraphic rhythm and layout, creating an immersive learning experience related to Chinese character culture. The flat design style maintains aesthetic appeal while reducing cognitive load for children [27]. The interface uses a fourfold cognitive load reduction strategy: (1) Synchronized voice readings accompany all characters to reinforce form-sound associations. (2) Increased spacing and fewer buttons minimize operational errors. (3) An escape hatch mode allows children to return to the main interface, preventing frustration. (4) Unlimited exploration encourages repeated practice to deepen understanding and memorization.

Scenography and Image Design. The WGIF system is set in the historical context of the Ming and Qing Dynasties, with a focus on Chinese classical gardens, particularly the Grand View Garden (Daguan Yuan) from *Dream of the Red Chamber*. This setting, enhanced with elements of Jiangnan gardens like bridges, streams, and bamboo forests, creates a culturally rich atmosphere, as shown in Fig. 5. Children take on the role of 'cultural messengers' within this virtual environment, learning Chinese characters through active participation and experiential interactions. Three modules—'鹿 (lú, 'deer')', '鸟 (niǎo, 'bird')', and '蝶 (dié, 'butterfly')'—integrate Chinese characters into narrative and scene nodes, as shown in Fig. 6 encouraging emotional engagement and knowledge construction [26].

Fig. 4. Scenario design comparison.

(a) Character 1 "鹿" (lù, "deer")   (b) Character 2 "鸟" (niǎo, "bird")   (c) Character 3 "蝶" (dié, "butterfly")

Fig. 5. Chinese Character Learning Module.

Virtual Character Design and System Construction. The character 'Xiao Cang Jie' is based on Cangjie, the legendary inventor of Chinese characters. His four-eyed features symbolize his deep connection with the evolution of Chinese characters. The design uses colors derived from oracle bones—brown, amber yellow, crescent white, and black—to evoke a sense of historical presence. His attire includes cultural symbols, such as the '心 (xīn, 'heart')' symbol, reinforcing the connection between the character and the origins of Chinese writing, as shown in Fig. 6. The character is reinterpreted as a 'cultural ambassador,' blending educational and symbolic elements to engage children.

The game system is built on Unreal Engine (UE) for its powerful graphics and virtual reality capabilities. The UI design prioritizes child-friendly interaction to enhance the immersive learning experience. The system's structure ensures a

Fig. 6. Virtual character 'Xiao Cang Jie' design

seamless interface for effective learning. The overall architecture of the system, as shown in Fig. 7. The system is divided into five hierarchical structures: access layer, UI presentation layer, front-end rendering layer, task interaction layer, and feedback response layer to support immersive learning for child users on different devices.

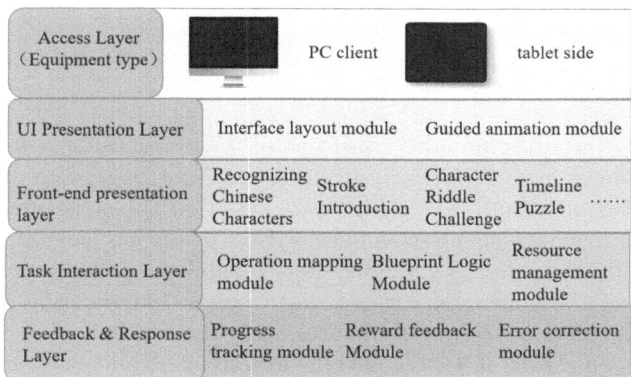

Fig. 7. The architecture of the 'WGIF' system

4 Empirical Analysis

4.1 Research Hypotheses

This study investigates the impact of the design method on children's learning of Chinese characters through a user study of the interactive serious game system 'WGIF' The research employed a pre-test and post-test controlled experimental design involving 95 first-grade students, aged 7–8 years, from two parallel classes in a public elementary school in Nanjing, China, with a relatively balanced male-to-female ratio. The pre-test results indicated no significant differences in the baseline language proficiency between the two classes (p = 0.76). The independent variables (IVs) included the 'WGIF' situational interactive Chinese character learning system (experimental group, N = 47) and the traditional classroom PPT teaching method (control group, N = 48). To evaluate the study's design objective—enhancing children's cognition of Chinese characters, fostering interest in learning, and improving knowledge retention through situational interactive serious games—the dependent variables (DVs) encompassed: (1) the effectiveness of Chinese character learning; (2) long-term knowledge retention; (3) children's depth of knowledge regarding Chinese characters and culture; and (4) interest in learning and participation. Based on analyses of prior studies, several research hypotheses were formulated for this investigation:

- H1: The WGIF system dramatically improves the immediate results of children's Chinese character learning.
- H2: Compared to traditional classroom instruction, the WGIF system is more conducive to the long-term retention of children's knowledge.
- H3: The WGIF system is effective in increasing the depth of children's knowledge of Chinese characters and culture.
- H4: The WGIF system dramatically increases children's interest and engagement in learning.

4.2 Questionnaire Data Acquisition

In this study, the questionnaire consisted of 15 items using a 5-point Likert scale [28], ranging from 1 (strongly disagree) to 5 (strongly agree), along with two open-ended questions. The design was based on the structural dimensions of the Game Engagement Questionnaire (GEQ) [29], with localization and age-appropriate adjustments. The validity and reliability of the scale were tested using Cronbach's α value, which was found to be 0.77, indicating good internal consistency. A total of 47 questionnaires were distributed, with 45 returned, yielding a response rate of 95.7%. After screening, 5 invalid questionnaires were removed, resulting in 40 valid responses, with an effective response rate of 85.1%. Cronbach's α value of 0.77 indicates good internal consistency, with values above 0.7 generally considered to indicate good reliability.

The study was conducted in a university laboratory environment, involving 95 first-grade students from a public elementary school in Nanjing. The participants included 49 boys and 46 girls, aged between 7 and 8 years (mean age: 7.4 years, SD = 0.5), maintaining a balanced male-to-female ratio. There was no significant difference in the overall proficiency levels of the students in the two classes based on the pre-language test (p = 0.76). Subsequently, 47 students were assigned to the WGIF system group (experimental group), while the remaining 48 students were assigned to the traditional classroom PPT learning method group (control group). The content and sequence of knowledge presented to both groups were kept identical to ensure fairness in the control.

Students in the experimental group engaged with an embodied game via the WGIF system, utilizing headphones and microphones to listen and interact with the game. In contrast, students in the control group received instruction from the teacher, learning Chinese characters through a conventional PowerPoint presentation. The researchers monitored the children's actions and behaviors on a computer screen, offering technical support as needed. Upon completing the learning tasks, all students were asked to complete a scale, and selected participants subsequently took part in semi-structured interviews and focus group discussions.

In terms of time, each student in the experimental group required approximately 30 min to engage with the game and complete the interactive tasks, while the control group also needed about 30 min to finish the PowerPoint learning session and associated exercises. Knowledge retention is a crucial indicator of the effectiveness of long-term learning [30], and Ebbinghaus' forgetting curve theory indicates that the most rapid rate of decay occurs within the first few days following initial learning [31], stabilizing after approximately one week [32]. To further assess the sustained impact of the WGIF system on children's learning of Chinese characters, a delayed test was conducted one week post-experiment. This test aimed to evaluate the long-term effects of the game system on knowledge retention and cultural cognitive transfer. To enhance the objectivity and empirical validity of the study, the following objective behavioral data were collected concurrently, in addition to subjective questionnaires and interviews:

(1) Task completion time: the total duration taken by each student to complete the learning session and interactive task was recorded as an indirect indicator of cognitive load and task proficiency;

(2) Eye-tracking data (experimental group only): Tobii Pro eye-tracking devices were utilized by a subset of the experimental group students ($N = 15$), recording their attention hotspots (Areas of Interest, AOIs) and gaze durations to further analyze the students' focus on key cultural elements.

- O1: High voluntary interaction frequency with cultural elements reflects strong user autonomy
- O2: High eye-tracking data indicates that gamified design significantly increased children's attention to cultural information

4.3   Statistical Analysis

The scale was first introduced by Lin et al. in their research on virtual reality and has since been widely used for evaluating subjective experiences in educational games, immersive systems, and virtual environments [33]. It is extensively employed to assess participants' sense of immersion, enjoyment, and engagement within virtual environments (UE). The choice of the EI scale as an assessment tool is primarily due to its suitability for studying learning experiences in virtual environments, as it comprehensively reflects users' subjective emotions and engagement with the context, tasks, and interactions. It is particularly well-suited for evaluating immersion and motivational states in younger children within gamified learning systems.

Through an in-depth analysis of the experimental data, the content of the table was derived. The table compares the WGIF system with traditional classroom teaching (PPT control group) across multiple academic indicators, including subjective questionnaire evaluations (e.g., validity, long-term knowledge retention) and objective behavior data (e.g., interaction frequency, gaze time). The results indicate that the experimental group outperforms the control group in most indicators, and statistical tests show that the differences are significant ($p < 0.05$ or smaller).

In terms of subjective questionnaire evaluations, the experimental group generally performs better across several dimensions. For example, the experimental group scores significantly higher than the control group on indicators such as "interaction" and "engagement," with many of these differences being statistically significant (e.g., $p < 0.05$, or even $p < 0.001$).

Regarding objective behavior data, significant differences were also found, particularly in interaction frequency and gaze time. The experimental group exhibited more active participation in interactive behaviors and longer gaze time. Additionally, the experimental group outperformed traditional classroom teaching in terms of gaze revisit frequency.

Further statistical analyses, including the Shapiro-Wilk test and Mann-Whitney U test, confirmed the reliability and statistical significance of the results. The majority of p-values were less than 0.05, indicating that the differences between the experimental and control groups are statistically significant in most cases.

These results suggest that the WGIF system significantly outperforms traditional teaching methods in terms of learning outcomes and interaction engagement. The detailed table content is provided in Table 1. Subjective questionnaire data support hypotheses and corresponding types: H1 (Validity), H2 (Long-term Knowledge Retention), H3 (Chinese Character Cultural Awareness), H4 (Interest and Engagement in Learning). Objective behavioural data supporting assumptions and corresponding types: O1 (Voluntary Interaction Frequency with Cultural Elements), O2 (Eye Tracking Data) (Fig. 8).

This study developed the WGIF Situational Interactive Chinese Character Serious Game System, which significantly enhances children's cognitive and memorization abilities regarding the shapes, sounds, and meanings of Chinese characters through the integration of multi-modal information and cultural elements. It also verifies the positive impact of gamified contexts on language learning. Furthermore, the system effectively increases children's interest and immersion in learning by utilizing contextual storytelling and interactive tasks. By addressing the monotonous nature of traditional literacy teaching, it stimulates children's willingness to engage with and disseminate culture by deepening their understanding of the cultural connotations of Chinese characters.

Experimental data and user feedback indicate that the system is effective in enhancing the depth of Chinese character instruction and optimizing the

Table 1. Comparison of WGIF System and Traditional Teaching

Explanation	Indicator	average(SD)		Shapiro-Wilk test or MannWhitney U test	
		WGIF (Experimental Group)	PPT (Control Group)	t/Z	p
H1	Serious Game	5.16(0.25)	4.92(0.20)	5.16	$1.51 \ times 10^-6*$
	Presence	4.96(0.30)	4.82(0.25)	1.73	0.087
	Enjoyment	5.83(0.72)	5.21(0.80)	−2.145	0.032*
H2	Interaction total	5.95(0.60)	5.10(0.85)	3.540	0.00063*
	Embodied cognition	5.66(0.35)	4.41(0.28)	19.200	0*
	Entertainment	5.88(0.90)	5.02(1.03)	−2.976	0.003
	Fluent	6.12(0.40)	5.25(0.38)	3.240	0.0016
H3	Chinese Character Knowledge total	0.79(0.15)	0.64(0.20)	2.512	0.014*
	Chinese Character Historical information	0.84(0.25)	0.68(0.23)	1.856	0.067
	Recall ability of "Oracle Bone Inscriptions"	0.72(0.20)	0.61(0.22)	1.681	0.097
H4	Awareness on Chinese Character	6.10(0.56)	5.42(0.72)	3.080	0.003
O1	Interaction Frequency	4.6(0.3)	1.2(0.6)	8.140	$6.16 \times 10^-6*$
O2	Gaze Time	7.82(2.1)	2.94(1.3)	13.590	0*
	Gaze Revisit Frequency	3.4(0.9)	1.1(0.6)	14.620	0*

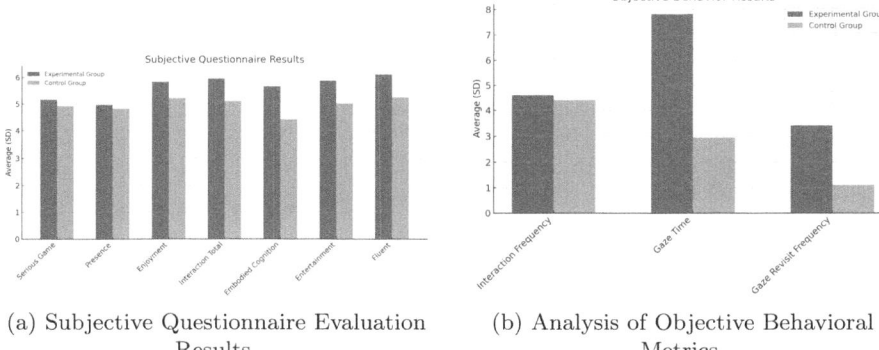

(a) Subjective Questionnaire Evaluation Results.

(b) Analysis of Objective Behavioral Metrics.

Fig. 8. User Experience Evaluation: Objective and Subjective Metrics

learning experience. This not only offers an innovative approach to Chinese character education but also provides a practical foundation for studying contextual interactive game-based learning.

4.4 Research Outlook

This study developed the WGIF Situational Interactive Chinese Character Serious Game System, which enhances children's understanding and memorization of Chinese characters by integrating multimodal information and cultural elements. The system leverages gamified contexts to improve language learning by increasing engagement, reducing the monotony of traditional literacy teaching, and stimulating interest in cultural knowledge. Experimental data and user feedback demonstrate that the system enriches Chinese character education and optimizes the learning experience, offering an innovative approach to Chinese character education. It also has potential for integration into classrooms, allowing teachers to select tasks based on educational objectives, track learning progress, and incorporate "Learning by Playing" into the curriculum. Future improvements can focus on the following areas: 1) Expanding cross-cultural applications by adapting the model to other writing systems (e.g., Egyptian hieroglyphics, Mayan script), enabling children to explore the historical evolution and cultural significance of different languages. 2) Enhancing technology integration and personalized learning through AR/VR to offer a richer experience, adaptive algorithms to optimize learning paths, and periodic reviews for long-term memory retention. 3) Strengthening classroom collaboration and teaching innovation by providing teachers with flexible access to task resources through modular content design and establishing a data-driven management platform for personalized teaching. These improvements will transform the system into a cross-cultural language learning platform, offering children globally an immersive, culturally rich, and effective educational experience.

Acknowledgments. This research was supported by the Teaching Research Special Project of the Inner Mongolia Autonomous Region Teaching and Research Office, under the Teaching Special Project of the Compulsory Education Master Teacher Workshop (Studio), titled "Design, Development, and Practice Research of the Metaverse System for Vocational Electromechanical Courses" (Project No.: NMKY14520135). The authors would like to express their sincere gratitude for this support, which has significantly contributed to the progress and completion of this study.

References

1. UNESCO, Texts of the Convention for the Safeguarding of the Intangible Cultural Heritage (2021). https://ich.unesco.org/en/convention
2. Spencer, H.: Social Statics. John Chapman, London (1851). https://doi.org/10.4324/9781003191919
3. Kulish, O., Cheng, Y.-Y.: How powerful are Chinese characters' effects on children's creativity? Think. Skills Creat. **49**, 101374 (2023)
4. Alotaibi, M.S.: Game-based learning in early childhood education: a systematic review and meta-analysis. Front. Psychol. **15**, 1307881 (2024)
5. Alomair, Y., Hammami, S.: Enhancing the achievement of learning outcomes for foreign language learners based on gamification and card games. Int. J. Comput. Games Technol. **2024**, 8084687 (2024)
6. Camuñas-García, D., Cáceres-Reche, M.P., Cambil-Hernández, M.D.L.E.: Mobile game-based learning in cultural heritage education: a bibliometric analysis. Educ. Train. **65**(2), 324–339 (2023)
7. Piaget, J., Gruber, H.E., Voneche, J.J.: The Essential Piaget (1977)

8. Jaramillo-Mediavilla, L., Basantes-Andrade, A., Cabezas-González, M., Casillas-Martín, S.: Impact of gamification on motivation and academic performance: a systematic review. Educ. Sci. **14**(6), 639 (2024)
9. Yang, L., Li, R.: Contextualized game-based language learning: retrospect and prospect. J. Educ. Comput. Res. **62**(1), 357–375 (2024)
10. Abt, C.C.: Serious Games. University Press of America, Lanham (1987)
11. Bado, N.: Game-based learning pedagogy: a review of the literature. Interact. Learn. Environ. **30**(5), 936–948 (2022)
12. Wulantari, N.P., Rachman, A., Sari, M.N., Uktolseja, L.J., Rofi'i, A.: The role of gamification in English language teaching: a literature review. J. Educ. **6**(1), 2847–2856 (2023)
13. Sadeghi, K., et al.: The effects of gamified instruction on vocabulary gain and motivation among language learners. Heliyon **8**(11), e11811 (2022). https://doi.org/10.1016/j.heliyon.2022.e11811
14. Palandi, J., Pudyastuti, Z., Molewe, K.: Enhancing english vocabulary through game-based learning: a case study of the scramword application. Int. J. Inf. Technol. Gov. Educ. Bus. **6**, 109–121 (2024)
15. Hwang, W.Y., Shih, T.K., Ma, Z.H., Shadiev, R., Chen, S.Y.: Evaluating listening and speaking skills in a mobile game-based learning environment with situational contexts. Comput. Assist. Lang. Learn. **29**(4), 639–657 (2016)
16. Wen, Y.: Chinese character composition game with the augment paper. Educ. Technol. Soc. **21**, 132–145 (2018)
17. Csikszentmihalyi, M.: Beyond Boredom and Anxiety. Jossey-Bass, San Francisco (2000)
18. Cruz-Martínez, G., Sainz, O.S., Sánchez, A.: Learning about political systems through role-play games. Revista Española de Ciencia Política **60**, 53–83 (2022)
19. Shen, S., Su, H., Shang, J.: How gamification affects knowledge retention: a meta-analysis. Mod. Distance Educ. Res. **36**(6), 55–68 (2024)
20. Zourmpakis, A.-I., Kalogiannakis, M., Papadakis, S.: A framework for adaptive gamification in physics education. AIP Conf. Proc. **2801**, 030001 (2023)
21. Vygotsky, L.S.: Mind in Society: Development of Higher Psychological Processes. Harvard University Press, Cambridge (1980)
22. Feng, F., Yang, W.: Effects of feedback types on cognitive load in game-based language learning. Educ. Inf. Technol. **29**(6), 2345–2360 (2024)
23. Chowdhury, M., et al.: Digital game-based language learning for vocabulary development. Comput. Educ. Open **6**, 100160 (2024)
24. Ishii, I.: The impact of Chinese character education on children's intelligence. Mod. Spec. Educ. (Youcai Edition) **1999**(3), 45–50 (1999)
25. Taguchi, N.: Immersive virtual reality for pragmatics task development. TESOL Q. **56**(1), 308–335 (2022)
26. Hwang, G.J., Chiu, L.Y., Chen, C.H.: A Contextual game based learning approach to improving students' inquiry based learning performance in social studies courses. Comput. Educ. **81**, 13–25 (2015)
27. Yang, W., Ng, D., Su, J.: The impact of story-inspired programming on preschool children's computational thinking. Think. Skills Creat. **47**, 101218 (2023)
28. Bandura, A.: Self-efficacy mechanism in human agency. Am. Psychol. **37**, 122 (1982)
29. Brockmyer, J.H., Fox, C.M., Curtiss, K.A., McBroom, E., Burkhart, K.M., Pidruzny, J.N.: The development of the game engagement questionnaire: a measure of engagement in video game-playing. J. Exp. Soc. Psychol. **45**(4), 624–634 (2009). ISSN 0022-1031. https://doi.org/10.1016/j.jesp.2009.02.016

30. Custers, E.: Long-term retention of basic science knowledge: a review study. Adv. Health Sci. Educ. **15**(1), 109–128 (2008). https://doi.org/10.1007/s10459-008-9101-y
31. Ebbinghaus, H.: Über das Gedächtnis: Untersuchungen zur experimentellen Psychologie. Duncker & Humblot, Leipzig (1885)
32. Murre, J., Dros, J.: Replication and analysis of Ebbinghaus' forgetting curve. PLoS ONE **10**(7), e0120644 (2015). https://doi.org/10.1371/journal.pone.0120644
33. Lin, J.W., Duh, H.B.L., Parker, D.E., Abi-Rached, H., Furness, T.A.: Effects of field of view on presence, enjoyment, memory, and simulator sickness in a virtual environment. In: Proceedings IEEE Virtual Reality, pp. 164–171. IEEE (2002)

Potential Representation Learning for Visible-Infrared Person Re-Identification in Virtual Surveillance Systems

Haoyuan Du[1(✉)], Xia Yu[1(✉)], Wei Yu[2], Dan Xue[1], and Yuhan Lin[1]

[1] School of Information Science and Engineering, Shenyang University of Technology,
No. 111, Shenliao West Road, Economic & Technological Development Zone,
Shenyang 110870, People's Republic of China
`duhaoyuanq@163.com, yuxia@sut.edu.cn`
[2] Neusoft Park, No. 2 Xinxiu Street, Hunnan District, Shenyang 110179,
People's Republic of China

Abstract. Visible-infrared person re-identification (VI-ReID) faces challenges in leveraging cross-modal semantic consistency within virtual-physical fusion systems. To address this, we propose PR-Net, a virtual surveillance-oriented framework that integrates spectral analysis with hierarchical feature fusion. The Fast Fourier Feature Transform (FFFT) aligns spectral distributions through frequency-domain correlation learning, establishing spectral-consistent representations for mixed reality rendering. The Super Token Aggregation (STA) captures both anatomical features and environmental context. Complemented by the Multi-Interaction Feature Extraction (MIFE) framework that fuses multiscale features through dual-channel interaction, our approach preserves identity discriminability for VR crowd simulation. Evaluations on SYSU-MM01 demonstrate 75.5% Rank-1 accuracy and 72.6% mAP under indoor search mode. This breakthrough provides a new paradigm for deploying ReID technologies in metaverse security systems requiring robust multimodal perception.

Keywords: VI-ReID · Diverse feature extraction · Latent common information · Modality difference

1 Introduction

The proliferation of virtual surveillance systems in smart cities demands reliable cross-modality perception capabilities, particularly for maintaining identity consistency between visible(VIS) and infrared(IR) modalities. This capability

Supplementary Information The online version contains supplementary material available at https://doi.org/10.1007/978-981-95-0100-7_12.

forms the foundation for critical applications ranging from metaverse security avatars to VR-based crowd behavior analysis, where heterogeneous sensor data must be seamlessly integrated in dynamic lighting conditions. Sole reliance on infrared imaging cannot achieve biometric-level unique identity authentication (e.g., facial recognition). The integration of metaverse security avatars enabl es cross-modal identity verification and real-time threat monitoring in mixed-reality environments, bridging physical sensors with virtual surveillance systems, while physics-based animation systems leverage multi-spectral inputs to simulate realistic thermal-textural interactions under dynamic lighting, enhancing crowd behavior analysis for public safety applications through synchronized visible-infrared physics rendering. Infrared thermal imaging is limited to capturing body contours (height, shoulder width, gait cycle) and thermal distribution patterns (local temperature gradients caused by clothing material variations). The core objective of this study is not to attain cross-modality unique identification, but rather to reduce candidate identities from full galleries (e.g., 10,000 individuals) to manually verifiable subsets (e.g., Top-10 candidates) through a multi-branch feature extraction architecture. This "coarse-to-fine" two-stage mechanism aligns with virtual surveillance systems' requirements for real-time responsiveness coupled with human-machine collaborative verification.

However, existing virtual surveillance frameworks face three fundamental challenges in cross-modality scenarios:

First, the inherent spectral discrepancy between VIS and IR sensors—VIS images capture detailed textures while IR images emphasize thermal profiles—creates significant feature misalignment. This gap hinders the deployment of robust AI visual generators for cross-modal avatar synthesis. Second, conventional methods predominantly focus on spatial feature extraction but neglect discriminative frequency patterns - distinctive characteristics in Fourier domain that capture periodic intensity variations (e.g., high-frequency edges vs low-frequency thermal contours) - limiting their effectiveness in physics-based animation systems requiring multi-spectral inputs. Third, the lack of hierarchical interaction mechanisms between low-level edge features - fundamental visual elements like clothing contours and texture boundaries - and high-level semantic representations - abstract identity-related attributes including body shape patterns and gait characteristics - leads to suboptimal performance in virtual crowd simulations where the preservation of both granular visual details (for VR rendering) and holistic identity semantics (for re-ID matching) is crucial.

To address these challenges, we propose the Potential Representation Learning Network (PR-Net). As illustrated in Fig. 1, this network's main innovation is its use of several feature extraction structures to extract features from various perspectives, which significantly reduces modal disparities and improves the capacity of feature maps to represent information. Our approach innovatively bridges computer vision fundamentals with virtual world requirements through three key technical contributions:

- A Fast Fourier Feature Transform (FFFT) module that resolves spectral discrepancies by learning frequency-domain correlations, providing essential support for mixed reality rendering systems requiring spectral consistency.
- A Super Token Aggregation (STA) mechanism that integrates global token attention with multi-scale dilated convolutions. This mechanism preserves the effective local information extraction from the DEE module in DEEN [22] while incorporating global information fusion, enabling effective feature alignment for virtual human path planning in multi-modal environments.

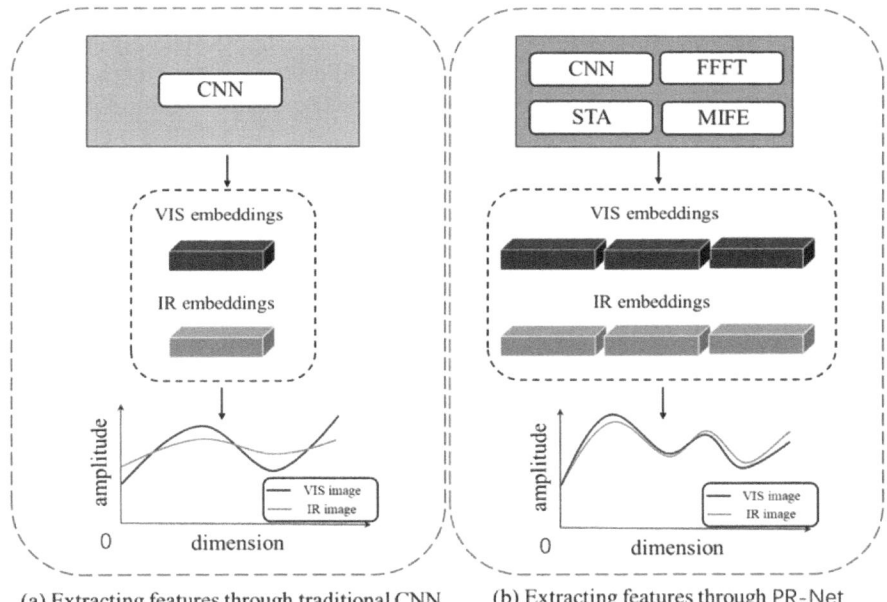

(a) Extracting features through traditional CNN   (b) Extracting features through PR-Net

Fig. 1. The motivation behind the proposed PR-Net is to generate diverse embeddings through diversified feature extraction structures, decreasing the modality difference between VIS and IR pictures by enabling the network to concentrate on acquiring latent modality-independent information.

- Inspired by the MFA block in DEEN [22], we propose a Multi-Interaction Feature Extraction (MIFE) framework that hierarchically fuses adjacent-stage features through dual-channel interactions, effectively aggregating low-level spatial details with high-level semantic context to enhance cross-modality feature discriminability.

2   Related Work

Generally speaking, the methods in VIReID can be mainly categorized into two types: image-level methods and feature-level methods.

The image-level VI-ReID methods typically endeavor to mitigate the modality discrepancies between visible light(VIS) and infrared(IR) imagery present in the image space by generating intermediate modality images (synthetic representations bridging VIS-IR spectral gaps through adversarial translation) or novel modality images (artificially generated hybrid spectra combining textural and thermal characteristics beyond original sensor captures), thereby enhancing the performance of the VI-ReID models through enhanced cross-modal consistency. To achieve this, some GAN-based methods of identity-preserving person image style transfer have been presented. Wei et al. [14] introduced a bidirectional image translation sub-network for generating intermediate modality images from the VIS and IR modalities. Li et al. [2] introduced a lightweight intermediate modality image generator to mitigate modality differences. These methods typically involved designing complex generative models to align cross-modal images. While they had successfully reduced the modality gap, GAN-based methods are prone to color inconsistencies or loss of image details, making the generated images potentially unreliable for subsequent network learning.

The goal of feature-level methods is to map features to a common feature space from various modalities, minimizing the modality gap between them. To achieve this, Liu et al. [5] attempted to learn cross-modal metrics in a bidirectional manner and then enhanced them via augmentation based on memory. Tan et al. [10] introduced cross-center loss to make intra-class distributions more compact compared to inter-class distributions. Sun et al. [9] pushed away negative pixels and promoted the proximity of positive pixels that have the same semantic information. Ling et al. [3] proposed a multi-constraint similarity learning approach to excavate the relationships between different modalities of information. Liu et al. [4] conducted effective data augmentation by constructing a generator to alter the original color information of the images, and introduced a novel channel-based local feature learning method to unify the feature representation across two modalities. Lu et al. [6] proposed a Progressive Modality-shared Transformer framework with progressive learning strategies and novel enhancement losses to extract reliable modality-invariant features for visible-infrared person re-identification. Zhang et al. [21] proposed a method based on Frequency Domain Nuances Mining that collaboratively mines cross-modality frequency domain information through amplitude-guided phase and amplitude nuances. However, learning a reasonable common feature space can be challenging due to the substantial modality gap between visible light and infrared images.

3   Method

3.1   Model Architecture

The overview of the proposed PR-Net is shown in Fig. 2. The components of PR-Net include a backbone network, multiple MIFE modules, an FFFT module, and a STA module. In this paper, we adopt a two-stream ResNet-50 network [8,17] as the backbone. We integrate the backbone network with an effective

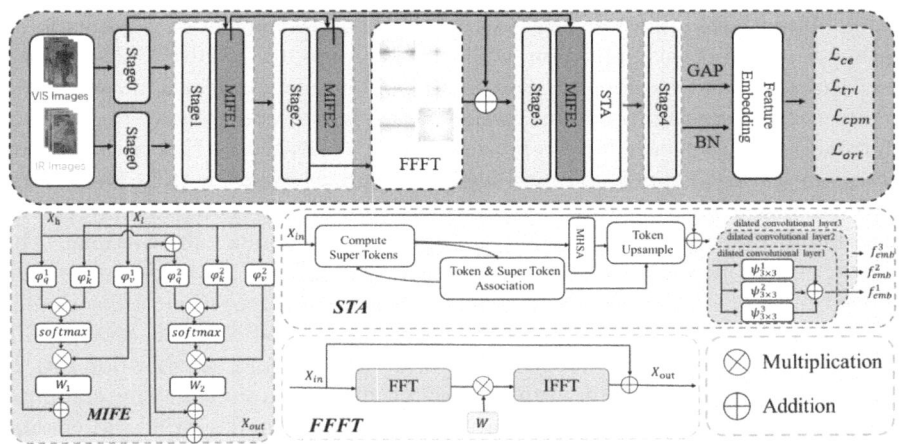

Fig. 2. Overview of the proposed PR-Net, including a backbone, a fast fourier feature transform (FFFT) module, a super token aggregation (STA) module, and three multi-interaction feature extraction (MIFE) modules.

MIFE module to aggregate features from several stages, combining information from low-level features' small receptive fields with high-level features to explore effective feature information in channels and spaces at different stages of the network. Meanwhile, in the network, we input the obtained features into the FFFT module, which learns the spectral information in images through fast Fourier transform to provide a more diversified feature extraction approach. Next, the STA module captures long-range dependencies between super tokens in the super token space using self-attention. Afterwards, different dilation rates of the dilated convolutional layers are employed to extract multi-scale contextual information and generate more diversified embeddings.

In practical deployment, PR-Net processes a single visible or infrared image as input to extract cross-modality features through the network architecture. The output is a 128-dimensional normalized feature vector, where cross-modality matching is achieved via cosine similarity computation. For instance, in virtual surveillance systems, the input could be real-time infrared frames captured by monitoring cameras. These extracted features are subsequently compared with pre-registered visible-light features in the gallery database through similarity ranking, generating a prioritized list of potential identity candidates.

3.2   Multi-Interaction Feature Extraction (MIFE) Module

Lower-level features have a small receptive field, focusing on detailed information and containing richer spatial details, while higher-level features have a larger receptive field, focusing on semantic information. Although every backbone network stage can make use of the global information of features, it only focuses on the current level of features and is unable to fully utilize the spatial and channel information of lower-level features, leading to the loss of valuable information. To address this limitation, while the MFA module in DEEN [22] employs two cascaded feature fusion structures with similar configurations, its sequential architecture inherently constrains the network's capacity to preserve task-critical information across hierarchical representations. Motivated by this critical observation, we propose the Multi-Interaction Feature Extraction (MIFE) module, which adopts a parallel feature integration paradigm to progressively consolidate lower-level spatial features into higher-level semantic abstractions. This architecture explicitly alleviates the information forgetting pathology commonly induced by cascaded fusion chains, ensuring persistent retention of discriminative features extracted at all granularities. The proposed MIFE is strategically embedded into three pivotal stages of the backbone network (as shown in Fig. 2), establishing coherent feature propagation pathways throughout the computational hierarchy. This module facilitates the propagation of spatial and channel information of lower-level features, while reinforcing higher-level features and enhancing the preservation of important information.

Specifically, after the first, second, and third stages of the backbone network, we fuse its high-level feature map $X_h \in \mathbb{R}^{C_h \times H_h \times W_h}$ with the low-level feature map $X_l \in \mathbb{R}^{C_l \times H_l \times W_l}$ from the previous stage using the MIFE module, where C, W, and H represent the channel number, width, and height of the feature maps, respectively. Initially, we convert X into three compact embeddings: $\varphi_q^1(X_h)$, $\varphi_k^1(X_l)$, and $\varphi_v^1(X_l)$ using three 1×1 convolutional layers, φ_q^1, φ_k^1, and φ_v^1. Using matrix multiplication and softmax, we obtain the channel similarity matrix $M_c^1 \in \mathbb{R}^{C' \times C'}$, C' represents the number of channels in the intermediate feature maps:

$$M_c^1 = f_{softmax}\left(\varphi_q^1(X_h) \times \varphi_k^1(X_l)\right) \tag{1}$$

Next, we restore the channel dimension by performing matrix multiplication between $\varphi_v^1(X_l)$ and M_c^1, achieving channel-wise multi-stage feature aggregation. Subsequently, we use another 1×1 convolutional layer W_1 to resize the above feature map to the size of X_h. Finally, we add X_h to it through matrix addition to obtain the output:

$$X_h^c = W_1(\varphi_v^1(X_l) \times M_c^1) \tag{2}$$

Afterward, we add the obtained X_h^c with the original high-level feature map X_h through matrix addition to obtain the new input X_h' for the next stage.

$$X_h' = X_h^c + X_h \tag{3}$$

Then, we use three new 1×1 convolutional layers, φ_q^2, φ_k^2, φ_v^2, to carry out the same spatial aggregation process on X_h' and X_l, resulting in a new channel-wise similarity matrix M_c^2 and the output X_h^s. The aggregation process is performed twice to creates a residual learning paradigm where the network learns additive refinements rather than overwriting features, preserving discriminative identity cues.

$$M_c^2 = f_{softmax}\left(\varphi_q^2(X_h') \times \varphi_k^2(X_l)\right) \qquad (4)$$

$$X_h^s = W_2(\varphi_v^2(X_l) \times M_c^2) + X_h' \qquad (5)$$

Finally, we obtain the result of the MIFE module by adding X_h^c and X_h^s together through matrix addition:

$$X_{out} = X_h^c + X_h^s \qquad (6)$$

3.3   Fast Fourier Feature Tansform (FFFT) Module

The purpose of using spectral information is to capture different frequency components of an image to understand local frequencies. This can be achieved using a spectral gating network, which includes a Fast Fourier Transform (FFT) layer, followed by weighted gating, and then an Inverse FFT layer. The spectral layer utilizes FFT to transform the feature map X_{in} from the physical space to the spectral space X_s. We use learnable weight parameters W to determine the weight of each frequency component, in order to properly capture the lines and edges of the image. Afterwards, the Inverse Fast Fourier Transform (IFFT) is used to bring X_s back from the spectral space to the physical space, and the final output of the module is obtained by adding it to the original feature map using matrix addition.

This process can be formulated as:

$$X_s = FFT(X_{in}) \qquad (7)$$

$$X_{out} = IFFT(W \times X_s) + X_{in} \qquad (8)$$

Then, all the generated embeddings are added to the output of the MIFE module through matrix addition and utilized as the input for the backbone network's subsequent phase.

3.4   Super Token Aggregation (STA) Module

Traditional VI-ReID methods frequently extract features using CNN or ViT (Vision Transformer). ViT is better at catching long-distance features and CNN is at capturing short-distance ones. In this paper, we adopt the STA module, which consists of the Super-Token Attention Branch (STAB) and the Dilated Convolution Branch (DCB). STAB includes Super-Token Sampling (STS), Multi-Head Self-Attention (MHSA), and Token Upsampling (TU). Super-Tokens are used in ViT to aggregate multiple adjacent tokens in a feature map into a larger unit. The Super-Token Attention Branch models global dependencies in super-token spaces by performing MHSA, while the Dilated Convolution Branch extracts multi-scale local dependencies by setting different dilation ratios. The DCB retains the DEE module from DEEN [22] that demonstrates superior local information extraction capabilities, which consists of three distinct dilated convolutional layers with varying receptive fields. Setting different dilation rates in the DCB aims to capture short-range dependency relationships of multi-scale context, and achieve performance improvement through diversified embedding.

Super-Token Attention Branch (STAB). In the STAB process, we convert the soft k-means based superpixel algorithm from pixel space to token space in SSN [1]. This branch will first convert the input feature map X_{in} into visual tokens. Given visual tokens $f \in \mathbb{R}^{N \times C}$ (where $N = H \times W$ is the token number), assuming each token $f_i \in \mathbb{R}^{1 \times C}$ belongs to one of m super tokens $f_s \in \mathbb{R}^{m \times C}$, it is necessary to compute the $f - f_s$ affinity mapping $Q \in \mathbb{R}^{N \times m}$. Each element Q[i,j] represents the association strength between the i-th original token and the j-th super token.

Super-Token Sampling (STS). First, we use the average of tokens in ordinary grid regions to sample the first super tokens f_S^0, $m = H/8 \times W/8$ is the number of super tokens, with the grid size set to 8×8 Then we do the next two phases of the sampling process iteratively:

Token and Super Token Association. Distinct from the SSN [1] pixel-super-pixel association calculation, we employ a more attention-like approach to compute the affinity mapping Q^t at iteration t, defined as:

$$Q^t = Softmax \left(\frac{f \times f_s^{t-1^T}}{\sqrt{d}} \right) \tag{9}$$

The number of channels in the equation is denoted by d.

Super Token Update. The column-normalized Q^t yields $\hat{Q}^t$, and the weighted total of tokens, which is represented as the updated super tokens, is as follows:

$$f_s = \left(\hat{Q}^t \right)^T \times X \tag{10}$$

X represents the input visual tokens derived from the original feature map.
    In order to expedite the sampling procedure, we limit the affinity calculation from every token to the nine super tokens that surround it, following SSN [1].

Multi-Head Self-Attention (MHSA). As super tokens represent essential information in a compact form, applying self-attention to them allows for a greater focus on global dependencies within the tokens rather than local features. We apply standard self-attention to the sampled super tokens $f_s \in \mathbb{R}^{m \times C}$ generated from the above process, defined as:

$$Att(f_s) = Softmax \left(\frac{q(f_s) \times k^T(f_s)}{\sqrt{d}} \right) v(f_s) = A(f_s)v(f_s) \tag{11}$$

where $A(f_s) = Softmax\left(\frac{q(f_s) \times k^T(f_s)}{\sqrt{d}}\right) \in \mathbb{R}^{m \times m}$ is the attention map, multiply the sampled super tokens by parameters W_q, W_k and W_v to obtain $q(f_s) = f_s \times W_q$, $k(f_s) = f_s \times W_k$ and $v(f_s) = f_s \times W_v$. For clarity, we have omitted the multi-head setting.

Token Upsampling (TU). While the long-range dependencies between super tokens may be efficiently captured by the self-attention, it also leads to the loss of most local details during the sampling process, and the subsequent DCB needs to extract local information. Therefore, we do not directly use them as inputs for subsequent layers, but instead map them back to visual tokens and ultimately add them to the initial feature map X_{in}. We upsample tokens from the super tokens f_s using the affinity mapping Q, which can be defined as:

$$X_{TU} = TU(Att(f_s)) = QAtt(f_s) \tag{12}$$
$$X' = X_{TU} + X_{in} \tag{13}$$

Dilated Convolution Branch (DCB). The proposed DCB extracts local features from the feature map by utilizing multi-branch dilated convolutions to generate structures, generating more embeddings to compensate for the limited ability of STAB in capturing local details.

Specifically, for the dilated convolution layers in DCB, we first use three 3×3 dilated convolutions, $\psi_{3 \times 3}^1$, $\psi_{3 \times 3}^2$, $\psi_{3 \times 3}^3$, with using inflation ratios of 1, 2, and 3, to cut down on the amount of features in the feature map X', to a quarter of its original size then combine them into a new feature map to extract local information from the feature map. Subsequently, ReLU activation function is used to enhance the non-linear representational capacity of DCB. Then, another 1×1 convolution layer θ is applied on the feature map that was obtained to match its dimensions with X'. Therefore, the generated embedding f_{emb}^i for the i-th dilated convolution layer can be expressed as follows:

$$f_{emb}^i = \theta\left(RELU\left(\psi_{3 \times 3}^1(X') + \psi_{3 \times 3}^2(X') + \psi_{3 \times 3}^3(X')\right)\right) \tag{14}$$

We will use three different dilated convolution layers to generate more embeddings, concatenate all the generated embeddings together, and use them as the final output of the STA module.

3.5   Multi-loss Optimization

To train our model we employ four loss functions that have demonstrated superior performance in the VI-ReID task: triplet loss [15], identity loss (utilizing cross-entropy loss [22] for identity classification), center-guided pair mining loss [7] (CPM), and orthogonal loss [7]. The expression for triplet loss is as follows:

$$\mathcal{L}_{tri} = \left[d(z_a, z_p) - d(z_a, z_n) + \alpha\right]_+ \tag{15}$$

Here, $z = \phi(x; \theta_a)$ represents the final generated embedding of the network, where θ_a is all the learnable parameters in the proposed network, the distance between two samples is represented by $d(\cdot, \cdot)$, α is a predetermined margin, and $[\cdot]_+$ stands for $max(\cdot, 0)$. z_a represents the anchor sample embedding - the feature vector of a query person image from one modality (either VIS or IR). z_p denotes the positive sample embedding - features of the same identity as z_a from the opposite modality (IR if z_a is VIS, and vice versa). z_n indicates the negative sample embedding - features of a different identity from either modality.

The identity loss is defined as:

$$\mathcal{L}_{ce} = \Sigma_i^N CE(\tau(z_i; \theta_c), y_i) \tag{16}$$

Here, $\tau(z_i; \theta_c)$ represents the identity classification module parameterized by θ_c, $CE(\cdot)$ is the standard cross-entropy loss, and the label y_i is the one for the i-th sample.

In the STA Module, different dilated convolution layers will generate different feature embeddings, which evolve into the ultimate output of the network as it progresses. We introduce the CPM loss to ensure that: (1) the network should be able to generate diverse embeddings to extract representative features from multiple perspectives, (2) the modality difference between images in the visible spectrum (VIS) and infrared (IR) should be reduced by the generated embeddings, and (3) the distance between intra-class should be smaller than the distance between inter-class.

For embeddings from the VIS, the CPM loss can be represented as:

$$\mathcal{L}_{vis} = \left[d\big(c_n^j, c_{v+}^{i,j}\big) - d\big(c_v^j, c_{v+}^{i,j}\big) - d\big(c_v^j, c_v^k\big) + \alpha \right]_+ \tag{17}$$

For embeddings from the IR, the CPM loss can be represented as:

$$\mathcal{L}_{ir} = \left[d\big(c_v^j, c_{n+}^{i,j}\big) - d\big(c_n^j, c_{n+}^{i,j}\big) - d\big(c_n^j, c_n^k\big) + \alpha \right]_+ \tag{18}$$

Therefore, the final CPM loss can be represented as:

$$\mathcal{L}_{cpm} = \mathcal{L}_{vis} + \mathcal{L}_{ir} \tag{19}$$

where c_v and c_n represent the embedding centers from the VIS and IR modalities, j and k are different identities in the mini-batch data, and c_{v+}^i is the embedding center of the i-th branch(STA outputs) from the VIS modality.

Furthermore, to guarantee that distinct information features should be captured by the embeddings generated by various branches, we aim for the different embeddings generated by different branches to be orthogonal to each other to minimize overlapping elements. As a result, the orthogonal loss has the following expression:

$$\mathcal{L}_{ort} = \sum_{m=1}^{i-1} \sum_{n=m+1}^{i} (f_{emb}^m{}^T f_{emb}^n) \tag{20}$$

Here, m and n represent original embeddings that, after passing through the m-th and n-th branches, produce new embeddings. The orthogonal loss enables the generated embeddings to extract representative features from various perspectives.

By optimizing the sum of the four aforementioned losses for end-to-end network optimization, the total loss is represented by:

$$\mathcal{L}_{total} = \mathcal{L}_{ce} + \mathcal{L}_{tri} + \theta_1 \times \mathcal{L}_{cpm} + \theta_2 \times \mathcal{L}_{ort} \tag{21}$$

4   Experiments

4.1   Datasets

We followed commonly used approaches and conducted experiments using two VI-ReID datasets that are accessible to the public.

The SYSU-MM01 dataset [23] includes 491 distinct person identities and offers two search modes: the all-search mode that tests all photographs, and the indoor-search mode that only uses images taken indoors. The RegDB dataset [13] contains 412 unique human IDs. Each individual has 10 visible light and 10 infrared photos taken. To achieve stable results, we performed ten independent training and testing splits on this dataset.

4.2   Implementation Details

All input photos are initially resized to $3 \times 384 \times 144$ during the training phase. Then, random erasing and random horizontal flipping are applied [20]. In the total loss, the parameters θ_1 and θ_2 are respectively set to 0.8 and 0.01. Throughout the first ten epochs, we employ a warm-up technique to gradually increase the learning rate from 1×10^{-2} to 1×10^{-1}. After that, over the course of 20 epochs, the learning rate decays to 2×10^{-2}. Until 150 epochs, the learning rate decreases to 1×10^{-3} at the 60th and 1×10^{-4} at the 120th epochs, respectively. As the optimizer, we employ SGD with a momentum parameter of 0.9. There will be 150 training epochs in all. We removed the stage-4 and MIFE3 modules and inserted the STA module before stage-3 when utilizing the RegDB dataset. Our evaluation measures are Cumulative Matching Characteristics (CMC) and Mean Average Precision (mAP).

4.3   Comparison with State-of-the-Art Methods

To prove that the suggested method is superior, We compared the proposed PR-Net with a number of state-of-the-art methods. Table 1 and Table 2 reports the experimental outcomes employing the RegDB and SYSU-MM01 datasets.

SYSU-MM01: As shown in Table 1, we found that in both search modes, our suggested PR-Net performed the best. Specifically, the PR-Net improved the mAP by approximately 10.8% and 9.8% compared to some image-level methods (such SMCL and JSIA-ReID) similarly improved the Rank-1 by approximately 8.1% and 13.6%, respectively, for all search modes and indoor search modes. PR-Net surpasses Transformer-based methods (PMT) and CNN-based methods (DDAG) by at least 8% in Rank-1 and 7.6% in mAP across all search mode. Additionally, it outperformed them by at least 10.7% and 8.9% for the indoor search mode. The outcomes demonstrate that PR-Net effectively reduces modality differences using diverse feature extraction structures and generates more diversified feature representations.

RegDB: Table 2 illustrates that, out of all the competing methods, our suggested PR-Net achieves superior or similarly. PR-Net obtains an mAP of 84.4% and a Rank-1 accuracy of 91.0% for the VIS to IR mode on RegDB. For the IR to VIS mode, PR-Net also achieves an mAP of 83.0% and a Rank-1 accuracy of 89.4%. The outcomes further demonstrate the robustness of our proposed method across various datasets and query modes.

Table 1. Comparison with state-of-the-art methods on the SYSU-MM01 datasets

Methods	SYSU-MM01							
	All Search				Indoor Search			
	R-1	R-10	R-20	mAp	R-1	R-10	R-20	mAp
JSIA-ReID [11]	38.1	80.7	89.9	36.9	43.8	86.2	94.2	52.9
AlignGAN [12]	42.4	85.0	93.7	40.7	45.9	87.6	94.4	54.3
X-Modality [2]	49.9	89.8	96.0	50.7	-	-	-	-
DDAG [20]	54.8	90.4	95.8	53.0	61.0	94.1	98.4	68.0
SMCL [13]	67.4	92.9	96.8	61.8	68.8	96.6	98.8	75.6
PMT [6]	67.5	95.4	98.6	65.0	71.7	96.7	99.3	76.5
DART [18]	68.7	96.4	99.0	66.3	72.5	97.8	99.5	78.2
CAJ [19]	69.9	95.7	98.5	66.9	76.3	97.9	99.5	80.4
MPANet [16]	70.6	96.2	98.8	68.2	76.7	98.2	99.6	81.0
DCLNet [9]	70.8	-	-	65.3	73.5	-	-	76.8
MAUM [5]	71.7	-	-	68.8	77.0	-	-	81.9
DEEN [22]	74.7	97.6	99.2	71.8	80.3	99.0	99.8	83.3
PR-Net(ours)	75.5	97.4	99.4	72.6	82.4	99.0	99.8	85.4

Table 2. Comparison with state-of-the-art methods on the RegDB datasets

Methods	RegDB							
	VIS to IR				IR to VIS			
	R-1	R-10	R-20	mAp	R-1	R-10	R-20	mAp
JSIA-ReID [11]	48.1	-	-	48.9	48.5	-	-	49.3
AlignGAN [12]	57.9	-	-	53.6	56.3	-	-	53.4
X-Modality [2]	62.2	83.1	91.7	60.2	-	-	-	-
DDAG [20]	69.3	86.2	91.5	63.5	68.1	85.2	90.3	61.8
SMCL [13]	83.9	-	-	79.8	83.1	-	-	78.6
PMT [6]	84.8	-	-	76.6	84.2	-	-	75.1
DART [18]	83.6	-	-	75.7	82.0	-	-	73.8
CAJ [19]	85.0	95.5	97.5	79.1	84.8	95.3	97.5	77.8
MPANet [16]	82.8	-	-	80.7	83.7	-	-	80.9
DCLNet [9]	81.2	-	-	74.3	78.0	-	-	70.6
MAUM [5]	87.9	-	-	85.1	87.0	-	-	84.3
DEEN [22]	91.1	97.8	98.9	85.1	89.5	96.8	98.4	83.4
PR-Net(ours)	91.0	97.9	99.0	84.4	89.4	97.2	98.7	83.0

Table 3. The impact of important PR-Net components on the SYSU-MM01 dataset performance

#	Methods	SYSU-MM01			
		All Search		Indoor Search	
		R-1	mAp	R-1	mAp
1	Baseline	68.8	65.5	76.6	80.6
2	+FFFT	69.6	66.0	77.3	81.0
3	+STA	71.6	68.2	78.1	81.9
4	+MIFE	70.8	67.9	79.4	82.5
5	+STA+FFFT	72.2	69.4	80.8	83.9
6	+STA+MIFE	74.9	71.8	80.6	83.8
7	+STA+FFFT+MIFE	75.5	72.6	82.4	85.4

4.4   Ablation Studies

Effectiveness of Key Components. Table 3 summarizes the results of the ablation study, with Method 1 denoting the standard ResNet-50 method.

STA: In all search mode and indoor search mode of SYSU-MM01, Method 3 achieved approximately 2.7% and 1.3% greater mAP than Method 1 by incorporating STA, respectively. **FFFT:** By incorporating FFFT into Method 3, Method 5 achieved improvements of 0.6%/1.2% and 2.7%/2.0% in Rank1/mAP on the two search modes, respectively. **MIFE:** Method 7 introduces MIFE into Method 5, resulting in improvements of 3.3%/3.2% and 1.6%/1.5% in Rank-1/mAP on the two search modes compared to Method 5.

Table 4. The influence of inserting the FFFT module after the MIFE module in the network

	SYSU-MM01			
Methods	All Search		Indoor Search	
	R-1	mAp	R-1	mAp
FFFT after MIFE1	74.6	71.3	82.0	84.8
FFFT after MIFE2	75.5	72.6	82.4	85.4
FFFT after MIFE3	41.6	41.4	44.4	54.5
FFFT after all MIFE	72.9	70.0	80.9	84.0

The Influence of Plugging and Unplugging the FFFT Module on the Network. At any stage across the network, the suggested FFFT can be plugged in and out. To enhance the diversity of network representation, we plugged it in parallel after MIFE. As Table 4 illustrates, when FFFT is plugged after MIFE1 and MIFE2, the performance gradually increases. The best feature extraction effect is achieved when FFFT is plugged after MIFE2. However, when FFFT is plugged after MIFE3, it interferes with the extraction of long-range and short-range dependencies in context. Finally, plugging FFFT after all MIFE layers introduces too much redundant information. Based on the above analysis, in unspecified cases, plug FFFT after MIFE3.

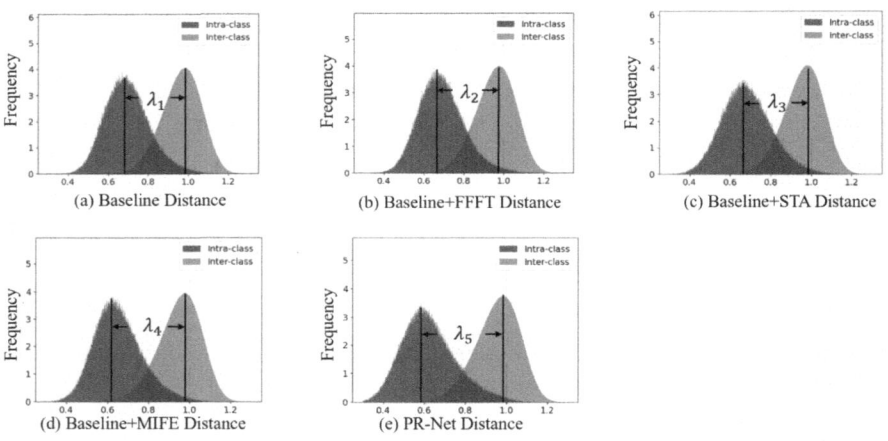

Fig. 3. Distances between cross-modal features Intra-class and inter-class. Green represents inter-class distances, and blue represents intra-class distances (Color figure online)

Feature Distribution. We used the SYSU-MM01 dataset to show intra-class and inter-class distances in order to investigate the efficacy of PR-Net. As shown in Fig. 3 comparing Fig. 3 (a) with Fig. 3 (b–e), evidently FFFT, STA, and MIFE push the mean values of inter-class and intra-class distances apart (represented by vertical lines), where $\lambda_1 < \lambda_2 < \lambda_5$, $\lambda_1 < \lambda_3 < \lambda_5$, and $\lambda_1 < \lambda_4 < \lambda_5$. This indicates that compared to the baseline features (Fig. 3(a)), PR-Net significantly reduces intra-class distances. The results demonstrate that our PR-Net can extract modality-agnostic features, decrease intra-class disparities and increase inter-class disparities compared to the baseline.

Visualization of Results. To evaluate the cross-modality retrieval capability of PR-Net, this study randomly selected multiple infrared and visible-light image pairs as query samples under the all-scenario mode of the SYSU-MM01 dataset, followed by visual analysis of their top-10 retrieval results (as illustrated in Fig. 4). Green borders annotate correctly matched cross-modality instances, while red borders highlight identity-mismatched cases, demonstrating the model's discriminative capability in complex cross-modal scenarios.

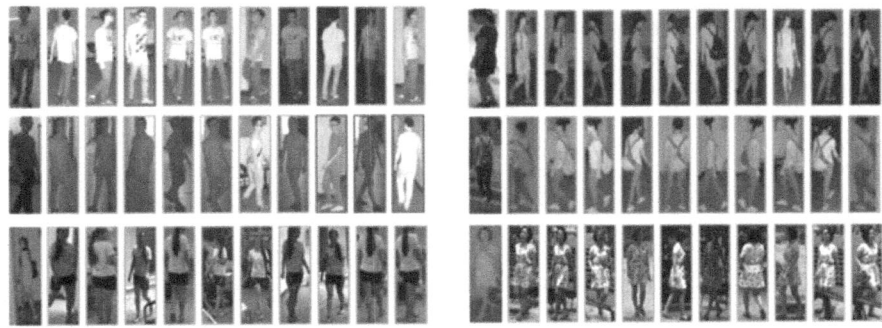

Fig. 4. Visualization of Results (Color figure online)

The visualization reveals significant modality discrepancies between infrared and visible-light images, particularly under nighttime conditions with drastic illumination variations (e.g., Row 3, Column 1), where textural details of pedestrians and background clutters jointly challenge the model. Notably, PR-Net achieved full matches in the latter four positions across most cases. For instance, in the visible-light query case of Row 3, Column 22, despite the target subject's side-view posture and partial occlusion, the model successfully identified identity-consistent matches across modalities through frequency-enhanced fabric wrinkle cues.

5   Conclusion

In this research, we present a novel PR-Net for VI-ReID, which consists of FFFT, STA, MIFE modules, and backbone network. Firstly, the FFFT module utilizes a fast fourier transform layer to learn spectral information within the images, providing a more diverse methods to feature extraction. Then, the STA module captures long-range dependencies between super tokens using self-attention, while also capturing multi-scale contextual short-range dependencies through dilated convolutional layers. Finally, the MIFE module extracts features from different stages, exploring effective feature information within the potential space and channels of the network.

Acknowledgments. This research received the National Natural Science Foundation of China [No. 62301339], the Applied Basic Research Project of Liaoning Provincial Science and Technology Program [No. 2023JH2/101700279].

Disclosure of Interests. The authors have no competing interests.

References

1. Hermans, A., Beyer, L., Leibe, B.: In defense of the triplet loss for person re-identification. arXiv preprint arXiv:1703.07737 (2017)
2. Li, D., Wei, X., Hong, X., Gong, Y.: Infrared-visible cross-modal person re-identification with an x modality. In: Proceedings of the AAAI Conference on Artificial Intelligence, vol. 34, pp. 4610–4617 (2020)
3. Ling, Y., Luo, Z., Lin, Y., Li, S.: A multi-constraint similarity learning with adaptive weighting for visible-thermal person re-identification. In: IJCAI, pp. 845–851 (2021)
4. Liu, J., Song, W., Chen, C., Liu, F.: Cross-modality person re-identification via channel-based partition network. Appl. Intell. 1–13 (2022)
5. Liu, J., Sun, Y., Zhu, F., Pei, H., Yang, Y., Li, W.: Learning memory-augmented unidirectional metrics for cross-modality person re-identification. In: Proceedings of the IEEE/CVF Conference on Computer Vision and Pattern Recognition, pp. 19366–19375 (2022)
6. Lu, H., Zou, X., Zhang, P.: Learning progressive modality-shared transformers for effective visible-infrared person re-identification. In: Proceedings of the AAAI Conference on Artificial Intelligence, vol. 37, pp. 1835–1843 (2023)
7. Nguyen, D.T., Hong, H.G., Kim, K.W., Park, K.R.: Person recognition system based on a combination of body images from visible light and thermal cameras. Sensors **17**(3), 605 (2017)
8. Park, H., Lee, S., Lee, J., Ham, B.: Learning by aligning: visible-infrared person re-identification using cross-modal correspondences. In: Proceedings of the IEEE/CVF International Conference on Computer Vision, pp. 12046–12055 (2021)
9. Sun, H., et al.: Not all pixels are matched: Dense contrastive learning for cross-modality person re-identification. In: Proceedings of the 30th ACM International Conference on Multimedia, pp. 5333–5341 (2022)
10. Tan, L., et al.: Exploring invariant representation for visible-infrared person re-identification. arXiv preprint arXiv:2302.00884 (2023)
11. Wang, G.A., et al.: Cross-modality paired-images generation for RGB-infrared person re-identification. In: Proceedings of the AAAI Conference on Artificial Intelligence, vol. 34, pp. 12144–12151 (2020)

12. Wang, G., Zhang, T., Cheng, J., Liu, S., Yang, Y., Hou, Z.: RGB-infrared cross-modality person re-identification via joint pixel and feature alignment. In: Proceedings of the IEEE/CVF International Conference on Computer Vision, pp. 3623–3632 (2019)
13. Wei, Z., Yang, X., Wang, N., Gao, X.: Syncretic modality collaborative learning for visible infrared person re-identification. In: Proceedings of the IEEE/CVF International Conference on Computer Vision, pp. 225–234 (2021)
14. Wei, Z., Yang, X., Wang, N., Gao, X.: RBDF: reciprocal bidirectional framework for visible infrared person reidentification. IEEE Trans. Cybern. **52**(10), 10988–10998 (2022)
15. Wu, A., Zheng, W.S., Yu, H.X., Gong, S., Lai, J.: RGB-infrared cross-modality person re-identification. In: Proceedings of the IEEE International Conference on Computer Vision, pp. 5380–5389 (2017)
16. Wu, Q., et al.: Discover cross-modality nuances for visible-infrared person re-identification. In: Proceedings of the IEEE/CVF Conference on Computer Vision and Pattern Recognition, pp. 4330–4339 (2021)
17. Yang, B., Chen, J., Ye, M.: Top-k visual tokens transformer: Selecting tokens for visible-infrared person re-identification. In: ICASSP 2023-2023 IEEE International Conference on Acoustics, Speech and Signal Processing (ICASSP), pp. 1–5. IEEE (2023)
18. Yang, M., Huang, Z., Hu, P., Li, T., Lv, J., Peng, X.: Learning with twin noisy labels for visible-infrared person re-identification. In: Proceedings of the IEEE/CVF Conference on Computer Vision and Pattern Recognition, pp. 14308–14317 (2022)
19. Ye, M., Ruan, W., Du, B., Shou, M.Z.: Channel augmented joint learning for visible-infrared recognition. In: Proceedings of the IEEE/CVF International Conference on Computer Vision, pp. 13567–13576 (2021)
20. Ye, M., Shen, J., J. Crandall, D., Shao, L., Luo, J.: Dynamic dual-attentive aggregation learning for visible-infrared person re-identification. In: Vedaldi, A., Bischof, H., Brox, T., Frahm, J.-M. (eds.) ECCV 2020. LNCS, vol. 12362, pp. 229–247. Springer, Cham (2020). https://doi.org/10.1007/978-3-030-58520-4_14
21. Zhang, Y., Lu, Y., Yan, Y., Wang, H., Li, X.: Frequency domain nuances mining for visible-infrared person re-identification. arXiv preprint arXiv:2401.02162 (2024)
22. Zhang, Y., Wang, H.: Diverse embedding expansion network and low-light cross-modality benchmark for visible-infrared person re-identification. In: Proceedings of the IEEE/CVF Conference on Computer Vision and Pattern Recognition, pp. 2153–2162 (2023)
23. Zhong, Z., Zheng, L., Kang, G., Li, S., Yang, Y.: Random erasing data augmentation. In: Proceedings of the AAAI Conference on Artificial Intelligence, vol. 34, pp. 13001–13008 (2020)

Improving Fidelity of Close Social Interaction Animations in Social VR with a Machine Learning-Based Refinement Framework

Alessandro Visconti[1]([✉]) [iD], Roberta Macaluso[1] [iD], Gabriele Di Bartolomei[2],
Davide Calandra[1] [iD], and Fabrizio Lamberti[1] [iD]

[1] Department of Control and Computer Engineering, Politecnico di Torino, Turin,
Italy
{alessandro.visconti,roberta.macaluso,davide.calandra,
fabrizio.lamberti}@polito.it
[2] Politecnico di Torino, Turin, Italy

Abstract. Social Virtual Reality platforms enable users to embody avatars and interact in virtual worlds. While research suggests that full-body avatar representations are generally preferred, high behavioral fidelity in avatar animations can be hard to achieve. Hardware-based tracking can be particularly effective but is costly, whereas Inverse Kinematics (IK) is more affordable but less accurate, leading to less realistic motion. Recent neural network-based approaches have shown promise in improving IK-based animations by predicting natural movements; however, guaranteeing high levels of fidelity in avatar-to-avatar interactions, particularly those involving close contact, remains challenging even with those approaches. With the aim to address such an issue, this paper proposes a neural network-based refinement framework to enhance behavioral fidelity in close social interactions. To investigate its effectiveness, hugging has been selected as a use case. The framework, trained on motion capture data, has been evaluated via a user study, showing improved behavioral fidelity in avatar social interactions.

Keywords: Social VR · avatar-based interactions · hugs · machine learning

1 Introduction

The rise of Social Virtual Reality (VR) platforms, driven by the increasing availability of affordable VR devices, has allowed users to embody avatars and interact in Virtual Environments (VEs) [16]. In these platforms, two primary factors contribute to the enhancement of realism and social presence: sensory fidelity,

Supplementary Information The online version contains supplementary material available at https://doi.org/10.1007/978-981-95-0100-7_13.

defined as the degree to which spatial, auditory, and haptic cues replicate real-world sensory experiences, and avatar fidelity, which encompasses both visual and behavioral dimensions. Specifically, visual fidelity refers to the degree to which avatar's appearance and movements resemble those of a human, while behavioral fidelity refers to the degree to which avatar's actions, gestures, and social interactions authentically emulate human behavior [13].

High sensory fidelity can be achieved, for example, through haptic and tactile interfaces (e.g., vests and suits) that provide a pseudo-physical sense of embodiment [3]. As for visual fidelity, full-body representations are generally preferred in Social VR settings to support more natural and immersive interactions [7].

To achieve behavioral fidelity in full-body avatars, various methods have been proposed. Methods relying on hardware-based tracking deliver superior realism but necessitate complex and expensive setups [19]; Inverse Kinematics (IK), in turn, offers a more cost-effective solution but tends to produce less natural movements [1]. Recent advancements in machine learning offer a promising alternative, generating more realistic and smooth animations by leveraging large motion datasets [9].

Despite advances in full-body animation, achieving realistic interactions with physical elements in VEs remains a significant challenge [12]. In this context, several studies have focused on improving hand-object interactions [11,17], in some cases leveraging neural network-based approaches to resolve overlaps and ensure realistic poses [11]. These methods have improved the accuracy [28] and plausibility [22] of hand-object interactions without significantly increasing application latency. However, research on direct avatar-mediated human-to-human interactions involving physical contact, particularly those utilizing neural networks, remains limited. This complexity arises from the need to manage social interactions involving multiple avatars, where each participant dynamically influences the other's movements rather than merely responding to predefined animations [14]. This issue is especially evident in Social VR, where close-proximity interactions such as handshakes, high-fives, and hugs often appear unnatural, reducing the sense of immersion [10,14].

To address this challenge and considering the positive effects of machine learning reported in previous studies on hand-object interactions, this paper proposes a neural network-based framework designed to simultaneously model and refine avatar motion during social interactions in real-time, ensuring more natural and synchronized movements between multiple avatars. The framework consists of two main components: a module that employs a base IK system to reconstruct the avatar body movements, followed by a neural network module implemented as a multilayer perceptron (MLP); the network processes motion data from user-controlled avatars, refining their synchronized movements during social interactions. The network needs to be trained on a dataset containing avatar social interactions like those mentioned above, so that it can learn and apply motion refinements dynamically.

In this paper, hugs are used as a case study, as they are considered one of the most emotionally charged forms of physical contact between humans and convey feelings of warmth, affection, and social affiliation [3]. In particular, hugging someone in Social VR requires making a hug movement in the real-life world, which strengthens emotional engagement in relationship [6]. The case study scenario aims to replicate a typical situation observed in Social VR, where two avatars perform a hug while being observed by external viewers within a VE. In this context, none of the users are physically co-located. For the training of the network, a dataset of avatar-mediated hugging interactions was utilized. At training time, motion capture data was used (following a preprocessing step, performed according to [9]), whereas at inference time the input consisted of animations generated using a base IK system. To assess the effectiveness of the proposed refinement framework, besides evaluating improvements in objective terms, a user study was also conducted, asking participants to subjectively assess improvements in behavioral fidelity by observing the animations of two avatars hugging in VR.

2   Background

The need to refine avatar animations primarily arises during physical-like interactions within VEs. When an avatar interacts with elements such as virtual objects [26], virtual agents [24], or avatars controlled by remote users [14], its movements should align with the ongoing physical action. However, the absence of a direct physical counterpart in the real world often causes inconsistencies between the movements of the avatar controlled by the user and the virtual elements in the environment, leading to unnatural and unrealistic animations [10]. Hence, avatar movements may need to be "refined".

2.1   Human-Object Interacton

One of the earliest studies in motion refinement, by Schmidl and Lin [20], introduced a geometry-driven physics approach that computes penetration depth and contact points when an avatar interacts with virtual elements. This information is used to adjust the avatar movements, resolving overlaps and ensuring realistic contact handling. Subsequently, Li et al. [11] introduced a grasp synthesis data-driven method using a shape-matching algorithm to align virtual hand shapes with objects. However, this approach was limited to single-hand interactions. Zhang et al. [28] extended this research by developing a bimanual interaction framework that uses a spatial representation combining object geometry with motion data. Their neural network-based approach demonstrated that incorporating object movement significantly improves the accuracy of hand-object interactions. A further step was taken by Taheri et al. [22] with GRIP, a learning-based model designed to generate realistic full-body grasping motions, synchronizing realistic motion for both hands before, during, and after object interaction based on predefined object interactions. These works highlight the importance of refining avatar motion to enhance the plausibility of interactions with virtual elements.

Besides hand-object interactions, some studies explored full-body motion refinement. Choi et al. [2] introduced a motion optimization technique for Mixed Reality environments, aimed at refining both locomotion and object interactions. Their approach included a penetration depth-based correction to minimize hand and foot intersection artifacts. However, their method did not incorporate learning-based techniques, which could further enhance realism. Similarly, Vogt et al. [24] proposed an optimization-based framework for virtual agents, leveraging prerecorded motion capture data of human interactions. Their system adapted and refined agent movements in real-time, enabling more natural interactions between human users and virtual agents.

2.2   Human-to-Human Interacton

While the above studies have contributed to improving avatar realism in object interactions, research on direct avatar-to-avatar interactions remains scarce. Oh et al. [14] tackled this issue by developing an avatar animation technique for remote handshakes. Their system refined avatar movements to maintain hand contact between users, improving social telepresence. However, their approach lacked fine-grained finger contact modeling. To address this limitation, Lee et al. [10] designed a framework enabling multifinger contact interactions, using a database of human hand gestures to refine avatar animations. Although their method improved realism for hand interactions, it did not extend to encompass full-body animations, which are essential for complex social interactions.

Hence, despite reported advancements, close-contact interactions in Social VR like handshakes, high-fives, hugs, etc. remain a significant challenge. Existing approaches have yet to fully address the bidirectional influence between interacting elements, such as avatars: most of the current methods refine avatar motion in isolation, without accounting for the dynamic interplay between two bodies during interaction.

To cope with the above limitation, this paper presents a neural network-based framework for real-time motion refinement enabling synchronized and realistic avatar interactions. The proposed refinement framework utilizes a network trained on virtual social interaction data to dynamically refine avatar motion. By jointly modeling the movements of the two interacting avatars it enhances behavioral fidelity, treating each avatar as an interactive entity rather than an independent object. This approach represents a step forward in improving the realism of complex social behaviors in VEs, ultimately providing a way to enrich the sense of presence and user experience in Social VR.

3   Materials and Methods

This section introduces the proposed refinement framework, designed to improve user's social interactions within a VE. Moreover, it outlines the use case that was devised to evaluate it.

3.1   Framework

The proposed framework, illustrated in Fig. 1, has been designed to be integrated into a Social VR platform accessible to users with consumer-grade VR

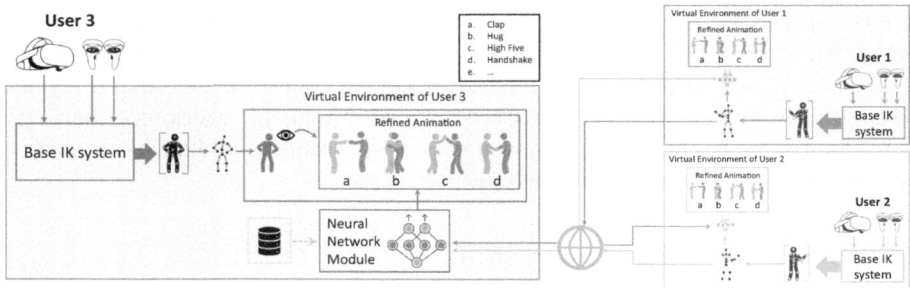

Fig. 1. Overview of the proposed refinement framework. In this case, User 3 acts as an observer, while User 1 and User 2 are engaging in a social interaction. The framework integrates a local neural network module for each user, which processes the structural information of the avatars and refines their animation by leveraging the output of a base IK system.

kits consisting of a headset and a pair of hand controllers. In the figure, User 3 is an external observer (the role played by the participants involved in the user study), while User 1 and User 2 are engaged in a social interaction.

When users wear the VR headset, the position and rotation of their head and hands are tracked. In a typical Social VR platform, this data is processed by an IK system that reconstructs the avatar's pose based on user input, providing a robust foundation for managing human motion. Consequently, a "base" IK system has been integrated into the proposed refinement framework, serving as a functional starting point for the second stage of the framework, which refines the motion. Although the base IK system module may introduce some errors and artifacts, it alleviates the need for the network to learn human motion from scratch, a highly complex task requiring also an extensive and well-prepared dataset. Thus, its integration helps mitigate the computational burden of neural network-based processing, which is performed locally on the user's machine. Furthermore, leveraging an existing IK system ensures adaptability, enabling the framework to integrate with various IK systems, rather than being limited to a specific one.

The second stage of the framework is the neural network module. The use of a neural network for pose refinement builds on the effectiveness of learning-based models and motion reconstruction methods. Neural networks offer high adaptability and the ability to learn complex motion patterns from data that would be impractical to encode manually. Additionally, running the neural network locally on each client rather than on a central server reduces computational load and enhances system scalability.

To limit computational load, the neural network module of a given user is activated only when proximity between two or more avatars is detected. Specifically, when proximity between User 1 and User 2 is detected, i.e. the distance between the users' hips is less than the so-called personal distance, set at 1.2 m, and avatars fall in the respective field of view, their local neural network modules are activated. Similarly, for User 3 the module is activated when the proximity between User 1 and User 2 is detected and when both User 1 and User 2 are within User 3's field of view. However, the locally activated module does not affect the User 3's own avatar, but instead refines the movements of other users involved in the interaction. Thus, from the perspective of User 3, who acts as an observer, the module refines the motions of both User 1 and User 2, while User 3's avatar remains unaffected. When the local neural network module is active, the IK-based reconstruction is used to extract the position and rotation of each joint for User 1 and User 2, which are then leveraged to compute per-joint velocities and angular velocities following the methodology from a previous study [9]. These four per-joint parameters define a numerical pose representation for each frame.

These pose representations are then processed by each user's local neural network module, which has been trained on a dataset of close social interactions. In this way, the network can refine motion with greater behavioral fidelity. In the current implementation, the network used is a MLP, chosen for its simplicity, flexibility, and effectiveness in learning complex motion patterns even with a single hidden layer, as shown in previous studies [21]. Specifically, in this framework, an MLP is used to infer full-body joint positions and orientations from partial input data, i.e., the positions and orientations of the head and hands. The model is optimized to minimize the difference between its predictions and the reference poses provided in the dataset, with the aim to provide a more realistic and coherent full-body avatar motion. The local neural network module is designed to reduce overlaps between avatars' virtual bodies and to suppress unnatural movements, particularly in the arms and torso, thereby improving the overall plausibility of the social interaction in the VE.

The refined poses generated by the neural network module correct artifacts or unnatural movements introduced by the base IK system reconstruction of User 1 and User 2. Refined poses are applied to the avatars of User 1 and User 2, making the updates visible to both users. Additionally, refinements applied to users engaged in the interaction are also visible to any close observer, like User 3 in this case.

The framework operates independently of avatars' global positions and orientations. To this purpose, a master-slave relationship is established between interacting avatars. The slave avatar's root position and rotation are expressed in the local coordinate system relative to the master's root, whereas all the other joints are represented in local coordinates relative to their respective parent joints. Additionally, during training, the master's global root position is zeroed out to ensure that the network learns motion patterns independently of absolute world positioning. At inference time, the master's root position and rotation are retrieved from the base IK system output, maintaining consistency between training and inference phases.

In this setup with User 3 acting as an observer, its neural network module dynamically applies the master-slave distinction to refine the social interaction between User 1 and User 2. Specifically, the avatar closest to the observer is identified as the master, while the other as the slave. Correspondingly, for the module running on each of the users directly engaged in the social interaction (User 1 and User 2 in this case), the master-slave distinction is applied such that the local user assumes the role of the master, while the other user is handled as the slave.

3.2 Use Case

As said, to evaluate the proposed refinement framework, hugs were considered as a use case. In the following, the use case is described by also making reference to all the technologies and settings used to implement, operate and assess the framework.

Hugging. Among social interactions, hugging involves very close interplay of the users limbs and bodies, making it a particularly complex case. The two most common types of hugs identified in real-life, the "criss-cross" and "neck-waist" [4, 5] hugs shown in Fig. 2, were considered when collecting the dataset. Additional variability was introduced during acquisition by modifying the crossing side of the heads and the positioning of the arms, whether over or under.

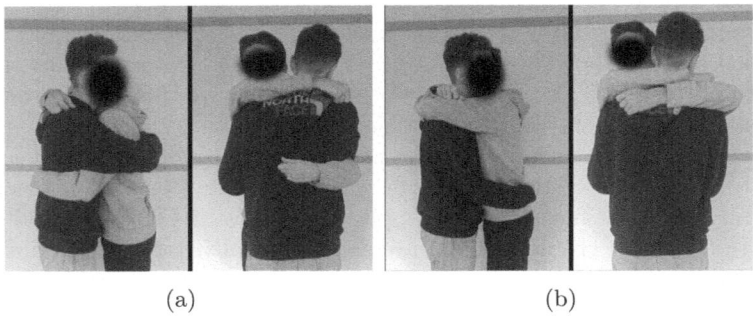

(a)   (b)

Fig. 2. The two types of hugs considered: (a) criss-cross, and (b) neck-waist.

Base IK System. In this work, the Final IK Unity asset by RootMotion[1] was selected as base IK system. Final IK is an IK solution for full-body character animation, featuring a VR-oriented IK solver for natural movement and real-time adaptation to user input given by head and hand tracking. It uses IK for the upper body and animation blending to manage walking. It is widely used in studies involving virtual avatars [23,25].

---

[1] Final IK: https://tinyurl.com/rMotionFinalIK.

Neural Network Module. To train the MLP, stochastic gradient descent with a MSE loss function was employed. Various configurations in terms of hidden layer sizes, along with other hyperparameters such as learning rate, batch size, and momentum were evaluated to determine the optimal settings for the network.

Dataset. The dataset was created using motion capture with the OptiTrack system[2], which has been used in previous studies [19]. The built-in re-targeting function from the OptiTrack streaming package for Unity was used to adapt the recorded movements to full-body avatars. In particular, full-body avatars downloaded from Mixamo[3] were used.

The dataset consists of the two most common types of hugs, i.e. "criss-cross" and "neck-waist". Specifically, each hug type was performed 29 times, with variations in hand, arm, and head positions between the two actors. Specifically, for each hug, the positions and rotations of both actors were recorded and then replicated in a mirrored way by switching the actors' movements in subsequent takes, ensuring complementary body positioning across all variations. This resulted in a total of 58 usable recordings, capturing different arm, hand, and head position combinations. The duration of each recording ranges from 5 to 7 s. To improve the robustness of the neural network, the dataset was further augmented by reversing the master-slave relationship for each hug sample, yielding 90 viable recordings. This augmentation ensured that the network can reconstruct the interaction regardless of which avatar assumes the master role.

Two simplifications were applied to the avatars for which motion data was collected. First, finger tracking was omitted, as finger movements are generally less relevant to the overall motion of a hug. Second, only avatars of the same height were considered; introducing height variations would have significantly increased the number of required recordings for each interaction type, with strong impacts on the data collection process.

For the data collection, the same two actors, both approximately 1.80 m tall and represented by virtual avatars of matching height, were involved in all usable recordings. Rotations and angular velocities from the collected data were converted to a 6D representation which has been shown to be effective for training neural networks [9,15,29].

The resulting dataset was split into three subsets for training (60%), validation (20%) and testing (20%).

To train the model, the input consists of the position and orientation of a set of bones (e.g., head, neck, etc.) obtained using Final IK, which receives head and hand positions from the dataset recorded with the OptiTrack system. The ground truth, used for supervision during training, consists of the positions and orientations of the same set of bones directly recorded via OptiTrack. The model outputs the predicted positions and rotations of these bones, which are then applied to the 3D avatar model.

---

[2] OptiTrack: https://www.optitrack.com/.
[3] Mixamo: https://www.mixamo.com/#/.

4   Evaluation

This section presents the evaluations conducted to assess the proposed refinement framework in both objective and subjective terms. Specifically, the rotation error with respect to the ground truth for both the selected base IK system and the proposed refinement framework was calculated. Additionally, a user study was conducted to determine whether the framework effectively enhances behavioral fidelity compared to the base IK system.

(a)   (b)   (c)

Fig. 3. Position of the users and viewpoints considered in the user study: (a) position of the participant as an external observer (red marker), (b) his or her viewpoint as an external observer, and (c) viewpoint as one of the users engaged in the hug. (Color figure online)

4.1   User Study

The user study was designed as a $2 \times 4 \times 10$ within-subjects experiment, with animation modality, type of hug, and point of view as independent variables, and involved 16 participants (12 males, 4 females) aged between 20 and 31 years. Participants were recruited from the student and staff population of the authors' university, volunteering as potential future users of Social VR. The VR experience for the user study was developed in Unity 2022.3, and the selected VR kit was a Meta Quest Pro.

The objective of the user study is to preliminarily investigate the potential effects on the visual perception of an external observer regarding the behavioral fidelity of hugging avatars in a VE, controlled by users who are not physically co-located. To this aim, two animation modalities were compared: a base IK system, specifically Final IK, and the proposed refinement framework, building upon Final IK.

At the beginning of the experiment, the participants filled in a demographic questionnaire covering age, gender, general experience with VR, and familiarity with multi-user Social VR. Most of the participants reported limited experience with VR technology, with approximately 50% rating their experience as 3 or lower on a 7-point scale (where 1 indicated almost no experience and 7 indicated daily use). Experience with social VEs was even lower, with about 94% of the participants stating they had little to no prior engagement with Social VR.

Afterwards, the participants were invited to enter a VE resembling a typical environment of Social VR platforms[4]. Within the VE, they watched four types of pre-recorded hug animations (each lasting a maximum of ten seconds): criss-cross right, criss-cross left, neck-waist high, and neck-waist low. The use of pre-recorded animations ensured reproducibility and consistency across the participants. Avatars with abstract representations were intentionally used to focus the attention on behavioral fidelity rather than visual fidelity [18].

Each animation was presented ten times, eight times from the perspective of an external observer with a 45-degree incremental rotation to allow for multiple viewpoints, and two times from a front-facing perspective of the hugger (one from the master and one from the slave viewpoint). The position of the users and the various viewpoints are illustrated in Fig. 3.

To balance exposure, a Latin square design was used to counterbalance both the order of hug animations and the sequence in which the two modalities were presented. After viewing an animation in a given modality, the participants answered questions aimed to assess the naturalness and realism of the hug. They were then shown the same animation in the second modality and asked to respond to the same set of questions, with the option to revise their previous answers. This approach enabled a direct comparison between the two modalities. A video illustrating the various hug types in the two modalities as seen in the VE is available for download[5].

Finally, the participants were invited to provide open-ended feedback.

4.2   Metrics

Evaluation metrics are reported in the following.

Objective Measures. As done in previous studies [9], the ability of the proposed framework to refine hugs compared to Final IK was measured in terms of Mean Per Joint Rotation Error (MPJRE), describing the mean rotation error of the joints in degrees.

Subjective Measures. As said, subjective evaluation was conducted using questionnaires aimed to assess the behavioral fidelity of the animations generated by the proposed refinement framework and to determine potential improvements over the base IK system. Custom questions were specifically designed to ask the participants to judge arm movements in relation to the use case, focusing on the following aspects: whether the beginning and end of the hug were well-coordinated, the hug appeared as visually harmonious, the postures and movements of the avatars were well-aligned, and the movement of the arms and hands appropriately adapted to the shape of the other body. These items were evaluated on a 7-point scale. Additionally, a question from [8] regarding perceived

---

[4] Sci-Fi Room: https://tinyurl.com/shifiRoom.
[5] Video of hug animations: https://tinyurl.com/2ja4zp7z.

collisions (in terms of avatars' mesh interpenetration) was included. Finally, to evaluate realism, the anthropomorphism section of the Godspeed Questionnaire Series [27] was used. The full questionnaire is available for download[6].

4.3   Results and Discussion

Various hyperparameter configurations were explored to optimize the neural network module. The best results came with a 1024-size hidden layer, momentum of 0.9, learning rate of 0.1, batch size of 32, 2000 epochs, and a downsampling factor (used to select a subset of frames from a recorded hug to increase variability and reduce overfitting) of 10.

For what it concerns objective results obtained on the trained network, the proposed refinement framework applied to Final IK yielded a MPJRE of 4.86°, whereas for Final IK alone MPJRE was equal to 17.83°. This outcome demonstrates that the proposed framework was able to produce an improvement of about 13° compared to Final IK in reproducing the ground truth poses.

For subjective results, the Shapiro-Wilk test was used to analyze normality of data. Since data was found to be normally distributed, T-test with a 5% threshold was used to identify significance differences (p-value $<.050$). For what it concerns custom questions (Fig. 4), scores regarding coordination of the beginning and end of the hug, visual harmony of the interaction, and alignment of the avatars postures and movements did not show significant differences between the two modalities.

This outcome suggests that the proposed refinement framework does not degrade the harmony and fluidity of the animations, which are already well-refined in Final IK. A significant difference in favor of the proposed refinement framework, instead, was observed in the evaluation of how well the movement of the arms and hands adapted to the shape of the other body (3.84 vs 4.22, $p = .036$). This improvement is likely due to the neural network, which, having been trained on a dataset of high-fidelity hugging interactions, refines the motion to better conform to the shape of the other avatar's body. Another statistically significant difference was found in the perception of perceived collisions, with the participants reporting fewer instances of unnatural visual collisions when watching the animations generated by the proposed refinement framework (3.27 vs 3.56, $p = .028$). This finding further supports an improvement in the behavioral fidelity of the hug, likely attributable to the neural network's ability to better adapt the movements of both the avatars, avoiding collisions and interpenetration.

In contrast, when analyzing the answers to the Godspeed questionnaire (Fig. 5) no significant differences were observed for most items, suggesting that the proposed refinement framework does not negatively impact the motion generated by Final IK. However, a notable exception was found in the assessment of the extent to which the movements appeared as human-like; in this case, animations generated by Final IK were perceived as more natural (4.52 vs 4.03,

---

[6] Questionnaire: https://tinyurl.com/54nbsaxu.

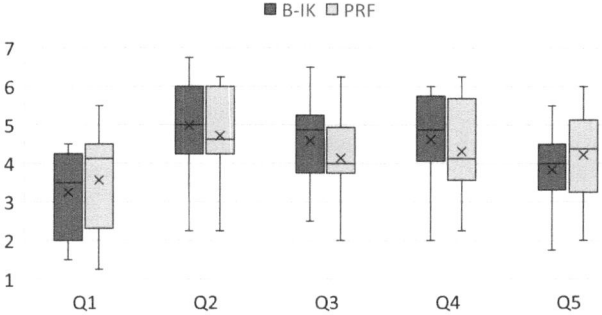

Fig. 4. Box plot showing the distribution of scores for the base IK system (B-IK) and the proposed refinement framework (PRF) in relation to custom questions assessing hug animations. Statistically significant results are marked with a * symbol. (Q1: I have never seen overlaps between the avatars; Q2: The beginning and end of the hug were well coordinated; Q3: The hug was visually harmonious; Q4: The postures and movements of the avatars were well aligned; Q5: The movement of the arms and hands adapted correctly to the shape of the other body).

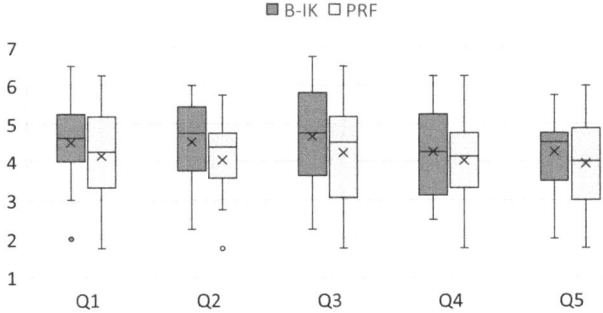

Fig. 5. Box plot showing the distribution of scores for the base IK system (B-IK) and the proposed refinement framework (PRF) in relation to items of the anthropomorphism section of the Godspeed questionnaire. Statistically significant results are marked with a * symbol. (Q1: Fake/Natural, Q2: Machinelike/HumanLike, Q3: Unconscious/Conscious, Q4: Artificial/Lifelike, Q5: Moving rigidly/Moving elegantly.)

$p = .032$). This outcome could be attributed to the fact that, while the proposed refinement framework improves natural adaptation, the resulting movements may have lacked smoothness, appearing slightly rigid and contributing to a more mechanical perception.

5   Conclusions and Future Work

In this work, a neural network-based framework has been designed to refine avatar animations during social interactions in real-time. The framework consists of two main components: a base IK system to reconstruct the avatar's body movements, followed by a neural network module implemented as a MLP. The neural network processes motion data from avatars controlled by users, refining their synchronized movements during social interactions. To achieve this goal, the network can be trained on a dataset containing motion capture recordings of avatar-to-avatar interactions, allowing it to learn and apply realistic motion refinements.

To evaluate framework's effectiveness in enhancing behavioral fidelity, hugs were chosen as a use case, and a user study was conducted to preliminary investigate the potential effects on the behavioral fidelity of the hugging avatars based on the visual perception of an external observer. In the study, both objective and subjective measures were collected. Objective results showed improvements in terms of MPJRE compared to a base IK system commonly used in VEs. Subjective results were gathered through the user study, in which participants evaluated two animations: one using the base IK system and the other using the proposed refinement framework. Subjective results indicated a reduction in perceived collisions and an improvement in animation harmony. However, participants noted a slight decrease in the humanlikeness of movements, likely due to the lack of smoothness in the refined movements despite the improvement in natural adaptation.

The study is affected by some limitations, including the limited sample, and suggests potential directions for future research. For instance, more advanced neural network models could be explored, balancing prediction accuracy and computational complexity. It would be interesting to investigate the latency introduced by the neural network, as it could potentially affect the perception of close-quarters interactions. The detection of social interactions used to trigger the neural network could be improved by incorporating classifiers capable of recognizing body gestures associated with specific interactions; this would enhance the scalability of the framework when handling multiple types of social interactions simultaneously, thereby reducing the risk of misinterpreting the users' intended behavior. In terms of scalability, it would be valuable to investigate the framework's ability to manage a large number of users connected at the same time. Future work could additionally focus on enhancing animation smoothness with motion filters to improve behavioral fidelity and evaluating the framework with a wider range of social interactions; this should also include investigating whether the refinement process enhances the sense of immersion. Building on that, new studies may investigate how the visual perception of an external observer is influenced by the nature of the human-human interactions occurring in the Social VE; specifically, such studies could explore the differences between typically more polished but inherently repetitive pre-recorded interactions, and real-time interactions, which, although potentially less refined in appearance, offer uniqueness and spontaneity that may enhance the sense of authenticity.

A further direction for future development would be to investigate user perception from a first-person perspective by integrating the framework in interactive applications and allowing users to actively engage in social interactions;

this would enable an assessment of the effects of such interactions from within the experience itself. Finally, the integration of haptic feedback systems or spatial audio technologies could be explored to further enhance sensory fidelity and enrich the overall sense of physical presence.

Acknowledgement. This work has been carried out in the frame of the VR@POLITO initiative.

References

1. Caserman, P., Achenbach, P., Göbel, S.: Analysis of inverse kinematics solutions for full-body reconstruction in virtual reality. In: Proceedings of the 7th IEEE International Conference on Serious Games and Applications for Health, pp. 1–8 (2019)
2. Choi, S., Hong, S., Cho, K., Kim, C., Noh, J.: Online avatar motion adaptation to morphologically-similar spaces. Comput. Graph. Forum **42**(2), 13–24 (2023). https://doi.org/10.1111/cgf.14740
3. Cui, D., Kao, D., Mousas, C.: Toward understanding embodied human-virtual character interaction through virtual and tactile hugging. Comput. Animat. Virtual Worlds **32**(3–4), e2009 (2021). https://doi.org/10.1002/cav.2009
4. Dueren, A.L., Vafeiadou, A., Edgar, C., Banissy, M.J.: The influence of duration, arm crossing style, gender, and emotional closeness on hugging behaviour. Acta Psychologica **221**, 103441 (2021). https://doi.org/10.1016/j.actpsy.2021.103441, https://www.sciencedirect.com/science/article/pii/S0001691821001918
5. Floyd, K.: All touches are not created equal: effects of form and duration on observers' interpretations of an embrace. J. Nonverbal Behav. **23**(4), 283–299 (1999). https://doi.org/10.1023/A:1021602926270, https://doi.org/10.1023/A:1021602926270
6. Freeman, G., Acena, D.: Hugging from a distance: building interpersonal relationships in social virtual reality. In: Proceedings of the ACM International Conference on Interactive Media Experiences, pp. 84–95 (2021). https://doi.org/10.1145/3452918.3458805
7. Freeman, G., Zamanifard, S., Maloney, D., Adkins, A.: My body, my avatar: how people perceive their avatars in social virtual reality. In: Proceedings of the CHI Conference on Human Factors in Computing Systems – Extended Abstracts, pp. 1–8 (2020)
8. Hoyet, L., Olivier, A.H., Kulpa, R., Pettré, J.: Perceptual effect of shoulder motions on crowd animations. ACM Trans. Graph. **35**(4) (2016). https://doi.org/10.1145/2897824.2925931, https://doi.org/10.1145/2897824.2925931
9. Jiang, J., et al.: Avatarposer: articulated full-body pose tracking from sparse motion sensing. In: Proceedings of the European Conference on Computer Vision, pp. 443–460 (2022)
10. Lee, Y., Lee, S., Lee, S.H.: Multifinger interaction between remote users in avatar-mediated telepresence. Comput. Animat. Virtual Worlds **28**(3–4), e1778 (2017). https://doi.org/10.1002/cav.1778
11. Li, Y., Fu, J.L., Pollard, N.S.: Data-driven grasp synthesis using shape matching and task-based pruning. IEEE Trans. Vis. Comput. Graph. **13**(4), 732–747 (2007)

12. Mangalam, M., Oruganti, S., Buckingham, G., Borst, C.W.: Enhancing hand-object interactions in virtual reality for precision manual tasks. Virtual Reality **28**(4), 166 (2024)
13. Narayanan, S., Polys, N., Bukvic, I.I.: Cinemacraft: exploring fidelity cues in collaborative virtual world interactions. Virtual Reality **24**(1), 53–73 (2020)
14. Oh, J., Lee, Y., Kim, Y., Jin, T., Lee, S., Lee, S.H.: Hand contact between remote users through virtual avatars. In: Proceedings of the 29th International Conference on Computer Animation and Social Agents, pp. 97–100 (2016). https://doi.org/10.1145/2915926.2915947
15. Oreshkin, B.N., Bocquelet, F., Harvey, F.G., Raitt, B., Laflamme, D.: ProtoRes: proto-residual network for pose authoring via learned IK. arXiv:2106.01981 (2022). https://arxiv.org/abs/2106.01981
16. Prattico, F.G., Checo, I., Visconti, A., Simeone, A., Lamberti, F.: Designing hand-held controller-based handshake interaction in Social VR and Metaverse. In: Proceedings of the 16th ACM SIGGRAPH Conference on Motion, Interaction and Games (2023). https://doi.org/10.1145/3623264.3624464
17. Rezzonico, S., Boulic, R., Huang, Z., Thalmann, N.M., Thalmann, D.: Consistent grasping in virtual environments based on the interactive grasping automata. In: Virtual Environments' 95: Selected papers of the Eurographics Workshops in Barcelona, Spain, 1993, and Monte Carlo, Monaco, 1995, pp. 107–118. Springer (1995)
18. Roth, D., et al.: Avatar realism and social interaction quality in virtual reality. In: Proceedings of the IEEE Virtual Reality, pp. 277–278 (2016). https://doi.org/10.1109/VR.2016.7504761
19. Roth, D., Waldow, K., Latoschik, M.E., Fuhrmann, A., Bente, G.: Socially immersive avatar-based communication. In: Proceedings of the IEEE Virtual Reality, pp. 259–260 (2017). https://doi.org/10.1109/VR.2017.7892275
20. Schmidl, H., Lin, M.C.: Geometry-driven physical interaction between avatars and virtual environments. Comput. Anim. Virtual Worlds **15**(3–4), 229–236 (2004)
21. Sharma, G., Chandra, S., Venkatraman, S., Mittal, A., Singh, V.: Artificial neural network in virtual reality: a survey. Int. J. Virtual Real. **15**, 44–52 (2016). https://doi.org/10.20870/IJVR.2016.15.2.2873
22. Taheri, O., et al.: Grip: generating interaction poses using spatial cues and latent consistency. In: Proceedings of the International Conference on 3D Vision, pp. 933–943 (2024)
23. Visconti, A., Calandra, D., Lamberti, F.: Comparing technologies for conveying emotions through realistic avatars in virtual reality-based metaverse experiences. Comput. Anim. Virtual Worlds **34**(3–4), 11 (2023). https://doi.org/10.1002/cav.2188
24. Vogt, D., Grehl, S., Berger, E., Ben Amor, H., Jung, B.: A data-driven method for real-time character animation in human-agent interaction. In: Proceedings of the 14th International Conference on Intelligent Virtual Agents, pp. 463–476 (2014)
25. Wagnerberger, L., Runde, D., Lafci, M.T., Przewozny, D., Bosse, S., Chojecki, P.: Inverse kinematics for full-body self representation in VR-based cognitive rehabilitation. In: Proceedings of the IEEE International Symposium on Multimedia, pp. 123–129 (2021). https://doi.org/10.1109/ISM52913.2021.00029
26. Wan, W., et al.: Learn to predict how humans manipulate large-sized objects from interactive motions. IEEE Robot. Autom. Lett. **7**(2), 4702–4709 (2022). https://doi.org/10.1109/LRA.2022.3151614

27. Weiss, A., Bartneck, C.: Meta analysis of the usage of the godspeed questionnaire series. In: Proceedings of the 24th IEEE International Symposium on Robot and Human Interactive Communication, pp. 381–388 (2015). https://doi.org/10.1109/ROMAN.2015.7333568
28. Zhang, H., Ye, Y., Shiratori, T., Komura, T.: ManipNet: neural manipulation synthesis with a hand-object spatial representation. ACM Trans. Graph. **40**(4) (2021). https://doi.org/10.1145/3450626.3459830
29. Zhou, Y., Barnes, C., Lu, J., Yang, J., Li, H.: On the continuity of rotation representations in neural networks. In: Proceedings of the IEEE/CVF Conference on Computer Vision and Pattern Recognition (2019)

Simulation of Ball Levitation with SPH

Sun-Lay Gagneux, Khalid Djado$^{(\boxtimes)}$, and Richard Egli

Université de Sherbrooke, 2500, boul. de l'Université, Sherbrooke,
Québec J1K 2R1, Canada
`{Sun-Lay.Gagneux,Khalid.Djado,Richard.Egli}@USherbrooke.ca`
`https://www.usherbrooke.ca/`

Abstract. We present a Smoothed Particle Hydrodynamics (SPH) simulation of a ball levitating in an air stream. We conducted experiments with various SPH techniques, such as Predictive-Corrective Incompressible SPH (PCISPH), Implicit Incompressible SPH (IISPH) and Divergence-Free SPH (DFSPH). However, the ball always escaped the air stream and fell onto the simulation floor. Therefore, we introduce a new heuristic to compute the Coandă effect that was shown to be missing in recent SPH works. Our method does not produce tensile and pairing instabilities typically found when negative pressure is involved. Since our method adds another external force to the Navier-Stokes equations, it can be generalized to any SPH-based method.

Keywords: SPH · ball levitating · fluid simulation · air stream ·
Coandă effect · Navier-Stokes equations

1 Introduction

Fluid simulation is a crucial component in the field of computer graphics, with applications in various industries such as film, video games, and engineering. Realistically simulating fluids is essential for creating convincing visual effects and animations. There are two main approaches to fluid simulation: Eulerian and Lagrangian. Eulerian methods use a grid to track the fluid and are better suited for simulating fluids with well-defined boundaries. Lagrangian methods, such as Smoothed Particle Hydrodynamics (SPH), represent fluids as a set of discrete particles and are better suited for simulating fluids with complex boundaries or that undergo large deformations.

In this paper, we focus on animating a ball levitating in an air stream as shown in Fig. 1 using a variant of SPH called Divergence-Free SPH (DFSPH), the current state of the art, from J. Bender et al. [1]. Additionally, modeling correct two-way coupling is essential for realistic ball animation, and we use the work of N. Akinci et al. [2] for that purpose.

Simulating the fluid as an air stream from a hair dryer using the incompressible form of the Navier-Stokes Eqs. 1 and 3 is acceptable if any particle of the fluid moves slower than 0.3 its speed of sound [3], which would be around $113 \, \mathrm{m \cdot s^{-1}}$ for air under normal pressure and temperature found on Earth (the air stream velocity of a hair dryer would be around $40 \, \mathrm{m \cdot s^{-1}}$).

C. Mousas et al. (Eds.): CASA 2025, LNCS 15915, pp. 220–229, 2026.
https://doi.org/10.1007/978-981-95-0100-7_14

Fig. 1. Simulation of ball levitation. (a) Real photo of our experiments with a hair dryer. (b) Image from the high-quality rendering of the simulator particles. (c) Image from our SPH-based simulator.

These equations consist of an equation that describes the conservation of momentum.

$$\frac{D\mathbf{u}}{Dt} = -\frac{1}{\rho}\nabla p + \nu\nabla^2\mathbf{u} + \mathbf{f} \tag{1}$$

where ρ is the density, $\mathbf{u}$ is the velocity, p is the pressure, ν is the kinematic viscosity and $\mathbf{f}$ is the external force; and a continuity equation which describes the conservation of mass:

$$\frac{D\rho}{Dt} + \nabla \cdot (\rho\mathbf{u}) = 0 \tag{2}$$

which is also known as the divergence-free constraint in case of an incompressible fluid since ρ is a constant.

$$\nabla \cdot \mathbf{u} = 0 \tag{3}$$

Additionally, the SPH method uses an artificial pressure term to enforce the divergence-free constraint of the Navier-Stokes equations, which is essential for maintaining stability.

The levitation of a ball is quite a challenge because we were unable to find recent works using SPH to simulate gases. Recent state-of-the-art Incompressible SPH (ISPH) techniques enforce the divergence-free constraint 3 of the Navier-Stokes equations by predicting the pressure component in the next timestep to correct the particle density ρ to the fluid rest density ρ_0 to be less than an acceptable compression level. Naturally, under such assumption, the artificial pressure is null when ρ is equal to ρ_0, positive when ρ is higher, and negative when it is lower. However, multiple articles highlight the importance of having a positive pressure to prevent tensile and pairing instabilities [1,4–9], [10, p.26] [11, p.558], which in turn leads to fixes that can be found in standard Equation Of State (EOS) solvers, i.e., to null the negative artificial pressure. Consequently, because the nulled out pressure component cannot correct the variation in density, the divergence-free constraint 3 is no longer respected.

By simulating the Coandă effect separately from the pressure force, our contribution provides the correct physical interactions between solids and gases under negative pressure, without creating tensile or pairing instabilities.

An alternative solution can be envisioned by filling the simulation domain to the brim to prevent voids from happening. This is not realistic because our tests showed that: first, it is not trivial to place particles in a natural setup that leaves no voids when initializing the scene; second, the simulation requires a tremendous quantity of particles, which in turn has a major impact on the simulation speed and memory consumption; third, it is only possible in an enclosed space; fourth, leaving no margin for correction quickly leads to an unstable simulation, unless we significantly reduce the simulation timestep.

To solve the problem, we propose a new heuristic that simulates the Coandă effect when the artificial pressure is negative. This allows us to prevent tensile and pairing instabilities without filling the domain to the brim, and without the need to compromise the divergence-free constraint of the Navier-Stokes equations.

Since this new heuristic is added to the Navier-Stokes equations under the external force term, it is independent of the SPH simulation technique used and can be easily plugged into any older algorithm. We evaluated our method by simulating a ball levitating in an air stream and comparing the results with real-world experiments as illustrated in the Fig. 1.

Section 2 will provide a brief overview of related works, then we will focus on our approach in Sect. 3. Experimental results will be detailed in Sect. 4, and limitations will be discussed in Sect. 5 before concluding.

2   Related Work

L.B. Lucy [12], R.A. Gingold, and J.J. Monaghan [13] are credited with the development of SPH, a meshless Lagrangian method for simulating fluid dynamics. Müller et al. [15] extended the SPH method to simulate free-surface flows with an EOS, but [16,17] described several artifacts in the method, including particle clustering and poor handling of fluid boundaries. Since SPH does not provide an explicit mechanism to enforce volume preservation, contrary to Eulerian approach, the challenge of these last decades has been to enforce $\rho - \rho_0$ to be less than a defined minimal error. M. Becker et al. [14] introduced weakly compressible SPH (WCSPH) based on [16]. They automatically computed the stiffness coefficient of the Tait equation from the speed of sound in the fluid. They ensured a compression level below 1% which made it more suitable for simulating free-surface flows. However, they had to reduce the simulation timestep, which increased the simulation time, because of the Courant-Friedrichs-Lewy condition [18]. Solenthaler et al. [19] proposed Predictive-Corrective Incompressible SPH (PCISPH) from the work of S.J. Cummins and M. Rudman [20], and S. Shao et al. [21]. PCISPH enforces the incompressibility constraint by correcting the position of the particles instead of solving the Pressure Poisson Equation (PPE). Thanks to this improvement, SPH has been widely adopted in the computer graphics community due to its ability to simulate highly detailed splashing effects [22, p.291]. M. Ihmsen et al. [5] extended PCISPH by solving the PPE for each particle, leading to more accurate pressure calculations. However, like standard EOS solvers, their work used a negative pressure clamping to solve the tensile and pairing instability. The divergence-free constraint 3 would not be respected in case $\rho < \rho_0$ which leads to incorrect two-way coupling in our case. To address the limitations of previous works, our work builds on the Divergence-Free SPH (DFSPH) method developed by J. Bender et al. [1]. DFSPH, in continuation with IISPH, solves two PPEs explicitly: one with density invariance as source term, and the other with velocity divergence. This results in more stable and accurate simulations as described in [1,4].

In terms of two-way coupling, SPH provides an intuitive way to handle interactions between fluids and rigid bodies. Rigid bodies are sampled in particles and interact with fluid particles in the same way as any other particles. N. Akinci et al. [2] improved the accuracy of two-way coupling with a correction coefficient accounting for missing or overly dense sampling. Furthermore, some research also proposed modeling rigid bodies with implicit surfaces, e.g., the work of J. Bender et al. [23] to remove artifacts due to non-uniform surface sampling that could result in trajectory biases or fluid particles penetrating the boundary.

Overall, these related works have contributed to the development of SPH as a powerful tool for simulating fluid dynamics in computer graphics. However, there are still challenges to be addressed, particularly in terms of handling two-way coupling and preventing tensile and pairing instabilities, which is what motivated our work.

3   Our Work

The main purpose of this research is to simulate a ball levitating in an air stream created by a hair dryer. Assuming that the simulation domain is large enough and walls are far enough from the region of interest (i.e., the area with the air stream and the ball), the enclosed wall should not affect the movement of the ball. We can thereby lower the particle count by not filling the simulation domain to the brim.

This paper uses boundary handling as described by Akinci et al. [2] with DFSPH [1]. This is because our contribution adds a component to the incompressible form of the Navier-Stokes Eq. 1 that can be computed separately from the main technique algorithm, along with the viscosity force or any external force that applies on the system.

The Coandă effect is an observation of a physical phenomenon happening when the pressure around a rigid body surface lowers due to a stream of moving particles [24]. From a microscopic point of view, under the influence of an incoming stream of fluid, the viscosity snatches fluid molecules resting within the direct vicinity of the rigid body's surface, thereby leaving gaps around the solid. The pressure drops and deviates the incoming molecules from the stream to fill those empty gaps. This deviation results in the stream of fluid sticking to the surface and moving along its curvature on a macroscopic level.

In our case, the drop in pressure leads to a negative pressure because the density is lower than the rest density. In this particular case, DFSPH, which nulls out the negative pressure, does not respect the divergence-free constraint Eq. 3. The technique loses the relationship between pressure and viscosity found in Coandă effect observations, and the ball leaves the stream to fall on the floor.

Since the Coandă effect is a physical observation, we propose a new heuristic to simulate this effect around the surface of a rigid body when the pressure is negative:

$$\mathbf{F}_{i_{Coand\breve{a}}} = \frac{m_i}{\Delta t^2} \sum_j C_j \mathbf{x}_{ij} \tag{4}$$

where $\mathbf{x}_{ij}$ is the distance between particle i and its neighbor j; Δt is the simulation timestep; m_i is the mass of the particle i; and C_j is a dimensionless user-defined constant to modulate the gain of the Coandă effect.

Equation 4 applies a magnetism force whose strength is proportional to the distance between each particle. The particles end up attracting each other, and we rely on the pressure component correction to separate them when a pair of particles start clustering. Therefore, that step is to be executed before computing the pressure component as shown in Algorithm 1.

Algorithm 1. Simulation

1: Initialize the simulation domain
2: **while** $t < t_{max}$ **do**
3:     **for all** particle i **do**
4:         Compute density
5:     **end for**
6:     **for all** particle i **do**
7:         Compute non-pressure forces $F_i^{adv}(t)$
8:         $F_i^{adv}(t) = F_i^{adv}(t) + \frac{m_i}{\Delta t^2} \sum_{j_b} C_j \mathbf{x}_{ij_b}$
9:     **end for**
10:     **for all** particle i **do**
11:         Apply pressure component correction scheme
12:     **end for**
13:     **for all** particule i **do**
14:         Euler integration to update particle position
15:     **end for**
16: **end while**

Applying the formula to all particles is an inefficient use of computational power since the correction brought by the pressure component would null out this attraction force. Our experiments prove that we achieved the same result by applying the Eq. 4 to only rigid body particles instead, but at lower computational cost.

We employed a two-way coupling strategy akin to the methodology outlined in N. Akinci et al. [2]. We evaluated the performance of two distinct rigid body sampling algorithms, namely a regular surface sampling technique outlined by M. Deserno [25], and a uniform Poisson disk sampling approach introduced by R. Bridson [26]. From our experimentation, the regular sampling technique seems to perform better for our needs. This can be attributed to the local non-uniformity of Poisson disk sampling within the kernel range, which leads to an irregular force application on the fluid particles. This asymmetry induces biases in the particle trajectories.

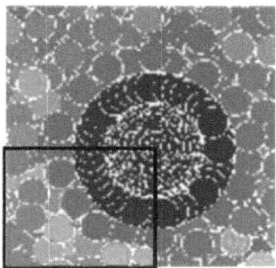

Fig. 2. Fluid particle aggregation around rigid body in red rectangle due to no-stick condition. (Color figure online)

Furthermore, we explored the Ghost particle method proposed by H. Schechter et al. [27], and the no-stick condition detailed in [28]. However, the no-stick condition presented compatibility challenges with our method. This is due to the restriction of particle velocity normal to the rigid body surface, resulting in an anomalous accumulation of fluid particles near the rigid body surface, as illustrated in Fig. 2. This is contradictory to Coandă effect, which allows particles to leave the boundary vicinity through the normal velocity component, but requests another particle to fill in the created gap, thereby creating the force required to push the ball back into the stream.

4   Result

Our implementation is performed in the C++ language using DirectX for the rendering. Since our research focuses on correcting two-way coupling simulation in an air stream, no effort was put into rendering the fluid. For debugging purposes and ease of development, we did not use the GPU for the simulation algorithm, but we made extensive usage of Single Instruction Multiple Data (SIMD) instructions.

Our approach does not require filling the entire simulation domain with fluid particles, nor does it require special particle layouts. We simply initialize the domain by spawning particles in an ordered manner, then remove the ones that collide or are inside rigid bodies.

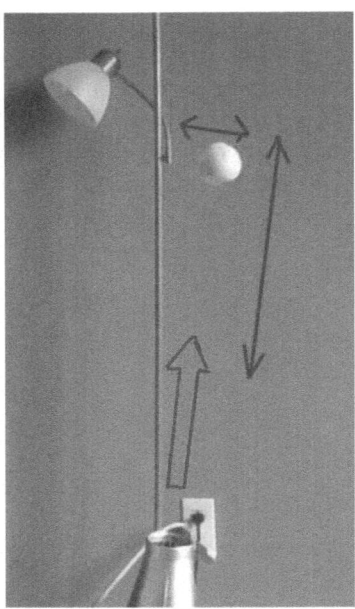

Fig. 3. A real-world experiment of a ping pong ball dropped over a hair dryer tilted by 7 °C. The thin and green arrows show the ball amplitude throughout the experiment, and the thick red arrow shows the air stream direction. (Color figure online)

Our work extends from DFSPH explained in [4], to which we added our new Coandă effect heuristic and compared to real-world experiments.

We experimented with the vertical tilt angle, and in the real-world experiment, our ball remained in the air stream from 0 to 10 °C as shown in Fig. 3. We succeeded in simulating this exact behavior with the same tilt angle at 0 °C and 7 °C as shown in Fig. 4.

5   Limitations

Since the Coandă effect force introduced by Eq. 4 does not use a valid kernel, the force comes to an abrupt halt beyond the kernel radius h, namely when $\mathbf{x}_{ij} > h$. Particles in the kernel radius are strongly attracted to the surface, while others located at a distance beyond the kernel radius are free to distance themselves. This results in artifacts where voids can still occur outside or at the surface vicinity.

Since there was no normalization of the weight of the rigid body sampling as described by [2], the method did not scale well with irregular sampling, e.g., Poisson Disk Sampling. This was acceptable because we chose to not use Poisson Disk sampling as it introduced biases in force trajectories leading to noisy movement of the ball.

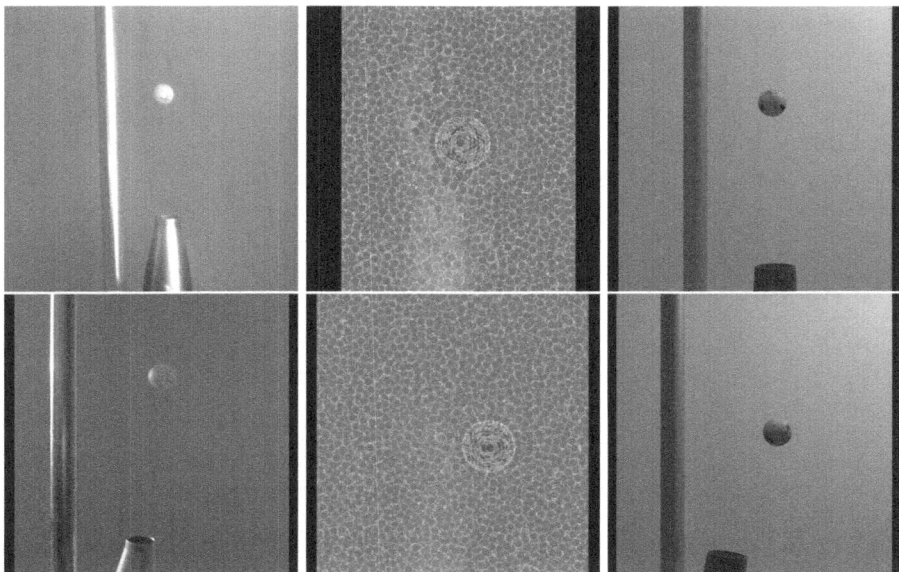

Fig. 4. Simulation of a ping pong ball dropped over a hair dryer tilted by $0\,^{\circ}\mathrm{C}$ ((a), (b), (c)), then $7\,^{\circ}\mathrm{C}$ ((d), (e), (f)). Red fluid particles are moving faster than blue fluid particles. Blue arrow shows the total force applied on the ball. (Color figure online)

Finally, the Coandă effect coefficient C_j found in Eq. 4 is a user-defined variable that needs fine-tuning. Too low a value reduces the Coandă effect correction, and its resulting force would not be enough to push the ball back into the stream. Too high a value would require stronger pressure, thereby increasing the pressure correction iteration needed per simulation step.

6   Conclusion

We implemented a fluid simulation engine based on the Smoothed Particle Hydrodynamics (SPH) method, a purely Lagrangian approach, to simulate the fluid-solid interaction required for the levitation scenario proposed. Recent SPH methods disallow pressure correction when the fluid particle density falls below the rest density. While this prevents tensile and pairing instabilities described in [29], it also hampers the ability to simulate the Coandă effect. Therefore, we could not achieve the desired effect of a ball levitating in an air stream with methods such as IISPH and DFSPH.

Our key contribution was identifying and rectifying this issue by introducing a new heuristic under external forces terms in Navier-Stokes Eq. 1 inspired by the Coandă effect to compensate for the lack of pressure force corrections. This added force is non-physical and relies on an empirical parameter. However, it introduces artifacts like a vacuum ring forming near the solid's boundary. An alternative solution could involve developing a method that generates a pressure force for cases where density is below the rest density while remaining wary of tensile and pairing instabilities.

Since our approach does not impede the pressure force correction, we validated that it still works on other common scenarios, such as waves carrying solids in their wake, or objects floating based on their density. The Coandă-inspired force is a step towards more intricate and realistic fluid-solid interactions.

References

1. Bender, J., Koschier, D.: Divergence-free smoothed particle hydrodynamics. In Proceedings of the 14th ACM SIGGRAPH/Eurographics Symposium on Computer Animation, SCA '15, pp. 147–155, New York, NY, USA, aôut 2015. Association for Computing Machinery (ACM)
2. Akinci, N., Ihmsen, M., Akinci, G., Solenthaler, B., Teschner, M.: Versatile rigid-fluid coupling for incompressible sph. ACM Trans. Graph. (TOG) **31**(4), 1–8. juillet (2012)
3. Anderson, J.D.: Fundamentals of Aerodynamics, Sixth Edition. Tata McGraw-Hill Education, New York, 6 edition, 2017
4. Bender, J., Koschier, D.: Divergence-free sph for incompressible and viscous fluids. IEEE Trans. Vis. Comput. Graph. **23**(3), 1193–1206 (2017)
5. Ihmsen, M., Cornelis, J., Solenthaler, B., Horvath, C., Teschner, M.: Implicit incompressible sph. IEEE Trans. Vis. Comput. Graph. **20**(3), 426–435 (2014)
6. Koschier, D., Bender, J., Solenthaler, B., Teschner, M.: Smoothed particle hydrodynamics techniques for the physics based simulation of fluids and solids. In: Jakob, W., Puppo, E. (eds.), Eurographics 2019 - Tutorials. Eurographics Association, 2019
7. Liu, M.B., Liu, G.R.: Smoothed particle hydrodynamics (sph): an overview and recent developments. Arch. Comput. Methods Eng. **17**(1), 25–76 (2010)
8. Macklin, M., Muller, M.: Position based fluids. ACM Trans. Graph. (TOG) **32**(4) (2013). juillet
9. Monaghan, J.J.: Sph without a tensile instability. J. Comput. Phys. **159**(2), 290–311 (2000)
10. Fulk, D.A.: A numerical analysis of smoothed particle hydrodynamics. PhD thesis, Air Force Institute of Technology, Department of the Air Force, Air University, Wright-Patterson Air Force Base, Ohio, September 1994
11. Monaghan, J.J.: Smoothed particle hydrodynamics. Annu. Rev. Astronomy Astrophysics **30**(1), 543–574 (1992)
12. Lucy, L.B.: A numerical approach to the testing of the fission hypothesis. Astron. J. **82**, 1013–1024 (1977)
13. Gingold, R.A., Monaghan, J.J.: Smoothed particle hydrodynamics: theory and application to non-spherical stars. Mon. Notices R. Astron. Soc. **181**(3), 375–389 (1977)
14. Becker, M., Teschner, M.: Weakly compressible SPH for free surface flows. In: Proceedings of the 2007 ACM SIGGRAPH/Eurographics Symposium on Computer animation, SCA '07, pp. 209–217, Goslar, DEU, August 2007. Eurographics Association

15. Muller, M., Charypar, D., Gross, M.: Particle-based fluid simulation for interactive applications. In: Proceedings of the 2003 ACM SIGGRAPH/Eurographics Symposium on Computer Animation, SCA'03, pp. 154–159, Goslar, DEU, July 2003. Eurographics Association
16. Monaghan, J.J.: Smoothed particle hydrodynamics. Rep. Progress Phys. **68**(8), 1703–1759 (2005)
17. Violeau, D., Rogers, B.D.: Smoothed particle hydrodynamics (SPH) for free-surface flows: past, present and future. J. Hydraul. Res. **54**(1), 1–26 (2016)
18. Courant, R., Friedrichs, K., Lewy, H.: On the partial difference equations of mathematical physics. IBM J. Res. Dev. **11**(2), 215–234 (1967)
19. Solenthaler, B., Pajarola, R.: Predictive-corrective incompressible SPH. In: ACM SIGGRAPH 2009 Papers, volume 28 of SIGGRAPH '09, pp. 1–6, New York, NY, USA, July 2009. Association for Computing Machinery (ACM)
20. Cummins, S.J., Rudman, M.: An SPH projection method. J. Comput. Phys. **152**(2), 584–607 (1999)
21. Shao, S., Lo, E.Y.: Incompressible SPH method for simulating newtonian and non-newtonian flows with a free surface. Adv. Water Resour. **26**(7), 787–800 (2003)
22. House, D., Keyser, J.C.: Foundations of Physically Based Modeling and Animation. AK Peters/CRC Press, New York, NY, USA, December 2016
23. Bender, J., Kugelstadt, T., Weiler, M., Koschier, D.: Volume maps: an implicit boundary representation for SPH. In: Motion, Interaction and Games, MIG '19, New York, NY, USA, October 2019. Association for Computing Machinery (ACM)
24. Tritton, D.J.: Physical Fluid Dynamics, chapter 22.7 Coanda effect, pp. 284–286. Van Nostrand Reinhold Company, New York, NY, USA, 1977
25. Deserno, M.: How to generate equidistributed points on the surface of a sphere. If Polymerforshung (Ed.), 99(2): sept. 2004
26. Bridson, R.: Fast poisson disk sampling in arbitrary dimensions. In: ACM SIGGRAPH 2007 Sketches, volume 10 of SIGGRAPH '07, p. 22, New York, NY, USA, August 2007. Association for Computing Machinery (ACM)
27. Schechter, H., Bridson, R.: Ghost SPH for animating water. ACM Trans. Graph. (TOG) **31**(4), 1–8 (2012)
28. Bridson, R.: Fluid Simulation for Computer Graphics, 2nd edn. AK Peters/CRC Press, New York, NY, USA, September 2015
29. Price, D.J.: Smoothed particle hydrodynamics and magnetohydrodynamics. J. Comput. Phys. Spec. Issue: Comput. Plasma Phys. **231**(3), 759–794 (2012)

Summon Arcane: An AI-Driven Pixel Art Game with Interactive Narrative and Immersive Summoning Experience

Siyao Du$^{(\boxtimes)}$, Haoxiang Yang, Yajie Deng, Liuxuan Xie, Yanzhe Kong, Haohan Zhang, and Hammadi Nait-Charif

National Center for Computer Animation, Bournemouth University, Bournemouth, UK
dusiyaosia@gmail.com,
{s5714695,s5714322,s5723229,s5645044,s5724327,hncharif}@bournemouth.ac.uk

Abstract. This paper introduces Summon Arcane, a 2D pixel-art interactive narrative game integrating AI-driven procedural content generation. Players act as summoners trapped within a mystical book, undertaking six summoning trials to inherit the Summoner's legacy. The core mechanic involves AI-powered speech-to-text summoning, where players verbally describe creatures to generate pixel-art visuals via Midjourney, processed using OpenCV for artistic consistency. The game also employs ChatGPT API for dynamic battle narration, enhancing interactivity and immersion. This study evaluates the impact of AI on interactive storytelling and procedural content generation in games.

Keywords: Game Design · AI Image Generation · AI Speech Recognition · ChatGPT · Pixel Art · Immersion

1 Introduction

The integration of generative artificial intelligence (AI) into game development has rapidly evolved in recent years, transforming traditional content creation workflows. From large language models (LLMs) enabling dynamic dialogue to diffusion models generating high-quality imagery, AI technologies have introduced new dimensions to player experience design. In particular, AI-driven procedural content generation (PCG) presents opportunities for player-driven creativity, enabling players to shape narrative, visuals, and interactions in real time.

However, existing implementations of AI in games are often limited to prescripted prompts, static image generation, or isolated interactions, which lack narrative coherence and real-time responsiveness. The challenge remains in how to seamlessly integrate multimodal AI systems—including speech recognition, image synthesis, and text generation—into a cohesive gameplay framework while maintaining aesthetic and narrative consistency.

In this paper, we introduce Summon Arcane, a 2D pixel-art interactive narrative game featuring a voice-activated AI summoning system, procedural image transformation pipelines, and ChatGPT-powered battle narration. Our system enables players to verbally describe creatures, which are dynamically generated through Midjourney and stylistically aligned through OpenCV and Unity pixelation techniques. Combat encounters are narrated by LLMs using structured prompts, enhancing immersion and replayability.

Our central research questions are: (1) How can AI-enhanced procedural content generation affect player immersion in narrative-based games? (2) How can visual post-processing ensure artistic consistency in AI-generated assets? (3) What are the technical and narrative implications of real-time multimodal AI integration in game design?

We conduct a mixed-method user evaluation (n = 15), analyzing usability, narrative immersion, and content quality. Results indicate strong player engagement with the voice-based summoning system (M = 4.5), and appreciation for dynamic combat narration. Based on our findings, we discuss challenges such as API latency, narrative coherence, and visual diversity, offering pathways for future work.

The remainder of the paper is organized as follows: Sect. 2 reviews related works in AI and game design; Sect. 3 details system architecture and implementation; Sect. 4 presents our evaluation method and findings; Sects. 5 and 6 discuss future directions and conclude the paper.

2   Literature Review

Interactive narratives and immersive experiences have become increasingly significant in contemporary game design. According to Parmar and Murari [1], AI-driven image generation techniques have significantly advanced the creation of customized characters, enhancing both player engagement and narrative depth. They highlight the transformative potential of AI-generated visuals in personalizing gaming experiences.

Pixel art has been widely adopted due to its aesthetic consistency and nostalgic appeal. Kopf and Lischinski [2] note that pixel art effectively masks visual imperfections, ensures stylistic unity, and contributes to visual clarity, crucial for maintaining coherence in interactive environments. They present methods for depixelizing pixel art, further enriching visual consistency across varied game scenarios. Our work adopts a similar stylistic direction but focuses on ensuring that AI-generated assets match the game's native aesthetic through post-processing methods like GrabCut segmentation and Unity-based pixelation.

Recent studies demonstrate that generative AI technologies significantly impact game development by enabling real-time content generation. Ratican and Hutson [3] emphasize AI's role in creating adaptive and personalized gaming experiences, such as dynamically generated levels and interactions tailored to individual player decisions. This aligns with our system's design, where speech-driven prompts result in unique creature generation and combat narratives.

In the domain of narrative design, large language models (LLMs) have revolutionized how stories are generated and adapted in games. Gallotta et al. [4] provide a comprehensive survey of LLM roles in gaming—from NPC behavior to automated design assistants and dynamic narrators—highlighting the transformative potential of LLMs while also noting current challenges, such as hallucination, memory limitations, and lack of narrative structure. Our work directly addresses this gap by designing structured prompts for ChatGPT to narrate turn-based combat in a consistent and contextually appropriate manner.

In SceneCraft, Kumaran et al. [5] demonstrate structured narrative scene generation using LLMs within a templated design framework, emphasizing narrative coherence. However, their work does not explore real-time player-driven inputs or voice interactions. Similarly, Sun et al. [6] propose the idea of "AI-Native" games, exemplified by 1001 Nights, where generative storytelling and gameplay mechanics are co-constructed by AI and players. Our system extends this lineage by introducing real-time voice-activated creature generation and ChatGPT-powered narrative feedback embedded in gameplay.

The StoryAgent framework by Sohn et al. [7] further addresses multi-modal consistency in long-form AI storytelling through hierarchical LLM agents and visual coordination. While their architecture is geared towards cinematic story production, our framework is optimized for lightweight game integration, ensuring that Midjourney-generated assets maintain visual coherence via pixelation and real-time post-processing.

Beyond text generation, LLMs have shown effectiveness in commentary generation. Nimpattanavong et al. [8] explore ChatGPT's role in fighting game commentary, demonstrating its capacity to dynamically generate engaging content. Although their study focuses on action-based gameplay, our work investigates LLM commentary in a turn-based RPG setting, combining it with narrative control and prompt engineering to improve consistency.

Voice interaction is another essential component of immersive gameplay. Mustaquim [9] discusses how automatic speech recognition systems enhance accessibility and engagement, particularly for players with disabilities. Allison et al. [10] provide a historical overview of voice interfaces in gaming, emphasizing their capacity to deepen emotional connection. Our system integrates Google Speech-to-Text for real-time creature summoning, enabling natural, voice-based interaction that complements narrative immersion.

AI's integration with non-player characters (NPCs) has also advanced, creating more realistic and engaging interactions. Tonini [11] explores generative AI-driven NPCs in VR, noting improvements in realism and dynamic response, though also identifying challenges in maintaining coherent conversational flow. Similarly, 1001 Nights and StoryAgent both employ structured reasoning and prompt control to maintain narrative believability, which we adopt in our system via predefined GPT dialogue templates.

Safadi et al. [12] propose a conceptual framework for game-independent AI behavior, advocating for generalizable, reusable AI systems. Our architecture, while customized, embraces this idea by designing reusable pipelines (voice-to-image, text-to-narrative) that can be repurposed for other narrative or summoning-based games.

Biswas [13] examines ChatGPT's broader role in gaming, noting its value in personalization and player analytics, but also its limitations in emotional nuance and creative originality. While Nimpattanavong et al. [8] focus on linear commentary tasks, our work explores LLMs in branching and reactive narrative generation during gameplay.

Collectively, these studies underline the transformative potential and current limitations of AI technologies—including generative models, LLMs, and speech interfaces—in creating deeply immersive and player-driven experiences. Our game, Summon Arcane, contributes to this discourse by presenting a voice-activated, multi-modal narrative system that leverages AI for personalized gameplay, while addressing stylistic coherence and narrative control.

3   Game Design

3.1   Project Background and Concept

"Summon Arcane" is a 2D pixel-art game that integrates AI-driven procedural content generation and interactive storytelling to craft a distinctive gameplay experience. Players begin their journey by customizing their summoner avatars through an interactive magic book interface, selecting both appearance and name. A seamlessly designed transition animation immerses the player into the richly developed narrative world.

The storyline follows a summoner who mysteriously descends into an ancient, European-style tower—a setting that serves as the backdrop for six critical summoning trials. Successfully completing these trials is the key to the protagonist's escape. The journey begins in a dimly lit subterranean chamber, where a floating magical staff guides the player through an introductory summoning task—invoking a luminous creature to illuminate the surroundings, thereby introducing the core summoning mechanics.

A defining aspect of gameplay is the voice-activated AI summoning system, which allows players to verbally describe their desired creature. The AI then dynamically generates corresponding visual representations. To mitigate latency in AI processing, a custom spell-casting animation sequence has been implemented, enhancing immersion and maintaining engagement throughout the summoning process.

3.2   Narrative and Level Design

"Summon Arcane" is structured around a coherent narrative comprising three distinct phases:

Opening Sequence: Players engage in character customization (illustrated in Fig. 1), gain familiarity with core mechanics, and are introduced to the game's overarching storyline, ensuring contextual immersion.

Fig. 1. Character Customization Page of Arcane Summon

Six Summoning Trials: Each trial presents carefully designed pixel-art environments and tactically structured enemy encounters, requiring players to devise strategic summoning approaches to advance.

Gallery and Conclusion: The final phase showcases the player's customized avatar and summoned creatures in a reflective gallery setting, reinforcing narrative closure while celebrating individual creativity (see Fig. 2).

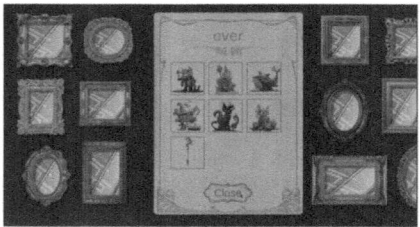

Fig. 2. Gallery Page of Arcane Summon

To maintain artistic consistency, all AI-generated visual assets undergo a systematic post-processing pipeline, particularly pixelation, ensuring a cohesive aesthetic throughout the game while preserving narrative and visual coherence.

3.3   AI-Driven Summoning System

The summoning system integrates advanced AI technologies, including natural language processing (NLP), generative AI image synthesis, and automated image processing, to facilitate an immersive and interactive summoning experience. The workflow is structured as follows:

1. **Speech-to-Text Processing**: The Google Speech-to-Text API transcribes player speech input into textual descriptions. Players initiate this process by holding a microphone button within the Unity interface, ensuring intuitive interaction. To enhance immersion, the system provides animated visual feedback, displaying real-time transcriptions as magical incantations.

2. **AI Image Generation**: The transcribed textual descriptions serve as input prompts for the Midjourney API, which generates four distinct creature images. To maintain stylistic consistency, prompt engineering techniques are employed, ensuring that AI-generated assets align with the game's pixel-art aesthetic. Players then select their preferred creature, reinforcing engagement and creative agency.

3. **Automated Background Removal via OpenCV**: To seamlessly integrate AI-generated creatures into gameplay, background removal is performed using OpenCV's GrabCut algorithm. This method segments the creature from its background by defining a rectangular bounding region and applying iterative refinement to isolate the foreground. The implementation is managed via Unity-integrated C# scripts, as demonstrated below:

Listing 1.1. Background Removal using OpenCV GrabCut

```
Cv2.GrabCut(inputImage, mask, rect, bgdModel, fgdModel, 5,
    GrabCutModes.InitializationWithRect);
```

4. **Pixelation for Artistic Consistency**: To maintain visual coherence, all AI-generated images undergo a pixelation process within Unity. This process involves downscaling and then upscaling textures, ensuring that the generated creatures seamlessly blend into the game's pixel-art aesthetic. Parameters such as pixel block size are adjustable for optimal visual fidelity. The core logic is implemented as follows:

Listing 1.2. Pixelation Algorithm in Unity

```
int newWidth = original.width / pixelSize;
int newHeight = original.height / pixelSize;
```

5. **Gameplay Integration**: The processed AI-generated creature assets are integrated into turn-based battles, where their behavior and interactions are dynamically influenced by ChatGPT-powered text generation. This system ensures narrative diversity, enhancing both immersion and replayability.

Figure 3 provides a visual representation of the AI-driven summoning workflow.

Automated Summoning Workflow. To seamlessly connect multiple AI modules into a cohesive gameplay experience, we implemented a centralized coordination system, encapsulated in the `AIWorkflowManager.cs` script. This component orchestrates the entire summoning sequence—from image generation to visual display—ensuring a fully automated, non-blocking pipeline. See Appendix A for representative code snippets from `AIWorkflowManager.cs`.

The manager monitors and controls the following components:

– **Image Generation** (`MjImageGenerator.cs`): Triggers Midjourney API and monitors image readiness.

- **Background Removal** (`AICharacterExtractor.cs`): Automatically segments the selected creature using OpenCV GrabCut.
- **Pixelation** (`ImagePixelationProcessor.cs`): Applies consistent pixel-art styling with optional animated transitions.
- **Display Coordination**: Dynamically manages visual stages (grid preview, single image, extracted sprite, pixelated result), with fade-in transitions and staged camera movement.

Each stage is initiated through Unity coroutines to avoid blocking the main thread. The system supports fallback display handling, debug logging, and visual reset between trials. This modular workflow design not only enhances maintainability but also ensures players experience the summoning ritual as a smooth, continuous visual sequence. A visual schematic of the pipeline is provided in Fig. 3.

The coroutine-based summoning orchestration logic is provided in Appendix A.2 and A.5.

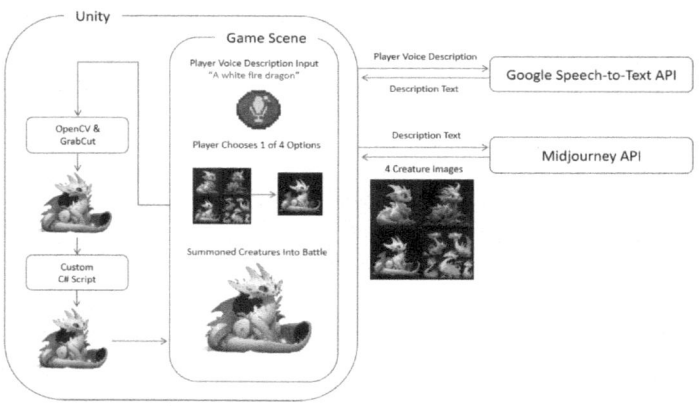

Fig. 3. Summoning System AI Workflow

3.4   Speech Recognition for Summoning

The integration of the Google Speech-to-Text API enables a natural language summoning interface, enhancing immersion by simulating vocal spellcasting—a familiar trope in fantasy narratives. Our Unity-based system supports *press-and-hold* voice recording, automatic transcription, and seamless pipeline triggering. To optimize usability and responsiveness, the system incorporates:

- **Press-to-speak recording**: A custom UI component allows players to hold a button to record, which automatically stops and sends audio upon release.

- **Transcription and filtering**: Audio is converted to WAV and sent to Google's API; results are filtered and auto-submitted to the image generator.
- **Latency masking**: While awaiting transcription and image generation, a dynamic dialogue box and visual volume meter keep players visually engaged.
- **Automatic flow control**: Once a transcription is returned, it is displayed in the corner UI, and a coroutine triggers the summoning animation without user re-confirmation.

3.5   AI Image Generation

The Midjourney API was chosen for its high-quality image generation, seamless integration capabilities, and efficient prototyping, making it an ideal solution for generating dynamic, AI-driven visual assets in Summon Arcane. We integrated the MetaChat Midjourney API [14], allowing text-to-image generation in near real-time. Players' speech is transcribed into descriptive prompts, which are dynamically injected into a reusable template and sent to the API.

To maintain artistic uniformity within the game's pixel-art aesthetic, a meticulously designed prompt engineering strategy is employed. This process involves:

- **Defining structured prompts** that specify key visual attributes, including creature morphology, texture details, color schemes, and composition. The prompt format—e.g., "game monster design, [player input: a white fire dragon] facing right, complete individual, 2D, cute, game-ready assets, pure black background, –s 750 –niji 5 –style expressive"—ensures that generated outputs align with the game's predefined artistic direction.
- **Adjusting model parameters** to refine aesthetic consistency. The "–niji 5" and "–style expressive" parameters are applied to achieve a cohesive and visually appealing style, ensuring that AI-generated creatures maintain uniformity within the game's world.
- **Generating multiple output variations** (typically four per summoning request), allowing players to select the most suitable creature for gameplay, thereby fostering player agency and personalized creativity.

To improve user experience during image generation, we implemented a progressive polling strategy and real-time feedback mechanisms. The system polls the result endpoint every 5 s, with a maximum of 60 attempts (i.e., 5 min timeout). If the task fails to return a URL within this window, a failure message is returned and the player is prompted to retry. During this waiting period, the game interface displays a looped animation and a dynamic dialogue box stating *"Waiting for summoning [CREATURE_NAME]..."*, keeping the player engaged. This strategy is crucial for masking API latency and preserving immersion in gameplay.

Since Midjourney's default rendering style may produce assets that do not fully conform to the pixel-art aesthetic, additional post-processing techniques are applied. These include background removal using OpenCV and pixelation adjustments via Unity scripts to ensure all AI-generated creatures seamlessly integrate into the game's visual environment. This multi-step approach preserves narrative coherence, artistic consistency, and gameplay immersion while leveraging AI to enrich Summon Arcane's dynamic content generation.

Once the final image is retrieved, the player selects one of four generated variations, triggering a separation API call to isolate the chosen creature. Upon success, the image is passed into the character extraction and pixelation pipeline, which is fully automated and handled asynchronously via multithreaded coroutines. This ensures that UI remains responsive and smooth, even under background processing load.

3.6   Procedural Image Processing

To ensure seamless integration of AI-generated assets within the game's pixel-art aesthetic, *Summon Arcane* employs a two-stage image processing pipeline: background removal and pixelation. This real-time pipeline ensures stylistic coherence without requiring manual asset curation.

Background Removal via OpenCV GrabCut. AI-generated creature images often contain complex backgrounds inconsistent with gameplay visuals. To isolate the foreground character, we implemented an OpenCV-based background removal system using the GrabCut algorithm, integrated into Unity through a custom multithreaded C# script (**AICharacterExtractor.cs**). The process includes:

– **Automatic bounding box estimation**: A margin-based ROI is defined around the input image center.
– **GrabCut segmentation**: Foreground-background separation is iteratively refined using GMMs.
– **Asynchronous task management**: All image processing is performed in a background thread to prevent UI blocking, coordinated via Unity coroutines.

Fallback strategies such as color-thresholding are used if GrabCut fails. The result is a transparent-cutout sprite preserving edge fidelity, as shown in Fig. 4. The extraction is triggered automatically after image download and does not require player input.

Pixelation for Visual Coherence. To enforce retro-styled consistency, we implemented a Unity-native pixelation module (**ImagePixelationPro cessor.cs**) that processes extracted creatures before they are added to the scene. The pixelation follows a controlled two-step pipeline:

– **Downsampling**: The extracted image is resized using adjustable block sizes (default: 13px) to reduce detail.
– **Upsampling with nearest-neighbor interpolation**: The image is scaled back to original dimensions, producing crisp pixel edges.

– **Animated transitions (optional)**: For visual polish, an optional coroutine animates the pixelation effect in steps.

This ensures that all summoned entities match the game's pixel-art style. The system supports dynamic reconfiguration of pixel size, and can adapt to different screen resolutions. Figure 4 showcases the visual difference before and after applying both background removal and pixelation.

Implementation details are included in the supplementary materials (`AICharacterExtractor.cs` and `ImagePixelationProcessor.cs`).

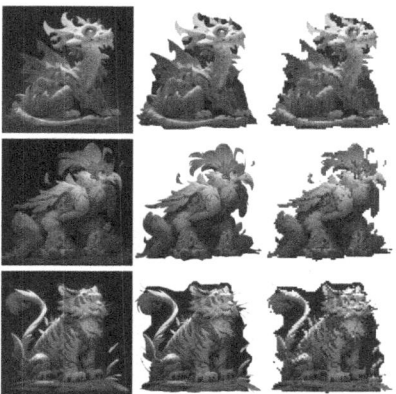

Fig. 4. Procedural Image Processing Result

3.7   Turn-Based Combat Mechanics

Summoned entities engage in structured turn-based battles, where combat interactions are dynamically generated using OpenAI's ChatGPT API. To ensure that battle descriptions are coherent, engaging, and strategically structured, a predefined prompt format is employed. This format specifies character roles, combat sequence, and outcome constraints, ensuring that the AI-generated narrative aligns with the game's mechanics.

The prompt structure follows a three-round battle format, where Player A (the summoner) ultimately defeats Boss B. Each round is described in one sentence, capturing key battle actions and their impact, culminating in a final justification for the player's victory. The structured prompt is as follows:

Listing 1.3. ChatGPT API Call for Combat Description

```
1  {
2      "model": "gpt-4-turbo",
3      "messages": [
```

```
4       {"role": "system", "content": "You are a game AI
            responsible for generating immersive turn-based
            battle descriptions."},
5       {"role": "user", "content": "Role 1: Player A Role
            2: Boss B Generate a battle between Role 1 and
            Role 2, and Role 1 wins in the end. There are
            three rounds in total. Describe the battle
            scene in one sentence for each round, and give
            the reason for victory based on the winner."}
6     ]
7   }
```

This dynamic narrative generation system produces varied, immersive, and strategically meaningful battle descriptions, as illustrated in Fig. 5.

Fig. 5. ChatGPT Battle Text Visualizations

By leveraging AI-driven storytelling, this approach creates unique and engaging combat experiences, significantly enhancing player immersion and replayability. The integration of ChatGPT-generated battle narration allows Summon Arcane to deliver an interactive, narrative-driven combat system that dynamically adapts to different encounters. This contributes to advancements in AI-assisted procedural content generation and deepens player engagement through responsive and immersive battle sequences.

3.8   Technical Challenges and Solutions

Integrating multiple AI modules in real-time gameplay presented several technical challenges, particularly around latency, visual consistency, and automation stability. We outline three key challenges and the corresponding solutions:

Managing API Latency. Speech-to-image and text-to-image generation APIs often introduce delays (up to 10 s), which can disrupt immersion. To mitigate this, we implemented:

– **Looped summoning animations** to engage players during wait times.
– **Progressive polling strategy** (5 s × 60 retries) to monitor task status.

– **Non-blocking coroutines** and multi-threaded image processing to keep the UI responsive.

These strategies maintain continuity in gameplay despite backend processing delays.

Ensuring Visual Style Consistency. Midjourney's outputs vary in style and resolution, potentially clashing with pixel-art aesthetics. Our solution involved:

– **Structured prompt engineering** to control pose, color, and composition.
– **Post-processing pipeline**: GrabCut (OpenCV) for background removal and pixelation with adjustable block sizes in Unity.
– **Visual gating**: Assets failing pixelation criteria were discarded or regenerated.

This ensured that all summoned creatures matched the retro visual theme.

Automating Sequential Pipelines. Coordinating speech recognition, image generation, extraction, and animation required tight synchronization. We addressed this by:

– Centralizing the entire pipeline in `AIWorkflowManager.cs`.
– Using Unity events and coroutines to trigger stage transitions (e.g., image download → segmentation → pixelation).
– Providing fallback error states and UI resets in case of API failure.

This robust pipeline enabled a seamless, one-click summoning experience for players.

4 Evaluation

To assess the effectiveness of Summon Arcane's AI-driven game mechanics, a mixed-method evaluation was conducted, incorporating both qualitative and quantitative analysis. This evaluation aimed to measure usability, AI-generated content quality, and narrative immersion, providing insights into the strengths and areas for improvement of the AI-enhanced gameplay experience.

4.1 Testing Environment and Participants

The evaluation was carried out in a controlled university lab environment. A total of 15 participants (8 male, 7 female, aged 18–30) were recruited, primarily university students with varying levels of gaming experience. Participants were classified into three experience groups:

Casual Gamers (5 participants, play games <5 h/week)

Regular Gamers (6 participants, play games 5–15 hours/week)

Experienced Gamers (4 participants, play games >15 h/week)

Each participant engaged in a 15-minute gameplay session, followed by a structured questionnaire and a semi-structured interview to gather both numerical ratings and subjective feedback.

4.2 Testing Parameters

The evaluation concentrated on three core parameters:

1. **Usability and Interaction Fluidity**: Players were asked about the intuitiveness and responsiveness of the game's interface, particularly focusing on the voice-driven summoning mechanism and general ease of navigation.
2. **AI-Generated Image Quality**: Participants assessed the visual coherence and stylistic consistency of AI-generated images. Additional questions addressed the perceived diversity of generated images and overall satisfaction with generation speed.
3. **Interactive Narrative and Immersion**: Players provided feedback on their perceived immersion and the effectiveness of the interactive narrative elements, emphasizing the impact of AI-driven storytelling and voice interaction on their gaming experience.

Each category was quantified using a 5-point Likert scale (1 = Poor, 5 = Excellent), alongside open-ended qualitative feedback.

4.3 Data Analysis

Quantitative Analysis. The questionnaire responses were analyzed to identify trends in user satisfaction. The following metrics summarize player feedback in Table 1

Table 1. Player Feedback Metrics

Evaluation Aspect	Mean Score (M)	Standard Deviation (SD)
Usability of Voice Summoning	4.5	0.7
Speech-to-Text Accuracy	4.2	0.8
AI Image Consistency	4.0	0.9
AI Image Diversity	3.8	1.0
Narrative Immersion	4.3	0.6
Combat Storytelling	4.1	0.8

The results indicate high satisfaction with the voice-driven summoning system (M = 4.5, SD = 0.7) and AI-generated storytelling (M = 4.3, SD = 0.6). However, some inconsistencies in AI-generated visuals were noted (M = 4.0, SD = 0.9), and image diversity was rated slightly lower (M = 3.8, SD = 1.0), suggesting room for improvement in prompt engineering and image generation parameters.

Qualitative Insights. From semi-structured interviews, participants provided the following feedback:

Usability and Fluidity: Players overwhelmingly found the voice-activated summoning mechanic intuitive and engaging. Most respondents indicated that this interaction significantly enhanced their sense of immersion, despite minor latency issues during image generation phases.

AI-Generated Content: The majority of players expressed satisfaction with the quality and diversity of generated images, appreciating the consistent pixel-art aesthetic achieved through post-processing techniques. However, a few participants noted slight discrepancies in style consistency, suggesting further refinement for future iterations.

Interactive Narrative Experience: Feedback regarding narrative immersion was strongly positive, with participants highlighting the effectiveness of AI-generated combat narratives and the novelty of voice interactions. Several participants mentioned that the interactive elements substantially enriched their narrative engagement.

Statistical Significance. A one-way ANOVA was conducted to analyze differences in player ratings based on gaming experience levels. Results showed no statistically significant differences across experience groups for narrative immersion ($p = 0.21$) or AI-generated image quality ($p = 0.34$), indicating that the AI-driven elements were consistently received across all player skill levels. However, experienced gamers reported slightly lower satisfaction with image diversity, suggesting that more advanced customization options could benefit replayability.

4.4   Summary and Future Improvements

The evaluation demonstrated that Summon Arcane's AI-driven gameplay mechanics significantly enhanced player immersion and interactivity, particularly through voice-based summoning and AI-generated combat narration. However, several areas for improvement were identified.

One key area is reducing AI latency, as delays in API response times occasionally disrupted the fluidity of gameplay. To mitigate this, future iterations should focus on optimizing API efficiency and implementing asynchronous processing techniques, ensuring that summoning actions occur seamlessly without perceptible delays.

Another critical improvement involves enhancing AI-generated image diversity. While the current system produces visually consistent pixel-art creatures, some participants noted a lack of variation in generated outputs. Addressing this issue could involve refining prompt engineering strategies to introduce greater creature variability and exploring advanced AI techniques, such as conditional generative adversarial networks (cGANs) or fine-tuned diffusion models, to increase the diversity and uniqueness of AI-generated creatures.

Finally, the expansion of AI-driven narrative personalisation provides an opportunity to make the storytelling experience more dynamic and player-centric. Future enhancements could include incorporating adaptive storylines that respond to player voice input, allowing for greater agency in the narrative progression. Additionally, ChatGPT's combat narrative could be improved by incorporating memory-based contextual tracking, allowing for more cohesive and contextual combat descriptions that evolve based on previous player interactions.

By addressing these areas, future iterations of Summon Arcane can further refine AI-generated content, creating an even more immersive, engaging, and personalized player experience.

5   Discussion and Future Work

The integration of artificial intelligence (AI) technologies with interactive storytelling in Summon Arcane has significantly enhanced player engagement, immersion, and content diversity. Player feedback highlighted a strong appreciation for the game's voice-driven summoning mechanics, procedurally generated narrative elements, and AI-powered combat storytelling, demonstrating the potential of AI-driven dynamic content generation in gaming. The seamless combination of natural language processing (NLP), AI-generated imagery, and adaptive narrative structures provided an interactive experience beyond what is achievable through traditional static game design.

Despite these advancements, the project encountered several technical challenges that require further refinement:

- **API Latency Issues**: The speed of AI-generated image processing occasionally led to delays in gameplay, momentarily disrupting immersion. Optimizing API response times or implementing asynchronous processing techniques could mitigate these latency concerns.
- **Visual Consistency in AI-Generated Content**: While the pixelation process effectively maintained stylistic coherence, minor inconsistencies in AI-generated assets were observed. Further refining prompt engineering techniques and post-processing algorithms can improve visual fidelity.
- **Narrative Flexibility and Player Agency**: The current AI-driven storytelling framework follows predefined parameters, limiting the extent to which players can influence the broader story arc. Future iterations could explore reinforcement learning-based narrative systems or more adaptive AI-generated branching storylines to enhance player-driven storytelling.
- **Narrative Memory**: Current GPT-based narration lacks persistent context, limiting continuity across sessions.

Future iterations will explore on-device image generation to reduce latency (e.g., Stable Diffusion), memory-augmented LLMs for persistent narrative context, and prompt learning or cGANs to enhance creature diversity. Additionally, adaptive narrative generation conditioned on player input will allow for more meaningful branching storylines.

6   Conclusion

This paper presents *Summon Arcane*, an AI-native 2D pixel-art game that fuses speech interaction, generative image synthesis, and LLM-driven storytelling into a cohesive, interactive narrative experience. Our modular design enables voice-based creature generation, real-time visual processing, and immersive battle narration. A mixed-method evaluation shows that players found the system highly usable and immersive, although opportunities remain to improve narrative adaptability and visual diversity. This work contributes a reproducible framework for integrating multimodal generative AI into games and demonstrates the potential of real-time player-driven content generation in shaping the future of interactive storytelling.

Disclosure of Interests. The authors have no competing interests to declare that are relevant to the content of this article.

Appendix A: Key AI Module Snippets

To support reproducibility and demonstrate modular integration, this appendix provides representative excerpts from the five Unity C# components that implement the core AI-driven pipeline in *Summon Arcane*. The full implementations are available as supplementary materials.

A.1   Speech Recognition Controller

File: PressHoldEnglishSpeechRecognition.cs

Listing 1.4. Press-and-hold speech recording setup

```
private void SetupRecordButton () {
    eventTrigger = recordButton.gameObject.AddComponent<
        EventTrigger >();
    ...
}
```

A.2   Midjourney Image Generator

File: MjImageGenerator.cs

Listing 1.5. Polling Midjourney task status

```
private IEnumerator PollTaskStatus (string taskId , bool
    isInitial) {
    string apiUrl = $"{resultApiUrl}/{taskId}";
    ...
}
```

A.3   AI-Based Background Removal

File: `AICharacterExtractor.cs`

Listing 1.6. OpenCV GrabCut segmentation

```
1  Cv2.GrabCut(inputImage, mask, rect, bgdModel, fgdModel, 5,
2          GrabCutModes.InitializationWithRect);
```

A.4   Pixelation Processor

File: `ImagePixelationProcessor.cs`

Listing 1.7. Pixelation downsampling and upscaling

```
1  int newWidth = original.width / pixelSize;
2  int newHeight = original.height / pixelSize;
3  ...
```

A.5   Summoning Workflow Manager

File: `AIWorkflowManager.cs`

Listing 1.8. Display stage management logic

```
1  public enum DisplayStage { None, QuadGrid, SingleImage,
     ... }
2  public void ShowPixelatedImageOnly() {
3      ...
4  }
```

References

1. Parmar, H., Murari, U.K.: Artificial intelligence in 2D games: analysis on customised character generation. In: Building Embodied AI Systems: The Agents, the Architecture Principles, Challenges, and Application Domains, pp. 321–342. Springer, 2025
2. Kopf, J., Lischinski, D.: Depixelizing pixel art. ACM Trans. Graph. **30**(4) (2011). ISSN: 0730-0301. https://doi.org/10.1145/2010324.1964994
3. Ratican, J., Hutson, J.: Adaptive worlds: generative AI in game design and future of gaming, and interactive media. ISRG J. Arts Humanit. Soc. Sci. **2**(5) (2024)
4. Gallotta, R., et al.: Large language models and games: a survey and roadmap. IEEE Trans. Games (2024)
5. Kumaran, V., et al.: Scenecraft: automating interactive narrative scene generation in digital games with large language models. In: Proceedings of the AAAI Conference on Artificial Intelligence and Interactive Digital Entertainment, vol. 19, no. 1, pp. 86–96, 2023

6. Sun, Y., et al.: Language as reality: a co-creative storytelling game experience in 1001 nights using generative AI. In: Proceedings of the AAAI Conference on Artificial Intelligence and Interactive Digital Entertainment, vol. 19, no. 1, pp. 425–434, 2023

7. Sohn, S.S., et al.: From Words to Worlds: Transforming One-line Prompt into Immersive Multi-modal Digital Stories with Communicative LLM Agent. arXiv preprint arXiv:2406.10478 (2024)

8. Nimpattanavong, C., et al.: Am i fighting well? Fighting game commentary generation with ChatGPT. In: Proceedings of the 13th International Conference on Advances in Information Technology, pp. 1– 7, 2023

9. Mustaquim, M.M.: Automatic speech recognition-an approach for designing inclusive games. Multimed. Tools Appl. **66**, 131–146 (2013)

10. Allison, F., Carter, M., Gibbs, M.: Word play: a history of voice interaction in digital games. Games Cult. **15**(2), 91–113 (2020)

11. Tonini, L.: Talk to me, Hal: A Study of Player Experience and Interaction in a Voice Interaction VR Game Featuring AI-driven Nonplayer Characters, April 2024. http://essay.utwente.nl/98788/

12. Safadi, F., Fonteneau, R., Ernst, D.: Artificial intelligence in video games: towards a unified framework. Int. J. Comput. Games Technol. **2015**(1), 271296 (2015)

13. Biswas, S.: Role of chatgpt in gaming: according to chatgpt. Available at SSRN 4375510 (2023)

14. MetaChat. Midjourney API Reference, 2025. MetaChat Knowledge Base. https://www.metachat.in/metachatknowledge-base/api/midjourney-api. Accessed 19 Apr 2025

STA-TAD: Spatial-Temporal Adapter on ViT for Temporal Action Detection

Zhongguang Zhang[1], Tingwei Wu[1,2], Qifei Zhang[1](✉), Li Wang[1], and Zhao Wang[2](✉)

[1] Zhejiang University, Hangzhou, China
cstzhangqf@zju.edu.cn
[2] Ningbo Innovation Center, Zhejiang University, Ningbo, China
zhao_wang@zju.edu.cn

Abstract. Temporal Action Detection (TAD) aims to localize all action instances and recognize their categories in a long untrimmed video. TAD plays an essential role in the long-term video understanding. Recently, TAD has achieved significant performance improvement with end-to-end training adapting pre-trained Vision Transformer (ViT) models. However, the memory bottleneck limits the implementation of powerful video models, which inevitably restricts TAD performance. In this paper, we present a novel Adapter based method, a typical parameter-efficient fine-tuning (PEFT) technique, to address this issue. The key to our approach lies in our proposed spatial-temporal adapter (STA), which is a novel lightweight module. The backbone can adapt to the TAD task during end-to-end training by only updating the parameters in STA. In addition, STA also leads to better TAD representation with its sparse self-attention design for exploiting local temporal information. We evaluate our model across 3 benchmark datasets THUMOS14, ActivityNet-1.3 and Charades. The proposed STA-TAD outperforms SOTA methods in most cases.

Keywords: Human Motion · Temporal Action Detection · ViT · Spatial-Temporal Adapter

1 Introduction

Temporal Action Detection (TAD) is essential for long-term video understanding. It localizes action instances and recognizes their categories in untrimmed videos. The task supports applications including highlight detection, video-language grounding, and action spotting [24, 28]. Beyond real-world video understanding, TAD can also benefit animation production and VR applications, e.g. generating character motions from sparse inputs.

Most TAD methods rely on the pre-trained backbone models to extract feature for each input video snippet and then apply the TAD heads on top of feature sequence for action detection. In such pipeline, the feature extracted from the backbone could conduct great effect on the final TAD performance. In order to obtain effective features, various backbones have been employed by previous TAD approaches. For instance, both CNN [10,11,29,36] based backbone and transformer [19,22,25,32] based backbones have been involved. Recent advances of ViT enables self-supervised masked pretraining on extensive video datasets,resulting in a more robust video representation learner. Unlike CNN, these powerful transformer backbones (e.g., VideoMAE [22]), present challenges when applied directly to untrimmed video modeling, especially in end-to-end training.

End-to-end training in TAD refers to jointly training the video backbone and action detector, which can effectively bridge the gap commonly found between pretraining and fine-tuning. Intuitively, combining the strengths of end-to-end training and large video backbone could be beneficial for improving TAD performance. However, such strategy could be limited by substantial GPU memory. Additionally, current end-to-end methods [7,30,33] in TAD may risk the issues of catastrophic forgetting and overfitting since the size of downstream TAD datasets is small.

Recent parameter-efficient fine-tuning (PEFT) strategies [3,4,8] effectively address computational and storage costs in full fine-tuning. These strategies typically update only a subset of network parameters. Adapters implement this by inserting lightweight modules resembling transformer feedforward networks. Only these adapter components require tuning during training. The AdaTAD method [14] demonstrates this potential, employing a standard adapter architecture for temporal action detection tasks.

To this end, a spatial-temporal adapter tuning for temporal action detection (STA-TAD) is introduced in this work. Our method successfully trains a TAD model in an end-to-end manner, utilizing a large pre-trained backbone model, e.g. VideoMAE. Specifically, we employ the following strategies to enhance the TAD performance while maintaining reasonable memory consumption. The PEFT is adopted to minimize memory usage and mitigate overfitting in transfer learning. The proposed STA is injected between backbone layers and is the only learnable component during fine-tuning. The proposed STA is tailored for the TAD task and integrates sparse self attention to aggregate local temporal informative context from adjacent snippets.

In particular, our STA-TAD yields state-of-the-art performance on the challenging datasets THUMOS14, ActivityNet-1.3 and Charades. In summary, our contributions are as follows:Our contributions could be summarizes as follows:

- An efficient end-to-end framework that utilizes the ViT backbone for TAD is presented. We have studied key design choices of improving training mechanism for TAD. The proposed framewrok can be trained in an end-to-end manner under limited GPU memory.
- A novel spatial-temporal adapter is proposed to improve training memory efficiency as well as aggregate the temporal context for TAD. Our STA has been validated by extensive ablation experiments.

– Our method achieves state-of-the-art performance across 3 major benchmark datasets and offers a solid baseline for TAD.

2 Related Work

2.1 Temporal Action Detection

Existing methodologies for temporal action detection (TAD), also referred to as temporal action localization, can be categorized along two orthogonal dimensions: architectural design and training paradigm. Based on methods' architectural design, they can be broadly classified into three categories, including one-stage, two-stage, and DETR-based methods.

One-stage methods (e.g., ActionFormer [32], TriDet [18]) directly predict action boundaries and categories through unified multi-scale feature pyramids, eliminating proposal generation stages by integrating classification and regression in a single network. Two-stage methods usually first generate candidate proposals via temporal anchors, then refine their features and classifications [10,34,37]. These methods often employ boundary-sensitive modules (e.g., BMN's boundary matching [35]) but incur higher computational costs. DETR-based methods leverage transformer decoders with learnable queries to model temporal relations, achieving end-to-end detection without hand-crafted anchors. Recently, there is a growing interest in such query-based methods [19,20]. These methods deploy a set of learned queries to interact with the feature maps and directly predict the actions' temporal boundaries and categories.

In addition to the aforementioned categories, TAD can also be divided into feature-based approaches and end-to-end approaches. Most aforementioned works could be categorized as feature-based approaches, which mainly relies on pre-extracted RGB features. Such methods can also optionally incorporates optical flow features. On the other hand, end-to-end methods take raw video frames as input and jointly optimize the video encoder and action detector [13]. We will detaily review end to end approaches in following paragraph.

2.2 End-To-End Temporal Action Detection

Traditional TAD methodologies [10,11,29,35] predominantly adopt a decoupled two-stage paradigm to alleviate GPU memory limitations. In this framework, pre-trained backbones (typically optimized for action recognition tasks) first extract fixed temporal features, followed by a separate detection stage. While computationally efficient, this task dissociation creates a feature-task misalignment that inevitably degrades detection performance, as the backbone remains unoptimized for temporal localization objectives.

Driven by this limitation, recent works [9,19,20,33] have shifted toward end-to-end trainable architectures that jointly optimize feature extraction and detection. However, simultaneous gradient updates for both backbone and detection modules impose prohibitive memory costs, especially for high-resolution video inputs. Current mitigation strategies diverge into two categories. resolution reduction techniques [9,13,20] that trade spatial-temporal fidelity for memory conservation, and architectural innovations preserving original resolutions through memory-efficient mechanisms.

Prominent examples of the latter category include TALLFormer [19], which employs an offline memory bank to asynchronously update partial network features during training, thereby circumventing full backward-pass computations. Re2TAL [33] introduces reversible transformer blocks that reconstruct intermediate activations during backpropagation, effectively halving memory consumption. The state-of-the-art AdaTAD [14] adopts parameter-efficient adaptation by freezing pre-trained backbone weights and exclusively training lightweight adapter modules, achieving competitive performance with minimal memory overhead.

A critical implementation challenge arises when adapting transformer-based backbones pre-trained at fixed spatial-temporal resolutions. Altering input dimensions disrupts positional encoding alignments, potentially degrading temporal localization accuracy. Current solutions exhibit divergent philosophies: TALLFormer [19] and Re2TAL [33] strictly preserve original backbone resolutions, whereas STPT [20] bypasses the issue through self-supervised pre-training on target domains. This dichotomy underscores an unresolved tension between resolution flexibility and computational efficiency âĂŞ a challenge exacerbated by increasing video resolutions in contemporary datasets.

Emerging hybrid approaches suggest dynamic resolution adaptation [13] and modular fine-tuning [14] as promising avenues. However, fundamental limitations persist in reconciling transformer architectures' rigid positional encoding schemes with variable-resolution inputs, leaving this as an open research frontier in end-to-end TAD optimization.

3   Methodology

3.1   Overview

In this section, We describe the details of proposed STA-TAD. The overall pipeline is shown in Fig. 1. In general, the proposed framework consists of the two stage components: Adaptive Feature Extraction and Multi-scale Temporal Decoding.

Formally, for each input of video $X \in \mathbb{R}^{B \times 3 \times T \times H \times W}$, where B denotes batch size, T denotes temporal duration, and (H, W) represent the spatial dimensions. Then, the input video X is divided into $N_s = \lceil T/T_s \rceil$ non-overlapping snippets, where T_s defines the snippet length with zero-padding applied to handle boundary cases. Hence the input X could be represented as Eq. 1

$$X = \{X_j\}_{j=1}^{N_s}, \quad X_j \in \mathbb{R}^{B \times 3 \times T_s \times H \times W} \tag{1}$$

Each non-overlapping snippet X_j undergoes spatial-temporal feature transformation through ViT blocks equipped with our Spatial-Temporal Adapters. The final backbone feature X_{out} could be defined as $X_{\text{out}} \in \mathbb{R}^{B \times C' \times D'}$, where (C', D') represent the channel and feature dimension.

The final backbone feature X_{out} is processed with a multi-scale encoder to produce n feature sequences at varying scales, denoted as Eq. 2

$$X'_{\text{out}} \in \mathbb{R}^{B \times C' \times \{D'_1, D'_2, \ldots, D'_n\}} \tag{2}$$

These multi-scale features are fused using a pyramid fusion strategy to generate action proposals. Finally, the prediction of start/end time (τ_j^s, τ_j^e), classification $\hat{a}_j$ and confidence score σ_j would be conducted through action localization and classification modules.

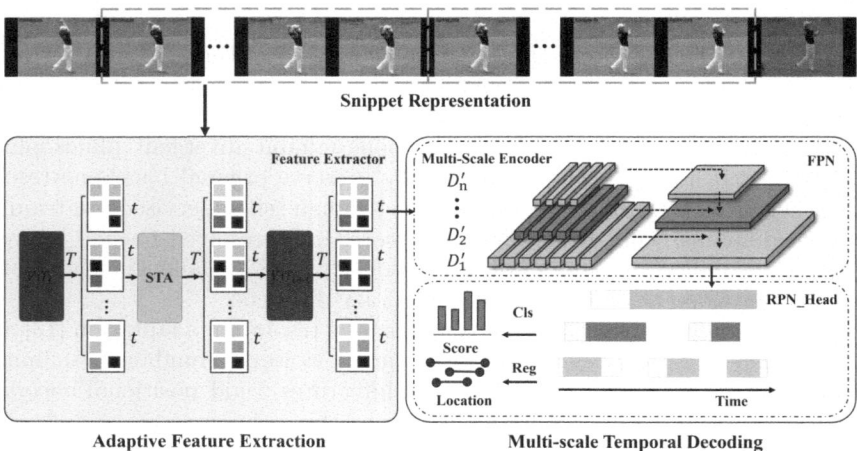

Fig. 1. Overview of STA-TAD. The proposed framework consists of the two stage components: Adaptive Feature Extraction and Multi-scale Temporal Decoding. For each input video snippet X_j, the start/end time (τ_j^s, τ_j^e), class $\hat{a}_j$ and confidence score σ_j would be predicted.

3.2 Adaptive Feature Extraction

Adapter Mechanism. Inspired by the recent success of Parameter-Efficient Fine-Tuning (PEFT) mechanism, we propose a fine-tune a plug-and-play module named Spatial Temporal Adapter (STA) to achieve efficient and effective transfer learning for temporal action detection.

The standard adapter [3] aims to leverage pre-trained models to effectively adapt to new tasks. The adapter utilize a modular and flexible architecture that bridges the gap between general-purpose feature extraction and task-specific learning. We first review the architecture of the standard adapter [3]. As shown in the Fig. 2(a), its architecture employs a bottleneck structure with three key components:

1. A dimensionality reduction layer $\mathbf{W}_{\text{down}} \in \mathbb{R}^{d \times r}$ that projects input features to a low-rank space ($r \ll d$).
2. A nonlinear activation function b $\sigma(.)$, typically ReLU or GELU
3. An ascending dimension layer $\mathbf{W}_{\text{up}} \in \mathbb{R}^{r \times d}$ to restore feature dimensionality.

The adapter operation can be formally expressed as:

$$f_{\text{adapter}}(\mathbf{h}) = \mathbf{W}_{\text{up}}^{\top} \cdot \sigma(\mathbf{W}_{\text{down}}^{\top} \cdot \mathbf{h}) \tag{3}$$

Note that such operation ensures dimensional consistency between input and output, enabling seamless integration into existing architectures while training only $2dr$ parameters, while traditional FFN layers require d^2.

Spatial Temporal Adapter. The standard adapter has demonstrated remarkable parameter efficiency in both natural language processing and computer vision. However, its inherent focus on on adapting channel information would neglects the temporal context vital for the TAD task. For instance, feature extraction usually splits long video sequences into small segments, then extract features from each segment, next fuse them to form a global feature representation. Such fragmented processing limits previous model's ability to capture long-range dependencies between adjacent segments. To address this limitation, we propose a spatial temporal adapter in this work.

The architecture of STA follows the general design of the standard adapter, where the overall structure of this component is depicted in Fig. 2. Assume that the input to the STA is denoted as $h \in \mathbb{R}^{B \times T \times C}$, where B denotes the batch size, T represents the sequence length, and C indicates the dimensionality of the feature space. Initially, the input passes through a dimensionality reduction layer followed by a nonlinear transformation layer, yielding $x \in \mathbb{R}^{B \times T \times C'}$. Subsequently, sparse attention is employed to extract feature information between fragments, producing $x' \in \mathbb{R}^{B \times T \times C'}$. Finally, the output is projected back to the original input dimensionality as $h' \in \mathbb{R}^{B \times T \times C}$ via a dimensionality expansion layer and is added to the original input h through a residual connection.

$$
\begin{aligned}
x &= \sigma(\mathbf{W}_{\text{down}}^{\top} \cdot h), \\
x' &= \mathbf{W}^{\top} \cdot \text{SA}(x) + x, \\
h' &= \mathbf{W}_{\text{up}}^{\top} \cdot x' + h
\end{aligned}
\tag{4}
$$

Compare with normal attention that computes the similarity between all pairs of positions, our method only considers the similarity between adjacent positions within a local window. Specifically, given the query Q and key K matrices, the sparse self-attention is computed within a local region by considering both the left and right neighboring positions (with $-w/2$ and $+w/2$ as the local window size), as shown below:

$$\text{SA} = \text{softmax}(\ell(Q, K))V \tag{5}$$

$$\ell(Q, K) = \left(\frac{Q_{\frac{-w}{2}} K_{\frac{-w}{2}}^{T} + Q_{\frac{+w}{2}} K_{\frac{+w}{2}}^{T}}{\sqrt{d_k} \cdot \lambda} \right) \tag{6}$$

where λ is the temperature coefficient, which controls the sharpness or smoothness of the attention distribution.

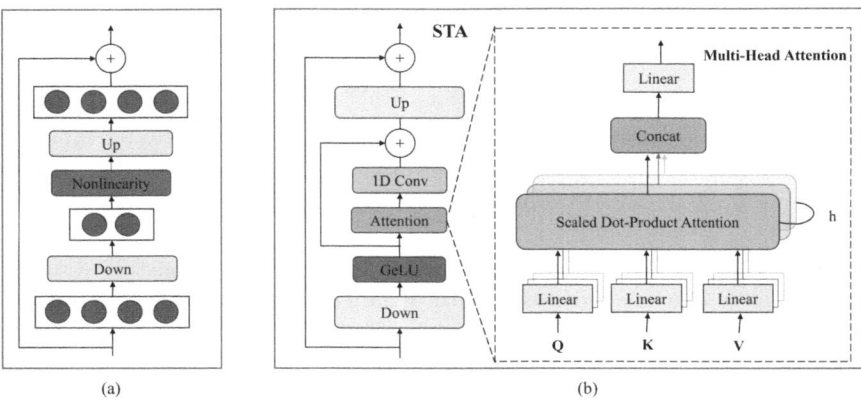

Fig. 2. Architecture of (a) standard adapter and (b) our spatial-temporal adapter.

As illustrated in Fig. 1, the proposed STA operates as a plug-and-play module strategically integrated between between backbone layers. For instance, it is inserted between ViT block of VideoMAE [22] in this work. By maintaining the original backbone parameters frozen while only updating the STA components, our proposed strategy achieves a massive reduction in trainable parameters compared to full fine-tuning. Our experimental results validate STA's efficacy in balancing temporal modeling capacity and computational efficiency. This parameter-efficient adaptation mechanism preserves the pre-trained model's spatial reasoning capabilities while injecting task-specific temporal awareness through lightweight spatial-temporal transformations.

3.3   Multi-scale Temporal Decoding

Our proposed STA-TAD framework establishes a streamlined and simple temporal action detection pipeline. In principle, it is compatible with any TAD head for converting features into predictions. Inspired by [14,25–27,32], we employ a general multi-scale temporal decoding module as temporal action detection head, which illustrated in Fig. 1.

Multi-scale Encoding. The multi-scale encoder take X_{out} as input. Our multi-scale encoding employ N_{scale} transformer layers, where each layer consisting of alternating layers of local multi-head self-attention (MSA) and MLP blocks. In addition, LayerNorm (LN) is applied before every MSA or MLP block, and residual connection is added after every block. The whole settings follow [23]. Our model combines D_n transformer blocks with downsampling in between, resulting in a feature pyramid $X'_{\text{out}} \in \mathbb{R}^{B \times C' \times \{D'_1, D'_2, ..., D'_n\}}$.

Temporal Decoding. the feature pyramid X'_{out} would be transferred into the sequence label using the decoder h. The decoder is a RPN head with a classification and a regression head. The RPN head is a lightweight convolutional network that widely used in Fast-RCNN [16] framework.

The classification head is a lightweight 1D convolutional network attached to each pyramid level with its parameters shared across all levels. A sigmoid function is attached to each output dimension to predict the probability of action categories. It examines each moment across all D_n levels on the feature pyramid X'_{out}, and predict the probability of action at every moment. In this work, the classification head is implemented using 3 layers of 1D convolutions with kernel size=3, layer normalization, and ReLU activation.

Compare with the classification head, the regression head predicts the distances to start/end time of an action (τ_j^s, τ_j^e) only if the current time step lies in an action. Similarly, the regression head is also implemented using a 1D convolutional network following the same design of the classification head, while a ReLU is attached at the end for distance estimation.

3.4   Loss Function

Generally, an end-to-end TAD pipeline is presented in the above paragraph. The ground-truth temporal annotations are represented as $\Gamma_{gt} = \{(t_i^{start}, t_i^{end}, a_i)\}_{i=1}^{K_g}$ where $t_i^{start} < t_i^{end}$ denote start, end times and $a_i \in \mathcal{A}$ the action class. The detector outputs predicted segments $\Gamma_{pred} = \{(\tau_j^s, \tau_j^e, \hat{a}_j, \sigma_j)\}_{j=1}^{K_p}$ with $\sigma_j \in (0,1]$ indicating detection certainty, designed to optimally match Γ_{gt} through temporal localization. The whole loss function consists of 2 terms, including classification loss $\mathcal{L}_{\text{cls}}$ and regression loss $\mathcal{L}_{\text{reg}}$.

Classification Loss. In the task of temporal action detection, most samples usually belong to the background class, while action instances are relatively sparse. In order to solve the problem of class imbalance, we use Focal Loss [12] as the action classification loss.

$$\mathcal{L}_{\text{cls}} = -\alpha_t (1 - p_t)^\gamma \log(p_t) \tag{7}$$

p_t represents the model's predicted probability for the correct category. α_t is a balancing factor used to balance the importance of positive and negative samples. γ is a regulating factor used to control the loss impact of easy-to-classify samples.

Regression Loss. In order to minimize the Euclidean distance between the center point of the predicted box and the true box, so that the bounding box not only overlaps as much as possible but also aligns with the center, we choose DIoU Loss [38] as the regression loss function. The formula is as follows:

$$\mathcal{L}_{\text{reg}} = 1 - \text{IoU} + \frac{\rho^2(b, b^g)}{c^2} \tag{8}$$

where $\rho^2(b, b^g)$ represents the Euclidean distance between the center point b of the predicted box and the center point b^g of the true box. c represents the diagonal length of the envelope box (i.e., the smallest box that contains both the predicted box and the true box). As mentioned in previous section, $\mathcal{L}_{\text{reg}}$ would only be active when positive sample is contained in current snippet.

Finally Loss. We control the impact of classification loss and regression loss by setting λ_{reg} and normalization factors T_+ , so that the model can focus on the accuracy of action category prediction and the precision of time boundary prediction at the same time. The final loss is as follows:

$$\mathcal{L}_{\text{final}} = \sum_t \left(\frac{1}{T}\mathcal{L}_{\text{cls}} + \frac{\lambda_{\text{reg}}}{T_+} 1_{c_t}\mathcal{L}_{\text{reg}} \right) \tag{9}$$

where $\mathcal{L}_{\text{final}}$ is the total loss term, $\mathcal{L}_{\text{cls}}$ is the Classification loss, $\mathcal{L}_{\text{reg}}$ is the Regression loss, T is the input sequence length, and 1_{c_t} is an indicator function that is 1 when the time step t belongs to an action instance and 0 otherwise.

4   Experimental Results

4.1   Datasets

THUMOS14. THUMOS14 [5] is a widely used dataset for action recognition and localization, featuring over 20 action categories and thousands of video clips. The training data is sourced from the UCF101 dataset, while the validation and test sets include annotations provided by THUMOS14 itself. For temporal action detection tasks, the dataset consists of 413 untrimmed videos spanning 20 action categories. Specifically, the training set includes 200 videos, and the test set contains 213 videos.

ActivityNet-1.3. ActivityNet-1.3 [2] is a large-scale video action recognition dataset featuring 200 categories of daily activities in complex scenarios, with a total of approximately 20,000 video clips. The dataset spans a wide variety of environments, actions, and temporal contexts, including both indoor daily activities and outdoor sports scenes. It is divided into three subsets: 10,024 videos for training, 4,926 videos for validation, and 5,044 videos for testing.

Charades. Charades [2] is a multi-label video dataset focused on daily indoor activities. It includes 157 action categories captured in diverse indoor scenarios, comprising a total of approximately 9,848 video clips. The dataset covers a variety of indoor environments, actions, and temporal contexts, including interactions with 46 object categories. It is divided into three subsets: 7,986 videos for training and 1,863 videos for validation.

4.2 Evaluation Metric and Implementation Details

Evaluation Metric. Following [7,14,18,30], we evaluate TAD performance using the standard mean average precision (mAP) at various temporal intersection over union (tIoU) thresholds for all datasets. For THUMOS14, the tIoU thresholds are set at $[0.3, 0.4, 0.5, 0.6, 0.7]$. On ActivityNet-1.3, the tIoU thresholds range from 0.5 to 0.95 in increments of 0.05. For Charades, the tIoU thresholds are selected from 0.1 to 0.9 with increments of 0.1.

Table 1. Comparison of action detection results on the Thumos14, measured by mAP(%) at different tIoU thresholds. E2E denotes end-to-end training.

Method	Publish	Backbone	E2E	0.3	0.4	0.5	0.6	0.7	Avg.
BSN [11]	ECCV'18	TSN	✗	53.5	45.0	36.9	28.4	20.0	36.8
BMN [10]	CVPR'19	TSN	✗	56.0	47.4	38.8	29.7	20.5	38.5
MGG [15]	CVPR'19	TSN	✗	53.9	46.8	37.4	29.5	21.3	37.8
G-TAD [29]	CVPR'20	TSN	✗	54.5	47.6	40.2	30.8	23.4	39.3
BU-MR [36]	ECCV'20	I3D	✗	53.9	50.7	45.4	38.0	28.5	43.3
ContextLoc [39]	CVPR'21	I3D	✗	68.3	63.8	54.3	41.8	26.2	50.9
ActionFormer [32]	ECCV'22	I3D	✗	82.1	77.8	71.0	59.4	43.9	66.8
ASL [17]	CVPR'23	I3D	✗	83.1	79.0	71.7	59.7	45.8	67.9
TriDet [18]	CVPR'23	I3D	✗	83.6	80.1	72.9	62.4	47.4	69.3
TE-TAD [7]	CVPR'24	I3D	✓	83.3	78.4	71.3	60.7	45.6	67.9
ViT-TAD [30]	CVPR'24	VideoMAE-B	✓	85.1	80.9	74.2	61.8	45.4	69.5
AdaTAD [14]	CVPR'24	VideoMAE-B	✓	**87.0**	**82.4**	<u>75.3</u>	<u>63.8</u>	<u>49.2</u>	<u>71.5</u>
Ours		VideoMAE-B	✓	<u>86.1</u>	<u>82.3</u>	**75.5**	**64.7**	**50.8**	**71.9**

Table 2. Comparison of action detection results on ActivityNet v1.3 and Charades, measured by mAP(%) at different tIoU thresholds.

Method	Backbone	ActivityNet v1.3				Charades			
		0.5	0.75	0.95	Avg.	0.2	0.5	0.7	Avg.
TAL-Net [1]	I3D	38.2	18.3	1.3	20.2	–	–	–	–
P-GCN [31]	I3D	42.9	28.1	2.5	27.0	–	–	–	–
PointTAD [21]	I3D	–	–	–	–	17.5	13.5	9.1	12.1
BMN [10]	TSN	50.1	34.8	8.3	33.9	–	–	–	–
G-TAD [29]	TSN	50.4	34.6	9.0	34.1	–	–	–	–
ActionFormer [32]	I3D	53.5	36.2	8.2	35.6	31.3	23.1	13.6	20.6
ASL [17]	I3D	54.1	37.4	8.0	36.2	24.5	16.5	9.4	15.4
TriDet [18]	R(2+1)D	54.7	38.0	8.4	36.8	–	–	–	–
ViT-TAD [30]	VideoMAE-B	55.9	38.5	8.8	37.4	–	–	–	–
AdaTAD [14]	VideoMAE-B	<u>56.8</u>	<u>39.4</u>	<u>9.7</u>	<u>38.4</u>	<u>40.8</u>	<u>31.8</u>	<u>20.1</u>	<u>28.0</u>
Ours	VideoMAE-B	**56.9**	**39.8**	**9.9**	**38.6**	**42.0**	**32.8**	**20.9**	**28.9**

Baselines. We compare our work on these three datasets with ActionFormer [32], ASL [17], TriDet [18], TE-TAD [7], ViT-TAD [30] and AdaTAD [14] which are the current state-of-the-art methods. All evaluations are under the same conditions to ensure a fair comparison. Besides, the code of ASL is not published, the best reported results from the paper are used [17].

Implementation Details. Our method is implemented using the PyTorch 2.0 with MMAction2 toolkit and trained on 8 NVIDIA GeForce RTX 3090 GPUs. The batch size is set to 1 for each GPU. For STA in the backbone, the learning rate ranges from $5e-4$ to $5e-5$. For THUMOS14 and Charades, we have used AdamW with a learning rate of $5e-4$ and a weight decay of 0.05. For ActivityNet-1.3, we train the model with a learning rate of $1e-3$. We randomly truncate a window of 768 frames with a time step of 4, which is split into segments of 16 frames. Frame pixels are cropped to 160×160. A sparse self-attention mechanism with w set to 4 is adopted.

4.3   Comparison with the State-of-the-Art Methods

Thumos14. Table 1 reports the comparison result of our method with other SOTA methods on THUMOS14 dataset. VideoMAE-B is selected as backbone model, which is a pre-trained models on Kinetics-400 [6] provided by [25]. For a fair comparison, we adopt the same parameter settings as ViT-TAD [30] and AdaTAD [14]. Specifically, all segments are trimmed to a resolution of 160×160, and the feature window size is set to 768. The results demonstrate that our method outperform the competitors in most cases, especially for the high tIoU threshold.

ActivityNet-1.3 and Charades. The results on ActivityNet-1.3 and Charades are presented in Table 2. These results demonstrate that our method outperforms existing approaches.

Table 3. Comparison results with Frozen, Full FT, and different STA modules. Mem. refers to memory usage (GB) per video.

adapter	Mem.	Avg. mAP	gains
Frozen	3.8G	64.3	+0.0
Full FT	5.7G	69.5	+5.2
Conv3d	5.0G	69.4	+5.1
GRU	5.1G	70.0	+5.7
Attention	5.3G	**71.9**	**+7.6**

4.4 Ablation Study

In this section, the result of ablation study is presented to further analyze the proposed method. All experimental results are obtained on the Thumos14 dataset.

STA Module. The Table 3 compares traditional fine-tuning with our STA module, incorporating various components. The results indicate that traditional fine-tuning incurs higher memory costs while delivering lower performance compared to the STA module. This demonstrates that our proposed module effectively addresses these limitations. Additionally, we visualize the performance of each module across different tIoU thresholds. As illustrated in the Fig. 3, the STA module consistently outperforms traditional fine-tuning, with a more pronounced advantage as the tIoU threshold increases.

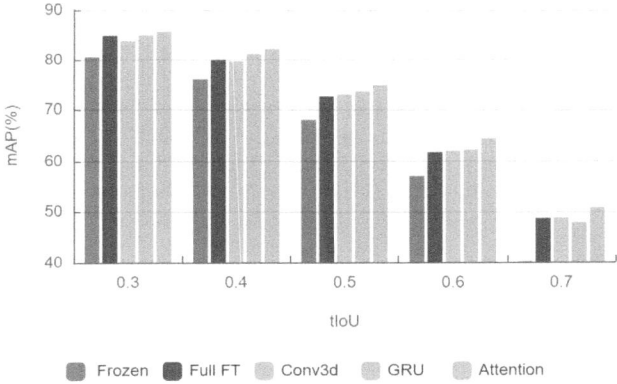

Fig. 3. Ablation study of STA module with different tIoU threshold.

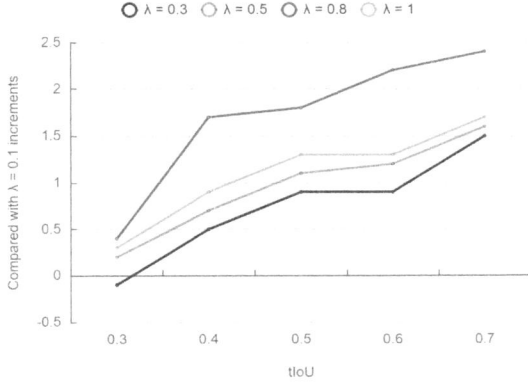

Fig. 4. Ablation study of Temperature Coefficient λ with different tIOU.

Temperature Coefficient λ. In order to examine the effect of the temperature coefficient λ of Eq. 6. As shown in Fig. 4, it achieves best performance when the temperature coefficient λ is set as 0.8

5   Conclusion

To sum up, this work introduces a memory-efficient and parameter efficient end-to-end method named STA-TAD. Our key innovation lies in the proposed spatial-temporal adapter, which is tailored for TAD with low computation costs that outperform SOTA performance while requiring much less trainable parameters compared to full fine-tuning. Our STA use sparse cross-snippet attention to grained temporal information across different snippets. Extensive evaluation results indicate that our work achieves new SoTA performance on the challenging datasets THUMOS14, ActivityNet-1.3 and Charades. In addition, we also perform in-depth ablation studies on the design of STA-TAD We hope the proposed STA-TAD will serve as a new TAD baseline for future research.

Acknowledgments. This research has been supported by Natural Key Research and Development Project of Zhejiang Province (Grant No. 2023C01043), and in part by the Major Program of The National Social Science Fund of China (Grant No. 24&ZD070), Ningbo Natural Science Foundation (Grant No. 2024Z148, 2024Z234).

References

1. Chao, Y.W., Vijayanarasimhan, S., Seybold, B., Ross, D.A., Deng, J., Sukthankar, R.: Rethinking the faster R-CNN architecture for temporal action localization. In: Proceedings of the IEEE Conference on Computer Vision and Pattern Recognition, pp. 1130–1139 (2018)
2. Caba Heilbron, F., Victor Escorcia, B.G., Niebles, J.C.: ActivityNet: a large-scale video benchmark for human activity understanding. In: Proceedings of the IEEE Conference on Computer Vision and Pattern Recognition, pp. 961–970 (2015)
3. Houlsby, N., et al.: Parameter-efficient transfer learning for NLP. In: International Conference on Machine Learning, pp. 2790–2799. PMLR (2019)
4. Hu, E.J., et al.: LoRA: low-rank adaptation of large language models. In: International Conference on Learning Representations (2022). https://openreview.net/forum?id=nZeVKeeFYf9
5. Jiang, Y.G., et al.: THUMOS challenge: action recognition with a large number of classes (2014). http://crcv.ucf.edu/THUMOS14/
6. Kay, W., et al.: The kinetics human action video dataset. arXiv preprint: arXiv:1705.06950 (2017)
7. Kim, H.J., Hong, J.H., Kong, H., Lee, S.W.: TE-TAD: towards full end-to-end temporal action detection via time-aligned coordinate expression. In: Proceedings of the IEEE/CVF Conference on Computer Vision and Pattern Recognition, pp. 18837–18846 (2024)
8. Li, X.L., Liang, P.: Prefix-tuning: optimizing continuous prompts for generation. arXiv preprint: arXiv:2101.00190 (2021)

9. Lin, C., et al. Learning salient boundary feature for anchor-free temporal action localization. In: Proceedings of the IEEE/CVF Conference on Computer Vision and Pattern Recognition, pp. 3320–3329 (2021)

10. Lin, T., Liu, X., Li, X., Ding, E., Wen, S.: BMN: boundary-matching network for temporal action proposal generation. In: Proceedings of the IEEE/CVF International Conference on Computer Vision, pp. 3889–3898 (2019)

11. Lin, T., Zhao, X., Su, H., Wang, C., Yang, M.: BSN: boundary sensitive network for temporal action proposal generation. In: Proceedings of the European Conference on Computer Vision (ECCV), pp. 3–19 (2018)

12. Lin, T.Y., Goyal, P., Girshick, R., He, K., Dollár, P.: Focal loss for dense object detection. In: 2017 IEEE International Conference on Computer Vision (ICCV), pp. 2999–3007 (2017). https://doi.org/10.1109/ICCV.2017.324

13. Liu, Q., Wang, Z.: Progressive boundary refinement network for temporal action detection. In: Proceedings of the AAAI Conference on Artificial Intelligence, vol. 34, pp. 11612–11619 (2020)

14. Liu, S., Zhang, C.L., Zhao, C., Ghanem, B.: End-to-end temporal action detection with 1B parameters across 1000 frames. In: Proceedings of the IEEE/CVF Conference on Computer Vision and Pattern Recognition, pp. 18591–18601 (2024)

15. Liu, Y., Ma, L., Zhang, Y., Liu, W., Chang, S.F.: Multi-granularity generator for temporal action proposal. In: Proceedings of the IEEE/CVF Conference on Computer Vision and Pattern Recognition, pp. 3604–3613 (2019)

16. Ren, S., He, K., Girshick, R., Sun, J.: Faster R-CNN: towards real-time object detection with region proposal networks. IEEE Trans. Pattern Anal. Mach. Intell. **39**(6), 1137–1149 (2016)

17. Shao, J., Wang, X., Quan, R., Zheng, J., Yang, J., Yang, Y.: Action sensitivity learning for temporal action localization. In: Proceedings of the IEEE/CVF International Conference on Computer Vision, pp. 13457–13469 (2023)

18. Shi, D., Zhong, Y., Cao, Q., Ma, L., Li, J., Tao, D.: TriDet: temporal action detection with relative boundary modeling. In: Proceedings of the IEEE/CVF Conference on Computer Vision and Pattern Recognition, pp. 18857–18866 (2023)

19. Shi, D., et al.: ReAct: temporal action detection with relational queries. In: European Conference on Computer Vision, pp. 105–121. Springer (2022)

20. Tan, J., Tang, J., Wang, L., Wu, G.: Relaxed transformer decoders for direct action proposal generation. In: Proceedings of the IEEE/CVF International Conference on Computer Vision, pp. 13526–13535 (2021)

21. Tan, J., Zhao, X., Shi, X., Kang, B., Wang, L.: PointTAD: multi-label temporal action detection with learnable query points. In: Advances in Neural Information Processing Systems, vol. 35, pp. 15268–15280 (2022)

22. Tong, Z., Song, Y., Wang, J., Wang, L.: VideoMAE: masked autoencoders are data-efficient learners for self-supervised video pre-training. In: Advances in Neural Information Processing Systems, vol. 35, 10078–10093 (2022)

23. Touvron, H., Cord, M., Douze, M., Massa, F., Sablayrolles, A., Jégou, H.: Training data-efficient image transformers & distillation through attention. In: International Conference on Machine Learning, pp. 10347–10357. PMLR (2021)

24. Wang, B., Zhao, Y., Yang, L., Long, T., Li, X.: Temporal action localization in the deep learning era: a survey. IEEE Transactions on Pattern Analysis and Machine Intelligence (2023)

25. Wang, L., et al.: VideoMAE V2: scaling video masked autoencoders with dual masking. In: Proceedings of the IEEE/CVF Conference on Computer Vision and Pattern Recognition, pp. 14549–14560 (2023)

26. Wang, Y., et al.: InternVideo2: scaling foundation models for multimodal video understanding. In: European Conference on Computer Vision, pp. 396–416. Springer (2024)
27. Wang, Y., et al.: InternVideo: general video foundation models via generative and discriminative learning. arXiv preprint: arXiv:2212.03191 (2022)
28. Xia, H., Zhan, Y.: A survey on temporal action localization. IEEE Access **8**, 70477–70487 (2020)
29. Xu, M., Zhao, C., Rojas, D.S., Thabet, A., Ghanem, B.: G-TAD: sub-graph localization for temporal action detection. In: Proceedings of the IEEE/CVF Conference on Computer Vision and Pattern Recognition, pp. 10156–10165 (2020)
30. Yang, M., Gao, H., Guo, P., Wang, L.: Adapting short-term transformers for action detection in untrimmed videos. In: Proceedings of the IEEE/CVF Conference on Computer Vision and Pattern Recognition, pp. 18570–18579 (2024)
31. Zeng, R., et al.: Graph convolutional networks for temporal action localization. In: Proceedings of the IEEE/CVF International Conference on Computer Vision, pp. 7094–7103 (2019)
32. Zhang, C.L., Wu, J., Li, Y.: ActionFormer: localizing moments of actions with transformers. In: European Conference on Computer Vision, pp. 492–510. Springer (2022)
33. Zhao, C., Liu, S., Mangalam, K., Ghanem, B.: Re2TAl: rewiring pretrained video backbones for reversible temporal action localization. In: Proceedings of the IEEE/CVF Conference on Computer Vision and Pattern Recognition, pp. 10637–10647 (2023)
34. Zhao, C., Ramazanova, M., Xu, M., Ghanem, B.: SegTAD: precise temporal action detection via semantic segmentation. In: European Conference on Computer Vision, pp. 576–593. Springer (2022)
35. Zhao, C., Thabet, A.K., Ghanem, B.: Video self-stitching graph network for temporal action localization. In: Proceedings of the IEEE/CVF International Conference on Computer Vision, pp. 13658–13667 (2021)
36. Zhao, P., Xie, L., Ju, C., Zhang, Y., Wang, Y., Tian, Q.: Bottom-up temporal action localization with mutual regularization. In: Vedaldi, A., Bischof, H., Brox, T., Frahm, J.-M. (eds.) ECCV 2020. LNCS, vol. 12353, pp. 539–555. Springer, Cham (2020). https://doi.org/10.1007/978-3-030-58598-3_32
37. Zhao, Z., Wang, D., Zhao, X.: Movement enhancement toward multi-scale video feature representation for temporal action detection. In: Proceedings of the IEEE/CVF International Conference on Computer Vision, pp. 13555–13564 (2023)
38. Zheng, Z., Wang, P., Liu, W., Li, J., Ye, R., Ren, D.: Distance-IoU loss: faster and better learning for bounding box regression. In: Proceedings of the AAAI Conference on Artificial Intelligence, vol. 34, pp. 12993–13000 (2020)
39. Zhu, Z., Tang, W., Wang, L., Zheng, N., Hua, G.: Enriching local and global contexts for temporal action localization. In: Proceedings of the IEEE/CVF International Conference on Computer Vision, pp. 13516–13525 (2021)

User Interface for Controlling Crowd in Metaverse Using Spatial Controller

Akira Miya, Kunio Yamamoto, and Masaki Oshita$^{(\boxtimes)}$

Kyushu Institute of Technology, Iizuka, Japan
miya.akira799@mail.kyutech.jp, {kunio,oshita}@ai.kyutech.ac.jp

Abstract. The Metaverse is a virtual space on the internet where users can gather, communicate, and enjoy events such as live performances using their avatars. Although the Metaverse has become more common, events often attract only a small number of participants, creating a deserted impression. To address this issue, we propose populating the Metaverse with crowds of virtual characters and allowing event organizers to control their movements. However, controlling a large number of characters in real-time is challenging, as it requires manipulating the parameters of individual characters. To overcome this, we have developed a novel user interface that uses a spatial controller. In our system, the user wears a head-mounted display to view the scene from above and uses a six degrees-of-freedom spatial controller to manage the movements of the crowd. The key idea behind our user interface is that the spatial controller allows users to simultaneously select target characters and manipulate their parameters. Characters are selected by pointing at them with the controller, while parameters—such as the motion magnitude— are adjusted based on the controller's height. Experimental results show that our interface is both efficient and intuitive for users.

Keywords: User interface · Crowd simulation · Spatial controller · Metaverse

1 Introduction

The Metaverse is a virtual space on the internet where many users can gather, communicate, and enjoy events such as live performances using their avatars. Although such virtual spaces have existed for over thirty years, the term 'metaverse' has recently become common, referring to easily accessible virtual spaces made possible by advances in hardware, software, and internet environments. However, despite its growing popularity, some Metaverse events still attract only a small number of participants, creating a deserted impression for those in attendance.

To address this issue, we propose populating the Metaverse with crowds of virtual characters and allowing event organizers to control their movements. By making these virtual crowds perform various motions, such as arm-waving

C. Mousas et al. (Eds.): CASA 2025, LNCS 15915, pp. 263–271, 2026.
https://doi.org/10.1007/978-981-95-0100-7_17

or hand-clapping, around participants, we can create the impression of a lively, well-attended event. Additionally, by directing the crowd to move toward certain locations within the scene can help guide participants on where to go.

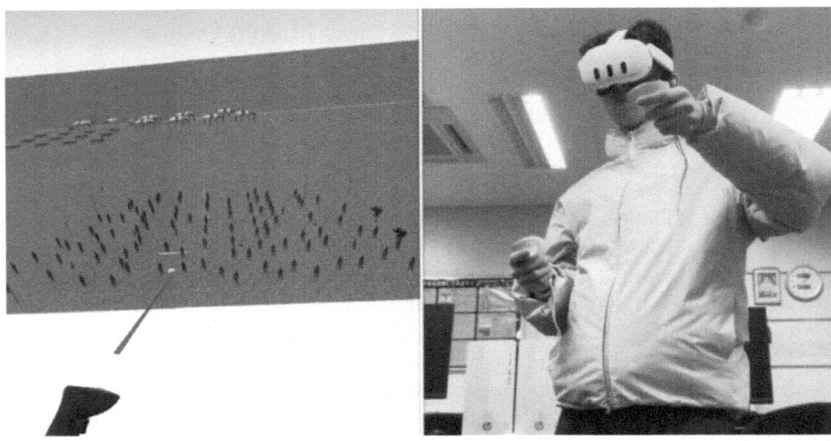

Fig. 1. Controlling crowd using a spatial controller.

However, controlling a large number of characters in real-time is challenging, as it requires manipulating parameters for each individual character. Although various methods exist for animating crowds, most still rely on manually setting parameters for individual characters to control their movements.

To solve this problem, we have developed a novel user interface for crowd control using a spatial controller. As shown in Fig. 1, the user wears a head-mounted display to view the scene from above and uses a six degrees-of-freedom spatial controller to manage the crowd. The key idea behind our interface is that the spatial controller enables the user to simultaneously select target characters and manipulate their parameters. Characters are selected by pointing at them using the spatial controller, while parameters, such as the magnitude of movements, are manipulated by the height of the spatial controller.

To animate the crowds, we use conventional methods. For in-place motions, such as arm-waving and hand-clapping with varying magnitudes, we use motion interpolation. For locomotion, we use the social force model, an agent based simulation, to move characters toward their target positions at specified speeds.

Our experimental results show that the interface is both efficient and intuitive for users.

2   Related Work

Many crowd simulation methods have been developed to generate animated characters. However, most of these methods do not consider interactive control during simulation. Instead, character behaviors are controlled by parameters set in advance. Moreover, most crowd simulation methods focus on navigating large groups of characters toward their goals while avoiding collisions [1,3,6,8,9,12,13]. These methods do not consider controlling motions other than walking, such as various motions in a position.

Several methods have been proposed for the interactive authoring of crowd animations. Ulicny et al. [14] proposed a crowd brush interface that allows users to assign motion types to multiple characters using a painting interface. However, their interface do not support the simultaneous specification of motion parameters alongside motion types. Therefore, users must perform multiple operations to specify motion types and then adjust the corresponding parameters. Oshita and Ogiwara [10] proposed a sketch-based interface that allows users to specify various parameters—such as the distances between characters, movements regularity, and individual paths for crowd simulation—based on multiple user trajectories. However, this interface is limited to specifying parameters for walking motions and requires multiple trajectories. Henry et al. [4] proposed a multitouch interface for controlling the formation of walking characters. However, this interface is also limited to the control of walking motions. Overall, specifying both the motion type and parameters simultaneously remains a challenge. Conventional interfaces require users to perform multiple operations, first assigning motion types and then adjusting the corresponding parameters separately.

Autonomously controlled characters can also be used to populate the Metaverse. Behavior Tree [7] are a common method for controlling such characters based on predefined combination of rules . However, autonomous characters may struggle to react appropriately to unexpected situations or various positions within a scene. Moreover, their motions may lack coordination across multiple characters. To address these limitations, we proposed providing event organizers with a user interface that enables direct control of characters according to the situational needs.

3   System Overview

The user wears a head-mounted display to view the scene from above and uses a six degrees-of-freedom spatial controller to control the crowd, as shown in Fig. 1. The user can also change the viewpoint and generate new characters as needed.

We implemented our system using Unity and Meta Quest 3. The scene and character models were created using the Unity editor. For motion control, we implemented two types of in a position motions arm-waving and hand-clapping as well as one type of walking motion, all based on motion capture clips. Although the system is intended for use in a Metaverse environment where multiple participants can connect using their avatars, full Metaverse functionality has not yet been implemented. Instead, we developed the system as a standalone application to evaluate the effectiveness of the proposed interface.

The system flow for crowd control is depicted in Fig. 2. Our system uses a single spatial controller to manage characters. The controller provides input data including its position $\mathbf{q}$, orientation $\mathbf{r}$, and buttons b_j where j denotes the button index. Each character i maintains internal parameters such as position $\mathbf{p}_i$, velocity $\mathbf{v}_i$, and motion type m_i. The motion type m_i indicates the character's current motion, either no motion (standing), one of the motions in a position, or one of the walking motions. Additionally, each character has motion parameters, including the magnitude of in a position motion w_i walking speed s_i, and target position $\mathbf{t}_i$ for walking motions. The user can assign a specific motion—either in a position or walking motions—to the selected characters using the controller buttons $\mathbf{b}_j$.

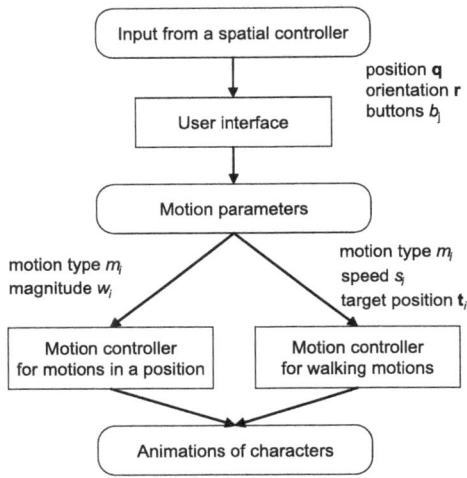

Fig. 2. System flow.

The motion controller contains two modules: one for in a position and another for walking motions. The in a position controller uses motion interpolation [11], where a small number of synchronized example motions is interpolated based on the motion magnitude w_i. The walking motion controller uses the social force model [3], an agent based simulation that guides characters toward their target positions $\mathbf{t}_i$ at specified speeds s_i, while avoiding collisions with other characters and obstacles.

4   Proposed Method

The key idea behind our interface is to enable the user specify multiple parameters of individual characters using a spatial controller. Using our interface, the user can simultaneously select target characters and manipulate their motion parameters, as shown in Fig. 3. First, the motion type m_i is selected using the buttons on the spatial controller. Next, characters are selected by pointing at them with the spatial controller. Simultaneously, motion parameter—such as the

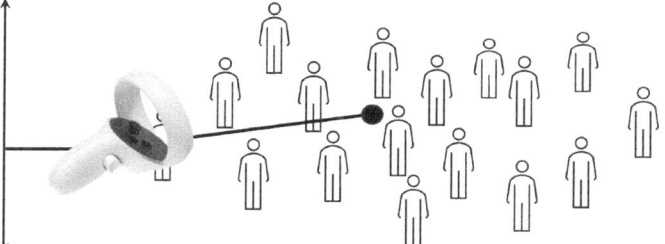

Fig. 3. Proposed user interface for crowd control using a spatial controller. Selecting characters and manipulating their motion parameters can be done simultaneously.

magnitude for motions in a position w_i or walking speed s_i for walking motions—are manipulated based on the height of the controller. The user selects characters using the orientation and horizontal position of the controller, while specifying motion parameter using the height of the controller, as shown in Fig. 3.

To implement this interface, the system computes the pointed position on the ground $\mathbf{o}$ and the height of the spatial controller h based on its position $\mathbf{q}$ and orientation $\mathbf{r}$. The height h is mapped within a range from 0.0 (the lowest) to 1.0 (the highest). Characters whose positions $\mathbf{p}_i$ fall within a certain distance of the pointed position $\mathbf{o}$ are selected. The motion type m_i and motion parameters, either w_i or s_i of the selected character are then modified. These parameters are computed based on the height h of the controller. As the user moves the spatial controller, both the pointed position $\mathbf{o}$ and height h are continuously updated, allowing real-time modifications of the motion types and parameters of characters near the pointed position $\mathbf{o}$.

When controlling in a position motions, the selected characters begin performing the motions using specified parameter w_i. In contrast, executing walking motions involves three steps. First, the user selects the characters and specifies their walking speed s_i using the proposed interface. Next, the user selects the center point for the target positions. The individual target positions $\mathbf{t}_i$ for each character are then computed such that the relative vectors from each character's current position to the group's center are preserved. Even if some target positions fall outside the walking area or within obstacles, the motion controller handles collision avoidance. Once the target positions are determined, the characters begin walking. During the walking motion, the user can continue to adjust each character's walking speeds through changing the height of the spatial controller.

5   Experimental Results

5.1   Experiment

We conducted experiments using the developed system to evaluate the effectiveness of our user interface, focusing particularly on controlling motions in

Fig. 4. Example of target scene that is presented to the subjects.

a position. Our interface was compared with two alternative approaches. The first alternative is a modified version of our interface, where the user selects characters and then sequentially specifies motion parameters using a button on the spatial controller. This sequential interface was introduced to compare the advantages of our simultaneous control approach. The second alternative interface uses a conventional screen and mouse to select characters and specify motion parameters. This interface was introduced to compare the differences between our spatial-controller interface and conventional input devices.

Four subjects participated in our experiments, all of whom were graduate students with moderate familiarity with virtual reality devices, including head-mounted displays and spatial controllers. We created a scene featuring a stage and an open stadium, populated with both controllable characters and dummy avatars representing remote participants, which the user could not control. Each subject was assigned three tasks involving target animations for the characters, as shown in Fig. 4. They were asked to reproduce the specified motions, each with one of three levels of magnitude, using all three interfaces in random order. Among the three tasks, Task 1 was relatively complex, while Task 3 was the simplest. We measured both the time taken to complete each task and the number of errors made in assigning the correct magnitude of motion parameters to the characters.

We also evaluated the usability of the interfaces using questionnaire-based usability tests: System Usability Scale (SUS) and Virtual Reality System Usability Questionnaire (VRSUQ) [2,5]. The SUS consists of 10 questions, while the VRSUQ includes 9 questions, each addressing various factors of usability. Subjects responded to each question using a 5 -point Likert scale, ranging from strongly agree (5) to strongly disagree (1). Usability scores were then calculated based on the aggregated responses to all questions.

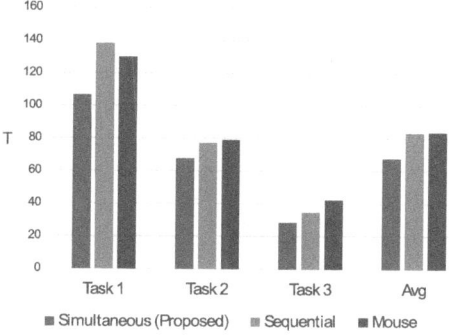

Fig. 5. The results of execution time in seconds in our experiment.

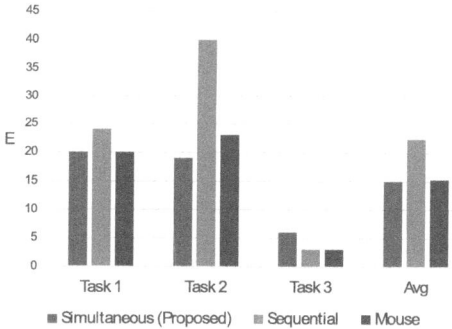

Fig. 6. The results of error counts in our experiment.

5.2   Results

The results for execution time and error counts are presented in Fig. 5 and Fig. 6, respectively. These results show that our interface achieved the shortest execution times and the fewest errors.

The usability scores based on the SUS and VRSUQ questionnaires are presented in Fig. 7. The results shows that our interface achieved the highest usability ratings compared to the alternative interfaces.

5.3   Discussion

Our interface achieved the shortest execution times and the fewest error compared to the alternative interfaces. In the sequential interface, subjects had to perform an additional step to specify motion parameters using buttons, which increased both execution time and error rates. With the mouse-based interface, although character selection was more precise, subjects needed additional time to adjust the view point for effective character selection. In contrast, changing the view point is more efficient in VR interfaces using a head-mounted display.

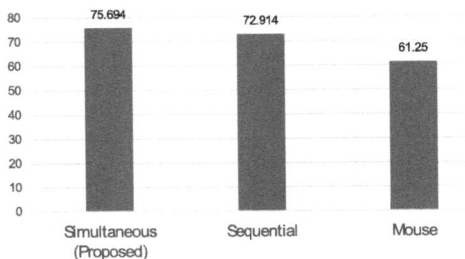

Fig. 7. The results of usability scores based on SUS and VRSUQ questionnaire in our experiment.

These results show the effectiveness of our simultaneous interface using a spatial controller.

Although our interface achieved higher usability scores in the SUS and VRSUQ tests compared to the alternative interfaces, it received relatively lower scores in the areas of responsiveness and ease of correcting errors. The responsiveness issue is attributed to the current unoptimized implementation of our system , which can be improved through performance optimization. The difficulty in correcting errors stems from the lack of undo / redo functionality, requiring users to perform additional steps to reverse unintended operation. This problem can also be addressed in future system updates. Overall, the result show that intuitiveness of our interface.

In this study, we developed a standalone system to evaluate our proposed interface. To evaluate the effectiveness of our approach, it is also necessary to conduct evaluation from the participants' perspective. We anticipate that our interface could help event organizers in the Metavers enhance participant engagement. Conducting a user study involving actual participants to confirm this approach is an important direction for future work.

6 Conclusion

In this study, we proposed a user interface for crowd control using a spatial controller. Experimental results showed that our interface is both efficient and intuitive for users. Future work includes improving the usability of the interface and evaluating its effectiveness within a Metaverse platform involving multiple remote participants.

Acknowledgement. This work was supported in part by a Grant-in-Aid for Scientific Research (No. 25K15404) from the Japan Society for the Promotion of Science (JSPS).

References

1. van den Berg, J., Guy, S.J., Lin, M.C., Manocha, D.: Reciprocal n-body collision avoidance. In: Robotics Research: The 14th International Symposium ISRR, pp. 3–19 (2011)
2. Brooke, J.: SUS: a quick and dirty usability scale, pp. 189–194 (1996)
3. Helbing, D., Molnár, P.: Social force model for pedestrian dynamics. Phys. Rev. E **51**(5), 4282–4286 (1995)
4. Henry, J., Shum, H.P.H., Komura, T.: Environment-aware real-time crowd control. In: 11th ACM SIGGRAPH/Eurographics Conference on Computer Animation, pp. 193–200 (2012)
5. Kim, Y.M., Rhiu, I.: Development of a virtual reality system usability questionnaire (VRSUQ). Appl. Ergon. **119**, 104319 (2024)
6. Lee, J., Won, J., Lee, J.: Crowd simulation by deep reinforcement learning. In: Motion, Interaction and Games (MIG) 2018, pp. 2:1–7 (2018)
7. Lim, C.U., Baumgarten, R., Colton, S.: Evolving behaviour trees for the commercial game DEFCON. In: Applications of Evolutionary Computation, pp. 100–110 (2010)
8. Narain, R., Golas, A., Curtis, S., Lin, M.C.: Aggregate dynamics for dense crowd simulation. ACM Trans. Graph. (ACM SIGGRAPH Asia 2009) **28**(5), 122:1–8 (2009)
9. Oshita, M.: Agent navigation using deep learning with agent space heat map for crowd simulation. Comput. Anim. Virtual Worlds **30**(3–4), 1–12 (2019)
10. Oshita, M., Ogiwara, Y.: Sketch-based interface for crowd animation. In: 9th International Symposium on Smart Graphics 2009, pp. 253–262 (2009)
11. Rose, C., Cohen, M.F., Bodenheimer, B.: Verbs and adverbs: multidimensional motion interpolation. IEEE Comput. Graphics Appl. **18**(5), 32–40 (1998)
12. Sakuma, T., Mukai, T., Kuriyama, S.: Psychological model for animating crowded pedestrians. Comput. Anim. Virtual Worlds **16**(3-4), 343–351 (2005)
13. Treuille, A., Cooper, S., Popović, Z.: Continuum crowds. ACM Trans. Graph. (ACM SIGGRAPH 2006) **25**(3), 1160–1168 (2006)
14. Ulicny, B., de Heras Ciechomski, P., Thalmann, D.: Crowdbrush: interactive authoring of real-time crowd scenes. In: 2004 ACM SIGGRAPH/Eurographics Symposium on Computer Animation, pp. 243–252 (2004)

The 6th Workshop on Next-Generation Computer Animation Techniques (AniNex 2025)

Immersion Discrepancies in Educational Serious Games Among Children's Age Groups

Hui Liang[✉], Yukun Li, and JiaLin Fu

Zhengzhou University of Light Industry, 136 Science Avenue, Zhengzhou 450001, Henan, China
hliang@zzuli.edu.cn

Abstract. With the development of virtual reality technology, serious games have become a new type of teaching tool, and exploring the differences in their sense of immersion is of great significance in enhancing user experience and promoting personalized education. In this study, we designed three educational-themed serious games and compared the power spectral densities (PSD) of immersion-related brain waves of children of different ages by using a difference analysis algorithm based on the game test model. The results showed that the PSDs of theta, alpha, and beta waves differed significantly in different age groups; in the tutor-guided experiment, only theta wave differed significantly. The younger group had higher levels of θ-wave and α-wave activity, and were more relaxed and creative during the game; the older children had higher levels of β-wave activity, and had better attention and cognitive level during the game. This study reveals the influence of age on children's cognitive and emotional participation in educational games from a neurophysiological point of view, and provides a neuroscientific basis for the development of personalized educational tools.

Keywords: VR education · serious game · EEG · immersion

1 Introduction

Serious games have gained widespread adoption in educational settings for school-age children, as they bolster the quality of the learning experience and academic performance. They offer a platform for knowledge exchange, collaborative learning, and social interaction [1–3]. When integrated with traditional educational resources, serious games offer unique visualization and interaction prospects [4], maintaining a high level of motivation, which, in turn, augments the overall learning experience [5, 6].

Successful serious games share a common trait: their capacity to engross players in an immersive experience. This phenomenon is commonly referred to as "immersion." To delve into the determinants of immersion, Brown et al. [7] conducted a qualitative study, confirming immersion as a descriptor of a player's engagement level in a game. The greater the engagement, the deeper the immersion, and correspondingly, the player's emotional responses are profoundly influenced by the game's immersive qualities, immersive environments lead to more positive emotions. Numerous studies emphasize the potential of serious games to augment learning by boosting motivation, thus

C. Mousas et al. (Eds.): CASA 2025, LNCS 15915, pp. 275–288, 2026.
https://doi.org/10.1007/978-981-95-0100-7_18

leading to enhanced learning outcomes [8]. Barclay et. al. [9] established a correlation between immersion and improved learning outcomes. Beyond its educational benefits, serious games serve as potent motivators in student education [10] while fostering the development of cognitive skills such as problem-solving, creativity, and critical thinking [11]. These advantages extend even to students prone to inattention [12]. Moreover, serious games facilitate the acquisition of skills including discovery-based learning [13], motor skills, spatial coordination [14], and expertise development [15]. Serious game affected positively the children's basic learning mechanisms (BLMs), by reinforcing balance, visual-motor, memory, attention, and spatial awareness abilities while interacting with the serious game [16].

Despite the availability of AI tools [17] and game design frameworks tailored to serious game design [18, 19], these resources remain insufficient in offering comprehensive guidance for the incorporation of immersion elements into serious games. In addition, there exists a paucity of in-depth studies concerning the variability of physiological markers of immersion in serious games for school-aged children, who constitute the primary demographic of serious game users.

This study combines neuroscience and education to investigate school-aged children's immersion in serious games. Section 1 presents the research background and objectives. Section 2 reviews relevant literature, focusing on correlation studies. Section 3 details the experimental design, covering the differential analysis algorithm based on the proposed serious game test model, EEG data collection methods, and game design. Section 4 describes the experimental procedures and data processing. Section 5 discusses the results, and Sect. 6 concludes the study.

2   Related Work

Serious games are experiencing rapid growth and are extensively employed in children's education. Cheng et al. [20] discovered a significant correlation between learning outcomes in educational games and the subjective experience of immersion. Achieving a balance between the effectiveness of serious games and the enjoyment of the experience poses a challenging task in contemporary game design. Investigating the emotional dynamics of players in the game environment has been proposed as an effective solution.

Barclay and Bowers [21] observed that the benefits of immersion in serious educational games are no longer solely attributable to highly available systems or exceptionally receptive learners. While some studies have applied game design principles to the educational process in serious games, there remains still a significant absence of systematic and empirically tested design methodologies [22]. Additionally, research has explored the variability in experiential perception and acceptance across different age groups in the context of serious gaming experiences. For instance, some researchers [23] assessed the performance and subjective experiences of three age groups in serious gaming, revealing significant differences in re-gaming experiences and processing speed among these age groups. Chiang et al. [24] created an EEG-based model to objectively gauge attention and learning capacities. Moreover, Wan et al. conducted an assessment of immersive learning in university students, providing evidence supporting the feasibility of predicting the level of learning immersion through physiological recordings.

The study focused on the child population's cognitive abilities, attention, and expression. Due to the unsuitability of children for questionnaire participation, subjective evaluations of the children were not collected. To ensure an accurate and objective assessment, brainwaves were utilized to physiologically measure the participants' brain activity. Previous research by scholars has assessed the brainwaves of individuals engaged in serious games. Alpha waves (18–12 Hz) are known to play a significant role in various sensory and cognitive processes and exhibit a negative correlation with attention [25] and cortical activation [26]. Beta band oscillations (15–30 Hz) have been proposed as indicators of cognitive processing, particularly in the upper part of the beta band. Theta EEG bands (4–7 Hz) have been linked to memory and cognitive abilities. In a study conducted by Škola et al. [27] on presence, engagement, and immersion in virtual reality, it was found that the total duration of a VR application was inversely related to technology adoption and negatively correlated with immersion. This suggests a negative association between the duration of VR application and the levels of presence, engagement, and immersion in virtual reality. These findings emphasize the potential of EEG as a viable and objective method for assessing immersion [28]. In terms of brainwave frequencies, alpha waves are consistently recorded and are sensitive to changes in task difficulty. They are the dominant waves in human EEG brain recordings in the range of 7.5–13.5 Hz. The evaluation of immersion comprises various aspects, including perception, control, attention, enjoyment, and self-awareness [29–32]. Indicators of immersion in different brain waves are shown in Fig. 1.

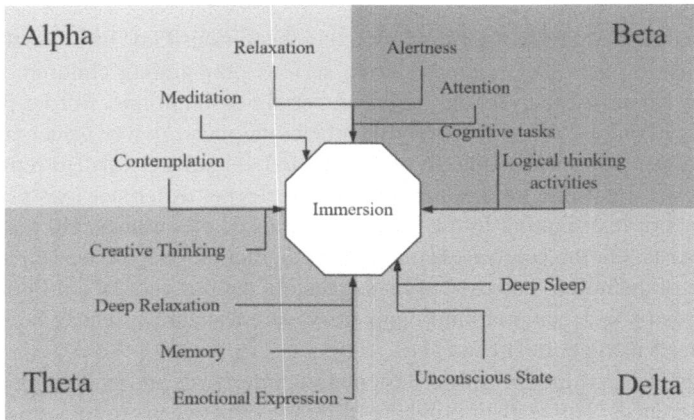

Fig. 1. Indicators of immersion in different brain waves

In summary, numerous studies have highlighted the benefits of serious games in enhancing children's learning abilities and immersive learning experiences. However, there remains a significant gap in research when it comes to understanding the differences in immersion at the physiological level in serious educational games. This gap is primarily due to differences in cognitive development, emotional responses, and levels of concentration among children of various age groups. There is a clear need for more comprehensive analyses into EEG indicators of immersion. To address this need, this study has developed a disparity analysis algorithm based on a serious game testing model. The primary objective is to verify the differences in immersion levels experienced by children of different age groups while engaging with serious educational games. To achieve this objective, we have designed three serious educational games with educational themes, which will be utilized to assess the participating children.

3 Research Design

3.1 Design of Variance Analysis Algorithm Based on Serious Game Testing Models

To investigate differences in the level of immersion among children of varying ages when engaging with serious games, a Variance Analysis algorithm is proposed, utilizing the Serious Game Test model. In this analytical framework, age serves as the primary independent variable. Employing the Serious Game Test model enables us to identify differences not only between different age groups but also in each age group. Our study categorizes children into high and low age groups, with their data hierarchically nested. Failing to acknowledge this nested relationship and conducting a simple comparison might result in an oversight of the relationship between individual and group data, leading to imprecise difference estimations. To address these potential issues, our proposed model, grounded in serious game testing, adeptly tackles the matter. It not only scrutinizes differences between groups but also within them, while also controlling for potential interfering factors.

The Variability Analysis algorithm, rooted in the Serious Play Test model, evaluates the variability in mean EEG signals during serious play among children. The inferences drawn from this analysis are based on certain assumptions. Before performing the Variability Analysis, it is necessary to subject the mean power values of the EEG signals, obtained from processing, to normality and chi-square tests.H0 represents the null hypothesis, signifying the assumption that no effect or difference exists in the overall parameters or distribution. In the context of analysis of variance, H0 posits that no difference exists. On the contrary, H1 signifies the alternative hypothesis, representing the opposite of the null hypothesis, often suggesting the presence of a difference. Prior to the analysis of variance, normality and chi-square tests are conducted, establishing hypothesis tests using both H0 and H1.

The statistical D-value is employed for making inferences and evaluating the significance of differences. This statistic compares differences between groups with differences in groups. In the framework of analysis of variance, a comparison is necessary between between-group differences, which reflect differences in group means, and in-group differences, which indicate the degree of variability in observations of each group. D-values are computed by contrasting between-group variance with in-group variance to measure the magnitude of between-group differences relative to in-group variance. Therefore, larger D-values indicate a significantly greater between-group variance compared to in-group variance, and vice versa. At the conclusion of the D-value analysis, it becomes essential to determine the criticality and make a statistical decision. Criticality pertains to the reference value employed in analysis of variance to determine the significance of the D-value. Statistical software, such as SPSS, is utilized to establish criticality and reach a statistical decision. To gain a comprehensive understanding of discrepancies in EEG metrics among children, taking into account EEG data's complexity and noise, repeated comparisons are conducted. This approach yields more exhaustive, profound, and stable findings. The following is the procedural outline:

(1) Statistical D-value

Means were calculated first: it represents the sample mean and the total mean for the ith overall level, with ni representing the number of sample observations for the ith overall level. Sum of Squared Errors: Calculate the sum of squared errors, which comprises the between-group sum of squares (Sa). Sa reflects the extent of difference between sample means of the overall levels and indicates the impact of differences in theoretical means of factor A. This is labeled as "the sum of squares of factor A" or "between-group difference."

In-Group Sum of Squares: it represents the in-group sum of squares (Se). Se is the sum of squared errors between the sample data of each group and its group mean, illustrating the dispersion of each observation in each sample and denoting the effect of random errors. It is referred to as "sum of squares of errors" or "in-group variance".

Total error sum of squares St: it represents the sum of the squares of errors across all observations and the overall mean, serving as an indicator of the dispersion among all observations. The between-group and in-group mean squares are obtained by dividing the sum of squared errors by their respective degrees of freedom. The Ma/Me ratio forms the basis of the D distribution.

(2) Critical value is determined and statistical decisions are made

After calculating the D statistic, one should locate the corresponding critical value, Alpha, in the D distribution table. This is achieved for a numerator with degrees of freedom of (k-1) and a denominator with degrees of freedom of n-k, according to the given significance level, Alpha.

When the value of D is greater than the critical D value, it is indicative of rejecting the null hypothesis in favor of the alternative hypothesis, supported by our data.

When the value of D is less than the critical D value, it is not advisable to conclude the acceptance of the null hypothesis. Instead, it is more appropriate to state that the null hypothesis was not rejected.

(3) Multiple comparisons

The difference between individual EEG indicator point estimates plays a role in reinforcing the conclusion mentioned above. If this difference is not sufficient to be practically significant, it further emphasizes that any existing differences between levels, if present, hold limited practical importance.

Should the difference in mean values between different levels reach a level of significance from an applied perspective, the original hypothesis H0 is accepted due to the significant effect of random error. Conversely, if this value is considered excessively large from an applied standpoint, it suggests that the present test lacks precision. In such cases, it is advisable to consider increasing the test size and improving the test to minimize the effect of random errors.

(4) Algorithm design

The sum of squares between age groups, denoted as Sa, is the sum of the squares of errors between the group means and the overall mean. This reflects the extent of difference among the sample means at each level of aggregation and signifies the effect of differences in the theoretical mean at each level of Factor A. It is also referred to as the "sum of squares of Factor A" or the "between-group difference." The calculation process of Sa is shown in Formulate 1.

$$Sa = \sum_{i=1}^{k} ni(\overline{x_i} - \overline{\overline{x}})^2 \tag{1}$$

On the other hand, the in-group sum of squares, Se, comprises the sum of the squares of errors in the sample data of each group and its respective group mean. This reflects the dispersion of each observation in each sample and indicates the effect of random errors. It is denoted as the "sum of squares of errors" or "in-group variation." The calculation process of Se is shown in Formulate 2.

$$Se = \sum_{i=1}^{k} \sum_{j=1}^{ni} \left(x_{ij} - \overline{x_i}\right)^2 \tag{2}$$

The total error sum of squares, St = Se + Sa, represents the sum of the squares of errors across all observations and the overall mean, reflecting the dispersion among all observations. The calculation process of St and D-value are shown in Formulate 3 and 4.

$$St = \sum_{i=1}^{k} \sum_{j=1}^{ni} (x_{ij} - \overline{\overline{x}})^2 \tag{3}$$

$$D = \frac{Ma}{Me} = \frac{Sa}{k-1} \Big/ \frac{Se}{n-k} = \frac{Sa \times Se}{(k-1)(n-k)} \sim F(k-1, n-k) \tag{4}$$

3.2 Design of Spectral Analysis

In this study, spectral features of electroencephalogram (EEG) signals are derived from four frequency bands: delta (0–3.5 Hz), theta (3.5–7.5 Hz), alpha (7.5–13.5 Hz), and beta (13.5–26 Hz). Given that EEG signals exhibit non-stationary characteristics over short periods, the Discrete Wavelet Transform (DWT) is adopted for feature extraction, as it outperforms the Fast Fourier Transform (FFT) in this context [32]. DWT utilizes scale and wavelet functions associated with low-pass and high-pass filters respectively. By passing the original signal X[n] through these filters and applying the Nyquist sampling rule to discard half of the samples, the signal is decomposed into different frequency bands. This subband coding process can be iterated, reducing time resolution by half while doubling the frequency resolution at each level, enabling detailed analysis of the signal across various resolutions and frequency bands.

Raw EEG data captured by the EEG device often contains artifacts from muscle activity, eye movements, and heart rate variability. To address this, BESA software is employed to remove these artifacts, yielding task-relevant raw signals. Subsequently, the targeted EEG waves are accurately extracted for further analysis.

3.3 Serious Game Design

We designed three serious games for elementary school age children. Among them, "Jing Ke Stabbing Qin" and "Grass Boat Borrowing Arrows" are inspired by Chinese culture, and "The Crow and the Water Jar" is inspired by Aesop's fables. The game is based on the story of Zhuge Liang's borrowing of arrows, in which the player has to control a thatched boat to collect 300 arrows and avoid bombs. The game adopts a cartoon interface, and is set up with three types of weather to increase the difficulty: sunny, rainy, and foggy, with gestures required to control the game in rainy and foggy days. Jing Ke Qin" reproduces the plot of Jing Ke's assassination of Qin by manipulating the shadow characters and utilizing five control points and depth sensors to complete the game. In "The Crow and the Water Jar", children have to use gestures to manipulate the puppet crow to pick up pebbles and put them into the water jar, and the game process provides feedback to assist in the measurement of EEG metrics. The games involved are shown in Fig. 2.

In each game, two modes of experience were set up, the lower age group was guided by an adult tutor, and the upper age group completed the game independently, in order to explore the differences in brain waves between the guided and unguided brain waves of different age groups, to understand the electroencephalographic mechanism of game immersion, and to compare the immersion indexes of the two groups, to explore the relationship between age and immersion.

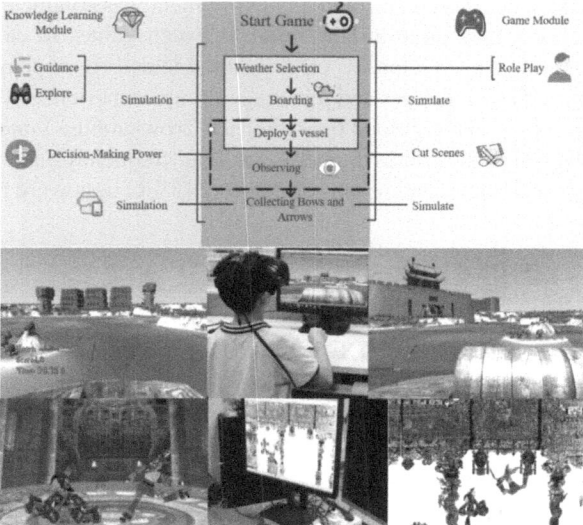

Fig. 2. Serious game design

4 Materials and Methods

4.1 Participants

The participants were 64 children of different school ages. According to the age division of primary school-aged children classified by the Ministry of Education of the People's Republic of China, our recruitment interval was set at 6–11 years old, and the participants were divided into a high age group (Group H) and a low age group (Group L) according to their age, with Group H's age range being 6–8 years old and Group L's age range being 9–11 years old. The age distribution of the participants was close to normal distribution to ensure the representativeness and reliability of the results.

4.2 Data Collection and Extraction

Prior to the experiment, children's parents will receive an information sheet and consent form containing detailed information about the purpose of the study, the game design, and the type of EEG data, and sign it after one week's consideration. The experiment follows the guidance of the UCLM Research Ethics Committee, which is in line with the ethical requirements of children's research.

   The experiment was conducted in the Serious Play Experience Laboratory, where children were accompanied by their parents and entered for ten minutes of interaction to familiarize themselves with the environment, followed by a three-minute break. After the children were relaxed, an immersion-inducing experiment was conducted, experiencing two identical games with a three-minute break between games to calm down. EEG signals were collected in a soundproof, electrically shielded room using a 60/64 EEG device (emotiv epoc X). Both upper and lower age groups experienced the three games, with the lower age group being guided by a tutor for Crow and the Water Jar (Game 3), and completing the rest of the games on their own. Four frequency bands of brain waves were recorded for each game, and a total of 24 sets of EEG data were recorded for the two groups.

4.3 Data Analysis

We used Discrete Fourier Transform (DFT) to calculate the power spectral density (PSD) of each participant's EEG waves, to get to its overall power and to assess whether there is a difference between the four waves of the participants in the high age group and the low age group, and we processed the PSD values we obtained, and according to the third section of this paper, it can be seen that the difference analysis algorithm based on the Serious Game Test Model we designed was used for the PSD values. Processing. When the data did not satisfy the assumption of normality or variance chi-square, appropriate nonparametric tests were used or the data were transformed and obtained to get the D-statistic, and finally its corresponding p-value was reported to determine whether there was a significant difference in power among different groups or under different conditions. The level of significance was set at 0.05. Based on the data obtained after processing, we summarized the calculated results. Game 1 refers to the game of Straw Boat Borrowing Arrows, and Game2 refers to the game of Thorng Khor Assassinate Qin. Groups H and L represent the high age group and low age group, respectively.

Table 1. Table analyzing the differences in power spectral density (PSD) values of the four brainwaves in Game1

Waves	Source of Variation	SS	df	MS	D-statistic	P-Value
α	Between Groups (Sa)	15.24	1	15.24	5.28	0.035*
	Within Groups (Se)	34.16	18	–	–	–
	Total	49.80	19	–	–	–
θ	Between Groups	22.40	1	22.40	12.89	0.003*
	Within Groups	31.20	18	1.73	–	–
	Total	53.60	19	–	–	–
β	Between Groups	22.50	1	22.50	12.00	0.004*
	Within Groups	33.75	18	1.875	–	–
	Total	56.25	19	–	–	–
δ	Between Groups	1.20	1	1.20	0.95	0.10
	Within Groups	25.30	18	0.66	–	–
	Total	26.50	19	–	–	–

As can be seen from Table 1, the p-value of α-wave obtained in Game1 is 0.035, which means that the difference of α-wave is significant ($p < 0.05$) on groups H and L. The p-value of θ-wave is 0.003, which is more significant compared to α-wave's 0.035, because the smaller p-value indicates that the result is less likely to be related to chance. β-wave has a p-value of 0.004, which is not very much different from θ-wave, and β-wave can be surely not happened by chance. There is not much difference, and theta and beta waves can be sure that they did not occur by chance. The p-value of δ-wave is 0.10, so the difference between δ-wave of group H and group L is not considered significant ($p > 0.05$), which means that the change of δ-wave in Game may be caused by random fluctuation only.

The p-value of α-wave obtained by group H and group L in Game2 is 0.033, which means that the difference between group H and group L in α-wave is significant ($P < 0.05$). The p-value of θ-wave is 0.004, which is more significant compared to 0.035 for α-wave. As mentioned in the analysis of Table1, the smaller p-value means that the result is less likely to be related to chance. The p-value of β-wave is 0.007, which is similar to the P-value of θ-wave, θ-wave and β-wave can be sure that they did not happen by chance. Unlike the δ-wave, the P-value of δ-wave is 0.10, so the difference between Group H and Group L in δ-wave is considered insignificant ($P > 0.05$), which means that the change of δ-wave in the Game may be caused by random fluctuation only.

The p-values of α, β and δ waves obtained in Game3 for Groups H and L were 0.06, 0.09 and 0.14 respectively, which were all > 0.05, which means that the difference between Groups H and L on these three waves was insignificant, while the p-value of θ wave was higher compared to that in Game1 and Game2, which indicates that although the difference between Groups H and L on θ wave is still significant, it is still not significant in comparison to the differences between Groups Game1 vs. Game2, the level of significance has decreased. By comparing with the data obtained in Game1 and Game2, it can be seen that external guidance has a greater impact on the brain waves of children in Group L during play, especially in the α and β waves, and these results suggest that guidance can help children in the younger age group to focus their attention and improve their thinking ability, especially when it comes to creative and problem-solving tasks, and the younger age group improved their cognitive load level under guidance. Theta waves, on the other hand, were related to children's memory processes and emotional responses, which were not significantly altered by external guidance.

5   Discussion

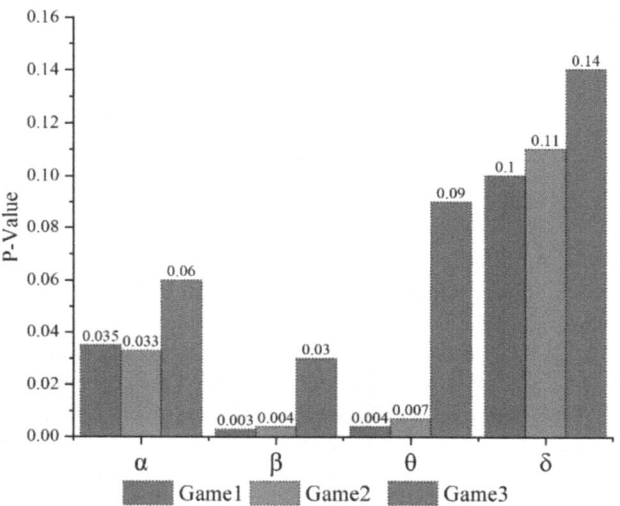

Fig. 3. Histogram of P-values for four waves in three games

Based on the 12 p-value results obtained from the experiments, we plotted a histogram of p-values (see Fig. 3), according to the histogram, we compared the p-values of the same waves in Game1 and Game2 two by two, the p-values of the same waves did not have much difference, they were all controlled within 0.1, while the p-values of the different waves differed significantly, which was due to the fact that the magnitude of the p-values received the influence of a variety of factors, and that different EEG waves were associated with different types of cognitive and neurophysiological processes, and each wave has different brain region activities, differences in electrode placement, signal processing and analysis methodology may also affect the p-value of a particular band, many reasons may cause this difference in p-values between different waves. The difference in p-values between group H and group L in the same wave is not large, this may be due to the similarity in effect sizes, sample sizes, and statistical power, and if the p-values of the two age groups have similar p-values, this means that the effect of age on that particular variable may be statistically similar when controlling for other variables. p-values are also affected by sample size. p-values for Game3 species differed significantly from those of Game1 and Game2 species, where the α, β, and δ waves were greater than 0.05, and the cause of this was related to the fact that Group L received bootstrapping in Game3 species that appropriate guidance mechanisms have a positive impact on younger children, especially in terms of enhancing their immersion and learning in games.

The aim of this study was to investigate the effects of serious games on brain waves (theta, alpha, beta and delta waves) in participants of different age groups. To this end, a well-designed serious game-based test model was used to analyze the effect of the game on EEG activity, and further difference-in-difference analyses were conducted to reveal statistically significant key findings. After taking a deeper look at the EEG waveforms recorded during gameplay, we noticed significant age-group differences.

For participants in the lower age group (Group L), the activity and amplitude of theta and alpha waves were relatively high, indicating that this group was more prone to deep attentional focus and reflective thinking during gameplay. This finding inspires us to emphasize the importance of adding elements that can capture attention and stimulate thinking when designing serious games for the L group. By doing so, we can expect to maintain and increase the interest and effectiveness of children in this age group. In contrast, participants in the older age group (Group H) showed higher beta-wave activity, reflecting a higher level of alertness, concentration, and information-processing abilities during play compared to younger children. Therefore, more complex challenges and tasks should be incorporated into the design of serious games for Group H children to promote their detailed attention and higher-order cognitive skill development.

In particular, when applied to children in the younger age group, our study also found that when using Game3, a game for intervention experiments, alpha and beta waves showed significant changes after appropriate instruction and guidance. This result suggests that the effectiveness of serious game design lies not only in the content of the game itself, but also in the accompanying guidance methods. Proper guidance plays an important role in enhancing children's immersion in the game in the younger age group, especially in expanding their cognitive ability, concentration, and immersion experience showing significant positive effects.

Taken together, our study highlights the unique role that serious games can play in the cognitive development of participants of different ages, and provides important insights into how to optimize game design and assistive guidance for specific age groups to promote effective learning and development.

6   Conclusion

In this study, we conceived and executed an educational experiment to investigate differences in immersion levels among primary school-aged children engaged in serious games. By creating a difference analysis algorithm based on a serious game test model, we delved into neurophysiological metrics associated with immersion, specifically power spectral density (PSD).

The results reveal significant differences in the neurophysiological facets of immersion among children in different age brackets. Younger children demonstrated more active relaxation and creative thinking patterns, as reflected in their brainwave activity. Conversely, older children exhibited increased focus and increased alertness. These findings not only deepen our understanding of the differences in immersion induced by serious games in virtual reality settings but also unveil a connection between cognitive developmental stages and electrophysiological indicators. Well-guided interventions can substantially enhance immersion in games for younger children.

Future studies may expand their scope to consist of a broader range of populations and game genres, building upon the findings of this project to verify and enrich our findings. Nonetheless, it is essential to acknowledge the limitations of this study, such as the relatively small sample size, which may constrain the generalizability of the findings. As the sample size grows and age stratification becomes more refined, we anticipate further validation and expansion of these findings. Additionally, the effects of various aspects of serious game design, such as difficulty level, storyline, or interactivity, on immersion and electrophysiological responses warrants further exploration.

In conclusion, research has demonstrated the significant potential of virtual reality technology and serious games in children's education. The creation and implementation of customized pedagogical tools tailored to the cognitive attributes of children in different age groups are necessary for realizing each learner's optimal learning potential. As technology continues to advance, we eagerly anticipate the development of more precise and captivating educational games capable of effectively stimulating children's interest in learning and unlocking their latent abilities. Clearly defining the target audience for serious games can specifically enhance their education.

Acknowledgments. This work is supported in part by the Research Project of Humanities and Social Sciences of the Ministry of Education with grant No. 24YJAZH075, International Cooperation Project of Henan Province with grant No.252102520012, the Research Project of Humanities and Social Sciences of Henan Province with grant No. 2025-ZZJH-370, the Research Project of Intangible Cultural Heritage of Henan Province with grant No. 24HNFY-LX149, the Postgraduate Education Reform and Quality Improvement Project of Henan Province with grant No. YJS2025AL39.

Disclosure of Interests. We declare that we have no financial and personal conflicts of interests with other people or other organizations that may inappropriately influence our work. There are no professional or personal conflicts of interests of any nature or any kind in any product, service and/or company that could be construed as influencing the position presented in, or the review in, the manuscript entitled.

Ethics approval all procedures performed in studies involving human participants were in accordance with the ethical standards of the institutional and/or national research committee and with the 1964 Hel-sinki declaration and its later amendments or comparable ethical standards. The IRB approval number is PMSM-20210227.

Availability of data and materials all data generated or analysed during this study are included in this published article (and its supplementary information files). Requests for material should be made to the corresponding authors.

References

1. Michaelis, J.E., Mutlu, B.: Supporting interest in science learning with a social robot. In: Proceedings of the 18th ACM International Conference on Interaction Design and Children, pp.71–82. (2019)
2. Bergin, D.A.: Social influences on interest. Educ. Psychol. **51**, 22–27 (2016)
3. Ahmadov, T., et al.: A two-phase systematic literature review on the use of serious games for sustainable environmental education. Interact. Learn. Environ. **33**(3), 1945–1966 (2024)
4. Žilak, M., Car, Ž: A framework for improving accessibility of serious games in handheld augmented reality based on user interaction data. Appl. Sci. **15**(4), 2161 (2025)
5. Villada Castillo, J.F., Bohorquez Santiago, L., Martínez García, S.: Optimization of physics learning through immersive virtual reality: a study on the efficacy of serious games. Appl. Sci. **15**(6), 3405 (2025)
6. Gundersen, S.W., Lampropoulos, G.: Using serious games and digital games to improve students' computational thinking and programming skills in K-12 education: a systematic literature review. Technologies **13**(3), 113 (2025)
7. Brown, E., Cairns, P.A.: A grounded investigation of game immersion. In: CHI EA '04, pp.1297–1300(2004)
8. Pange, J., Lekka, A., Katsigianni, S.: Serious games and motivation. In: Conference on Interactive Mobile Communication Technologies and Learning, pp.240–246(2017)
9. Barclay, P.A., Bowers, C.A.: Associations of subjective immersion, immersion Subfactors, and learning outcomes in the revised game engagement model. Int. J. Game Based Learn. **8**, 41–51 (2018)
10. Hsiao, H.: A brief review of digital games and learning. In: 2007 First IEEE International Workshop on Digital Game and Intelligent Toy Enhanced Learning (DIGITEL'07), pp.124–129(2007)
11. Goli, A., Teymournia, F., Naemabadi, M., Garmaroodi, A.A.: Architectural design game: a serious game approach to promote teaching and learning using multimodal interfaces. Educ. Inf. Technol. **27**, 11467–11498 (2022)
12. Cone, B.D., Thompson, M.F., Irvine, C.E., & Nguyen, T.D.: Cyber security training and awareness through game play. In: IFIP International Information Security Conference, pp.432–436(2006)
13. Kroustalli, C., **nogalos, S.: Studying the effects of teaching programming to lower secondary school students with a serious game: a case study with Python and CodeCombat. Educ. Inf. Technol. **26**(5), 6069–6095 (2021)
14. Gros, B.: Digital games in education: the design of games-based learning environments. J. Res. Technol. Educ. **40**(1), 23–38 (2007)
15. VanDeventer, S.S., White, J.A.: Expert behavior in children's video game play. Simul. Gaming **33**(1), 28–48 (2002)
16. Cornejo, R., et al.: Serious games for basic learning mechanisms: reinforcing Mexican children's gross motor skills and attention. Pers. Ubiquit. Comput. **25**, 375–390 (2021)
17. Westera, W., et al.: Artificial intelligence moving serious gaming: presenting reusable game AI components. Educ. Inf. Technol. **25**(1), 351–380 (2020)
18. Lindberg, R.S., Laine, T.H.: Formative evaluation of an adaptive game for engaging learners of programming concepts in K-12. Int. J. Serious Games **5**(2), 3–24 (2018)
19. Sajjadi, P., Broeckhoven, F.V., Troyer, O.D.: Dynamically adaptive educational games: a new perspective. In: International Conference on Serious Games pp. 71–76(2014)
20. Cheng, M.T., She, H., Annetta, L.A.: Game immersion experience: its hierarchical structure and impact on game-based science learning. J. Comput. Assist. Learn. **31**(3), 232–253 (2015)

21. Barclay, P.A., Bowers, C.: Associations of subjective immersion, immersion Subfactors, and learning outcomes in the revised game engagement model. Int. J. Game-Based Learn. **8**(1), 41–51 (2018)
22. Antonaci, A., Klemke, R., Specht, M.M.: Towards design patterns for augmented reality serious games. In: International Conference on Mobile and Contextual Learning, pp.273–282(2015)
23. Greipl, S., Moeller, K., Kiili, K., Ninaus, M.: Lifelong learning with a digital math game: performance and basic experience differences across age. In Games and Learning Alliance: 8th International Conference, GALA 2019, Athens, Greece, November 27–29, 2019, Proceedings 8, pp. 301–311. Springer International Publishing(2019)
24. Wan, B., Huang, W., Bai, L., Guo, J.: Using support vector machine on EEG signals for college students' immersive learning evaluation. In 2021 7th International Conference of the Immersive Learning Research Network (iLRN), pp. 1–5. IEEE (2021)
25. Ray, W.J., Cole, H.W.: EEG alpha activity reflects attentional demands, and beta activity reflects emotional and cognitive processes. Science **228**(4700), 750–752 (1985)
26. Laufs, H., et al.: EEG-correlated fMRI of human alpha activity. Neuroimage **19**(4), 1463–1476 (2003)
27. Škola, F., et al.: Virtual reality with 360-video storytelling in cultural heritage: study of presence, engagement, and immersion. Sensors **20**(20), 5851 (2020)
28. Tauscher, J.P., et al.: Immersive EEG: evaluating electroencephalography in virtual reality. In 2019 IEEE Conference on Virtual Reality and 3D User Interfaces (VR), pp. 1794–1800. IEEE (2019)
29. Shu, Y., Huang, Y., Chang, S., Chen, M.: Do virtual reality head-mounted displays make a difference? A comparison of presence and self-efficacy between head-mounted displays and desktop computer-facilitated virtual environments. Virtual Reality **23**, 437–446 (2018)
30. Barrett, A.J., Pack, A., Quaid, E.D.: Understanding learners' acceptance of high-immersion virtual reality systems: insights from confirmatory and exploratory PLS-SEM analyses. Comput. Educ. **169**, 104214 (2021)
31. Huang, W., Roscoe, R.D., Johnson-Glenberg, M.C., Craig, S.D.: Motivation, engagement, and performance across multiple virtual reality sessions and levels of immersion. J. Comput. Assist. Learn. **37**(3), 745–758 (2021)
32. Acharya, R.U., et al.: Symptomatic vs. asymptomatic plaque classification in carotid ultrasound. J. Med. Syst. **36**, 1861–1871 (2012)

Unsupervised Salient Object Detection with Pseudo-Labels Refinement

Yanfeng Zheng[1], Pengjie Wang[1,2], Hao Liu[1], and Xiaosong Yang[2(✉)]

[1] Dalian Minzu University, Dalian 116650, China
202412054063@stu.dlnu.edu.cn
[2] Bournemouth University, Fern Barrow, Poole, Dorset BH12 5BB, UK
xyang@bournemouth.ac.uk

Abstract. In Salient Object Detection (SOD), most methods rely on manually annotated labels, which are costly. As a result, unsupervised methods have gained significant attention. Existing methods often generate noisy pseudo-labels using traditional techniques, which can affect model performance. To address this, we propose an unsupervised method for RGB image salient object detection that generates high-quality pseudo-labels without manual annotation and uses them to train the detection model. The method generates initial pseudo-labels and improves their quality by introducing contrastive learning pretrained weights and a pseudo-label self-updating strategy. Additionally, we design a detection network with a Multi-Feature Aggregation (MFA) module and a Context Feature Interaction (CFI) module to enhance the model's ability to detect salient objects in complex scenarios. The model we proposed, trained with our pseudo-labels, shows significant improvement on USOD and achieves excellent scores on public benchmarks.

Keywords: Unsupervised · Salient Object Detection · Contrastive Learning · Pseudo-Labels

1 Introduction

The development of deep learning has significantly advanced salient object detection, with fully-supervised methods achieving notable breakthroughs. However, these methods are highly dependent on large-scale, accurately labeled data. To reduce the annotation burden, weakly-supervised methods have emerged, such as class labels [1] text descriptions [2],bounding boxes [3], scribbles [4] and point annotations [5]. Despite progress, human annotation is still required. Unsupervised methods aim to eliminate the need for human annotations altogether, offering better applicability in real-world scenarios where labeled data is scarce. A key challenge for unsupervised methods is generating high-quality pseudo-labels through image modeling, which is essential for training effective models.

C. Mousas et al. (Eds.): CASA 2025, LNCS 15915, pp. 289–303, 2026.
https://doi.org/10.1007/978-981-95-0100-7_19

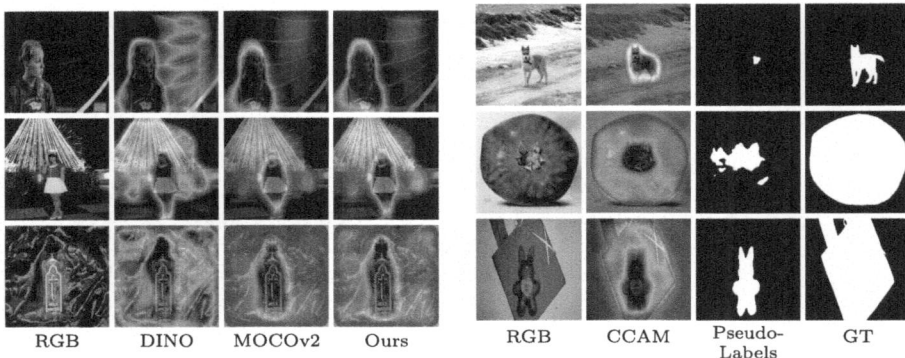

| RGB | DINO | MOCOv2 | Ours | RGB | CCAM | Pseudo-Labels | GT |

Fig. 1. (a) Visualisation of class-agnostic activation maps for different pre-trained weights. (b) Incorrect pseudo-labeling results.

Before the rise of deep learning, unsupervised methods mainly relied on hand-crafted features like color contrast to identify salient regions, but these methods struggled in complex scenes. Today, most unsupervised methods generate initial pseudo-labels using traditional techniques and refine them with various strategies. However, traditional methods often produce low-quality pseudo-labels, limiting detection performance. Researchers are exploring advanced algorithms to improve pseudo-label accuracy and overall detection. Few methods use deep learning for pseudo-label generation, but Zhou et al. [6] showed that pre-trained weights from convtrastive learning can provide supervision for salient object detection models, yielding impressive results. One such method, CCAM [7], uses unsupervised contrastive learning to identify foreground regions by contrasting foreground and background in different images. As shown in Fig. 1, CCAM trained with MOCOv2 [8] weights achieves good foreground localization but incomplete coverage, while CCAM trained with DINO weights [9] provides full coverage but with redundancy. These issues affect the quality of the final pseudo-labels.

In generating category-agnostic activation maps and refining them with a dense conditional random field (DCRF) to produce pseudo-labels, several challenges arise, as shown in Fig. 1. While activation maps highlight target regions, they often lack precise edges, and complex scenes present further refinement difficulties. Additionally, some activation regions may not be suitable for salient object detection, leading to inaccurate pseudo-labels. To address these issues, this paper proposes a two-stage model for salient object detection. The first stage generates pseudo-labels in two steps: enhancing the original CCAM using offline distillation for the initial pseudo-label network, and refining the labels with a self-updating strategy. The second stage focuses on salient object detection, where the model is primarily supervised by the generated pseudo-labels. Key components of this model include: 1) a multi-feature aggregation module to enhance high-level features, and 2) a context feature interaction module for improved feature fusion, boosting detection performance.

Our main contributions can be summarized as follows:

(1) This work introduces an updated pseudo-label generation method, leveraging different pre-trained weights for complementary learning and a self-updating strategy to improve label quality.
(2) A salient object detection network is designed to boost detection performance, incorporating a multi-feature aggregation module and a context feature interaction module.
(3) Experiments on four common RGB image saliency detection datasets demonstrate that the proposed method performs comparably to current weakly-supervised and unsupervised approaches.

2   Related Work

2.1   Fully-Supervised Method Salient Object Detection

The majority of Salient Object Detection (SOD) methods are rely on extensive pixel-level manual annotations as the foundation for training and optimization. Qin et al. [10] proposed the BASNet method, which incorporates boundary-aware mechanisms to enhance the accuracy of salient object detection by focusing on the boundaries of objects. Liu et al. [11] proposed a feature aggregation module structure based on the U-net structure, combining coarse-level and high-level information. Pang et al. [12] proposed a multi-scale interactive network that uses multi-scale features and interactive mechanisms to improve the accuracy of salient object detection. Xu et al. [13] proposed PA-KRN, a progressive architecture for salient object detection that first locates objects globally using a coarse module, then segments them locally with a fine module, and uses an attention-based sampler to highlight salient regions. Liang et al. [14] proposed ExPert, a parameter-efficient fine-tuning method for salient object detection that uses adapters and injectors in a frozen transformer encoder to incorporate external prompt features, achieving superior performance with fewer parameters.

2.2   Weakly-Supervised Method Salient Object Detection

The prevailing state-of-the-art techniques for salient object detection are heavily dependent on extensive datasets that require precise pixel-level manual annotations. The creation of such annotations is both time-consuming and labor-intensive. Consequently, weakly-supervised approaches are emerging as a prominent and increasingly favored research trajectory. Piao et al. [15] employed an iterative calibration strategy to mitigate the pseudo-labeling error within the network. Zhang et al. [4] conducted supervised training by annotating simple pairs of images with foreground and background labels. Piao et al. [16] introduced a multiple pseudo-label fusion framework that leverages richer information from multiple labels to diminish the impact of the algorithmic process. Gao et al. [17] presented a point-supervised approach that initially acquires pseudo-labels via an adaptive masking algorithm and subsequently generates the final prediction saliency maps through a Transformer-based network.

2.3   Unsupervised Method Salient Object Detection

In the field of salient object detection, weakly-supervised methods have played a significant role, but unsupervised methods have also garnered considerable attention. Unsupervised methods aim to detect salient objects without any explicit annotations. Nguyen et al. [18] proposed the DeepUSPS method, which uses self-supervision to leverage the input image itself as a natural supervisory signal for robust unsupervised saliency prediction. Yan et al. [19] introduced an uncertainty-aware pseudo-label learning approach for unsupervised domain adaptation in salient object detection, enabling the model to adapt to the target domain without labeled data in that domain. Wang et al. [20] proposed a method for deep unsupervised saliency detection that mines multi-source uncertainty to select reliable labels from multiple noisy labels, thereby improving the performance of unsupervised saliency detection. Zhou et al. [6] introduced a method called "Activation to Saliency", which forms high-quality labels for unsupervised salient object detection by leveraging activation information, leading to better detection results. Zhou et al. [21] proposed a texture-guided saliency distilling method by matching textures around the predicted boundaries for unsupervised salient object detection.

3   Method

The unsupervised saliency object detection process discussed in this paper mainly consists of two key stages: the first is the pseudo-label generation stage, where pseudo-labels are generated based on RGB images; the second is the saliency object detection stage, which differs from fully-supervised methods in that it uses the pseudo-labels generated in the first stage for learning and supervision. In this section, we will first describe the method for generating pseudo-labels, and then introduce the two core modules that constitute the saliency object detection network, namely the Multi-Feature Aggregation module (MFA) and the Contextual Feature Interaction Module (CFI).

3.1   Pseudo-Label Generation Model

This study proposes a novel method for generating pseudo-labels using class-agnostic activation maps, which automatically identify and locate salient objects. Instead of directly using the CCAM method, the network is enhanced with different pre-trained weights. A CCAM model trained with DINO pre-trained weights serves as an auxiliary supervision signal, providing additional guidance to improve training and combine the strengths of both weight sets.

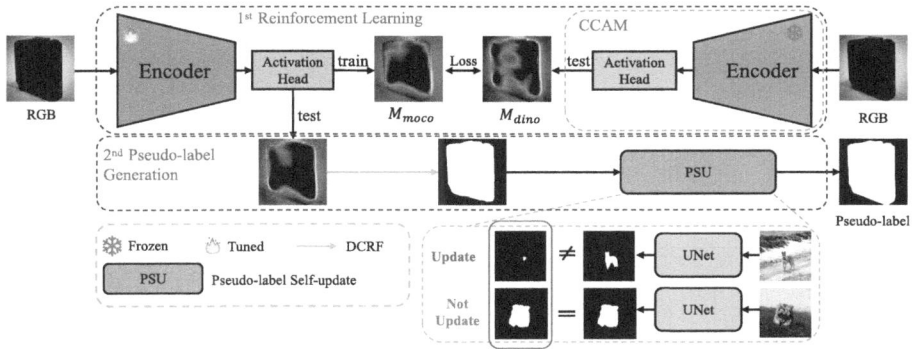

Fig. 2. Pseudo-label generation method structure.

As shown in the upper part of Fig. 2, in the specific implementation, Resnet-50 is used as the encoder of the backbone network. An RGB image is input, and after being processed by the encoder of the backbone network, four sets of feature maps F_1, F_2, F_3, and F_4 are obtained. This process can be represented as:

$$F_1, F_2, F_3, F_4 = Encoder(I_m) \tag{1}$$

Here, I_m represents the input RGB image, and Encoder represents the encoder. Then, the feature maps F_3 and F_4 are concatenated along the channel dimension and then processed through the CBS operation to generate the class-agnostic activation map M_{moco}, This process can be represented as:

$$M_{moco} = CBS(Contact(F_3, F_4)) \tag{2}$$

Here, $Concat(\cdot)$ denotes the concatenation operation along the channel dimension, and CBS represents a sequence of operations including a 3×3 convolution, BatchNorm, and a Sigmoid activation function. Additionally, based on the aforementioned process, the encoder is pre-trained using DINO pre-trained weights to generate a class-agnostic activation map represented as M_{dino}.

$$\mathcal{L} = \mathcal{L}_{POS} + \mathcal{L}_{NEG} + \alpha\mathcal{L}_{SSIM} + \beta\mathcal{L}_{IoU} \tag{3}$$

Here, $\mathcal{L}_{POS}$ and $\mathcal{L}_{NEG}$ are the original CCAM losses, $\mathcal{L}_{SSIM}$ is the structural similarity loss, and $\mathcal{L}_{IOU}$ is the intersection over union loss. The values of α and β are set to 0.2.

After generating the final class-agnostic activation maps using the aforementioned strategy, Dense Conditional Random Fields (DCRF) are further employed to process these activation maps to generate the initial pseudo-labels Y_{PL}. This process aims to refine the saliency maps from the original activation maps, providing more accurate labels for subsequent training. However, although DCRF can improve the quality of the labels to some extent, the pseudo-labels still have imperfections in detail, as shown in the first and second columns of the third row in Fig. 1. Due to the characteristics of the class-agnostic activation maps, some activated regions may not be entirely suitable for the task of salient object detection, as shown in the third and fourth columns of the third row in Fig. 1. These incomplete or incorrect refinements, if used as the basis for long-term network training, may lead the model to learn these inaccurate pieces of infor-

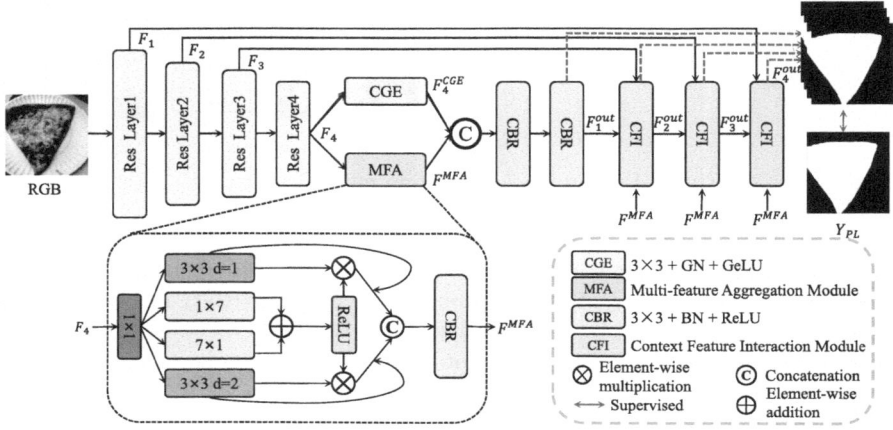

Fig. 3. The structure of the salient object detection network.

mation, ultimately affecting the detection performance of the network. Despite the potential inaccuracies in the pseudo-labels, network training remains an iterative learning and optimization process. Even with imperfect labels, they still guide the salient object detection network towards the correct targets, providing a generally valid learning direction. This demonstrates that the network can learn effective saliency information by capturing statistical patterns in large datasets, even with imprecise labels. In the early stages of training, the network is highly sensitive to the saliency information in the pseudo-labels, highlighting the importance of effective pseudo-label updating strategies. A well-designed updating strategy enhances the network's ability to capture saliency features, improving detection performance. Based on this, we propose a pseudo-label self-updating algorithm, as shown in the lower part of Fig. 2. Specifically, the generated pseudo-labels Y_{PL} are used to train a simple U-shaped network, and the saliency map Y_{PL}' produced by the network is used to update the pseudo-labels. In the early stages, the model can more accurately identify and correct errors in the pseudo-labels, and iteratively updating them improves both their accuracy and detail, ultimately enhancing the detection performance.

In this algorithm, the pseudo-labels are self-updated using different evaluation criteria at different training stages to improve the model's performance. Specifically, in the 2nd to 5th rounds of training, the algorithm uses the intersection over union (IoU) to measure the similarity between the model's current predictions and the previous pseudo-labels.If the result is below the threshold, the pseudo-labels are updated using the current model predictions. In the later stages of training, the pseudo-labels are updated using the Structure Similarity Index Measure (SSIM) [32] as the update criterion.

Here, the threshold is initially set to 0.9 for each evaluation criterion, and starting from the second epoch it is continuously updated during training, increasing by 0.1 each epoch over a total of 10 epochs. By dynamically adjusting the update strategy during training, the pseudo-labels are continuously refined, thereby enhancing the model's understanding of the data and the accuracy of its predictions.

3.2   Unsupervised Salient Object Detection with Pseudo-Labels

To better enhance the performance of salient object detection, this paper designs a salient object detection model that uses Resnet-50 as the backbone network for feature extraction. An input RGB image is processed through the backbone network to obtain four features, namely F_1, F_2, F_3, and F_4, which are used as inputs for the multi-feature aggregation module and the context feature interaction module. The overall architecture is shown in Fig. 3.

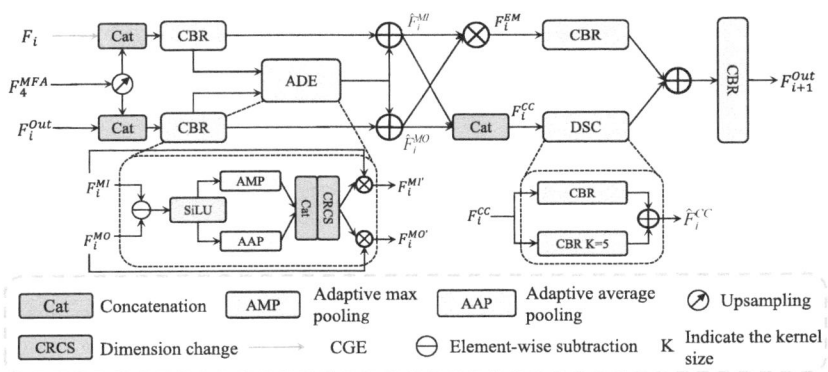

Fig. 4. Contextual Feature Interaction Module (CFI)

Multi-feature Aggregation Module. In deep learning tasks, the shallow layers of a network extract low-level features, while higher convolutional layers extract more advanced features. Among these, high-level semantic features are crucial as they provide a deep and abstract understanding of the image content. The abstract nature of these features enables them to effectively capture complex concepts and entities within the image, ensuring robustness against variations. By enhancing high-level semantic features, the model can more accurately understand and represent complex structures and abstract concepts within the image. Chen et al. [25] used dilated convolutions to expand the receptive field of convolutional layers, significantly improving the model's ability to recognize objects of different sizes without increasing the number of parameters or computational burden. To this end, this paper designs a multi-feature aggregation module that primarily enhances the high-level feature F_4 from the encoder. By employing convolutional kernels of various sizes and shapes, the module enhances the feature representation and adapts to the processing needs of objects of different shapes. Specifically, as shown in the MFA (Multi-feature Aggregation) module in Fig. 3, the input is F_4. First, a 1×1 convolution is applied to reduce the dimensionality of the feature, resulting in F_4'. F_4' is then processed through 3×3 convolution operations with different dilation rates to obtain the features $\tilde{F}_4$ and $\bar{F}_4$. The process can be represented as:

$$\begin{aligned} \tilde{F}_4 &= \text{Conv}_{d=1}(F_4') \\ \bar{F}_4 &= \text{Conv}_{d=2}(F_4') \end{aligned} \tag{4}$$

Here, Conv denotes a convolution with a 3×3 kernel, and d represents the dilation rate. By combining vertical and horizontal convolution kernels, the model can more comprehensively capture spatial information in the image. Compared to using traditional 3×3 and 7×7 convolution kernels, this method not only reduces the number of parameters and the risk of overfitting but also increases the model's processing speed and efficiency. For this reason, F_4' is also processed through convolution kernels in different directions to obtain spatial information in the image and then passed through a ReLU layer to obtain F_{HW}. The process can be represented as:

$$F_{HW} = \text{ReLU}(\text{Conv}_H(F_4') \oplus \text{Conv}_W(F_4')) \tag{5}$$

Here, $Conv_H$ denotes a vertical convolution with a 7×1 kernel, and $Conv_W$ denotes a horizontal convolution with a 1×7 kernel. The symbol $\otimes$ represents element-wise addition. To better integrate the features from dilated convolutions and the spatially enhanced features, the feature map F_{HW} is element-wise multiplied with the dilated features $\tilde{F}_4$ and $\bar{F}_4$ of different dilation rates. Additionally, skip connections are applied to each set of features to fuse the original features. This approach not only enhances the spatial representation but also maintains the integrity of the original features, thereby providing the network with a richer and more effective feature representation.

$$\begin{aligned} \tilde{F}_4 &= \tilde{F}_4 \copyright (F_{HW} \otimes \tilde{F}_4) \\ \bar{F}_4 &= \bar{F}_4 \copyright (F_{HW} \otimes \bar{F}_4) \end{aligned} \tag{6}$$

Here, $\oplus$ denotes element-wise multiplication. Finally, $\tilde{F}_4$ and $\bar{F}_4$ are concatenated and then passed through a CBR to obtain the feature F_{MFA}. The process can be represented as: Through the aforementioned operations, convolutional kernels of different shapes and sizes are effectively integrated, thereby significantly enhancing the feature representation capabilities. By expanding the receptive field, this method enables the network to learn richer spatial attributes, thereby deeply exploring and utilizing the complexity and diversity of image content. This enhances the high-level feature F_4 and provides richer and more effective input features for subsequent modules.

Context Feature Interaction Module. In salient object detection, the U-shaped structure is commonly used for its strong performance. However, as high-level features pass upwards in this structure, their information density decreases, impacting detection capability [11]. To address this, we propose a Context Feature Interaction Module that enhances feature interaction across levels, mitigating the dilution of high-level features during transmission.

As shown in Fig. 4, the inputs to this module are F_{MFA}, F_i^{Out}, and F_i, which originate from different stages of the model and each contain unique information and data representations. First, F_{FMA} is concatenated with F_i^{Out} and F_i respectively. Then, these concatenated features are processed through two separate CBRs to obtain two new features F_i^{MI} and F_i^{MO}. These features are then fed into the Adaptive Difference Enhancement Module (ADE).

The primary function of the ADE module is to calculate the differences between the two input features and process these difference features using the SiLU function to highlight important information and suppress less important information. Subsequently, the ADE module further processes these difference features through adaptive average pooling and adaptive max pooling operations. These two types of pooling operations extract features from different perspectives, and combining the pooled features helps to integrate their respective advantages. By applying these combined features to the original input features through element-wise multiplication, the expressive power of the input features is further enhanced. Additionally, skip connections are introduced to prevent information loss during the weighting process, resulting in $\hat{F}_i^{MI}$ and $\hat{F}_i^{MO}$. The process is as follows:

$$
\begin{aligned}
F_i^{MI'}, F_i^{MO'} &= ADE(F_i^{MI}, F_i^{MO}) \\
\hat{F}_i^{MI} &= F_i^{MI'} + F_i^{MI} \\
\hat{F}_i^{MO} &= F_i^{MO'} + F_i^{MO} \\
F_i^{CC} &= \text{Cat}(\hat{F}_i^{MI}, \hat{F}_i^{MO})
\end{aligned}
\tag{7}
$$

In the feature interaction operation, $\hat{F}_i^{MI}$ and $\hat{F}_i^{MO}$ are element-wise multiplied to generate F_i^{EM}, which helps to capture and enhance the interactions and dependencies between the two features.

$$
F_i^{EM} = \hat{F}_i^{MI} \otimes \hat{F}_i^{MO}
\tag{8}
$$

To enhance the representation capability of the feature $\hat{F}_i^{CC}$, a multi-scale convolutional kernel strategy is employed to capture different scale information from the input features. Specifically, convolutional kernels of different sizes are applied to $\hat{F}_i^{CC}$ to extract features at different scales, and these features are then element-wise added to obtain F_i^{CC}. The process can be represented as:

$$
\hat{F}_i^{CC} = CBR(F_i^{CC}) + CBR_{k=5}(F_i^{CC})
\tag{9}
$$

By integrating features from different scales, the expressiveness and adaptability of the features are further enhanced. Finally, to combine multiple feature representations, $\hat{F}_i^{CC}$ and F_i^{EM} are element-wise added and then processed through a

CBR operation to obtain the final output feature F_{i+1}^{Out} of the Context Feature Interaction Module. The process can be represented as:

$$F_{i+1}^{Out} = CBR(\hat{F}_i^{CC} + F_i^{EM}) \tag{10}$$

This paper replaces the traditional U-shaped structure's decoder with the Context Feature Interaction Module, which more effectively integrates feature information across different levels, particularly during upsampling and resolution restoration. This module combines deep semantic information with shallow detail, enhancing the model's ability to capture target details and improving overall feature representation. As a result, the model better incorporates both contextual and local information during decoding, boosting performance.

3.3   Loss Function

In this paper, a combined loss function is used for training, which includes the intersection over union loss ($\mathcal{L}_{IoU}$) and the local saliency coherence loss ($\mathcal{L}_{lsc}$) [23]. Additionally, this paper employs a deep supervision strategy, which introduces supervision signals at different network layers to further improve the model's performance. The formula for the total loss in this paper is as follows:

$$\mathcal{L} = \sum_{i=1}^{4} \left(\mathcal{L}_{IoU} \left(Y_i^{out}, Y_{pl} \right) + \mathcal{L}_{lsc} \right) \tag{11}$$

4   Experiments and Results

4.1   Datasets

In the experiments of this paper, DUTS-TR [28], is used as the training dataset. The pixel-level pseudo-labels generated by the proposed method serve as supervision signals for network training. For testing, the method is evaluated on ECSSD [29], DUTS-TE [28], DUT-OMRON [30], and HKU-IS [31] datasets.

4.2   Experimental Details

Experiments were conducted on a NVIDIA GTX 3090 GPU using the PyTorch framework. The first stage's hyperparameters match those of CCAM, while the second stage uses a DINO pre-trained ResNet-50 as the backbone. Training images are resized to 256×256, with the Adam optimizer and a batch size of 32. The model trains for 15 epochs, starting with a learning rate of 1e-4, which decays by 10% every 5 epochs.

4.3   Evaluation Metrics

This paper employs three commonly used evaluation metrics in salient object detection, to assess the performance of different models. These include the F-measure (F_β) [26], Mean Absolute Error (MAE) [27], E-measure [24].

Table 1. Quantitative comparisons on four datasets

Method	Sup	DUTS-TE			HKU-IS			ECSSD			DUT-OMRON		
		$MAE\downarrow$	$E_m\uparrow$	$F_\beta\uparrow$	$MAE\downarrow$	$E_m\uparrow$	$F_\beta\uparrow$	$MAE\downarrow$	$E_m\uparrow$	$F_\beta\uparrow$	$MAE\downarrow$	$E_m\uparrow$	$F_\beta\uparrow$
RBD [10]	T	0.162	0.664	0.428	0.176	0.716	0.54	0.206	0.705	0.577	0.165	0.654	0.416
BASNet [22]	F	0.048	0.884	0.791	0.032	0.946	0.895	0.037	0.921	0.88	0.056	0.869	0.756
MINet [12]	F	0.037	0.917	0.828	0.029	0.96	0.909	0.033	0.953	0.924	0.056	0.873	0.755
KRN [13]	F	0.034	0.926	0.851	0.028	0.959	0.916	0.036	0.92	0.922	0.049	0.889	0.783
WSSA [4]	W	0.062	0.869	0.742	0.047	0.932	0.86	0.059	0.917	0.870	0.068	0.845	0.703
MFNet [16]	W	0.079	0.832	0.692	0.058	0.919	0.839	0.084	0.880	0.844	0.098	0.784	0.621
SCWS [23]	W	0.049	0.907	0.823	0.038	0.943	0.896	0.049	0.931	0.900	0.060	0.870	0.758
USPS [18]	U	0.068	0.85	0.747	0.045	0.923	0.88	0.067	0.893	0.873	0.062	0.848	0.738
UDASOD [19]	U	0.05	0.897	0.795	0.035	0.947	0.883	0.043	0.94	0.895	0.059	0.849	0.733
UMNet [20]	U	0.067	0.863	0.752	0.041	0.939	0.889	0.064	0.904	0.879	0.063	0.860	0.743
A2S [6]	U	0.069	0.847	0.729	0.041	0.936	0.868	0.056	0.921	0.882	0.079	0.818	0.688
A2SV2 [21]	U	**0.047**	0.903	0.81	0.037	0.948	0.903	**0.044**	**0.940**	**0.917**	**0.061**	**0.864**	0.746
OURS	U	0.048	**0.905**	**0.822**	**0.033**	**0.953**	**0.915**	0.048	0.936	0.916	0.064	0.862	**0.752**

4.4   Comparison Experiments

This section compares the method proposed in this paper with fully-supervised, weakly-supervised, and unsupervised methods for salient object detection, including: RBD [10], BASNet [22], MINet [12], KRN [13], USPS [18], UDA-SOD [19], A2S [6], A2SV2 [21], MFNet [16], SCWS [33], UMNet [20], USPS [18] and WSSA [4]. The effectiveness of each method is evaluated by comparing the saliency maps they generate, either using the original code or directly provided by the authors. The comparisons aim to highlight the performance gap between unsupervised methods, which do not require manual annotations, and other supervised approaches. Additionally, the section emphasizes the performance of the proposed method, which operates without any manual annotations. All methods are evaluated using the same evaluation code to ensure fairness.

Quantitative Analysis. The assessments are shown in Table 1. "Method" indicates the model name. "Sup" denotes the supervision method of the model, where "T" represents traditional methods, "F" indicates fully-supervised methods, "W" stands for weakly-supervised methods, and "U" signifies unsupervised methods. Results in bold font represent the best performance among unsupervised methods.

Qualitative Analysis. As shown in Fig. 5, compared with the current mainstream weakly-supervised and unsupervised methods, the method proposed in this paper demonstrates significant advantages on various types of images. Particularly in the first to second rows of images, the method in this paper performs excellently in detecting the salient object "door", almost accurately completing the segmentation of the region while maintaining the complete edges and detailed

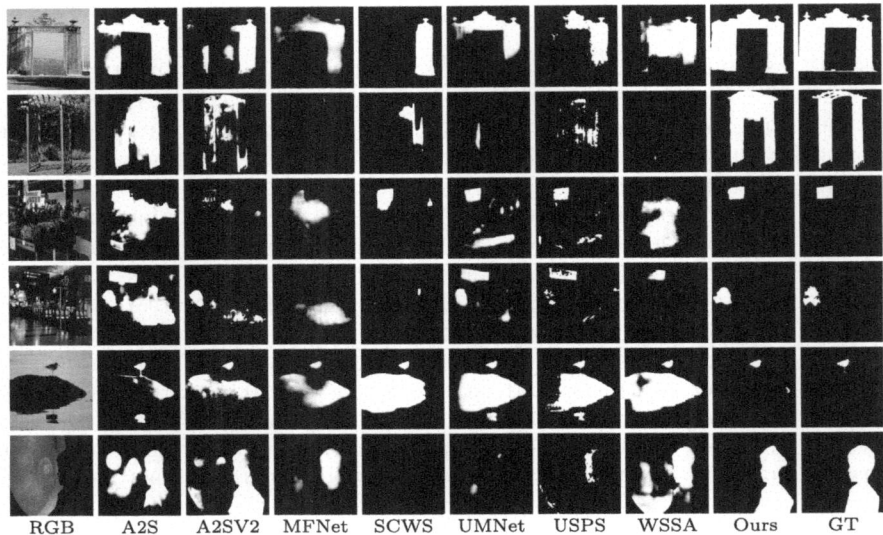

RGB   A2S   A2SV2   MFNet   SCWS   UMNet   USPS   WSSA   Ours   GT

Fig. 5. Qualitative comparison of the methodology in this paper with other methods

features of the "door". Compared with previous methods, they have deficiencies in detecting the details and edges of the "door". Furthermore, the method in this paper can accurately segment salient objects in complex scenes, as shown in the third to fourth rows. Additionally, it can precisely segment salient objects when they are small or when the input images have insufficient lighting. The above experimental results demonstrate the excellent performance of the method in this paper for salient object detection in complex tasks.

4.5 Ablation Studies

To evaluate the contributions of the various modules in the proposed method, this paper first established a baseline model. This model only uses CCAM and DCRF to generate pseudo-labels for supervision and excludes the Multi-feature

Table 2. Ablation experiments on DUT-OMRON dataset

MOCO	DINO	PSU	MFA	CFI	$F_\beta \uparrow$	$E_m \uparrow$
✓	×	×	×	×	0.716	0.835
✓	×	✓	×	×	0.727	0.838
✓	✓	×	×	×	0.726	0.835
✓	✓	✓	×	×	0.731	0.840
✓	✓	✓	✓	×	0.743	0.848
✓	✓	✓	✓	✓	**0.752**	**0.862**

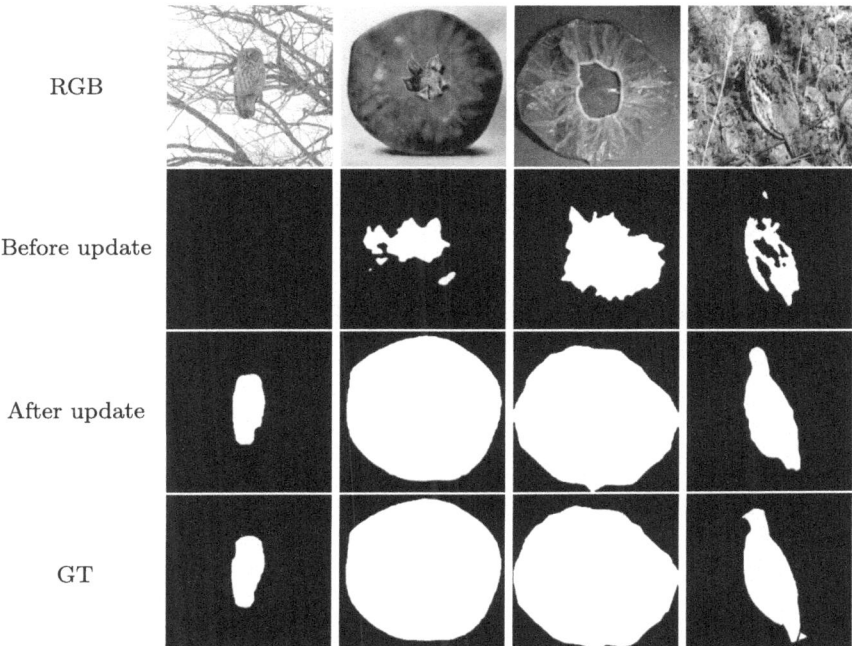

Fig. 6. Comparison of pseudo-labels before and after the update.

Aggregation Module (MFA) and the Context Feature Interaction Module (CFI), serving as the baseline model. Subsequently, this paper incrementally added the proposed modules to the baseline model and analyzed the contributions of each module in detail. As shown in the results in Table 2, each module introduced into the model plays a decisive role in achieving the final excellent performance. It can be concluded that the method proposed in this paper makes significant contributions to salient object detection.

As shown in Fig. 6, the visual differences between the pseudo-labels before and after updating are displayed. It is evident that the pseudo-labels updated using the self-updating method are closer to the ground-truth labels and better suited for the salient object detection task.

5   Conclusion

The comprehensive evaluation across multiple datasets demonstrates the robustness and effectiveness of the proposed method. Our approach consistently delivers competitive performance compared to both unsupervised and mainstream methods. Specifically, it matches the performance of fully-supervised and weakly-supervised methods on some datasets, while maintaining comparable results with mainstream methods on others. These findings highlight the potential of our method to bridge the gap between unsupervised and supervised learning in salient object detection. Future work will focus on optimizing the model architecture further and exploring its application in more diverse and complex scenarios.

References

1. Li, G., Xie, Y., Lin, L.: Weakly supervised salient object detection using image labels. In: AAAI, vol. 32, no. 1, pp. 7024–7031. AAAI Press (2018)
2. Zhang, L., Zhang, J., Lin, Z., Lu, H., He, Y.: Capsal: leveraging captioning to boost semantics for salient object detection. In: IEEE CVPR, pp. 6024–6033. IEEE (2019)
3. Liu, Y., Wang, P., Cao, Y., Liang, Z., Lau, R.: Weakly-supervised salient object detection with saliency bounding boxes. IEEE TIP **30**, 4423–4435 (2021)
4. Zhang, J., Yu, X., Li, A., Song, P., Liu, B., Dai, Y.: Weakly-supervised salient object detection via scribble annotations. In: IEEE CVPR, pp. 12546–12555. IEEE (2020)
5. Gao, S., et al.: Weakly-supervised salient object detection using point supervision. In: AAAI, vol. 36, no. 1, pp. 670–678. AAAI Press (2022)
6. Zhou, H., Chen, P., Yang, L., Xie, X., Lai, J.: Activation to saliency: Forming high-quality labels for unsupervised salient object detection. IEEE TCSVT **33**(2), 743–755 (2022)
7. Xie, J., Xiang, J., Chen, J., Hou, X., Zhao, X., Shen, L.: C2am: contrastive learning of class-agnostic activation map for weakly supervised object localization and semantic segmentation. In: IEEE CVPR, pp. 989–998. IEEE (2022)
8. Chen, X., Fan, H., Girshick, R., He, K.: Improved baselines with momentum contrastive learning. arXiv preprint arXiv:2003.04297 (2020)
9. Caron, M., et al.: Emerging properties in self-supervised vision transformers. In: IEEE International Conference on Computer Vision, pp. 9650–9660. IEEE (2021)
10. Zhu, W., Liang, S., Wei, Y., Sun, J.: Saliency optimization from robust background detection. In: IEEE CVPR, pp. 2814–2821. IEEE (2014)
11. Liu, J.J., Hou, Q., Cheng, M.M., Feng, J., Jiang, J.: A simple pooling-based design for real-time salient object detection. In: IEEE CVPR, pp. 3917–3926. IEEE (2019)
12. Pang, Y., Zhao, X., Zhang, L., Lu, H.: Multi-scale interactive network for salient object detection. In: IEEE CVPR, pp. 9413–9422. IEEE (2020)
13. Xu, B., Liang, H., Liang, R., Chen, P.: Locate globally, segment locally: a progressive architecture with knowledge review network for salient object detection. In: AAAI, vol. 35, no. 4, pp. 3004–3012. AAAI Press (2021)
14. Liang, W., et al.: External prompt features enhanced parameter-efficient fine-tuning for salient object detection. In: International Conference on Pattern Recognition, pp. 82–97. Springer (2024)
15. Piao, Y., Wang, J., Zhang, M., Ma, Z., Lu, H.: To be Critical: Self-Calibrated Weakly Supervised Learning for Salient Object Detection. arXiv preprint arXiv:2109.01770 (2021)
16. Piao, Y., Wang, J., Zhang, M., Lu, H.: Mfnet: multi-filter directive network for weakly supervised salient object detection. In: IEEE International Conference on Computer Vision, pp. 4136–4145. IEEE (2021)
17. Gao, S., et al.: Weakly-supervised salient object detection using point supervision. In: AAAI (2022)

18. Nguyen, T., et al.: Deepusps: deep robust unsupervised saliency prediction via self-supervision. In: NIPS, vol. 32 (2019)
19. Yan, P., Wu, Z., Liu, M., Zeng, K., Lin, L., Li, G.: Unsupervised domain adaptive salient object detection through uncertainty-aware pseudo-label learning. In: AAAI, vol. 36, no. 3, pp. 3000–3008. AAAI Press (2022)
20. Wang, Y., Zhang, W., Wang, L., Liu, T., Lu, H.: Multi-source uncertainty mining for deep unsupervised saliency detection. In: IEEE CVPR, pp. 11727–11736. IEEE (2022)
21. Zhou, H., Qiao, B., Yang, L., Lai, J., Xie, X.: Texture-guided saliency distilling for unsupervised salient object detection. In: IEEE CVPR, pp. 7257–7267. IEEE (2023)
22. Qin, X., Zhang, Z., Huang, C., Gao, C., Dehghan, M., Jagersand, M.: Basnet: boundary-aware salient object detection. In: IEEE CVPR, pp. 7479–7489. IEEE (2019)
23. Yu, S., Zhang, B., Xiao, J., Lim, E.G.: Structure-consistent weakly supervised salient object detection with local saliency coherence. In: AAAI, vol. 35, no. 4, pp. 3234–3242. AAAI Press (2021)
24. Fan, D.P., Gong, C., Cao, Y., Ren, B., Cheng, M.M., Borji, A.: Enhanced-alignment measure for binary foreground map evaluation. arXiv preprint arXiv:1805.10421 (2018)
25. Chen, L.C., Papandreou, G., Schroff, F., Adam, H.: Rethinking atrous convolution for semantic image segmentation. arXiv preprint arXiv:1706.05587 (2017)
26. Achanta, R., Hemami, S., Estrada, F., Susstrunk, S.: Frequency-tuned salient region detection. In: IEEE CVPR, pp. 1597–1604. IEEE (2009)
27. Perazzi, F., Krähenbühl, P., Pritch, Y., Hornung, A.: Saliency filters: contrast based filtering for salient region detection. In: IEEE CVPR, pp. 733–740. IEEE (2012)
28. Wang, L., Lu, H., Wang, Y., Feng, M., Wang, D., Yin, B., Ruan, X.: Learning to detect salient objects with image-level supervision. In: IEEE CVPR, pp. 136–145. IEEE (2017)
29. Yan, Q., Xu, L., Shi, J., Jia, J.: Hierarchical saliency detection. In: IEEE CVPR, pp. 1155–1162. IEEE (2013)
30. Yang, C., Zhang, L., Lu, H., Ruan, X., Yang, M.H.: Saliency detection via graph-based manifold ranking. In: IEEE CVPR, pp. 3166–3173. IEEE (2013)
31. Li, G., Yu, Y.: Deep contrast learning for salient object detection. In: IEEE CVPR, pp. 478–487. IEEE (2016)
32. Wang, Z., Bovik, A.C., Sheikh, H.R., Simoncelli, E.P.: Image quality assessment: from error visibility to structural similarity. IEEE Trans. Image Process. **13**(4), 600–612 (2004)
33. Yang, T., Wang, Y., Zhang, L., Qi, J., Lu, H.: Depth-inspired label mining for unsupervised rgb-d salient object detection. In: ACM Multimedia, pp. 5669–5677. ACM (2022)

Intelligent Compilation System for Chinese Character Animation Based on Dynamic Data Sets

Xin Luo[1,2,3](✉) and Qingsheng Li[1,2]

[1] Communication University of Zhejiang, Hangzhou 310018, Zhejiang, China
luoxin020228@163.com
[2] Hangzhou Liangyun Intelligent Technology Co., Ltd., Hangzhou 310023, Zhejiang, China
[3] University College London, London WC1E6BT, UK

Abstract. With the rapid evolution of AI and human-computer interaction technologies, Chinese character animation has gained wide applications in film/TV effects, digital education, and cultural heritage digitization. Current methods relying on static datasets face critical limitations in generation efficiency, style diversity, and real-time responsiveness. We address these challenges through an intelligent animation system incorporating three interconnected innovations: a dynamic dataset architecture supporting real-time updates for over 3,000 characters, a style-adaptive character description library, and a decoupled compilation-rendering framework that independently manages content generation and visual execution. By integrating stroke feature extraction with stroke-order reconstruction algorithms, our system automatically converts input characters into customizable animations with parametric control of curve smoothness and motion dynamics. Experimental validation confirms substantial efficiency improvements over conventional approaches, coupled with robust cross-platform compatibility and enhanced interactive capabilities across diverse usage scenarios. This work establishes a new paradigm for dynamic dataset-driven character animation systems.

Keywords: Chinese character animation generation · dataset · real-time rendering

1 Introduction

1.1 Background

With the rapid development of digital artificial intelligence and human-computer interaction technology, Chinese character animation, as a fusion form of visual communication and semantic expression, is showing important application value in many fields. In the scenes of film and television special effects production, digital education platform, digital human voice synchronous display, and cultural heritage visual display, the demand

Supplementary Information The online version contains supplementary material available at
https://doi.org/10.1007/978-981-95-0100-7_20.

for fine and stylistically diversified Chinese character animation is becoming more and more urgent. For example, in film and TV post-production, anthropomorphic Chinese character animation can enhance the expressive power of the screen; while in Chinese language education, dynamic Chinese character animation can help to improve learners' understanding of the stroke order, structure, and meaning, which is especially inspiring and interactive for non-native language learners.

However, most of the mainstream Chinese character animation generation methods rely on static datasets, such as existing stroke order character databases, standard vector data or fixed calligraphic style character databases. These datasets are mostly designed to serve the needs of standard Chinese character display at the early stage of design, and they have the following three core problems in animation generation:

1. Low generation efficiency: static data need to be parsed and interpolated to form animation sequences, which is difficult to meet the demand for real-time or batch generation.Recent studies have proposed methods like StrokeGAN to address efficiency issues by incorporating stroke encoding into generative models, thereby enhancing the generation process [1].
2. Single style: most datasets only support canonical writing styles and cannot express artistic and diverse expressions of Chinese characters [2].To overcome this limitation, approaches such as ZiGAN have been developed, enabling fine-grained Chinese calligraphy font generation through few-shot style transfer, thus allowing for a broader range of stylistic expressions [3].
3. Weak extensibility: it is difficult to extend new characters, variant characters or specific stroke styles, and the animation generation lacks universal adaptability.Innovative models like the one proposed by Chen et al. utilize generative adversarial networks to learn one-to-many stylized Chinese character transformations, enhancing the system's adaptability to new characters and styles [4].

To cope with the above problems, this paper focuses on the potential application of dynamic datasets in Chinese character animation. Dynamic datasets not only record stroke paths and time series information, but also integrate the stylistic features of different writers to achieve time-sensitive and expressive animation generation [5]. With the introduction of dynamic data in the generation system, it can be combined with deep learning models for real-time modelling and style migration, thus significantly improving the efficiency and diversity of animation generation [6].

For example, dynamic stroke libraries constructed based on online writing data have been widely used in handwriting recognition and personalised handwritten font synthesis, providing a theoretical and practical basis for the development of intelligent animation systems. There are also research attempts to apply Generative Adversarial Networks (GAN) or Transformer models to style migration and motion trajectory prediction of dynamic Chinese character stroke data, which have achieved preliminary results [2].

1.2   Background

This research aims to construct a dynamic dataset-driven intelligent compilation system for Chinese character animation for various application scenarios, such as film and television special effects, educational digitisation, and cultural communication. Specific objectives include: to propose a dynamic dataset architecture that supports real-time addition, deletion, and modification of Chinese characters, which can record stroke paths, time series, and style information, and achieve efficient management and flexible expansion of Chinese character data; to design a set of intelligent compilation processes with dynamic data as the core input, which integrates structural parsing and animation generation models, to improve the system's generation efficiency and degree of intelligence, and have the capability of adapting to multi-terminal, multi-style, multi-context, and multi-directional animations. The system has the ability to adapt to multiple terminals, styles, and contexts.

The technical innovation of this research mainly reflects the dynamic incremental updating mechanism, which breaks through the limitation of static font and realises the real-time addition, deletion and style customization of Chinese character data to provide the data basis for the diversity animation.

2   Related Work

2.1   Chinese Character Animation Generation Technology

Currently, the generation of Chinese character animation can be mainly classified into three types of technical paths: keyframe-based interpolation, physical simulation methods, and deep learning generation.

Early animation production relied on keyframe interpolation, such as the use of commercial tools such as Adobe After Effects for manual keyframe annotation and path adjustment [7]. Although the accuracy of this method is high, the production cost is large, the generality is weak, and it is difficult to meet the needs of large-scale batch generation.

The physical simulation method simulates the writing process through physical engines such as Mass-Spring Model, which tries to restore the trajectory of the brush strokes on the physical level.

In recent years, deep learning techniques have been widely used in the field of Chinese character animation generation. Researchers have proposed a variety of models based on Generative Adversarial Networks (GAN) and Recurrent Neural Networks (RNN) for style migration and dynamic generation of Chinese characters. For example, the Auto-Encoder Guided GAN model proposed by Lyu et al. is able to convert standard fonts into calligraphic fonts with specific styles [8], which enhances the diversity and artistry of generated Chinese characters.

2.2   Dynamic Data Set Techniques

Dynamic dataset management is one of the key technologies in the system supporting real-time generation of Chinese character animation. Traditional graphic data are mostly managed by static version, such as Git-LFS and other tools have basic tracking ability in image and font data management, but synchronisation delays and access conflicts often occur when dealing with large-scale and multi-version graphic files, which makes it difficult to meet the demands of real-time animation synthesis.

2.3 Existing Challenges

Although some progress has been made in Chinese character animation generation and dynamic data management, there are still a number of technical bottlenecks in practical applications:

Firstly, there is a contradiction between data dynamics and animation stability. Frequent data updates may lead to unstable animation generation and style jumps, affecting visual coherence.

Secondly, the real-time compilation of large-scale glyph data is not efficient enough, and the existing methods are difficult to meet the immediate response requirements in multi-threaded concurrent environments, especially in educational platforms or interactive media that exhibit latency problems.

Finally, the consistency guarantee of cross-platform animation generation is still a difficult problem. In different terminals (e.g., Web, mobile, VR devices), the animation rendering mechanism varies greatly, resulting in the generation of results that are difficult to unify in terms of time synchronisation and visual style.

3 Approaches

3.1 Chinese Character Glyph Description Library

This study needs to extract the core data of Chinese characters based on the dynamic description library of Chinese character glyphs [9, 10], and to organise and structure the data reasonably to ensure the efficiency and scalability of the subsequent processing.

The system adopts a structured glyph description library to store the stroke information of each Chinese character. Each Chinese character consists of multiple strokes, each stroke is represented by a series of two-dimensional coordinate points (x, y), and the storage format has been standardised to ensure the consistency of machine reading and parsing. The first 3 bits of the data file are the header information, describing the basic attributes of the character, and the 4th bit is the coordinate data of the strokes. Among them, the boundary point is marked by (–64, 0), which is used to separate neighbouring strokes, and the end point is marked by (–64, –64), which indicates the end of all the feature point data of the Chinese character. This glyph library supports accurate reconstruction at the stroke level and provides data support for subsequent dynamic rendering and interactive applications.

In the system, the glyph parsing process is realised by cyclically reading the data array, extracting and caching the coordinate points of each stroke, and drawing them as a continuous trajectory as soon as the stroke termination symbol is encountered. The advantage of this structure is that it can not only accurately restore the traditional writing process, but also provide the basic data unit for animation speed control (Fig. 1).

Fig. 1. Dynamic description library of Chinese character glyphs (partial)

3.2 Chinese Character Dynamic Datasets

The animation generation module is based on the point-by-point drawing strategy, which realises the dynamic reconstruction and multi-speed playback of the stroke structure of Chinese characters. The system first receives the coordinate points of the characters and plots them in the MATLAB graphical interface. The plotting is done by the 'plot(x, y)' command, which sets the line thickness and marker size to enhance the visual expression. The animation process is controlled by the 'pause(t)' control interval, where the time can be set by the user to adjust the animation speed. The system supports switching from point-by-point drawing (slow demonstration) to instantaneous drawing of the whole stroke (fast presentation), which makes the animation suitable for both calligraphy and brushstroke teaching, as well as high-speed special effects generation and other application scenarios.

In the complete process, the system first receives the content of the Chinese character to be queried through the input interface, then loads its corresponding stroke data, decodes and draws it through the animation algorithm, and renders it stroke by stroke in the graphic window according to the set speed, and ultimately outputs a complete animation of the Chinese character writing process. The whole compilation and rendering process is completely automated, with good real-time response capability and user interaction experience.

4   Experiments

This system aims to build an experimental platform that can efficiently generate, dynamically invoke and intelligently render Chinese character animations. The overall process consists of three key steps: dataset generation, dynamic query and animation rendering. The following is a detailed description of the experimental process using the Chinese character "皂" as an experimental object:

Step 1: Generate dynamic Chinese character dataset.

Firstly, the curvature of the basic character description model built into the system is adjusted by setting different curve control parameters, and dynamic data representations of more than 3,000 commonly used Chinese characters, including "皂" are generated in batch. Each Chinese character is indexed by a standard code, and each piece of data consists of feature points arranged in stroke order and automatically labelled with the corresponding Chinese character for subsequent retrieval (Fig. 2).

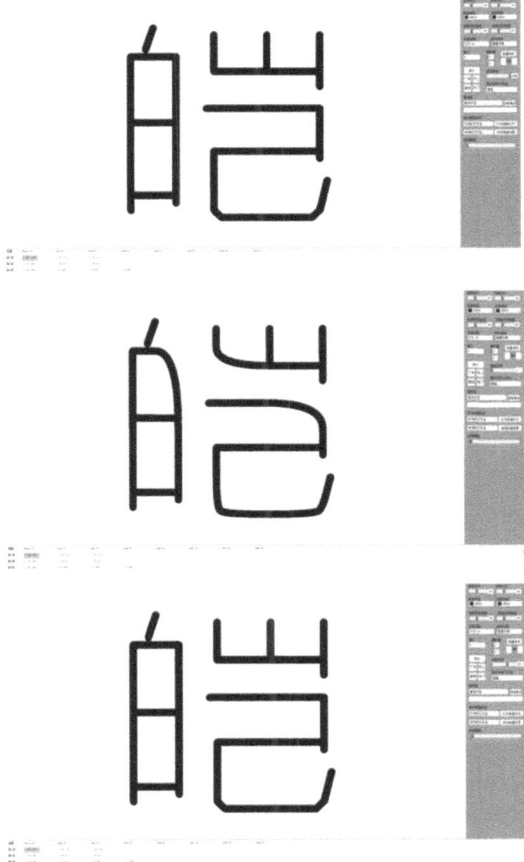

Fig. 2. Dynamic Chinese character datasets generated by different curves ("皂")

Assuming that the feature point data of Chinese character "㧃" in the generated dynamic dataset is variable C, which represents the feature point information of Chinese character "㧃":

C =

"104, –64, 0, –10, –14, –11, –11, –11, –11, –64, 0, –13, –10, –13, 11, –13, 11, –64, 0, –13, –10, –7, –10, –7, 10, –7, 10, –64, 0, –13, –1, –1, –1, –1, –1, –1, –1, –7, –1, –64, 0, –13 9, –7, 9, –7, 9, –64, 0, 5, –13, 5, –8, 5, –8, –64, 0, –2, –13, –2, –8, 12, –8, 12, –8, –64, 0, 12, –13, 12, –6, 12, –6, –64, 0, –3, –3, 12, –3, 12, –3, 12, 4, 12, 4, –64, 0, –2, 3. 12, 3, 12, 3, –64, 0, –2, 3, –2, 11, –1, 12, 11, 12, 12, 11, 13, 7, 13, 7, –64, –64,,,,,"

The system automatically parses the data, separates the strokes, and writes them into the dynamic dataset in a standardised format, realising a basic data system for Chinese character animation with a clear structure, rapid retrieval and flexible updating.

Step 2: Dynamic reading of Chinese character data.

When the user inputs the Chinese character "㧃" into the system, the system immediately locates the corresponding entry in the glyph description library through the tag search mechanism and reads the complete coordinate point data of the Chinese character "㧃" (Fig. 3).

```
Please enter the Chinese character you want to query: 㧃
Chinese character: 㧃
complete description of the data:
,"104,-64,0,-10,-14,-11,-11,-11,-11,-64,0,-13,-10,-13,11,-
```

Fig. 3. Dynamic reading of the data of the Chinese character "㧃"

Step 3: Separation of Chinese Strokes.

The reading module parses the stroke structure according to predefined rules, where:

The feature point marker (–64, 0) indicates the end of a stroke;

The feature point (–64, –64) indicates the termination of the entire word;

All point information is organised in stroke order and temporarily stored in set S.

For example, the parsed set S is shown below (only partially):

S = {

s0 = {(–10, –14), (–11, –11), (–11, –11)},

s1 = {(–13, –10), (–13, 11)},

s2 = {(–13, –10), (–7, –10), (–7, 10)},

...

}

This data provides the raw graphic path data for subsequent animation drawing modules.

Step 4: Generate Chinese Character Animation.

The animation generation module receives the stroke data in the set S and generates animation by drawing the strokes one by one in accordance with the stroke order. The system performs the following operations for each stroke:

1. Extract all the coordinate points of the current stroke from the set S;

2. Based on the number and arrangement of points:

- If the number of points is two, connect them directly with a straight line;
- If the number of points is more than three, the path is fitted using a polyline or smooth curve;

3. Draw each stroke frame by frame at a set speed to form an animation (Figs. 4 and 5).

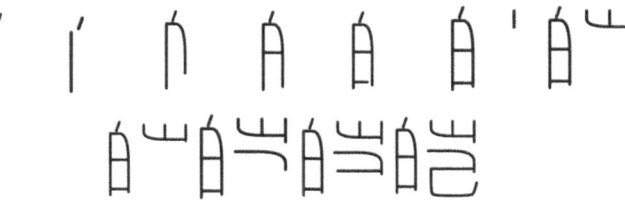

Fig. 4. Animation of Chinese character strokes ("皑")

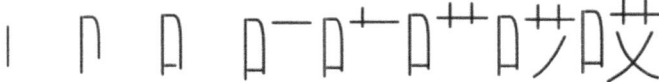

Fig. 5. Animation of Chinese character strokes ("哎")

Plotting is implemented using the MATLAB graphics engine or equivalent graphics APIs, and rendered in real time using the 'plot' function; the tempo of each stroke can be controlled by setting the speed of the plot, thus enabling flexible switching between slow teaching and fast visual presentation (Figs. 6, 7, 8 and 9).

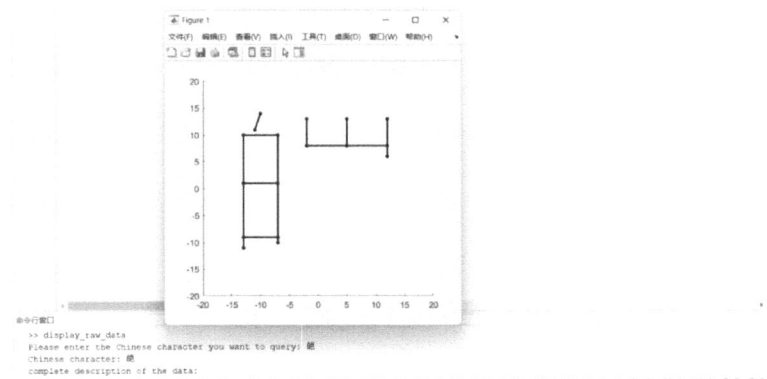

Fig. 6. Searching Chinese character "皑" and generating Chinese character animation in real time.

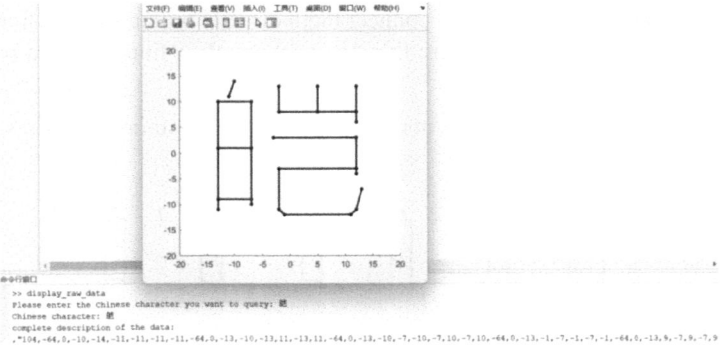

Fig. 7. End of animation generation of Chinese character "皑"

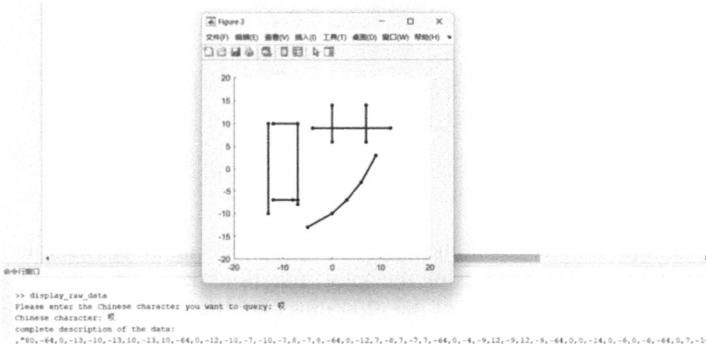

Fig. 8. Searching Chinese character "哎" and generating Chinese character animation in real time.

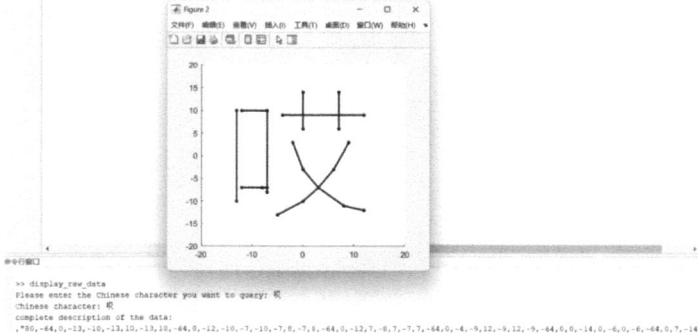

Fig. 9. End of animation generation of Chinese character "哎"

In the end, the system synthesises all the strokes in S into the dynamic structure C of a complete Chinese character, and realises the animated writing display of the Chinese character "皑". This process supports efficient rendering, speed adjustment, and real-time user interaction, and provides a technical foundation for subsequent deployment in multiple scenarios such as educational platforms and special effects engines.

In order to enhance the robustness and versatility of the system, the system constructs specialized stroke data sets for complex font styles such as cursive and semi-cursive.

Cursive script dataset: it is collected from the cursive script glyph database, covering a large number of characteristic strokes such as continuous strokes, omissions, deformations and so on. The system extracts the connection patterns between strokes through the trajectory deconstruction algorithm, and introduces the curvature analysis and stroke direction modeling technology to restore the free-flowing and rhythmic dynamic strokes of cursive script;

Semi-cursive Script Data Set: Constructing a transitional font style based on cursive writing, taking into account the actual writing characteristics of structural normality and stroke deformation. The system can combine the standard stroke template with the actual writing trajectory, automatically determine the starting and stopping point fuzzy situation, and carry out flexible stroke synthesis and dynamic fitting to ensure the balance between style restoration and recognition (Figs. 10, 11 and 12).

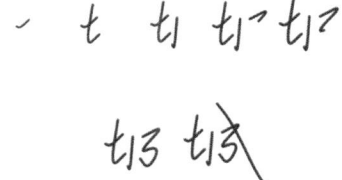

Fig. 10. Animation of semi-cursive strokes("城")

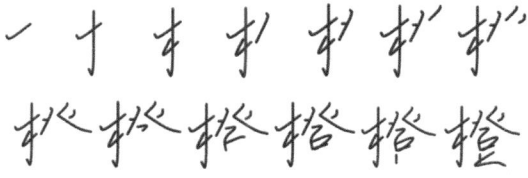

Fig. 11. Animation of semi-cursive strokes("橙")

Fig. 12. Animation of cursive strokes("啊")

5 Conclusion

This study demonstrates the clear advantages of an intelligent Chinese character animation system based on a dynamic dataset in terms of generation efficiency, scene adaptability, and user interaction. Leveraging a decoupled compile-render architecture and dynamic data-driven approach, the system achieves high efficiency, with an average generation time of just 0.15 s per character. It also supports flexible control of curve parameters and animation speed, enabling smooth adaptation to various scenarios—such as digital education, film effects, and human-computer interaction—while maintaining consistent performance across platforms like web and mobile.

Acknowledgments. This study was funded by Key R&D Project of Zhejiang Province, China (grant number 2021C03137).

Disclosure of Interests..   The authors have no competing interests to declare that are relevant to the content of this article.

References

1. Zeng, J., Chen, Q., Liu, Y., Wang, M., Yao, Y.: StrokeGAN: reducing mode collapse in chinese font generation via stroke encoding. In: AAAI Conference on Artificial Intelligence (2020)
2. Pan, Z.: A method for generating Chinese calligraphy fonts based on generative adversarial networks. Hangzhou Dianzi University (2023). https://doi.org/10.27075/d.cnki.ghzdc.2023.000953
3. Wen, Q., Li, S., Han, B., Yuan, Y.: ZiGAN: fine-grained Chinese calligraphy font generation via a few-shot style transfer approach. In: Proceedings of the 29th ACM International Conference on Multimedia (2021)
4. Chen, J., Ji, Y., Chen, H., Xu, X.: Learning one-to-many stylised Chinese character transformation and generation by generative adversarial networks. IET Image Process. **13**, 2680–2686 (2019)
5. Li, Y., et al.: Fast and robust online handwritten Chinese character recognition with deep spatial and contextual information fusion network. Multimedia, IEEE Trans. on (T-MM), **25**(000), 13 (2023)
6. Wang, Z.R., Du, J., Wang, J.M.: Writer-aware CNN for parsimonious HMM-based offline handwritten Chinese text recognition (2020)
7. Burtnyk, N., Wein, M.: Interactive skeleton techniques for enhancing motion dynamics in key frame animation. Seminal graphics: pioneering efforts that shaped the field (1998)
8. Lyu, P., Bai, X., Yao, C., Zhu, Z., Huang, T., Liu, W.: Auto-Encoder Guided GAN for Chinese Calligraphy Synthesis (2017)
9. Xiong, J., Liu, X., Li, Q.: Ontology description of Chinese character semantics. In: 2015 IEEE International Conference on Computer and Information Technology; Ubiquitous Computing and Communications; Dependable, Autonomic and Secure Computing; Pervasive Intelligence and Computing, pp. 709–713 (2015)
10. Li, Q., Liu, Q.: A Novel Dynamic Description and Generation Method for Chinese Character, pp. 719–724 (2015). https://doi.org/10.1109/CIT/IUCC/DASC/PICOM.2015.1

Author Index

The manufacturer's authorised representative in the EU is Springer
Nature Customer Service Centre GmbH, Europaplatz 3, 69115 Heidelberg,
Germany. If you have any concerns regarding our products, please
contact ProductSafety@springernature.com

Printed and bound by CPI Group (UK) Ltd, Croydon, CR0 4YY

29/04/2026

02099551-0002